The Nuclear Weapons Industry

by Kenneth A. Bertsch and Linda S. Shaw
Investor Responsibility Research Center

The Investor Responsibility Research Center was founded in 1972 as an independent, not-for-profit corporation to conduct research and publish impartial reports on contemporary social, economic and public policy issues and the impact of those issues on major corporations and institutional investors. IRRC's work is financed primarily by annual subscription fees paid by more than 170 investing institutions. IRRC is governed by a 21-member board of directors, most of whom represent subscribing institutions. Executive Director: Margaret Carroll. Deputy Director: James E. Heard. Editor: Carolyn Mathiasen.

Copyright 1984, Investor Responsibility Research Center Inc.
1319 F St., N.W., Suite 900, Washington, DC 20004
Telephone: (202) 833-3727

LIBRARY
The University of Texas
At San Antonio

The Nuclear Weapons Industry

TABLE OF CONTENTS

Introduction

Corporations participate in all aspects of the production of nuclear weapons and support equipment in the United States. Under contract to the Department of Energy, 13 corporations operate most of the facilities that research, produce and test nuclear warheads. Under Department of Defense contracts, thousands of companies work to design, research and manufacture the equipment that could take the warhead to its target.

The Investor Responsibility Research Center initiated the study that led to this report in mid-1982, as the debate over nuclear weapons production and deployment intensified, and as institutional investors were drawn into that debate because of the implications of its outcome for their stock portfolios. IRRC believed that a body of information about the corporate role in nuclear weapons production, such as this report supplies, would illuminate the debate.

A full understanding of the production of nuclear weapons in the United States requires consideration of Defense and Energy Department programs in tandem. To produce this study, IRRC analyzed in detail the contracts and contractors of both departments. As a result of this analysis, IRRC has:

-- drawn a picture of the nuclear weapons industry and discussed major issues of strategic policy.

-- written profiles of 26 leading companies in the industry.

-- developed an extensive guide to strategic and tactical nuclear weapons and support systems currently under production.

The report consists of three sections. The first section contains six chapters that give concise overviews of major issues in the debate over nuclear weapons: strategic policy, arms control, the nuclear weapons industry, the relationship between military contractors and the government, the economic effects of military spending and the concept of economic conversion.

The second section contains profiles of 26 companies that produce nuclear weapons and related systems, including the largest producers.

These profiles center around a discussion of each company's nuclear weapons-related production, but they also include general information on the company's business and history as a military contractor.

The third section, Appendix A, contains a guide to nuclear weapons-related systems produced by the leading contractors.

This report was written by Kenneth A. Bertsch, program director of IRRC's defense project, and Linda S. Shaw, research analyst at IRRC. Peter Rogoff assisted in the research for Chapter IV and, along with Paul Ferrari, wrote several company profiles. Kenneth Propp also assisted in the preparation of company profiles. Judi Christy assisted with the manuscript, and Shirley Carpenter prepared it for publication. Research assistance was provided by Marilyn Jonnes, Karen Mathiasen and Tracey Durham. The cover was designed by Peter Beck.

The authors are grateful to a number of reviewers who commented on all or part of this report.

IRRC acknowledges with gratitude the support of Carnegie Corporation of New York in the publication of this report.

Chapter I
U.S. Strategic Policy and Nuclear Weapons Systems

Eleven months before the first atomic bomb was dropped on Hiroshima, a committee of scientists associated with the Manhattan Project issued a report entitled "Prospectus on Nucleonics." In the report, the committee said:

> The most that an independent American nucleonic rearmament can achieve is the certainty that a sudden total devastation of New York or Chicago can be answered the next day by an even more extensive devastation of the cities of the aggressor, and the hope that the fear of such a retaliation will paralyze the aggressor.... [However,] the whole history of mankind teaches that this is a very uncertain hope, and that accumulated weapons of destruction 'go off' sooner or later, even if this means a senseless mutual destruction.[1]

This statement may have been the first official postulation that in the atomic age, America's only protection from the danger of nuclear devastation would be the threat to respond in kind against any nuclear attack. Such a policy would later be enshrined as "assured destruction" and become the foundation of the central military concept of the new era, "deterrence."

While suggesting that the American nuclear monopoly would be short-lived, and that deterrence might be the only defense, the committee's words also implied an imperative to find an alternative to that prospect. Defense through the threat of retaliation with these new and horrible weapons posed its own moral dilemma. And if the moral qualms were not enough, the committee's pessimism about the long-term instability of a "balance of terror," as Winston Churchill later called it, suggested that another alternative must be found.

The United States first pursued the possibility of placing all nuclear weapons under some kind of international control. When this short-lived proposal was rejected by the Soviet Union, a torrent of suggestions on how the United States should structure its nuclear-era defense policies burst forth. Since 1945, strategists, soldiers, politicians and other citizens have issued voluminous writings proposing various ways to escape reliance on a balance of terror.

Nuclear Explosive Power, from 'Little Boy' to the SS-18

Nuclear warheads are measured in kiloton and megaton equivalents of TNT. A megaton is equal in explosive power to a million tons of TNT. A kiloton is equal to a thousand tons of TNT. The bomb that destroyed Hiroshima, nicknamed "Little Boy," was about 12.5 kilotons, very small by today's standards. The largest explosives in today's arsenals apparently are 20 megaton warheads carried by some Soviet SS-18 land-based missiles, according to the London-based International Institute for Strategic Studies. Thus, the SS-18 is 1,600 times as large as Little Boy.

The largest warheads in the U.S. arsenal are 9 megatons. In recent years, though, the United States has emphasized developing less powerful but more accurate warheads. Yields in weapons not being retired range from a kiloton or less in several "tactical" weapons designed for use in battle, to the Minuteman II missile, which has a yield up to 2 megatons.

The total combined U.S. and Soviet stockpiles have a yield of 13,000 megatons or more.

The overriding facts that all would-be strategists had to confront were, as Bernard Brodie pointed out in 1946: 1) that the "bomb" exists and 2) that its destructive power is enormous and unprecedented.[2] This second consideration became even more emphatic after the explosion of the hydrogen (thermonuclear) bomb by the United States in 1952. This technology provided the potential for bombs more than 1,000 times as powerful as the Hiroshima atomic blast. Thermonuclear bombs employ fusion, as opposed to fission energy, to release energy much more efficiently.

A third overriding fact of the new age became apparent in 1949, when the Soviet Union detonated its first atomic explosion. Two great powers, none too friendly toward each other, were to build up nuclear arsenals (later to be joined by at least three smaller powers). Robert Oppenheimer in 1953 suggested the metaphor of "two scorpions in a bottle, each capable of killing the other, but only at the risk of his own life."[3] Later, the notion that each side deterred the other through the threat of devastating retaliation became known as "mutual assured destruction," or MAD.

Proposed alternatives to MAD have ranged from hard-line prescriptions for preemptive attack against America's chief rival, the Soviet Union, to proposals for complete and immediate unilateral disarmament. The nuclear policy debates in the four decades since Hiroshima have been incessant--and frequently repetitive--within the U.S. defense community. In the view of some experts, little has been learned from or resolved in these debates, except perhaps that engineering any credible alternative to indefinite reliance on mutual assured destruction may be impossible.

One result of the evident inadequacy of all nuclear options has been a legacy of ambiguous U.S. nuclear weapons policies. U.S. administrations have issued contradictory public statements on strategic goals and methods, and actual weapons targeting policies often have been on yet another track.

As a practical matter, negotiations between the nuclear powers have been the focus of most official efforts to control the arms race. Ostensibly, the ultimate goal of these arms control efforts has been total nuclear disarmament. Critics on the left and right, however, have said that the actual proposals offered in recent arms control talks would only regulate the arms race, not eliminate reliance on terror. Early in 1983, President Reagan proposed another way to escape reliance on the threat of nuclear retaliation, through the long-term development of an impregnable defense against nuclear attack. Much of this defense would rely on space-based weapons systems. The President supported this concept by noting that even with substantial reduction in nuclear warheads, "it will still be necessary to rely on the spectre of retaliation, on mutual threat," to maintain peace, unless new alternatives are found.[4]

Many experts doubt that a reliable defense against nuclear attack could ever be developed, and they view the President's proposal as destabilizing. The technological obstacles to building a 100 percent effective defense are enormous, as even the President admitted. Reagan's reaching for this alternative, even in the face of such long odds, is but another chapter in the search for a way out of the nuclear dilemma.

Reagan, Weinberger and the New Nuclear Debate

Despite Reagan's proposal for long-term development of defensive systems, the core of his military program is the buildup of nuclear offensive capabilities, combined with improvements in the command and control of nuclear forces. The administration views this effort as necessary to redress a potential imbalance of terror in favor of the Soviet Union. During the last 20 years, the USSR has invested a great deal of effort in catching up to the U.S. nuclear arsenal, and Reagan believes that the Soviet Union now has greater power in some areas than does the United States. While critics view differences in nuclear capability as meaningless, given the continued mutual ability of the two sides to destroy each other, administration officials fear that the Soviets would take advantage of any perceived superiority, perhaps precipitating superpower conflict. Thus, a host of new U.S. nuclear systems are planned for the 1980s and 1990s.

The nuclear arms buildup, along with pronouncements and policies adopted by the Reagan administration, have provoked critical public reaction, most notably through the broad-based movement for a bilateral halt--or "freeze"--of further nuclear weapons production. Reagan's critics do not share his view that the Soviets are ahead in any meaningful sense, and they have been alarmed by certain provocative public statements by Reagan and his allies.

The 1980 Republican platform, for example, promised a new nuclear regime, explicitly calling for military superiority over the Soviets--a goal that recent administrations had considered unrealistic. Moreover, the Republican platform rejected the notion that nuclear war must mean mutual suicide, as implied by the theory of mutual assured destruction.[5]

During their first two years in office, Reagan administration officials made public statements about whether it is possible to "win" a nuclear war, the possibility of limited use of nuclear weapons, and what Reagan termed the culpability of the "evil Soviet empire." In addition to castigating the Soviet leadership in the strongest terms, the President suggested that limiting a nuclear exchange to Europe was possible. This comment was not well-received by Europeans or by those American strategists who believed that any nuclear exchange was likely to escalate rapidly.

Secretary of Defense Caspar Weinberger stressed to a House committee the need to build up nuclear forces "across the full range of plausible nuclear war-fighting scenarios." Weinberger's top deputy, Frank Carlucci, similarly emphasized in his confirmation hearings the need for a nuclear war-fighting capability. Harvard historian Richard Pipes, named as senior Soviet specialist on the National Security Council, stated early in 1981 that "Soviet leaders would have to choose between peacefully changing their Communist system...or going to war."[6]

Among the most noted comments suggesting a new view of nuclear war were those of T.K. Jones, a former Boeing official whom Reagan had appointed Deputy Under Secretary of Defense for Research and Engineering. In an interview with reporter and author Robert Scheer, Jones said that, with appropriate civil defense measures to protect people and industry, the recovery time from an all-out nuclear war "could be two to four years" and that 90 percent or more of the American population could survive.[7]

These and similar assertions by other Reagan administration leaders ran counter to the popular and orthodox view that nuclear war would be cataclysmic. In the view of many observers, these officials seemed to be saying that nuclear war should be reevaluated as a more reasonable and usable foreign policy option.

Three strategic documents prepared by the administration served to confirm this impression in the minds of critics. Most notably, in May 1982, a five-year Defense Guidance Plan issued by Secretary Weinberger came to light. The document, the first complete outline of Reagan administration military policy, ordered preparation for "protracted nuclear war," and indicated that the U.S. nuclear forces "must prevail and be able to force the Soviet Union to seek earliest termination of hostilities on terms favorable to the United States." One critic commented that "the idea of 'prevailing in a nuclear war' looks a lot like the idea of winning a nuclear war," but after the guidance plans came out, Weinberger insisted that prevailing and winning were different.

The Defense Guidance Plan stressed a nuclear targeting strategy known as "decapitation." This strategy to "render ineffective the total Soviet (and Soviet-allied) military and political power structure" was especially alarming to many observers because it raised the question of how to negotiate with the enemy if its leadership were gone. Administration officials responded that decapitation already was the Soviet strategy.

The guidance also emphasized research on ballistic missile defense and space-based weapons systems.[8] A year later, as noted above, President Reagan would take up this theme.

Late in 1982, author Scheer reported that the White House had drawn up a National Security Decision Document (NSDD 13) which he said was "the first declaratory policy statement of a U.S. administration to proclaim that U.S. strategic forces must be able to win a protracted nuclear war."[9]

In addition to these actions, the administration established a new Single Integrated Operations Plan (SIOP 6). Since 1961, SIOP has been the single plan establishing targets, options and weapons allocation for the strategic nuclear force. Every SIOP is classified, but administration critic William Arkin of the Institute for Policy Studies says he has information that the new SIOP was adopted to create greater capacity for fighting and ultimately prevailing in a protracted war, and to provide more options for limited use of nuclear weapons.[10]

The various personnel and policy statements by the new administration set off substantial controversy. In his 1982 book, With Enough Shovels: Reagan, Bush and Nuclear War, Scheer argued that American strategic policy had shifted dramatically under Reagan. In Scheer's view, which some other critics share, "Either the Reagan administration, while believing that nuclear war is catastrophic, has chosen to play nuclear chicken with the Soviets with the intention of changing their political system and challenging their empire, or the United States really has abandoned the view that nuclear war is inevitably cataclysmic and believes that nuclear weapons can be detonated as viable instruments of policy."[11]

Needless to say, Scheer's thesis did not win universal endorsement. Chief among those who disagreed were Secretary Weinberger and other administration officials, who do not view their policies as dangerous or as representing a sharp departure from past concepts of deterrence. Weinberger has been at pains to establish the precedents for current administration policy. In his most recent annual report to Congress, Weinberger cited annual reports by then-Defense Secretaries Robert McNamara (1961-68) and James Schlesinger (1973-75) to show that current policy is based on concepts "squarely in the mainstream of American strategic thinking for over two decades."[12]

To a substantial degree, Weinberger is joined in this view by some of the Pentagon's harshest critics, who believe that the government long has evinced a willingness to use nuclear weapons for a variety of purposes, not just as a last resort for the most serious aggression. Moreover, these defense critics say, almost all the nuclear weapons and related equipment to be built in the "Reagan" build-up--from the MX, Trident and cruise missiles to improvements of command and control of nuclear weapons in order to enhance warfighting capability--actually were begun in the Nixon, Ford and Carter administrations.

Over the history of strategic policy, disagreement has stemmed from its ambiguities. Neither Weinberger nor his critics appear to present a wholly accurate picture of the history of strategic policy, and the truth seems to be much less clear than either side would contend. Robert McNamara, for example, did push early in the Kennedy administration for providing a flexible menu of strategic options, a policy for which Weinberger is criticized. In fact, much of the strategic thinking of the early Kennedy administration resembles the path taken 20 years later by Reagan and his appointees. Later, however, McNamara backed away from the implications of "flexible response" for limited nuclear war and for a protracted exchange. He ended his tenure as defense secretary providing a thoroughgoing case for reliance on mutual assured destruction, which Weinberger rejects.[13]

The ambiguities of nuclear warfare policy have a number of sources. One is the need for secrecy and perceived requirements (at times plainly stated in government documents) to present a "declaratory" policy for public consumption that may be at variance with actual deployment and weapons employment policies. Thus, while the emphasis of U.S. declaratory policy usually has been on the validity of deterrence through assured destruction, actual targeting policies have emphasized military targeting, which is not consistent with the assured destruction theory.

A second reason for ambiguous government weapons policy is that "the government" is not as homogeneous as is sometimes thought. Some Air Force leaders, for example, believed that victory in nuclear war was possible and an appropriate goal, when civilian leadership thought otherwise. Another source of ambiguity is the difficulty or impossibility of ever coming up with a morally, strategically and economically acceptable nuclear weapons doctrine. This third factor at times has led to rapidly changing policies (at least in public discussion) that resulted in notable and frequent contradictions and backpedaling.

A fourth factor is confusion in government officials' thinking about questions of nuclear policy. That decisionmakers should have difficulty in considering the new strategic issues should not be surprising, for nuclear weapons turned traditional military thinking on its head, and planning for thermonuclear war has its own distinctive paradoxes. To consider these paradoxes, one must look at the major concepts that have defined strategic thinking about nuclear weaponry.

Deterrence, MAD and Counterforce

The concept of deterrence: The military notion of deterrence is not new, of course. Discouraging attack through threat of retaliation is at least as old as war. In essence, one strategic expert explains, "deterrence means discouraging the enemy from taking military action by posing for him a prospect of cost and risk which outweighs his prospective gain."[14] While the concept is straightforward, its application in the nuclear age posed entirely new and paradoxical problems.

In theory, there is a difference between arming to deter and arming to wage war. Before the advent of the nuclear bomb, however, the difference had little practical effect, at least for a defensive power. A nation's armed forces served both to deter attack and, if that failed, to fight battles with the aggressor.

In the view that came to dominate postwar strategic thought, the enormous destructive power of the atomic bomb--and even greater power of the hydrogen bomb--drove a wedge between deterrence and war-fighting. Strategists came to feel that, while nuclear weapons could be the ultimate deterrent, their practical military application was limited or nonexistent. Even in the event that deterrence should fail most grievously with the enemy's launch of an all-out nuclear attack, it was not clear that carrying out the threatened retaliation would be a rational action. After a calamitous attack, retaliation could only serve as revenge and perhaps to provoke further attack. (It is of interest to note that the forerunners of the superpowers' intercontinental nuclear missiles were German World War II conventional missiles named Vergeltungswaffe, or revenge weapon.)[15]

Thus, the military's most important function--fighting wars--became secondary to deterring wars with equipment that was unsuited to actual use. In the first major book on nuclear policy, Bernard Brodie wrote:

> The first and most vital step in the American security program for the age of the atomic bomb is to take measures to guarantee ourselves in case of attack the possibility of retaliation in kind. Thus far the chief purpose of a military establishment has been to win wars. From now on its chief purpose must be to avert them. It can have no other useful purpose.[16]

Under these conditions, nuclear arms were not so much military weapons as political and psychological tools. Thus, over the years each power has had to convince the other of the credibility of its deterrent--of its willingness actually to carry out the nuclear threat if provoked.

The all-important psychological factors provided a source for instability on several fronts. For example, early thought about nuclear warfare focused on the possibly decisive advantage to be gained by striking first in a nuclear exchange in order to pre-empt the enemy's forces, thus blunting the enemy's ability to counterattack. American strategist Thomas Schelling noted that each side's moderate fear that its opponent might try such a surprise attack could be compounded and increase the chances of such an attack through "successive cycles of 'He thinks we think he thinks we think...he thinks we think he'll attack; so he thinks we shall; so he will; so we must.' "[17]

A second new factor to be considered for nuclear deterrence was the apparent impossibility of any effective defense. Most strategists have felt from the beginning and continue to feel that establishing a foolproof defense against nuclear warheads would always be impossible, in part because the system must be completely effective; 99 percent is not good enough with such extraordinarily destructive weapons. Thus, the historic cycles of offensive and defensive innovations overtaking each other seemed to have ended.

The dominance of offensive weapons meant that the military had to accept the vulnerability of the nation's citizens. In a bizarre twist of traditional thought, strategists came to believe that if either side were to be lulled into thinking that it could defend itself against attack, the stability of mutual terror would break down, and both sides could be in jeopardy. In part, it is on this ground that many experts oppose President Reagan's efforts to develop a space-based defense against nuclear missiles.

Recently, one journalist called nuclear deterrence a "world of paradoxes," in which "weapons purely for defense of helpless populations, like the antiballistic missile systems, became the greatest threat to peace. Weapons aimed at people lessen the risk of war; weapons aimed at weapons increase it."[18]

Most strategic thinkers eventually came to feel that nuclear weapons destroyed traditional concepts of military superiority. As long as each side held the capability to respond with massive retaliation to nuclear attack, numbers did not seem to matter. As Henry Kissinger remarked during his tenure as Secretary of State:

> What in the name of God is strategic superiority? What is the significance of it politically, militarily, operationally at these levels of numbers? What do you do with it?[19]

The deterrence concept, with all its paradoxes and difficulties, came to dominate thinking about nuclear weapons. The term is used with reverence by all sides of the nuclear debate. Unfortunately, deterrence is a vague term that serves to obscure as well as to illuminate.

The word begs the question--deter what? The popular conception is that nuclear deterrence serves one purpose--to deter nuclear attack. Some officials and government publications use the term in this sense. For example, the U.S. budget for fiscal year 1984 says that strategic nuclear capabilities must be maintained to "make nuclear war with us an unacceptable option."[20]

U.S. policy, however, holds that the nation's nuclear deterrent exists to prevent both conventional and nuclear attack on the United States or its allies. The threat of using nuclear weapons in response to any conventional Soviet aggression in Europe is a linchpin of the North Atlantic Treaty Organization alliance.

Both supporters and opponents of the theory of mutual assured destruction claim that they speak in the name of deterrence. Theodore Draper has commented, with reference to Reagan's policies, that the number of crimes committed in the name of deterrence may yet equal the number committed in the name of liberty.[21]

The debate over MAD and counterforce: The complexity of the debate over deterrence is illustrated by two conflicting theories about the general requirements for effective deterrence--mutual assured destruction (MAD) and counterforce. As noted earlier, the theory of mutual assured destruction holds that stability between the superpowers will reign as long as each side has the assured capacity to "destroy" the other. (Definitions of the word "destroy" vary, but in general it is thought that the ability to bomb the enemy's largest cities--thereby killing a large portion of the population and demolishing much of the economic infrastructure--would suffice.) MAD in its pure form would involve using nuclear weapons only to target the enemy's cities in the event of nuclear attack.

Critics of the theory of mutual assured destruction believe that it has a fundamental flaw--that it lacks credibility. These critics say that reliance on MAD would mean suicide or surrender in an actual nuclear confrontation. Opponents of MAD assert that the United States should be able to respond to Soviet provocation with a range of nuclear options, and that America should be in a position to "win" a nuclear exchange and end hostilities on terms favorable to the United States. A key component of any such strategy is "counterforce," which means the targeting of Soviet military installations. Counterforce advocates believe that a U.S. threat to respond to attack (nuclear or otherwise) through destruction of selected or widespread Soviet military targets is much more credible than threatening destruction of cities.

Then-Defense Secretary James Schlesinger, the author of a major 1974 public policy shift to emphasize counterforce, put the debate over counterforce in the context of Soviet policy:

> The Soviet Union now has the capability in its missile forces to undertake selective attacks against targets other than cities. This poses for us an obligation, if we are to ensure the credibility of our strategic deterrent, to be certain that we have a comparable capability in our strategic systems and targeting doctrine.[22]

Counterforce critics charge that military targeting--particularly the targeting of Soviet nuclear forces--threatens the USSR with a preemptive first strike that could demolish Soviet forces. Since counterforce theory requires the United States to maintain secure "second-strike" forces to use if necessary--that is, sufficient counterforce weapons to wipe out remaining Soviet forces after an initial Soviet attack on U.S. missiles--an "inescapable dilemma" may result. A 1978 Congressional Budget Office paper noted that a U.S. counterforce arsenal "large enough to attack Soviet ICBMs after having absorbed a Soviet first strike would be large enough to threaten the Soviet ICBM force in a first strike."[23] Such a capability encourages the Soviet Union to continue its buildup and puts the atomic button on a hair-trigger, since both sides might feel in a crisis situation that they have to "use or lose" their nuclear forces.

Counterforce critics also point out that mutual adoption of counterforce theory by both superpowers could fuel an endless arms race. Each side must build ever-increasing numbers of missiles in order to keep up with the opposition's deployment. The theory of assured destruction, in contrast, suggests a limit to the effectiveness of nuclear weapons. Moreover, say counterforce opponents, the theory ignores the fact that a large number of military targets are in or near cities, reducing to theoretical irrelevance the distinction between military and population or economic targeting.

Moreover, there is substantial evidence that the general environmental damage caused by a large-scale nuclear exchange could exceed the immediate effects. Supporters of military targeting sometimes suggest that a nuclear exchange is likely to take the form of a counterforce war of attrition. The environmental results of such an exchange are not fully predictible but are very likely disastrous. For years, experts have debated the long-term effects of a nuclear war, with some conservatives pointing out that, contrary to popular perceptions, it is not at all certain that even an all-out war would result in complete destruction of civilization. Several studies released in the fall of 1983, however, suggest that nuclear war would indeed be catastrophic. (See box.)

Nevertheless, even many critics of U.S. counterforce policy also are alarmed by Soviet policies and capabilities. As in the case of the United States, official Soviet policies and military theories about nuclear weapons have been contradictory and ambiguous. And because the USSR is a closed society, speculation about military policies is even more difficult than in the case of the United States. Nonetheless, the fact is that in the last two decades, the Soviets have built an enormous land-based intercontinental ballistic missile (ICBM) force. ICBMs are superior counterforce weapons because of their accuracy and speed. Submarine-launched ballistic missiles (SLBMs), in contrast, lack the accuracy (at this time) to destroy hardened military targets, and nuclear bomber aircraft lack the speed to pose the threat of surprise attack.

Soviet military strength is subject to exaggeration by Western governments, but there can be no doubt that the USSR has superior ICBM strength. The Stockholm International Peace Research Institute, which attempts to document arsenals from an independent standpoint, reported that at the end of 1982 the Soviets had the ICBM capability to launch 5,678 warheads, compared with 2,151 for the United States.[25] (Most observers agree that the United States continues to have stronger sea- and air-based strategic forces.)

Thus, one conclusion of the Commission on Strategic Forces that reported to President Reagan in April 1983 was that:

> While Soviet operational missile performance in wartime may be somewhat less accurate than performance on the test range, the Soviets nevertheless now probably possess the necessary combination of ICBM numbers, reliability, accuracy, and warhead yield to destroy almost all of the...U.S. ICBM silos, using only a portion of their own ICBM force. The U.S. ICBM force now deployed cannot inflict similar damage, even using the entire force.[26]

Some commentators fear that there is no way out of the MAD/ counterforce dilemma. British strategist Lawrence Freedman,

The Environmental Effects of Nuclear Warfare

Ground-breaking studies presented at a November 1983 conference on the effects of nuclear war drew grim pictures of a postwar world. The studies assumed the explosion of 5,000 megatons, about a third of existing stockpiles. The World Health Organization has estimated that about one billion people would be killed outright in such an exchange, and another billion would be severely injured.

The new studies look at what would happen next. The most dire consequence of a nuclear exchange, previously ignored, is that it would throw up into the atmosphere enormous quantities of dust, and fires started by bombs would add tremendous quantities of smoke to the atmosphere as well. Based on the assumption that 80 percent of the nuclear megatonnage exploded at military sites and 20 percent on urban and industrial targets, a study by chemist Richard P. Turco, astronomer Carl Sagan and three other scientists found that sunlight over much of the earth largely would be eliminated at ground level--making it "too dark," wrote Sagan, "for plants to make a living from photosynthesis." One result would be a sharp reduction in land temperatures. Except for narrow coastline areas warmed by the ocean, Turco predicts land temperatures will drop to minus 13 degress Fahrenheit, and stay below freezing for months, even in the summer.

A study by Soviet scientists predicted an even greater temperature drop--an average of 61 degrees in the midwestern and eastern United States 40 days after the initial atomic blast. A third study, by scientists at the Lawrence Livermore Laboratory, predicted a 50 degree drop for inland areas.

The Turco study also found that radiation effects would be far greater than previously predicted, because 225 million tons of radioactive debris would be spread over the earth in a few days. The debris also would carry large amounts of toxic chemicals. In addition, as some previous studies have predicted, there would be substantial destruction of the atmosphere's ozone layer, said the Turco report, which concluded that "These long-term effects, when combined with the direct casualties from the blast, suggest that eventually there might be no human survivors in the Northern Hemisphere." Turco and associates found that the effects were almost as powerful with the explosion of 3,000 megatons, and also would be signficant at lower levels of conflict.[24]

author of a book on the evolution of nuclear strategy, agrees with counterforce advocates that a credible strategy for "what happens if deterrence fails" must be found to make the deterrence concept work. He concluded:

> It now seems unlikely that such an answer can be found. No operational nuclear strategy has yet to be devised that does not carry an enormous risk of degenerating into a bloody contest of resolve or a furious exchange of devastating and crippling blows against the political and economic centers of the industrialized world.[27]

Freedman, who doubts the potential for disarmament, adds that the belief that the current order "can go on indefinitely without major disaster requires an optimism unjustified by any historical or political perspective." Thus, his conclusions come full circle to those of the Manhattan Project committee cited at the beginning of the chapter.

The U.S. Nuclear Weapons Arsenal

The U.S. nuclear arsenal is much more diversified than most Americans generally perceive. In its new book, The Nuclear Weapons Databook, the Natural Resources Defense Council identified 24 nuclear warheads and bombs known to have been deployed by the United States in 1982.[28] The weapons range from atomic demolition munitions of less than a kiloton yield, to nuclear depth charges for attacking enemy submarines, to nuclear howitzer shells, to the large strategic weapons that receive most public attention.

The variety of nuclear weapons sometimes confuses even the experts, as March 1983 discussion before the House Subcommittee on Procurement and Military Nuclear Systems of the House of Representatives showed.[29] Participants in the exchange were Rep. Samuel Stratton (D-N.Y.), chairman of the subcommittee and one of the most knowledgeable members of Congress when it comes to nuclear weapons; Adam Klein, counsel to the committee; Major Gen. William W. Hoover, director of the Office of Military Applications at the Energy Department; and Troy Wade, the Energy Department's principal deputy assistant secretary for defense programs. Stratton began by asking about nuclear weapons likely to be deployed on ships that will be located at a new New York City naval base:

> Mr. STRATTON: What nuclear weapons would be likely to be carried on [these] ships...? The only thing I could think of would be Tomahawk [cruise missiles] and conceivably a nuclear depth charge. Is there anything else?
> Mr. KLEIN: Torpedos.
> Mr. STRATTON: We have nuclear torpedos?
> Gen. HOOVER: The official policy, sir, is to neither confirm

> nor deny the status of weapons, but we can certainly hypothesize what might be. [Deleted.]
> Mr. STRATTON: What about Asroc [an antisubmarine weapon deployed on surface ships]? [Deleted.]
> Gen. HOOVER: [Deleted.]
> Mr. WADE: [Deleted.]
> Mr. STRATTON: Maybe we will get into a nuclear war after all. We have a hell of a lot of things that can be fired.

While much of this discussion has been classified and therefore deleted from the written transcript, the gist is clear. Even after one realizes the variety of the U.S. and Soviet arsenals, however, it still is difficult to describe the nuclear warfare apparatus, since much more is involved than warheads.

Definitional problems: Any description of the U.S. nuclear weapons arsenal poses definitional problems. The question of what constitutes a nuclear weapons system is not so simple as it appears at first blush. To begin with, no matter what strategic theory may be in vogue, on a procurement basis the Pentagon does not make a distinction between its nuclear and conventional systems, as an official with the Pentagon office that provides contracting information warned IRRC.

Second, even if the government did provide a handy reference to nuclear systems, the reference would have to be examined critically. Commentators on the nuclear debates use widely varying definitions of nuclear weapons systems. Those choosing the narrowest definition count only nuclear warheads. By this accounting, the "nuclear weapons" designation does not include delivery systems and "launch platforms," such as missiles, submarines and bombers, but only the actual warheads, as a distinct category. All warheads are manufactured under the auspices of the Department of Energy, not the Pentagon. IRRC found that some manufacturers of delivery systems and launch platforms prefer this definition.

Other observers prefer a broader definition that includes delivery vehicles and launch platforms. While such a definition is more realistic--one cannot deliver warheads without delivery vehicles of one sort or another--it also poses several problems. One problem for the analyst relates to the Defense Department's construction of a "seamless web" of conventional and nuclear systems. A large portion of the U.S. nuclear arsenal is carried by ostensibly tactical "dual-capable" aircraft and submarines. Dual-capable systems are equipped to carry both conventional and nuclear armaments. Some missiles and launching systems also are dual-capable, as are howitzer guns and other battlefield weapons. By the same token, bombers and submarines primarily used for strategic weapons also carry conventional armaments.

At the same time that this broader definition runs into problems on the dual-capable systems front, it does not include some of the "nonweapons" systems that are essential in the operation of nuclear weapons, particularly many of the more advanced weapons. These systems include satellite and command and control systems. As a 1983 Worldwatch Institute study notes:

> Nonweapons such as sensors, communications systems and computers have become as important to the strategic balance as weapons improvements. As a result, the measure of military strength has shifted away from the power and speed of weapons to the ability to detect and target the enemy's forces and to hide and communicate with one's own.[30]

Two examples of strategic satellite systems are Navstar and the Air Force Satellite Communications System (Afsatcom). Navstar eventually will consist of a network of 18 satellites that will permit aircraft, ships and missiles to locate their positions precisely. While this has defense-wide applications, one result will be to give the Trident II missile, scheduled for deployment beginning in 1989, an unprecedented accuracy for sea-launched missiles. The Trident II will be the first sea-launched missile with the accuracy to destroy hardened military targets, and thus will be a counterforce weapon.

The Afsatcom satellite system provides data communications for command and control of Air Force nuclear-capable forces. The system provides integral support for Minuteman intercontinental ballistic missiles, strategic bombers, and other forces.

U.S. military satellites also provide crucial data on Soviet nuclear forces, as do land-based radar systems and reconnaissance aircraft. By the same token, U.S. and Soviet antisatellite (Asat) weapons, now in development, threaten those systems, and therefore would play an important role in nuclear warfare.

In addition to the high-tech systems mentioned above, other equipment, including aerial tankers and antisubmarine and anti-aircraft weaponry, play important roles in planning for nuclear warfare, and must be considered.

So there is no clear line dividing nuclear and conventional weapons systems. For the purposes of analyzing corporate involvement in nuclear weapons and related production for this report, IRRC developed two categories for classifying nuclear-related systems. With this system, IRRC could include both a broad and a relatively narrow definition. "Primary" systems include strategic nuclear weapons and support systems (satellites, aerial tankers and other equipment primarily designed to support strategic nuclear systems) and tactical nuclear weapons. The "secondary" category includes dual-capable systems and certain "defense-wide" support equipment that affects both nuclear and conventional systems. To take the satellite examples mentioned above, Afsatcom is considered a primary nuclear weapons system, since its main role is to provide support for nuclear systems. Navstar, on the other hand, provides support for "defense-wide" systems, and therefore is classified by IRRC as secondary.

Appendix A discusses various systems in detail within this framework, and the table on page 397 specifies which systems are considered primary and which are secondary. It is important to note here that this classification system is not meant to gauge the moral, political or military significance of particular military systems. Radars built to watch for Soviet attack are not controversial, but their role clearly is in the realm of nuclear warfighting, and IRRC does not exclude them from the primary category. Any attempt to make distinctions based on moral or political grounds poses difficulties, in large part because, as noted above, nuclear weapons obliterate conventional notions of defense and offense. The single distinction of importance for this study is between nuclear weapons and their support systems and purely conventional weapons and their support systems.

It should also be noted that the primary/secondary categorization has its limitations. One of the most important current U.S. nuclear arms programs is the Tomahawk cruise missile program. However, because Tomahawks come in both nuclear and conventional varieties, and because contracts for conventional and nuclear versions for the most part are grouped together by the Pentagon, Tomahawks are considered "secondary" systems.

The remainder of this chapter outlines briefly the main U.S. nuclear forces, including delivery vehicles and launch platforms.

Nuclear force structure: The strategic deterrent forces of the United States are a "triad" of nuclear forces, a three-part arsenal that consists of long-range bombers, submarine-launched ballistic missiles and land-based intercontinental ballistic missiles. A fourth category, air-, sea- and ground-launched cruise missiles, are coming on line, further muddying an already tenuous Pentagon distinction between "strategic" and "tactical" forces. The Defense Department considers cruise missiles to fall in both categories.

The International Institute for Strategic Studies estimated in 1982 that U.S. strategic forces included 9,268 warheads, compared with 7,300 for the Soviet Union.[31]

In addition to the strategic forces, the United States maintains many tactical nuclear warheads and bombs, including nuclear artillery shells, land mines, depth charges, and antiship and antisubmarine missiles. The United States has 6,000 "battlefield" nuclear warheads in Europe, and NATO is preparing to deploy 572 new intermediate-range nuclear weapons there.

The number of warheads in the U.S. stockpile is classified. The Defense Department states only that the number stands "at a few tens of thousands."[32] The Natural Resources Defense Council estimated the total U.S. nuclear stockpile as of January 1982 at 26,000 warheads.[33] Some other estimates are higher. The NRDC suggests that after 10,000 or more warheads for currently planned weapons are built (and after some older weapons are retired), the total stockpile will increase to about 32,000.

The Defense Department notes that the stockpile is smaller today than it was in the 1960s. The number of weapons in the inventory was one-third higher in 1967 than it is now. If NRDC estimates are correct, that would place the 1967 stockpile at about 35,000 bombs and warheads. The Pentagon also points out that in terms of yield, or megatonnage, the U.S. force has been reduced by 75 percent since 1960.[34] This largely is because huge older warheads have been retired as greater missile accuracy--and U.S. emphasis on counterforce as opposed to industrial targeting--have led to smaller warheads on strategic missiles.

Strategic systems:[35]

Intercontinental ballistic missiles (ICBMs)--The current ICBM force includes 450 single-warhead Minuteman II missiles, 550 three-warhead Minuteman III missiles, and about 40 single-warhead Titan II missiles, which are being retired between now and 1987. Since 1966, the Air Force has made some 15 major changes in Minuteman missiles including the installation of multiple warheads. All 550 Minuteman III missiles have been fitted with a guidance system designed to deliver each warhead within 600 feet of its target. Some 300 Minuteman IIIs have been fitted with Mark-12A warheads that double the explosive power of the missiles.

The total American ICBM force consists of 1,040 missiles carrying about 2,150 warheads.

Beginning in 1986, the Pentagon plans to deploy the controversial MX missile. The MX was designed to offer counterforce capability to U.S. forces. Its basing mode was supposed to reestablish ICBM invulnerability to Soviet attack, but, after consideration of more than three dozen possible basing modes, the Pentagon has yet to find one that is politically, economically and strategically acceptable. As a result, current plans call for basing 100 MX missiles--each with 10 warheads--in existing missile silos, while research and development work begins on a small, possibly mobile, single-warhead missile.

The proposed follow-on to the MX is the small ICBM, popularly known as "Midgetman." This single-warhead missile was advocated by President Reagan's Commission on Strategic Forces. The missile as planned will weigh 30,000 pounds, compared with the MX's weight of

190,000 pounds. A Pentagon advisory committee has said that the favored deployment of the Midgetman would be in hardened mobile launchers. The missile as now planned would incorporate the Avco-produced Mark 21 warhead (which also is being deployed on MX missiles) and would use a yet to be developed lightweight guidance system. Until late in 1984, several companies will receive funding for competing design ideas. The missile is planned for deployment beginning in 1992.[36]

Submarine-launched ballistic missiles (SLBMs)--The nation's existing SLBMs are carried by 31 Poseidon and two Trident ballistic missile submarines. Nineteen of the Poseidon submarines each carry 16 Poseidon (C-3) missiles, and each missile features 10 warheads. Another 12 Poseidon submarines each carry 16 of the more accurate, longer-ranged and higher-yield Trident I (C-4) missiles, and each Trident missile carries eight warheads.

The first two Trident-class submarines have been deployed in the last year. Each of these submarines initially carries 24 Trident I missiles. Three more Trident submarines are undergoing sea trials.

In total, just short of 5,000 warheads are deployed on 544 SLBMs. Eventually, the government plans to deploy at least 13 Trident submarines, thus providing for an additonal 264 SLBMs. (Dismantling of Poseidon submarines may begin in the 1990s, however, possibly keeping the total number of SLBMs somewhat below 800.) The first eight Trident submarines will carry the Trident I missile. The other Trident subs will carry the Trident II (D-5) missile, which will be deployed beginning in 1989. The Trident II will be the first sea-based counterforce weapon. It will have a range of 6,000 nautical miles and the ability to carry 14 warheads. Eventually, the first eight Trident subs are to be retrofitted with the Trident II missile.

Strategic bombers--The current strategic bomber force consists of 330 B-52 bombers and 60 FB-111 bombers. These aircraft carry a total of 2,580 warheads, about evenly split between short-range attack missiles (SRAMs) and gravity bombs.

Beginning in 1982, the Air Force has been reconfiguring B-52s to carry air-launched cruise missiles (ALCMs). Eventually, 2,500 ALCMs will be deployed on B-52s and the new B-1 bomber. Later, radar-evading versions of the cruise missile will also be deployed on the bombers.

As part of its strategic modernization effort, the Reagan administration is developing two new bombers. The B-1, which had been rejected by President Carter, will now be deployed beginning in 1985. The government plans to build 100 of the aircraft. In addition to cruise missiles, the B-1 will be equipped to carry SRAMs and gravity bombs.

The second bomber now under development is based on new radar-evading "Stealth" technology. Currently labeled the Advanced Technology Bomber (ATB), the aircraft will be deployed in the 1990s.

Sea-launched cruise missiles (SLCMs)--In addition to the bomber-carried cruise missiles mentioned above, the government considers sea-launched cruise missles to be "strategic" weapons. The nuclear versions of the missiles will be deployed beginning in 1984 on attack submarines and surface ships.

Tactical and theater systems: As noted above, there are a variety of "tactical" nuclear weapons designed for use on the battlefield and/or in particular areas of the world. Some 1,000 Terrier and Nike Hercules nuclear warheads are designed for anti-aircraft purposes. Some 1,750 to 3,400 nuclear depth charges and Asroc and Subroc missiles are held in reserve for antisubmarine warfare. Between 4,000 and 5,000 warheads are carried on Navy and Air Force strike aircraft.[37] And, as discussed earlier, some 6,000 nuclear weapons (counting some of those mentioned above) are deployed in Europe, although NATO plans to reduce that number to between 4,000 and 4,600 over the next five to six years.

The government has plans to develop and deploy a number of new tactical nuclear systems over the next few years. By far the most important of the plans are those to deploy under NATO auspices 108 new Pershing II medium-range ballistic missiles and 464 ground-launched cruise missiles in Europe, providing a counter to the 315 Soviet missiles that have been aimed toward Western Europe in recent years. The NATO missiles, scheduled for deployment beginning in December 1983, but facing strong opposition in Europe, will give the Western allies the capability of hitting targets within the Soviet Union.

Critics of the program argue that it will increase the possibilities of a nuclear war and that it fails to meet the major weaknesses of NATO conventional forces. Proponents say that the new missiles are needed to ensure that NATO has a full range of responses to Soviet aggression.

Strong European protests against the planned 1983 deployment of the cruise and Pershing missiles helped to prod the United States and the Soviet Union into negotiations over European-based intermediate missiles, but those negotiations have not brought results to date, and it is almost certain that the initial deployment plans for the missiles will be fulfilled.

The Debate over Battlefield Nuclear Weapons

Since the late 1940s, the United States has provided Europe with a nuclear "umbrella" in the face of what generally has been viewed as superior Warsaw Pact conventional capabilities. By 1951, the United States was working toward possession of "atomic weapons in almost as complete a variety as conventional ones, and a situation where we can use them in the same way," said then-Atomic Energy Commission Chairman Gordon Dean. He added that capabilities "would include artillery shells, guided missiles, torpedoes, rockets and bombs for ground support amongst others...."[38]

Among those pushing development of tactical weapons in the 1950s were Robert Oppenheimer and other scientists who hoped such weapons would be pursued instead of the hydrogen bomb--which was labeled a "weapon of genocide"--and the concept of massive retaliation. Oppenheimer expressed the hope that "battle could be brought back to the battlefield" through development of such weapons. Oppenheimer and others hoped to establish a new division between limited and all-out war, with tactical nuclear weapons.[39]

In the mid-1950s, some academics argued that tactical nuclear weapons could be useful weapons that would have greater credibility than the threat of massive retaliation. Henry Kissinger, among others, helped to make his reputation in arguing this case. As these options were explored, however, severe doubts about such tactical use arose, and gradually many of its advocates, including Kissinger, reversed their positions. The largest problem was the difficulty of protecting the civilians whom these armaments were supposed to defend from the effects of the weapons. War games "using" tactical nuclear weapons invariably resulted in horrible effects on the population, usually with little military gain. An exercise in Louisiana called Operation Sage Brush ended when all life in the state was judged to have "ceased to exist."[40]

Scenarios and war games using tactical weapons continued to be posed through the 1960s. Alain Enthoven, then an assistant secretary of defense, said in 1975 that over "eight years of studying the problem," he never saw a convincing scenario for the use of such weapons.[41] Critics of battlefield weapons emphasized also that the break between nuclear and nonnuclear weapons was much clearer than that between "battlefield" and other nuclear weapons. Greater availability of smaller weapons would tempt one side or the other into use, destroying the concept of a nuclear "firebreak."

Despite such arguments and evidence, tactical nuclear weapons continued to be built and deployed, and NATO planned (and continues to plan) to use them in the event of Soviet conventional attack. The overriding stated reason for this policy has been the belief that the Soviets have overwhelming conventional superiority in Europe. Periodically, NATO governments have resolved to correct the perceived imbalance, only to falter in the face of the massive costs involved. Whatever the hazards of nuclear weapons, they are much cheaper than maintaining more divisions.

Chapter I Footnotes

1. Lawrence Freedman, The Evolution of Nuclear Strategy, New York, St. Martin's Press, New York, 1981, p. 41.
2. Ibid., p. 396.
3. Ibid., p. 94.
4. Congressional Quarterly Weekly Report, March 26, 1983, p. 632.
5. Congressional Quarterly Almanac, Congressional Quarterly, Washington, 1980, p. 77B.
6. Robert Scheer, With Enough Shovels: Reagan, Bush & Nuclear War, Random House, New York, 1982, p. 5, 8.
7. Ibid., p. 18, 21.
8. Richard Halloran, "Pentagon Draws Up First Strategy for Fighting a Long Nuclear War," The New York Times, May 30, 1982.
9. Scheer, op. cit., p. 10.
10. Bulletin of the Atomic Scientists, April 1983, p. 9-10.
11. Scheer, op. cit.
12. "Report of the Secretary of Defense Caspar W. Weinberger to the Congress on the FY 1984 Budget," in the "Defense Department Authorization and Oversight Hearings on HR 2287," House Committee on Armed Services, 1983, p. 67.
13. Freedman, op. cit., p. 245-56.
14. Glenn Snyder, "The Theory of Deterrence," in American Defense Policy: Fifth Edition, ed. John F. Reichert and Steven R. Sturm, Johns Hopkins University Press, Baltimore, 1982, p. 154.
15. Freedman, op. cit., p. 13.
16. Ibid., p. 44.
17. Ibid., p. 164.
18. Charles Krauthammer, "How to Prevent Nuclear War," The New Republic, April 28, 1982, p. 15.
19. Laurence Martin, "Is Military Force Losing Its Utility," in American Defense Policy, op. cit., p. 35.
20. Budget of the United States Government, Fiscal Year 1984, Government Printing Office, Washington, 1983, p. 5-7.
21. Leon Wieseltier, "Nuclear War, Nuclear Peace," The New Republic, Jan. 10-17, 1983, p. 20.
22. Quoted in Weinberger, op. cit., p. 311.
23. Congressional Budget Office, "Counterforce issues for the U.S. Strategic Nuclear Forces," January 1978, p. 32.
24. The most noted of these studies is entitled "Global Atmospheric Consequences of Nuclear War," by R.P. Turco, V.B. Toon, T.P. Ackerman, J.B. Pollack and Carl Sagan. Findings of this and the other studies were reported in The Washington Post, Nov. 1 and 2, 1983; The New York Times, Oct. 30, 1983; and Parade Magazine, Oct. 30, 1983.
25. Stockholm International Peace Research Institute, World Armaments and Disarmaments: Sipri Yearbook 1983, Taylor & Francis, New York, 1983, p. 48-9.
26. "Report of the President's Commission on Strategic Forces," April 1983, p. 4.
27. Freedman, op. cit., p. 395.
28. William M. Arkin, Thomas B. Cochran and Milton M. Hoenig, The Nuclear Weapons Databook, Ballinger, Boston, 1983.
29. "Hearings on Department of Energy National Security and Military Applications of Nuclear Energy Authorization Act of 1984," House Armed Services Subcommittee on Procurement and Military Nuclear Systems, March 1 and 2, 1983, p. 369-70.
30. Deudney, Daniel, "Whole Earth Security: A Geopolitics of Peace," Worldwatch Institute, Washington, 1983, p. 3.
31. International Institute for Strategic Studies, The Military Balance: 1982-1983, London, 1982, p. 138-41.

32. Office of Assistant Secretary of Defense (Public Affairs), News Release, Aug. 25, 1983.
33. William M. Arkin, Thomas B. Cochran and Milton M. Hoenig, "The U.S. Nuclear Stockpile," Arms Control Today, April 1982.
34. Office of Assistant Secretary of Defense (Public Affairs), op. cit.
35. Sources for this section are The International Institute for Strategic Studies, The Military Balance, 1982-83, London, 1982; Stockholm Peace Research Institute, op. cit.; and Congressional Budget Office, Modernizing U.S. Strategic Offensive Forces: The Administration's Program and Alternatives, U.S. Government Printing Office, Washington, 1983.
36. Office of Assistant Secretary of Defense (Public Affairs), News Release, Sept. 30, 1983.
37. Randall Forsberg, "A Bilateral Nuclear-Weapons Freeze," Scientific American, November 1982, p. 54-5.
38. Freedman, op. cit., p. 64.
39. Ibid., p. 66-9.
40. Ibid., p. 109.
41. Solly Zuckerman, Nuclear Illusion and Reality, Viking Press, New York, 1982, p. 70.

Chapter II
Curbing Nuclear Weapons: Arms Control and Disarmament

Only 41 days after the June 1945 signing of the United Nations Charter, the Hiroshima atomic blast fundamentally altered international relations. When the UN General Assembly first met in January 1946, its first resolution, unanimously approved, set up an Atomic Energy Commission to make proposals "for the elimination from national armaments of atomic weapons and of all other major weapons adaptable to mass destruction."[1]

In June 1946, the United States proposed to the United Nations the establishment of an International Atomic Development Authority, which would control or own all atomic resources and be responsible for all stages of nuclear production, and the eventual destruction of all nuclear weapons. (At the time, the United States was the only nuclear power.) A large majority of UN members endorsed the proposal (known as the Baruch plan), but the Soviets--suspicious of a United Nations that at that time appeared to be dominated by the United States--objected to ownership and enforcement provisions. The Soviet Union proposed that national authorities control nuclear technology, and that an international ban on nuclear weapons be verified by periodic inspection of declared nuclear facilities. The Truman administration, along with most other member governments, found these verification procedures inadequate. Negotiations faltered, and the United States conducted its first postwar atomic test over the island of Bikini on July 1, 1946. The opportunity to foreclose the nuclear arms race before it gained momentum was lost.[2]

Thus began the long--and to date largely fruitless--struggle to control and reduce nuclear arms through international agreement.

In the early years of the nuclear era, the United Nations continued to stand at the center of negotiating efforts, which were aimed at general disarmament--that is, the reduction and eventual elimination of all weapons of warfare, including nuclear, conventional and chemical. As part of one such general disarmament proposal, and partially in response to pressure from nonaligned nations, in 1955 the USSR proposed a nuclear test ban. Subsequently, the Soviets advocated a separate test ban, not contingent on a more general control agreement. The three western nuclear powers--the United States, Britain and

France--argued that the test ban proposal should not be separated from more general discussions. However, in 1958 the United States, Britain and the USSR each unilaterally placed a moratorium on testing. The Soviet Union broke the moratorium and resumed testing in 1961, setting back the most important area of progress.[3]

Despite the testing setback, later in 1961 the Soviet Union and the United States concluded a "Joint Statement of Principles," calling for:

- establishment of reliable procedures for the peaceful settlement of disputes...[and] to strengthen institutions for maintaining peace.

- disarmament...in an agreed sequence, by stages...[and] balanced so that at no stage...could any state...gain military advantage.

- strict and effective international control...[to] provide firm assurance that all parties are honoring their obligations,...the nature and extent of such control depending on the requirements for verification...in each stage.

- an International Disarmament Organization...assured [of] unrestricted access without veto to all places as necessary for the purpose of effective verification.[4]

This statement, which became known as the McCloy-Zorin Agreed Principles, after the U.S. and Soviet negotiators, was approved in December 1961 by the UN General Assembly. Subsequently, each of the two superpowers prepared detailed proposals to fulfill the principles. U.S. Ambassador Arthur Dean said the idea of the U.S. plan was "that the nations of the world should seize a moment in time to stop the arms race, to freeze the military situation as it then appears, and to shrink it to zero."[5]

The U.S. plan called for cutting nuclear delivery vehicles, including missiles, airplanes and other equipment which can deliver nuclear weapons, by 65 percent in two stages to be enacted over a six-year period. In a third stage over an unspecified period, all nuclear weapons and most conventional armaments would be eliminated, and nuclear weapons production facilities and materials would be converted to peaceful uses. The proposal also called for strengthening of the United Nations and of peacekeeping arrangements.

Despite the idealism expressed in both the U.S. and the Soviet proposals, the arms race was heating up even as these discussions were held. The United States, for example, was deploying a wide range of nuclear weapons under the doctrine of "flexible response," suggesting that nuclear warheads might be used in a wide variety of contingencies. And both nations were attempting to place nuclear weapons in geographic locations close to the opposing power (in Cuba and Turkey, for example). The Soviet attempt to place missiles in Cuba in the fall of 1962 touched off one of the gravest crises of the nuclear era.

Nuclear Test Ban Negotiations

While the ambitious efforts for general disarmament fell by the wayside, negotiations toward a comprehensive test ban proceeded, in part because of concerns about the environmental effects of fallout from atmospheric tests. Multilateral negotiations under UN auspices made important progress on a comprehensive test ban in 1962 and 1963, but agreement was not reached. The United States, Britain and the Soviet Union instead negotiated a limited test ban in the summer of 1963, prohibiting testing in the atmosphere, in space and under water.[6]

The agreement won wide praise, and 124 nations signed or acceded to the treaty; the signatories indicated that it was but a prelude to a comprehensive test ban. That goal has eluded negotiators since then, and since 1963 there have been 887 nuclear explosions, including 63 atmospheric tests by France and China, which have not signed the limited test ban treaty. From 1963 to 1982, the United States exploded 407 nuclear bombs, and the Soviet Union 336, according to the Stockholm International Peace Research Institute.[7]

The United States and the Soviet Union did agree in 1974 to a Threshold Test Ban Treaty, limiting undergound tests to 150 kilotons. In 1976, a companion agreement limiting underground nuclear explosions for peaceful purposes was signed by the United States and the Soviet Union.[8] Neither agreement has been ratified by the Senate, and allegations have been made by some administration officials and by several members of Congress that the Soviets have exceeded the limit.

The United States, Great Britain and the Soviet Union made substantial progress on a comprehensive test ban in negotiations conducted during Jimmy Carter's presidency, when the three parties tentatively agreed to place tamperproof seismic sensors in each country.[9] Many experts believe that such sensors would provide high confidence in verifiability. The three countries also agreed to provisions for on-site inspections. The Reagan administration nevertheless canceled the negotiations, in part, officials said, because the administration was not confident of the verification methods. Later, officials added that the desire to test a new generation of U.S. warheads and bombs played an important role in the decision to withdraw from the talks.

Advocates of the test ban believe that a ban would be important precisely because it would inhibit the development of new weapons, since nations could not be confident about the reliability of any new warheads. Over time, they suggest, even confidence in existing stockpiles might erode, although some scientists disagree. Thus, nations would be even more reluctant to use nuclear weapons.[10]

Despite opposition from the Reagan administration, pressures for securing a test ban persist, and it is likely that a Democratic administration would revive the negotiations. If the three nations that conducted the last round of negotiations allow tentative agreements reached at that time to stand, the outlook for a comprehensive test ban would be promising, despite strong opposition to a test ban from some military officials in each country.

Outer Space Treaty

A second successful 1960s initiative was the Outer Space Treaty of 1967. The United States had been concerned since 1957 with limiting the possibility of space warfare. The Soviet and American proposals of the early 1960s for general disarmament included provisions to ensure the peaceful use of outer space. The United Nations passed a resolution in 1963 calling for states to refrain from using space for weapons of mass destruction, and in 1966, U.S. and Soviet negotiators reached agreement on a treaty banning weapons of mass destruction from space and limiting the moon and other celestial bodies exclusively to peaceful purposes. The treaty was signed or acceded to by 110 nations, including the major powers, and it was quickly ratified by the Senate.[11]

A petition now being circulated by leading American scientists calls for the banning from space of all weapons, including antisatellite weapons.[12] The U.S. government was expected to test an antisatellite device in the fall of 1983.

Soviet President Yuri Andropov announced in August 1983 a unilateral moratorium on the deployment of antisatellite weapons as long as other states "will refrain from stationing in outer space antisatellite weapons of any type."[13]

Strategic Arms Limitation Talks

Salt I: The bilateral Strategic Arms Limitation Talks of 1969 to 1972 (Salt I) resulted in a treaty limiting antiballistic missile (ABM) systems and an interim agreement on the levels of offensive nuclear weapons. The origins of these talks date to 1964, when the United States suggested consideration of strategic arms separately from the general disarmament proposals. The United States suggested that the two superpowers "explore a verified freeze of the number and characteristics of their strategic nuclear offensive and defensive vehicles."[14]

In 1966, the USSR began deploying an ABM system around Moscow, and in 1967, the United States announced that it also would deploy a limited ABM system. Critics argued that these systems introduced a dangerous new element to the arms race, since one side or the other might be tempted into nuclear attack under the misapprehension that defense against the enemy was possible. Critics added that no such foolproof defense would ever be possible.

In July 1968, President Johnson announced that the superpowers had agreed to begin discussions on limiting both offensive and defensive strategic systems, but the Soviet invasion of Czechoslovakia one month later caused the talks to be postponed. The two sides finally met in November 1969, after the Nixon administration had come to office.

When the Salt I talks were concluded in May 1972, the United States and the Soviet Union agreed to an ABM Treaty of unlimited duration, under which each party could withdraw on six months' notice. The treaty limited each side to two ABM deployment areas--and a later protocol limited the number to one site--"so restricted and so located that they cannot provide a nationwide ABM defense or become the basis for developing one," as the Arms Control and Disarmament Agency describes the treaty. The treaty also limited development, testing or deployment of ABM launchers or of sea-based, air-based or space-based ABM systems. (Despite this limitation, both sides are conducting research on alternative ballistic missile defense possibilities.)

The interim agreement on strategic offensive arms prohibited starts on construction of additional fixed land-based ICBM launchers during the five-year period of the agreement. Modernization was allowed, except that launchers for older ICBMs could not be converted to support modern heavy ICBMs, and the dimensions of the launchers could not be significantly increased. The agreement also limited launchers for SLBMs and the number of modern ballistic missile submarines at a level somewhat above the number each side then had.[15]

Salt II: As agreed to in the Salt I interim agreement, Salt II negotiations began in November 1972. At a Vladivostok meeting in November 1974, President Ford and General Secretary Brezhnev reached agreement on a basic framework for a Salt II treaty. The proposed framework included a limit on each nation of 2,400 on strategic delivery vehicles, with a sublimit of 1,320 on missiles with multiple warheads (or MIRVed missiles).

Despite this understanding, disagreements over inclusion of cruise missiles and the Soviet Backfire bomber prevented agreement, and when Jimmy Carter became president in 1977, a new comprehensive proposal including new reductions and qualitative limitations was proposed by the United States. The Soviets balked, and an agreement was not concluded until 1979.

The MIRVing of Missiles

In the 1960s, the United States developed the technology to place more than one independent warhead on the same missile. Missiles with this capability are said to have multiple independently targetable reentry vehicles, or MIRVs. The Soviets later developed the same technology. MIRVing missiles was an inexpensive way to add great numbers of warheads.

It is widely conceded today that reliance on MIRVed missiles places both U.S. and Soviet strategic forces in peril, and has destabilized the arms balance. As both sides have MIRVed their missiles, both have become more vulnerable to a first strike. MIRVing missiles creates many more warheads with which to threaten the other side's nuclear forces. At the same time, reliance on fewer missiles carrying more warheads increases the vulnerability of a nation's own forces. A single missile with 10 warheads makes a more inviting target to a hostile enemy than do 10 missiles each with a single warhead.

Moreover, because it is thought that it would take two attacking warheads to have any confidence in destroying a single missile, it would not be possible for either side to have confidence in first-strike capability if each has roughly equal numbers of single-warhead ICBMs. (This equation will change as sea-launched and perhaps other missiles achieve the accuracy to destroy hardened military targets.)

Thus, President Reagan's Commission on Strategic Forces recommended that a new, single-warhead small ICBM be developed, and that negotiations with the Soviets stress a move away from MIRVed missiles. These proposals have won substantial, if grudging, support from long-time advocates of arms control, as well as from Reagan and the Pentagon.

Under the Salt II accord, each side was to reduce its total missiles and bombers to 2,250, with a combined limit of 1,320 on MIRVed missiles and heavy bombers carrying cruise missiles. Each side was allowed only 1,200 missiles armed with MIRVs, including up to 820 land-based launchers firing MIRVs. Each allowed cruise missile bomber could carry no more than 28 cruise missiles. The agreement also limited each side to the development of one new land-based ballistic missile system. Existing systems could be modernized. The treaty would be in effect until 1985.

A protocol to the treaty limited mobile missiles and land- and sea-based cruise missiles with extended ranges. The protocol expired at the end of 1981.

The U.S. Senate never ratified the treaty, but both the United States and the Soviet Union have said that they will abide by the treaty as long as the other side does the same.[16]

Strategic Arms Reduction Talks

While the Reagan administration agreed to abide by Salt II limits, its first meeting with the Soviets on a new round of strategic arms talks took place almost a year and a half after the administration took office. At that meeting, the United States proposed in the new Strategic Arms Reduction Talks (Start) that the two sides agree to reductions to fewer than 5,000 ballistic missile warheads on no more than 850 deployed ballistic missiles. No more than half the warheads could be on ICBMs, a requirement that would require the USSR, with its heavy reliance on ICBMs, to restructure its forces. The United States contended that less reliance on ICBMs would promote strategic stability, since ICBMs are both accurate and particularly vulnerable.

In the summer of 1983, the United States amended its Start proposal to remove the sublimit of 850 missiles; reportedly, the new proposal specified a sublimit of 1,200.[17] This change could accommodate a shift toward small single-warhead ICBMs, as recommended by the President's Commission on Strategic Forces (the Scowcroft commission). The commission suggested that a long-term bilateral shift to single-warhead missiles and away from MIRVed warheads would promote strategic stability, and some members of Congress made their continued support for the MX missile contingent on the President's commitment to the small, single-warhead missile option.

The United States also proposed in mid-1983 that the two countries limit long-range strategic bombers to 400, each to carry no more than 20 cruise missiles. The bomber limit was an important concession to the Soviets, given U.S. strategic bomber superiority and the earlier U.S. decision to exclude bombers from Start.

The United States also proposed that first-phase reductions be followed by reductions in aggregate "throwweight" to equal levels. With its heavy reliance on large ICBMs, the Soviet Union has a four to one throwweight advantage. Since the initial Start discussions, the United States has modified its position by offering several options on throwweight. (Throwweight is the maximum weight of the warhead and related equipment that can be delivered over a particular trajectory by a missile.)

The Soviets reportedly have pursued a continuation of the Salt framework, with further reductions. The Soviets would limit missile launchers and heavy bombers to 1,800 by 1990, of which no more than 1,080 could be MIRVed missiles. No more than 680 of the MIRVed missiles could be land-based. At the end of 1982, the Soviets had 930 and the Americans 450 strategic land-based MIRVed missiles. Both sides would be limited to 120 bombers carrying ALCMs. The Soviets have said that they would withdraw the proposal if NATO begins, as planned for December 1983, to deploy the Pershing II and ground-launched cruise missiles in Europe.

According to the Congressional Budget Office, enactment of the administration's Start proposal in its present form would have no effect on the current modernization program if sufficient numbers of older systems were retired, including all Minuteman missiles and Poseidon submarines, and some B-52s.[18]

While U.S. Start negotiator Edward Rowny is optimistic that at least a basic framework for agreement can be reached in the near future, the recent heightening of tensions between the superpowers, and the apparently slow progress in negotiations to date, make the Start prospects appear uncertain at best. If installation of the new NATO theater nuclear missiles begins in the winter of 1983-84, as seems likely, negotiations will be further complicated.

INF Negotiations

In 1977, NATO governments approved a proposal to deploy 464 ground-launched cruise missiles and 108 Pershing II intermediate-range ballistic missiles in Europe. At the same time, NATO supported bilateral negotiations between the United States and the Soviet Union aimed at reducing intermediate-range missiles in the Soviet Union. The particular threat to Western Europe has been the Soviet deployment since 1976 of more than 300 SS-20 missiles, each of which has three warheads.

The Soviet Union agreed to separate negotiations with the United States over so-called intermediate range nuclear forces (INF). While both sides have shown some signs of accommodation, the talks have not borne fruit, and the Soviets have said they would withdraw if deployment of the Pershing and cruise missiles began, as scheduled, in December 1983.

The United States initially insisted on total elimination of SS-20s, and two other intermediate range missiles from the Soviet arsenal, in exchange for no NATO deployment of the Pershing and cruise missiles. The Soviets rejected this "zero option," in large part because it ignored the presence of independent French and British nuclear forces. Britain has 64 Polaris missiles, each with three warheads, and is preparing to replace them with eight-warhead Trident II missiles. France rapidly is upgrading its force de frappe, which currently includes 18 intermediate range land-based missiles and 80 submarine-launched missiles. The Soviets insisted that French and British forces must be included in the equation.[19]

The most promising avenue for agreement probably was the proposal outlined in the Nitze-Kvitsinsky compromise of July 1982. Named for the U.S. and Soviet negotiators, this framework would have allowed 75 GLCM launchers (with 300 warheads) and 75 Soviet SS-20s in Europe. The Pershing II, which the Soviets find particularly threatening, would not be allowed, and the Soviets could not increase deployment of SS-20s in the far eastern USSR.[20] The latter requirement was generated by U.S. fears that Soviet reduction of European SS-20s might be accomplished by moving them east. Both nations rejected the Nitze-Kvitsinsky framework.

Nuclear Weapons Freeze

During the Reagan administration, a proposal for a nuclear freeze has proven to be a popular rallying point for opponents of continued arms buildup, who suggest in a direct manner that the superpowers must stop production of new (and more capable) systems before a reduction of the nuclear threat can be achieved. The freeze proposal has been approved by numerous local groups and governments, by many private organizations, and by voters in nine of 10 states that voted on freeze referenda in 1982. In the spring of 1983, a freeze proposal was approved by the House of Representatives.

There are a variety of nuclear freeze proposals, but all call for a mutual and verifiable cessation of further arms production. It is difficult to identify precisely which military programs would be affected by an agreed-upon freeze; it depends on the details. In a study of the economic effects of a nuclear freeze, the Nuclear Weapons Freeze Campaign identified weapons systems that would be directly affected by a freeze as advocated by the campaign. The systems include the B-1B and Stealth bombers, MX missile, Trident I and II missiles, nuclear-armed cruise missiles and Pershing II missile. The Freeze Campaign suggested that new investments in ballistic missile defense, strategic air defense, command, control, communications and intelligence (C^3I) and the Trident submarine would not be prohibited by a freeze, but could be expected to be reduced or eliminated once a freeze took effect.[21]

Negotiations over a freeze probably would not stop with consideration of these major weapons. It is likely that the two sides would have to discuss other systems. In particular, nuclear-capable tactical forces are of major concern to the Soviets. These dual purpose systems include many attack and fighter planes, as well as various ships that are equipped with nuclear weapons. New investments in antisatellite weapons, as well as anti-aircraft and antisubmarine programs that would affect the strategic balance, also could complicate the negotiation of a freeze.

Despite complications, freeze advocates believe that an agreement --which would be followed by negotiations to reduce arsenals--could be reached within a relatively short time compared with the length of Salt and Start talks.

Chapter II Footnotes

1. Alva Myrdal, The Game of Disarmament (Revised Edition), Pantheon, New York, 1982, p. 73.
2. For text of Baruch statement, see United Nations, "Atomic Energy Commission, First Meeting, June 14, 1946." For discussion, see Myrdal, op. cit., p. 74; U.S. Arms Control and Disarmament Agency (ACDA), Arms Control and Disarmament Agreements, Washington, 1982; ACDA, Toward a World Without War: A Summary of United States Disarmament Efforts--Past and Present, Government Printing Office, Washington, 1962, p. 5-7.
3. Myrdal, op. cit., p. 84-8; Bulletin of Atomic Scientists, August/September 1983, p. 36-8.
4. ACDA, Toward World Without War, op. cit., p. 10-11.
5. Ibid., p. 15.
6. For text of treat and signatories, see ACDA, Arms Control and Disarmament Agreements, op. cit., p. 41-7.
7. Stockholm International Peace Research Institute, World Armaments and Disarmament: Sipri Yearbook 1983, Taylor & Francis, New York, 1983, p. 100.
8. For text of treaties, see ACDA, Arms Control and Disarmament Agreements, op. cit., p. 167-70; 173-89.
9. Scientific American, October 1982, p. 47-55.
10. For discussion of test ban, see Myrdal, op. cit.; Bulletin of Atomic Scientists, August-September 1983, p. 36-42; Scientific American, op. cit.; Sipri, op. cit., and earlier Sipri yearbooks.
11. For discussion and text of treaty, see ACDA, Arms Control and Disarmament Agreements, op. cit., p. 45-48.
12. For petition and partial list of signatories, see Bulletin of Atomic Scientists, November 1983, p. 2-3.
13. Arms Control Association, Arms Control Today, September 1983, p. 5.
14. ACDA, Arms Control and Disarmament Agreements, op. cit., p. 132.
15. Ibid. for discussion and text of treaty, p. 132-63.
16. Ibid. for discussion and text of treaty, p. 239-77.
17. Arms Control Today, op. cit., p. 5.
18. Congressional Budget Office, "Counterforce Issues for the U.S. Strategic Nuclear Forces," January 1978.
19. Sipri, op. cit., p. 3-25.
20. Arms Control Today, op. cit., p. 5.
21. National Clearinghouse--Nuclear Weapons Freeze Campaign, The Freeze Economy (1983), p. 13.

Chapter III
The Nuclear Weapons Industry

The producers of nuclear weapons and related systems and of tactical nuclear weapons form a rapidly growing industry that in 1983 will have received at least $30 billion in new orders. Calling this group of companies an "industry" may be a misnomer, in that a wide assortment of companies are involved in producing nuclear weapons and their various support systems. Producers range from highly sophisticated electronics companies to shipbuilders to metals manufacturers.

While these companies are diverse, they can be broken down into two groups: (1) companies that manage or do other work for government-owned facilities that participate in the production of nuclear warheads and materials under contract to the Department of Energy, and (2) Defense Department contractors that develop and produce weapon delivery and related systems.

In a recent study, the Center for Defense Information (CDI) estimated that nuclear forces consumed $51.8 billion in U.S. fiscal year 1983, or 21 percent of total military expenditures.[1] (See Table 1.) Based on administration budget projections, that figure can be expected to rise to $94.7 billion in 1988. Overall between 1983 and 1988, the cost of nuclear forces is projected at $457.6 billion.

In terms of dollars, the Defense Department program is much more important than is the Energy Department's. The DoD share of the 1984 nuclear budget is $58.1 billion, according to CDI, compared with $6.2 billion for DoE and $386 million for the Federal Emergency Management Administration (FEMA), which is responsible for civil defense.

The Defense Department's "strategic forces" budget for FY 1983 was $20.6 billion, and President Reagan recommended an increase to $28.1 billion in FY 1984. Correcting for inflation, the strategic forces budget grew by 29 percent in 1983.[2] Currently, nuclear weapons systems are the fastest growing part of the defense budget.

Budget authority for the Energy Department defense program (including naval nuclear reactors) was $5.7 billion in FY 1983 and $6.6 billion in FY 1984, a 14 percent increase. The 1983 budget included $3.3 billion

Table 1
National Defense and Nuclear Forces Budgets, 1983-88
(dollar figures in billions)

Fiscal year	National defense budget	Costs for nuclear forces	Nuclear budget as a percentage of total	DoD nuclear costs	DoE nuclear costs*
1983	$245.5	$51.8	21.1%	$46.2	$5.3
1984	$280.5	$64.7	23.1%	$58.1	$6.2
1985	$330.0	$77.5	23.5%	$69.6	$7.4
1986	$364.8	$81.5	22.3%	$73.6	$7.3
1987	$397.0	$87.4	22.0%	$79.3	$7.5
1988	$432.7	$94.7	21.9%	$86.9	$7.1

Source: Center for Defense Information.

* Does not include naval reactor program.

NOTE: Total national defense and nuclear forces figures include budget of the Federal Emergency Management Agency (FEMA). All figures are based on total obligational authority as projected by the administration.

for weapons activities and $1.2 billion for materials production related to those weapons and to the naval reactors program. Another $527 million is allocated to the development of naval atomic reactors for submarines and surface ships such as aircraft carriers and cruisers.[3]

While the Energy Department's portion of the nuclear systems budget is smaller than the Defense Department's program, the DoE complex produces the actual warheads and bombs, the core of the nation's nuclear armaments system. Shortly after World War II, the Atomic Energy Commission, one of DoE's predecessor agencies, was given responsibility for both civilian and military applications of atomic technology, in large part to assert civilian control. The responsibility for nuclear programs rested with the AEC until it was abolished in 1975. At that time, the new Energy Research and Development Administration took responsibility, followed by the Energy Department when it was created in 1978. In 1981, the Reagan administration proposed abolishing the Energy Department, shifting its nuclear programs, including defense, to the Commerce Department. Those plans since have been shelved.

This chapter describes the two parts of the nuclear warfare industry, beginning with the Defense Department contractors.

Department of Defense Nuclear Warfare Systems Contractors

In October 1981, President Reagan and Secretary Weinberger announced the administration's strategic program. Reagan's priorities included strategic command, control, communications and intelligence systems (C^3I in military lingo), and such programs as the MX and Trident II missiles and B-1B bomber. The course charted by President Reagan would accelerate an expansion of the nuclear weapons industry that President Carter had initiated.

The overall DoD procurement and research and development budget in fiscal year 1983 was $85 billion, including $21 billion for strategic systems. Not including inflation, the procurement budget is expected to increase 113 percent between calendar year 1982 and 1987, compared with a 48 percent increase in the defense budget overall, the Commerce Department says. By 1987, the procurement budget should consume 34¢ of every defense dollar, compared with 24¢ in 1982.[4] (See Figure 1.) A major reason for the increasing procurement budget is substantial investment in strategic forces.

This dramatic procurement increase should be a boon to the defense business and its employees. In 1981, an estimated 2.6 million employees of private companies worked on military contracts, about 3 percent of the nation's total employed labor force. (Another 2.2 million people served in the armed forces.) In the next five years, the private defense work force can be expected to increase in all 30 leading defense industries. (See Table 2.)

Table 2 presents estimates of the value of 1983 production by the leading defense industries, along with projections for 1988. The estimates are used by the Defense Department and are based on Data Resources Inc. economic models. As the table indicates, the most important final suppliers of unique goods and services used to support the nation's nuclear defense forces are the aircraft, radio and TV communication equipment, shipbuilding, electronic components and guided missiles and space vehicles industries. Each of these industries is expected to grow substantially in the next few years, and employment on military projects in the five industries is projected to grow from 800,000 in 1983 to 1.1 million in 1988.[5]

The leading industries involved in the production of nuclear weapons and related products are described below.

Figure 1
National Defense Purchases by Program, 1982 and 1987: Dollar Breakdown

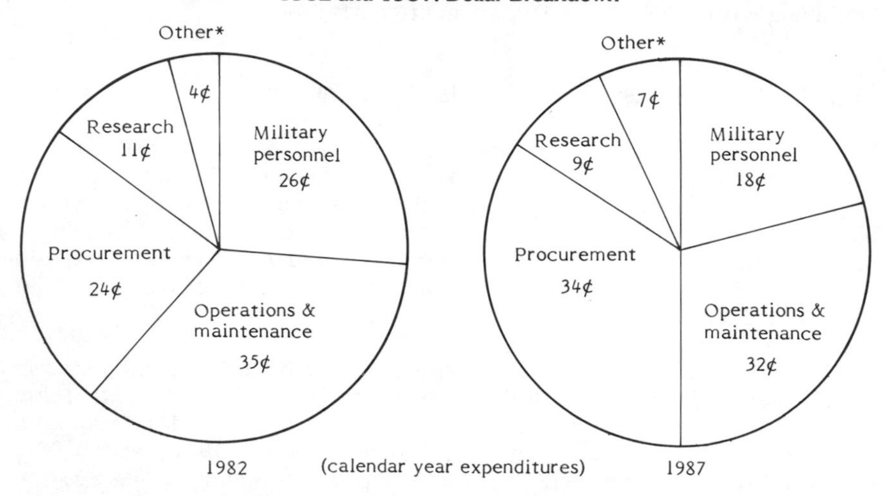

*Includes military construction, family housing and non-DoD defense programs, including Energy Department nuclear weapons and materials programs.

Source: U.S. Department of Commerce, U.S. Industrial Outlook 1983, p. XLI.

Aerospace: The largest defense industry and the most substantial producer of nuclear weapons-related systems and equipment is the aerospace industry. Aerospace production for the military (excluding foreign military sales) was expected to total $27.1 billion in 1983. In 1982, DoD purchases of aerospace products and services reached the highest level (in constant dollars) since the peak Vietnam war year of 1969, according to the Aerospace Industries Association.[6] The aerospace category includes aircraft and aircraft engines, along with missiles and space vehicles and their propulsion systems.

For purposes of this analysis, the military aerospace industry is broken down into two product groups: One group is aircraft; the other is missiles and space vehicles. Military demand for both product groups has grown rapidly since 1979. Overall, the Defense Department increased its aerospace purchases by 38 percent (after accounting for inflation) between 1979 and 1982, and they are expected to increase by another 50 percent by 1987. This growth reverses the rapid post-Vietnam shrinkage of the military aerospace market that took place in the early 1970s. (See Figure 2.)

Table 2
Leading 30 Defense Industries
(millions of 1982 dollars)

Industry	Defense Production		Defense production as percentage of Total Domestic Prod.		Avg. annual Growth in Def. Prod.	Defense employment (in thousands)	
	1983	1988	1983	1988	1983-88	1983	1988
AIRCRAFT*	**$21,879**	**$33,191**	**50.1%**	**54.6%**	**8.7%**	**239**	**313**
RADIO & TV COMMUNICATION EQUIPMENT	**17,996**	**29,588**	**47.3**	**55.2**	**10.5**	**247**	**326**
Miscellaneous business services	8,578	13,227	6.0	6.7	9.0	259	354
SHIPBUILDING & REPAIRING	**8,020**	**11,370**	**69.9**	**72.8**	**7.2**	**144**	**173**
Petroleum refining & related products	7,757	10,236	5.0	6.4	5.7	8	10
ELECTRONIC COMPONENTS	**6,284**	**11,527**	**21.4**	**24.3**	**13.0**	**117**	**176**
GUIDED MISSILES & SPACE VEHICLES	**5,229**	**8,269**	**55.2**	**65.4**	**9.6**	**62**	**85**
Crude petroleum & natural gas	4,998	6,407	4.9	6.5	5.1	12	17
Steel mill products	4,848	7,412	8.6	10.0	8.9	32	41
Inorganic & organic chemicals	4,605	6,955	7.9	9.1	8.6	23	29
Ammunition & ordnance (exc. small arms) n.e.c.+	4,262	7,523	75.8	88.1	12.5	78	114
Electric utilities	4,159	6,047	3.0	3.9	7.8	15	19
Electric measuring instruments	4,081	6,158	43.8	43.9	8.6	66	93
Computers	3,909	7,927	10.6	11.9	15.2	44	63
Air carriers & related services	3,500	4,994	6.3	6.9	7.4	28	35
Motor freight	3,218	4,549	5.2	5.7	7.2	44	49
Motor vehicles, including parts & accessories	3,026	4,948	3.0	3.5	10.4	18	25
Communications, except radio & TV	2,811	4,547	2.6	2.7	10.1	31	39
Gas utilities	2,728	3,644	2.3	3.3	6.0	4	6
Aluminum^	2,228	3,752	10.1	12.2	11.0	15	22
Measuring & control instruments	1,969	2,928	24.6	26.8	8.3	43	55
Water transportation & related services	1,765	2,081	8.4	9.0	3.3	15	16
Miscellaneous machinery	1,690	2,632	11.8	13.8	9.3	30	40
Miscellaneous plastic products	1,571	2,878	4.0	4.9	12.9	19	29
Engineering & scientific equipment	1,378	2,089	41.7	45.7	8.7	24	31
Railroads & rail-related services	1,293	1,881	4.2	4.9	7.8	16	19
Power boilers & steam generators	1,076	1,674	10.4	12.7	9.5	14	18
Tanks & tank components	1,061	1,453	65.4	77.3	6.5	10	15
Plastic materials & resins	1,036	1,794	5.1	5.9	11.6	4	5
Iron & steel foundries & forgings	1,021	1,552	8.3	9.6	8.8	15	19

Source: DoD's Defense Economic Impact Modeling System, except where noted. Figures exclude foreign military sales.

Five leading suppliers of equipment for strategic and other nuclear weapons forces appear in all caps.

* Includes engines and parts, along with space propulsion systems and space vehicle equipment.
\+ N.e.c. = not elsewhere classified.
^ Excludes wire drawing and insulation.

Figure 2
Aerospace Sales to the Defense Department, 1967-1983

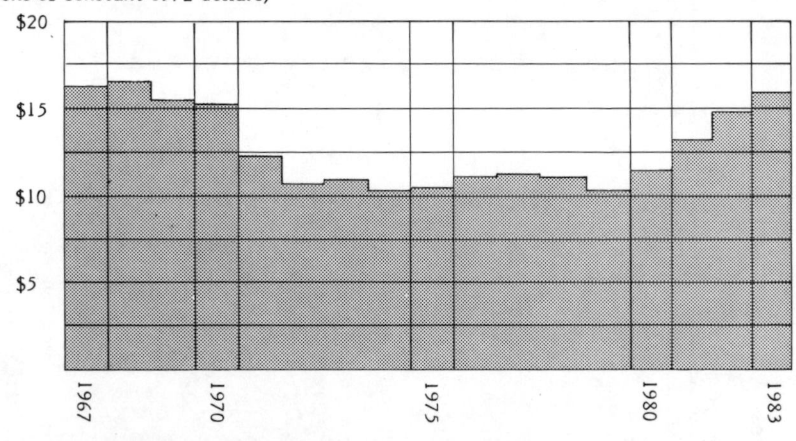

Source: Aerospace Industries Association.

Despite the increase in DoD aerospace purchases between 1981 and 1982, a plunge in civilian aircraft sales resulted in a net decline in total aerospace business in 1982. Aerospace Industries Association figures show a sharp increase in the defense share of aerospace business since 1981.[7] Using a somewhat different definition of the industry, the AIA has provided data on the breakdown of the aerospace industry among customers. (See Figure 3.) (The AIA used a broader definition of the aerospace industry than do the other organizations cited here.)

Defense should continue consuming a greater portion of the nation's aerospace expenditures through the decade (although a recovery in civilian aerospace is expected, assuming interest rates are not excessive). The Defense Department calculates that aerospace defense sales (excluding foreign military sales) will increase 53 percent between 1983 and 1988, compared with a 40 percent increase in commercial aerospace sales.

Aerospace employment totaled 687,000 in 1982, according to the Commerce Department, equal to about 0.8 percent of all U.S. employment. Some 362,000 of the industry's employees (53 percent) were production workers, and another 194,000 were scientists and engineers. Defense Department figures indicated that 45 percent of aerospace workers were employed on defense projects in 1982; that is projected to increase to 56 percent by 1988.

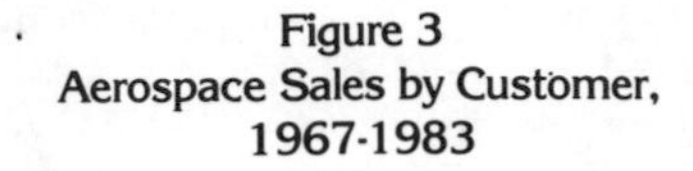
Figure 3
Aerospace Sales by Customer,
1967-1983

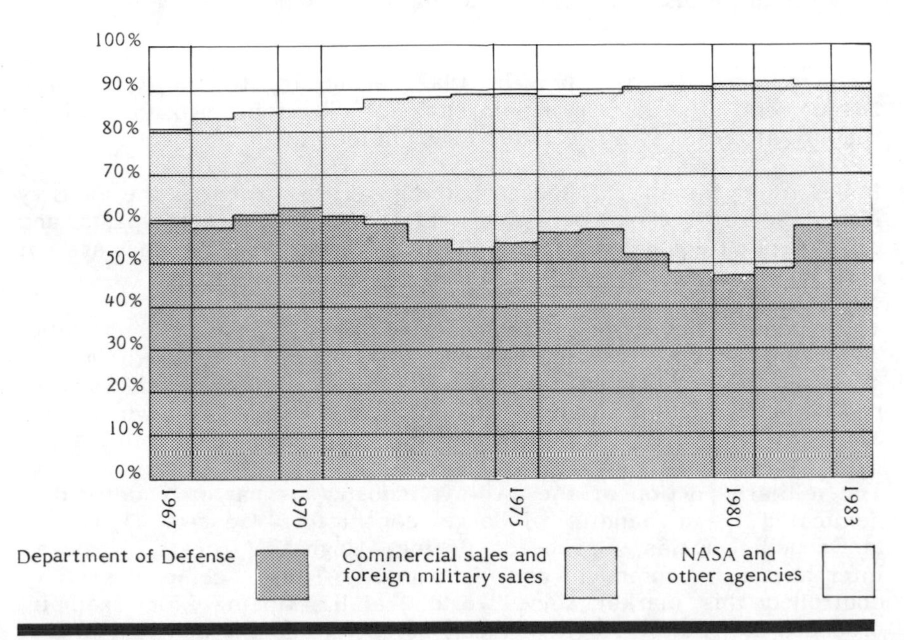

Source: Aerospace Industries Association.

Aerospace workers are well-paid--average hourly compensation for aircraft production workers was $12.50 in 1982--and many of the production workers are organized by the Machinists and other unions.

As measured against sales and assets, industry profits usually have lagged behind profit rates for manufacturing industries overall, although as a percentage of equity, aerospace earnings have exceeded the average in recent years. (Moreover, among the Fortune 500, aerospace companies provided the highest return to investors of any industry over the 1972-82 period.[8]) In 1982, estimated aerospace profits after taxes were equal to 3.3 percent of sales, compared with 4.0 percent for all manufacturing industries.[9] The Commerce Department and other sources indicate that military programs generate lower profits than do civilian projects, although frequently less investment is required because the government often provides factory space and equipment. In addition, military work may involve less risk for the company than do commercial projects, which the company must fund itself. Research and development on prospective military programs is funded largely by the government, although some firms, such as Northrop, prefer to rely mostly on their own resources for preliminary research.

The aerospace industry is highly concentrated. The four largest companies account for 61 percent of shipments. The most important aerospace facilities are located in just five states--California, Connecticut, Kansas, Texas and Washington.

Aircraft--Total sales by the aircraft segment of the aerospace industry were $41.5 billion in 1982, according to the Commerce Department. The industry employed 521,400 persons. Roughly half of the aircraft business is accounted for by defense.

In describing the aircraft industry, the government divides the industry into three categories: aircraft, aircraft engines and engine parts, and other aircraft equipment. (See Table 3.) By and large, engines are not made by the same companies that produce the aircraft.

The aircraft portion of the industry (minus engines and other equipment) accounts for the majority of shipments and is expected to grow by 59 percent between 1982 and 1987. The current wave of production is expected to peak after U.S. fiscal year 1986, when 1,082 aircraft will be ordered by the government (according to current plans).

The military portion of the aircraft industry as narrowly defined is dominated by a handful of large contractors--General Dynamics, McDonnell Douglas, Lockheed, Boeing, Hughes Aircraft, Rockwell International, Grumman and Northrop. These companies have controlled this market since World War II. Boeing, for example, produced the first strategic (nuclear) bombers, and the company still is a major factor in the B-52, B-1B and Stealth bomber programs.

The engines segment of the industry--accounting for $11.2 billion in sales in 1982--is dominated by three companies: United Technologies' Pratt & Whitney subsidiary, General Electric and Rolls Royce, the British corporation. Pratt & Whitney and GE control all of the U.S. market for large military aircraft engines. In 1982, Pratt & Whitney won 73 percent of that market; GE took the other 27 percent. Despite the few participants in the market, competition between GE and Pratt & Whitney is keen. GE has been increasing its market share in recent years, and the company's contract to produce the B-1B engines should be a major boon.

The aircraft equipment segment is more diffuse, involving hundreds of companies. The most important suppliers, however, are those that dominate the aircraft market. Shipments of aircraft equipment not elsewhere classified totaled $9.4 billion in 1982.

It is important to note that, despite the dominance of a few firms in the aircraft market, thousands of subcontractors and suppliers are involved. It is estimated that the major firms subcontract as much as half the value of their prime contracts (although often to each other).

Table 3
Aircraft Industries, 1982

Industry	Shipments (in millions of dollars)	Employment	Production Workers
Aircraft	$21,791	252,300	137,800
Aircraft engines and engine parts	9,222	127,100	76,100
Aircraft equipment, not elsewhere classified	10,469	142,000	84,300

Source: Commerce Department, Bureau of Industrial Economics.

Military aircraft and related production has been marked by substantial cost escalation in recent years, including a price level increase of 23 percent between the first quarters of 1982 and 1983. Overall, aircraft price levels increased 178 percent between 1972 and the beginning of 1983, compared with only a 107 percent increase in price levels in the economy as a whole.[10] Factors contributing to this inflation include rising raw materials prices and increasing wage rates. In addition, a large body of critics, including some officials within the Pentagon, believe that aircraft and related equipment are becoming much too complicated, inflating costs and creating performance problems. This factor is reflected only indirectly in the price level increases cited above.

Expenditures on aircraft primarily developed for nuclear warfare purposes have constituted relatively small portions of the defense aircraft budget in recent years, but that is changing with the development of the B-1B and advanced technology (or Stealth) bombers. In U.S. fiscal year 1981 (IRRC's base year for studying contractors), procurement costs for major "primary" nuclear warfare aircraft totaled $807 million, only 6 percent of the procurement budget for all major aircraft. By 1983, the procurement budget for primary nuclear warfare aircraft, not including the classified Stealth bomber, had risen to $6.1 billion, primarily because of the B-1 bomber. (See Table 4.) These procurement commitments totaled 25 percent of the budget for major aircraft systems. (It is important to note that procurement dollars are actually spent--and actually show up in industry sales--for some period after the commitments are made.) It is likely that primary nuclear systems will account for a quarter or more

Table 4
FY 1983 Procurement and R&D Funds
for Primary Nuclear Warfare Aircraft
(in millions of dollars)

System	Budget*	Lead Contractors
B-1B bomber	$4,787	Rockwell International, GE
KC-135 aerial tanker	496	Boeing, GE
B-52 bomber	447	Boeing
EC-130 communications aircraft	36	Lockheed, Collins Radio
ECX communications aircraft	37	Boeing
"Stealth" advanced technology bomber+	?	Northrop, Boeing, GE

Source: "Program Acquisition Costs by Weapon System," Department of Defense, Jan. 31, 1983.

* Includes procurement and research and development costs.
+ Classified.

NOTE: Procurement budgeted in any one year usually are spent over several years.

of military aircraft sales--and at least 15 percent of total aircraft sales--for the next several years, unless the B-1B is canceled.

As noted in Chapter I, and as detailed in the company profiles, IRRC has developed a "secondary" classification for nuclear warfare-related systems and for dual-capable (that is, conventional and nuclear) delivery and launch systems. A large number of aircraft built for conventional warfare also are equipped to carry nuclear weapons. These include such fighters as the McDonnell Douglas F-15, the General Dynamics F-16 and the McDonnell Douglas/Northrop F/A-18, as well as attack aircraft such as the Grumman A-6. Weapons in this secondary category account for $11.5 billion of the FY 1983 budget for major aircraft programs, or 50 percent of the total. Thus primary and secondary nuclear systems combined account for 75 percent of the total.

Missiles and space--Missiles and space systems together accounted for about 25 percent of aerospace business in 1982, with shipments totaling $15.1 billion, according to the Commerce Department. These industries employed 165,400 persons in 1982, including 63,400 production workers.

The military missile and space markets are expected to be among the fastest growing markets in the next few years, to a substantial degree because of anticipated production runs for a number of large nuclear missile programs, including the MX, Trident, Pershing II and various cruise missiles. The Commerce Department expects the military's demand for guided missiles and space vehicles to grow by 64 percent between 1982 and 1987. If President Reagan's proposals for expanded military use of space, including defense against ICBMs, are developed, and if the proposed Midgetman mobile ICBM is developed, missile and space sales can be expected to continue to grow at a rapid clip after 1987.

It is possible that this sector will experience bottlenecks during this military buildup. The growth rate for all missile and space vehicle products, including both military and nonmilitary, is projected by the Commerce Department to average 5.6 percent a year over the next five years, the highest rate for any of the aerospace industries.

Sales of missile systems and parts, excluding propulsion systems and research and development expenditures, were valued by the Census Bureau at $5.4 billion in 1982, a substantial increase over 1981 sales levels. As might be expected, 97 percent of missile shipments were to the military, including 88 percent to the U.S. government.

A large portion of missiles are equipped with nuclear warheads and are otherwise designed for strategic war. Table 5 shows the major primary nuclear warfare missiles now being produced or developed, the FY 1983 budget for each missile, and the lead contractors. The 1983 budget authority for these primary systems (to be spent over several years) totaled $5.7 billion, 53 percent of the government's total budget for major missile systems. The only secondary system is the Tomahawk cruise missile, which is being developed in both nuclear and conventional versions. The Tomahawk FY 1983 appropriation is $330 million, or 3 percent of the total missile budget. (A second dual-capable system, General Dynamics' extended range Standard Missile-2, will have both conventional and nuclear versions, but apparently all the missiles ordered in 1983 will be conventional.)

In 1982, for the first time since 1960, the military bought more space vehicle systems and parts than did NASA. Sales of these products (not including propulsion systems and research and development work) added up to $4.8 billion in 1982, up 20 percent from 1981. Military space purchases, which were up 49 percent to $2.5 billion, accounted for all of the increase.

Table 5
Procurement and R&D Funds
for Primary Nuclear Missiles, FY 1983
(in millions of dollars)

System	Budget*	Lead Contractors
MX missile	$2,506	TRW, Martin Marietta, Northrop, Rockwell International, Boeing, Avco, Morton Thiokol, General Tire & Rubber, Hercules
Trident I missile	677	Lockheed
Air-launched cruise missile	574	Boeing
Pershing II missile	565	Martin Marietta
Ballistic missile defense	519	McDonnell Douglas, Rockwell
Ground-launched cruise missiles	487	General Dynamics, McDonnell Douglas, Williams International
Trident II missile	370	Lockheed
Advanced strategic missile systems	50	GE, Avco, others
Minuteman II & III missiles	11	Boeing, GE, GTE, Rockwell
Advanced cruise missile+		General Dynamics

Source: "Program Acquisition Costs by Weapon System," Department of Defense, Jan. 31, 1983.

* Includes procurement and research and development costs.
\+ Classified.

NOTE: Listing does not include the proposed small ICBM, or Midgetman missile, which is budgeted at $604 million in research and development for fiscal 1984.

The trend toward greater military activity in space relative to nonmilitary activity is illustrated in Figure 4, which shows the NASA and DoD space activities budgets.

It is important to note at this point that the industry sales figures exclude satellite and other equipment that is produced by the "radio and TV communications industry." (See p. 48. The space activities budgets

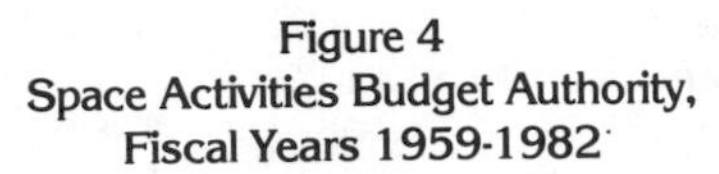

Figure 4
Space Activities Budget Authority,
Fiscal Years 1959-1982

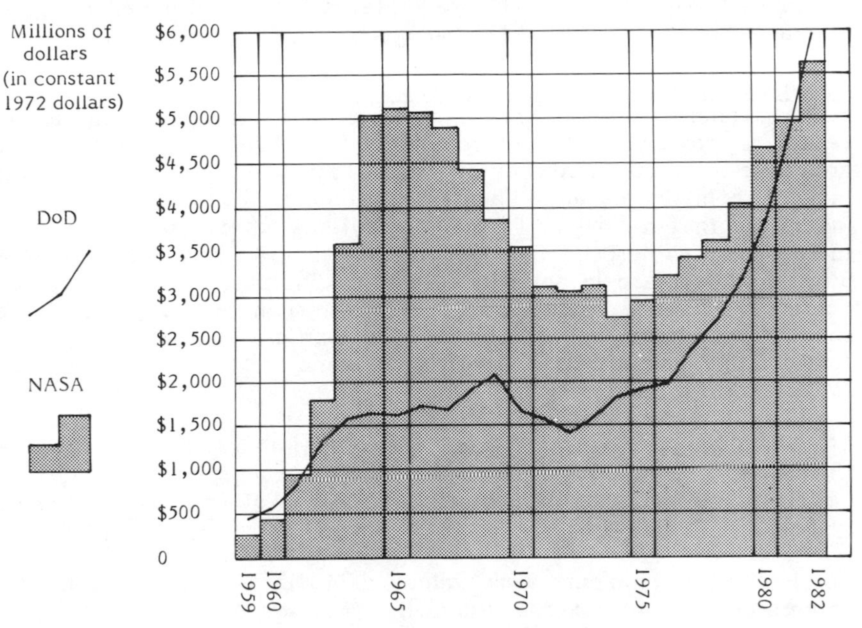

Source: Aerospace Industries Association.

in Figure 4 include these satellite systems.) In addition, there is substantial blurring between military and civilian space programs. For example, the Space Shuttle has been produced by NASA, but it has both military and civilian purposes. The Defense Department now makes its own payments on shuttle programs, but NASA expenditures may have substantial value to DoD.

Major space vehicle programs that have implications for both nuclear and conventional forces include the Space Shuttle (FY 1983 DoD budget: $492 million); Boeing's Inertial Upper Stage vehicle and McDonnell Douglas's Payload Assist Module (combined budget of $169 million); and Martin Marietta's Titan III booster ($86 million).

Major space vehicle producers are Rockwell International, Martin Marietta, General Dynamics, McDonnell Douglas, LTV, Lockheed, Fairchild Industries and Boeing.

Producers of engine and propulsion systems for missile and space vehicles sold $1.6 billion in such goods during 1982. The industry employs 28,700. The government developed space and large missile propulsion systems at the same time, and many of the same systems are used for both ICBM and satellite launches. Major producers include General Dynamics, General Tire & Rubber's Aerojet General subsidiary, Hercules, Morton-Thiokol, Rockwell International, McDonnell Douglas, Martin Marietta, and United Technologies.

Radio and television communications equipment: The radio and television communications industry grew by 10 percent in 1982 and is expected to grow by another 13 percent in 1983. To a large extent, this growth is being stimulated by increased defense requirements for this kind of sophisticated and expensive equipment. The Defense Department says that radio and TV communications defense production will increase by 64 percent between 1983 and 1988, compared with a 36 percent increase in nondefense output. In 1981, the U.S. military consumed 45 percent of this sector's production; by 1988, the figure should rise to more than 55 percent. (Foreign military sales accounted for another 8 percent of the total in 1981 and are expected to account for 7 percent in 1988.)

The radio and TV communications equipment industry includes more than its name implies. It consists of a wide range of non-communications electronic systems, including ICBM and other missile guidance systems.

Total industry shipments were valued at $31.3 billion (and domestic defense production at $18.0 billion) in 1982, and employees numbered some 454,000, including 233,000 production workers. Wages were somewhat lower than those earned by aerospace workers; a production worker earned an average of $9.96 an hour in 1982.

Inflation rates also have been lower in the communications industry than in aerospace; prices for defense communications goods increased only 87 percent between 1972 and 1983, half the rate of aerospace price inflation. Between the first quarters of 1982 and 1983, prices increased 1.9 percent.[11] (Nevertheless, in the view of Pentagon critics, the increasingly complicated systems in this category account for much of the price escalation of aerospace products on a unit basis.)

The communications industry is somewhat concentrated, with four companies accounting for 20 percent of sales. Major portions of the industry are located in four states: California, New York, Texas and Florida, in order of importance. A total of 2,121 establishments are classified in this industry.

Communications equipment accounted for more than 20 percent of the DoD procurement budget in 1982. The military's $18 billion expenditure on radio and TV communications products included radars and sonars, navigation systems, missile guidance systems, gunfire control components, satellites, electronic countermeasures equipment and simulators to train pilots in the use of aircraft.

Much of this equipment is used in relation to nuclear weapons, as well as for systems used for the whole spectrum of defense needs, but accurate breakdowns between nuclear and nonnuclear sales are not available.

The administration considers improvement of command, control, communications and intelligence (C^3I) systems to be the most important strategic priority at present, and this accounts for much of the current growth in the radio and TV communications industry. The Defense Department's budget for strategic surveillance, warning, command and communications programs--which by no means includes all systems that affect nuclear warfighting ability--was $1.6 billion in FY 1983, including $860 million for research and development.

Perhaps the best way to illustrate the industry's contribution to strategic and other nuclear weapons systems is to look at the industry's five product groups. Three of the five--search, detection, navigation and guidance systems; communications systems; and electronic systems not elsewhere classified--involve significant military and strategic production. (The other two groups are "broadcast, studio and related electronic equipment" and "intercommunications systems.")

Search, detection, navigation and guidance systems: Shipments of these mostly military products totaled $18 billion in 1982, more than half of the overall industry. This product group includes many systems used on missile and space vehicles, radar and sonar systems, electronic warfare systems and navigation devices. Many of these products are indispensable to the operation of nuclear weapons. For example, the most important advancement in missile technology in recent years has been improved accuracy. The inertial guidance systems on the Minuteman III, MX and Trident I missiles make possible their unprecedented accuracy. Leading guidance manufacturers for these missiles are Rockwell International, Northrop, Honeywell, General Electric, Draper Laboratories, Raytheon and Hughes Aircraft. Another guidance system that tracks terrain during the course of the missile's flight is produced by McDonnell Douglas for the cruise missile. Goodyear Aerospace is producing the guidance system for the highly accurate Pershing II missile, to be deployed in West Germany.

Radar and sonar systems are required for the successful operation and tracking of aircraft and submarines. Notable producers of radar and sonar systems for nuclear weapons "launch platforms" such as strategic bombers and submarines include Lockheed, Raytheon, Sperry, AT&T, General Electric, GTE, Honeywell, Westinghouse and RCA.

Land-based radar, such as the Distant Early Warning (DEW) line across the northern tier of the continent, provides essential tracking of potential nuclear threats. Major producers of such systems include Raytheon, Allied's Bendix subsidiary, and GE. In addition, the mobile Awacs system, including Westinghouse radar systems, provides similar defensive warning capability.

Table 6
The Electronic Warfare Industry's
Leading Contractors in 1981

Rank	Company	Estimated EW sales (in millions of dollars)
1	E-Systems	$216
2	Loral	203
3	TRW	185
4	Raytheon	170
5	Northrop	166
6	GTE	165
7	Sanders Associates	150
8	Westinghouse	140

Source: Lexicon, EW market data, 1981.

The importance of electronic communications--and the gains to be had from disrupting the enemy's communications--have spawned the burgeoning field of electronic warfare (or EW). EW includes systems to track the enemy's electronic devices, electronic countermeasures (ECM) to deceive or disrupt the enemy's electronic systems, and electronic counter countermeasures, to disrupt the disrupters. The sophistication of electronic surveillance systems was revealed in the recent controversy over the Soviet destruction of a Korean jetliner. American and Japanese surveillance systems picked up all the conversations between the Soviet fighters involved and their ground commanders, and the United States released tapes of the discussions to document its allegations.

The EW industry is very dynamic, and many medium-sized and smaller firms are finding great potential for growth. Among these are E-Systems, which provided the highest return to investors of any company among the Fortune 500 over the years 1972-82.[12] Loral and Sanders Associates are other examples of such successful EW companies. (The top EW companies are listed in Table 6.)

The EW industry grew by 39 percent in 1981, although sales are expected to level off over the next few years.

Communications systems--The communications systems product group within the industry was responsible for $5.9 billion in sales in 1982. Products within this category include fiber optics systems and equipment, radio communication equipment, space satellite communications systems, and such commercial products as CB and other radios and antennas.

Fiber optics systems are poised for rapid growth in both the commercial and military spheres. Such high-speed and reliable communications lines are being installed to improve C^3I systems, particularly in connection with ICBM systems. A spokesman for one of the leaders in this field, GTE, told IRRC that access to military technological progress in this area is an important aid to the company's commercial fiber optics pursuit.

While fiber optics are one way to maintain command and control over ICBMs, other communications systems produced by this industry segment are essential to maintaining command and control of strategic bombers and SLBMs. GTE's new ELF network, a huge underground antenna system being built in Michigan's upper peninsula, will be used for reliable communication with strategic submarines.

Space satellite communications systems provide crucial support for nuclear warfare as well as defense-wide weapons systems. Table 7 includes major satellite systems that play key roles in the nation's strategic defense. Satellite systems provide essential command, control and communications links between command authorities and strategic forces, and, increasingly, satellites such as those in the Navstar network will assist in the guidance of missiles. The systems listed in the table accounted for about $800 million of the nation's 1983 defense budget. Leading satellite contractors include General Electric, Rockwell, General Dynamics, TRW, RCA, Ford and Hughes Aircraft.

Radio systems, of course, are used by the full spectrum of the military.

Other electronic systems--Shipments within this "catch-all" category were valued at $3.1 billion in 1982, up 12 percent from 1981. This product group includes such defense systems as ultrasonic equipment, particle accelerators, simulators, and laser systems. Much of the equipment produced by this industry is used in research and development laboratories, including those of the Energy Department's nuclear weapons complex. Simulators have become increasingly popular with the military, because they are tremendously helpful in training, and are much cheaper than using the aircraft and other equipment that they simulate. Leading producers of this equipment are Singer, Boeing and Raytheon.

Electronic components: Electronic components are the building blocks of electronic systems such as those produced by the radio and TV communications industry. Electronic components include such items as integrated circuits, semiconductors, capacitors, sensors and transducers. This high-tech industry has been growing very fast, and in 1982, sales of electronic components totaled $27.8 billion. Some 15 percent of those sales, or $4.1 billion, were of military equipment, according to

Table 7
FY 1983 Procurement and R&D Funds
for Major Satellite Systems
Affecting Nuclear Warfighting Capability
(in millions of dollars)

System	Budget*	Lead Contractors
Navstar Global Positioning System	$276	Rockwell, General Dynamics
Navy Fleet Satellite Communications System (FLTSATCOM)	234	TRW, Aerospace Corp.
Defense Satellite Communications System (DSCS)	233	GE
Defense Meteorological Satellite Program (DMSP)	192	RCA, Westinghouse Electric
Air Force Satellite Communication System (AFSATCOM)	74	GE

Source: "Program Acquisition Costs by Weapon System," Department of Defense, Jan. 31, 1983.

* Includes procurement and research and development costs.

the Commerce Department. Electronic components production is expected by the Defense Department and Data Resources to increase 61 percent by 1988. The growth will be strong in both the commercial and the military markets, although somewhat stronger in the latter, which will increase some 83 percent over the five-year period.

Military C^3I and electronic warfare systems make extensive use of electronic components, particularly semiconductors, electron (especially microwave) tubes, and integrated circuits. The Defense Department played a crucial role in assisting these technologies by providing early markets. Because the military is not particularly price-sensitive, it is able to create markets for innovative products before prices are reduced to commercially marketable rates. The government purchased 100 percent of the integrated circuits produced in 1962, 55 percent of those produced in 1965, and 10 percent of those produced in 1978.[13] (Since then, the government's share has increased slightly to 12.5 percent.) As two MIT scientists have asserted:

> Missile guidance systems were an early source of support for integrated circuit development; requirements for satellite-tracking radars have supported the development of surface acoustic-wave technology and charge-coupled devices, as well as modern signal processing techniques.[14]

(Despite the military's role in assisting these technologies, there is considerable question about whether the military did more to aid or hinder progress in these technologies, given the military's extensive claim to research and development funding. The Council on Economic Priorities' Robert DeGrasse asserts that "none of the major innovations in this field was directly supported by military research.")[15]

The strongest growth in military demand for electronic components in the next few years is likely to be for certain microwave tubes and cathode ray display tubes, as well as semiconductors and advanced integrated circuits. Advances in integrated circuits are being pushed along by the military's Very High Speed Integrated Circuit (VHSIC) research and development program, which was budgeted at $66 million in FY 1983 and $125 million in FY 1984.

Shipbuilding and repair: With the merchant shipbuilding business in a severe depression, and with the Navy adding 133 new ships in order to build a 600-ship armada, military orders have come to play a much more important role in in the shipbuilding business in the last few years. Despite a 22 percent increase in defense purchases of shipbuilding services in 1982 (according to Commerce Department calculations), the overall industry's business declined by 10 percent. Total employment dropped from 184,500 to 170,000, and employment was expected to drop to 160,000 by the end of 1983. Only 18 commercial vessels were under construction at the beginning of 1983, 17 fewer than one year earlier.

Data Resources estimates a total value for shipbuilding production of $11.5 billion in 1983, including $8.0 billion for the U.S. military. There are a total of about 180 privately owned and eight government owned shipbuilding and repair facilities. All the government yards have been engaged exclusively in naval repair work since 1967. The government yards employ about 67,000 persons.

Only 15 of the privately owned yards build naval ships. Two shipyards predominate: The General Dynamics-Electric Boat shipyard in Groton, Conn., and Tenneco's Newport News shipyard in Newport News, Va., account for 50 percent of major shipyard employment and more than 50 percent of dollar value contracts. A third shipyard is almost in the Electric Boat/Newport News league: Litton Industries' Ingalls Shipbuilding yard in Pascagoula, Miss. The nine major shipyards that currently are building or have on order major naval vessels are listed in Table 8.

Table 8
Major Private Military Shipyards

Shipyard	1980 Employment
Avondale Shipyards Inc. New Orleans, La.	7,500
Bath Iron Works Corp. Bath, Maine	4,950
Electric Boat Division General Dynamics Corp. Groton, Conn.	22,100
Ingalls Shipbuilding Div. Litton Industries Pascagoula, Miss.	19,150
Lockheed Shipbuilding & Construction Co. Seattle, Wash.	3,270
National Steel & Shipbuilding Co. San Diego, Calif.	6,400
Newport News Shipbuilding & Dry Dock Co. Newport News, Va.	22,500
Todd Shipyards Corp. San Pedro, Calif.	2,650
Todd Shipyards Corp. Seatle, Wash.	2,425

Source: Polmar, Nelson, The Ships and Aircraft of the U.S. Fleet, Naval Institute Press, Annapolis, Md., 1981.

The shipyard with the strongest involvement in nuclear weapons-related production is General Dynamics's Electric Boat subsidiary. (General Dynamics maintains another, predominantly commercial, yard in Quincy, Mass.) Electric Boat produces the Trident nuclear-powered ballistic missile submarines (SSBNs), which account for 23 percent of the Defense Department's total appropriation for ships in 1983 (not counting aircraft carriers, which were provided with multi-year funding and distort the FY 1983 budget figures). The only other primary nuclear weapons-related ship appropriation was $4 million for two small SSBN supply ships. Electric Boat is the only yard equipped to produce the Trident submarines.

Major secondary systems include attack submarines (SSNs) produced by Electric Boat and Newport News, and aircraft carriers, produced exclusively by Newport News. In fiscal 1983, Congress budgeted $7.3 billion for the construction of two huge nuclear-powered aircraft carriers. The two carriers will be produced over the next decade, providing more than $1 billion in business annually to Newport News. Other major nuclear-capable ships under production or development in 1983 include: the Aegis CG-47 cruiser, produced by Bath Iron Works and Litton (FY 1983 appropriation: $2.9 billion); and the FFG guided missile frigate, built by Bath Iron Works and Todd Shipyards (FY 1983 appropriation: $819 million).

As noted earlier, industry employment at the end of 1982 was 170,000, including 134,300 production workers. The major private yards employed about 105,000 workers including approximately 70,000 working on new ships. Of the latter, 86 percent were employed on Navy projects. Average hourly earnings of production workers was $10.05 in 1982.

Department of Energy Defense Activities

The Energy Department nuclear weapons complex includes five laboratories, seven production and testing facilities and four nuclear material production facilities. The nuclear weapons program facilities and contractors are listed in Table 9. This complex is responsible not only for production of new nuclear warheads and bombs, but also for the management of the existing U.S. nuclear weapons stockpile.

Nuclear warheads and bombs currently in production are:

- B61 gravity bomb,
- W76 Trident I missile warhead,
- W79-1 8-inch artillery shell,
- W80-0 sea-launched cruise missile warhead,
- W80-1 air-launched cruise missile warhead,
- B83 gravity bomb,
- W84 ground-launched cruise missile warhead,
- W85 Pershing II missile warhead.

The Defense Department incurs most of the cost of any nuclear weapons system in building the delivery and launch systems. The Center for Defense Information (CDI) estimates that warheads typically consume 10 to 20 percent of the cost of the total weapons system. For example, the cost of the warheads for 560 nuclear-armed, ground-launched cruise missiles (GLCMs) is expected to be $630 million, 19 percent of the total cost of $3.3 billion.[16]

Overseen by DoE's Assistant Secretary for Defense Programs, most of the nuclear weapons operations report to three field operations offices,

Table 9
Department of Energy Nuclear Weapons Program Facilities, Contractors

(U.S. fiscal year 1982 data; dollar figures in millions)

Facility/Principal Defense Responsibility	Place	Operator	Budget	Employees
LABORATORIES				
Lawrence Livermore National Lab.: nuclear weapons design	Livermore, Calif.	University of California	$421	7,200
Los Alamos National Lab.: nuclear weapons design	Los Alamos, Calif.	University of California	473	7,000
Sandia National Labs.: design of firing, fusing components, weapons management research	Albuquerque, N.M.	Western Electric (subs. of AT&T)	540	7,900
Savannah River Lab.: research and development assistance on nuclear weapons materials in all areas of nuclear fuel cycle	Aiken, S.C.	Du Pont	90	900
New Brunswick Lab.: research on measuring and safeguarding of nuclear materials	Argonne, Ill.	Energy Dept.	3	52
PRODUCTION AND TESTING AND NUCLEAR MATERIALS PRODUCTION/HANDLING FACILITIES				
Kansas City Plant: manufacture of electronic, mechanical and other non-nuclear components for nuclear warheads	Kansas City, Mo.	Allied	322	7,116
Pinellas Plant: production of neutron generators that start nuclear reaction; other components	St. Petersburg, Fla.	General Electric	75	1,741
Pantex Plant: fabrication of chem. explosive and other components necessary to assemble, repair and test nuclear warheads; assembling, repair and modification of all U.S. nuclear warheads	Amarillo, Texas	Mason & Hanger-Silas Mason	94	2,150
Mound Facility: detonators and timers for nuclear warheads	Miamisburg, Ohio	Monsanto	107	2,099
Nevada Test Site: underground nuclear testing, waste management	Mercury, Nev.	Energy Dept. (mgr.)	NA	
		[Contractors incl.:		
		Reynolds Electrical & Engineering (subs. of EG&G)	260*	
		EG&G	112*	
		Holmes & Narver	39*	
		Fenix & Scisson	14*	
		Wackenhut Services]	10*	
Rocky Flats Plant: fabrication of plutonium triggers; production of other nuclear and non-nuclear components for nuclear warheads	Rocky Flats, Colo.	Rockwell International	212	4,714
Y-12 Plant: production of components for nuclear warheads; test devices for weapons R&D agencies	Oak Ridge, Tenn.	Union Carbide+	NA	5,903
Savannah River Plant: production, processing of plutonium, tritium; waste storage & reclamation	Aiken, S.C.	Du Pont	372	5,716

(Table 9 continued)

Facility/Principal Defense Responsibility	Place	Operator	Budget	Employees
Feed Materials Production Center: production of uranium products	Fernald, Ohio	NLO (subs. of NL Industries)	33	670
Extrusion Plant: processing of depleted and slightly enriched uranium	Ashtabula, Ohio	RMI (jointly held subs. of U.S. Steel and Nat'l. Distillers & Chemical)^	3	93
Hanford Production Operations: reactor fuel fabrication, plutonium production, waste mgt.	Richland, Wash.	Rockwell Intl. and UNC Resources**	268	5,523
OTHER WEAPONS-RELATED FACILITIES				
Idaho National Engineering Lab.++: naval nuclear propulsion reactor work; materials and fuel reprocessing; waste management	Idaho Falls, Idaho	EG&G and Westinghouse Electric	260	4,094
Bettis Atomic Power Lab.***: research and development of naval nuclear propulsion plants	West Mifflin, Pa.	Westinghouse Electric	197	3,570
Knolls Atomic Power Lab.***: design and development of naval nuclear propulsion plants	Schenectady, N.Y.	General Electric	126	3,050

Other major DoE weapons program contractors in FY 1982 included Bechtel ($18 million in contract awards for waste management, other work), Wheelabrator-Frye ($39 million for miscellaneous construction work), Westinghouse Electric ($12 million for waste management work), Air Products & Chemicals ($36 million for construction work), M-K National ($13 million for construction management).

Notes

NA Not applicable or not available.
* FY 1982 contract awards.
\+ Union Carbide is withdrawing as operator of the Y-12 Plant and other Energy Department facilities in the Oak Ridge complex, early in 1984. Companies that are bidding to replace Union Carbide are Martin Marietta, Westinghouse and Rockwell International.
^ U.S. Steel and National Distillers & Chemical plan to sell RMI.
** Co-managed by subsidiaries of Rockwell International and UNC Resources. Contract awards for Hanford operations in FY 1982 included $208 million to Rockwell and $130 million to UNC Resources.
++ The Idaho National Engineering Laboratory (INEL) is not a part of the Energy Department's defense division. INEL has broad responsibilities in all areas of DOE operations.
^^ At press time, facility co-managed by subsidiaries of EG&G and Exxon. However, Westinghouse Electric will take over Exxon's role early in 1984. INEL is not part of Energy Department's defense division.
*** Bettis and Knolls laboratories are not part of the Energy Department's defense division.

in Albuquerque, N.M., Las Vegas, Nev., and Aiken, S.C. These offices, along with the laboratories and other facilities in the complex, employed about 52,500 persons in weapons activities in FY 1983.

The weapons complex: The DoE "weapons activities" program includes the laboratories and facilities that contribute directly to the manufacture of the nuclear warheads and bombs. The facilities that produce nuclear materials used in warheads--such as plutonium and tritium--are treated separately. (See below.) Employment on nuclear weapons activities at the laboratories and production and testing facilities averaged 38,500 in FY 1983. The Reagan weapons budget is $3.7 billion in FY 1984, up from $3.3 billion in FY 1983.[17]

There are 11 major weapons sites within this complex, including three laboratories. In addition, two small laboratories provide research assistance on nuclear testing. To illustrate the contributions made by the major sites, it is useful to look at the development of one weapon.

The production of the B61 bomb--Table 10 shows the origin of the 1,800 component parts that make up the B61 bomb, a 100 to 500 kiloton nuclear weapon which is deployed on tactical and strategic aircraft. The B61 can serve to illustrate the nuclear weapons production process.[18]

The B61 nuclear device itself was designed by the Los Alamos National Laboratory in Los Alamos, N.M. All nuclear explosives are designed by either Los Alamos or the Lawrence Livermore National Laboratory (in Livermore, Calif.), both of which are operated by the University of California.

The weapon ordnance design was provided by Sandia National Laboratories, which is operated by AT&T's Western Electric subsidiary in Albuquerque, N.M. In the words of its president, Sandia does "those things which make a nuclear explosive into a weapon." In addition to designing the weapon, LANL and Sandia contribute three small items to the B61's actual hardware.

The nuclear materials for the B61 are provided by Du Pont from its Savannah River Weapons Facility near Aiken, S.C. (The defense nuclear materials cycle is described below.) Most final nuclear materials are produced by Savannah River and by the Hanford Production Operations in Richland, Wash. UNC Resources and Rockwell International operate the Hanford facilities.

Most of the components for the final weapon are produced by Bendix, a subsidiary of Allied Corp., at the Kansas City (Mo.) Plant. This plant is the largest of the production facilities, and it provides 101 "end item components" for the B61. The end components, in turn, are built from 1,555 items provided by 387 suppliers. The components produced by Bendix include fuzing and firing elements, radar systems, mechanical

Table 10
Contractors and Parts for the B61 Nuclear Bomb

Contractor	Parts	Number of components produced for B61	Number of suppliers to contractor
Los Alamos (Univ. of Calif.)	Nuclear design, nitrogen valve	2	1
Sandia (AT&T)	Weapon ordnance design, thermal fuse	1	1
Savannah River (Du Pont)	Nuclear materials	2	3
Kansas City (Allied)	Fuzing and firing components, radar, hardware, mechanical and electrical subassemblies, cases, light machining	101	387
Oak Ridge Y-12 (Union Carbide)	Misc. components	6	43
Pinellas (General Electric)	Neutron generators	1	80
Mound (Monsanto)	Spin rocket, detonators, gas generator	3	6
Rocky Flats (Rockwell)	Nuclear components	6	22
Pantex (Mason & Hanger-Silas Mason	Final assembly	1	6

Source: Procurement and Military Nuclear Systems Subcommittee of the House Committee on Armed Services, "Hearings on H.R. 2496, Department of Energy National Security and Military Applications of Nuclear Energy Authorization Act of 1984", March 1 and 2, 1983, p.41.

and electrical subassemblies and other hardware. None of the Kansas City components is nuclear.

Most of the nuclear components are provided by Rockwell International's Rocky Flats Plant, near Golden, Colo. Rocky Flats fabricates and assembles plutonium parts and also disassembles the plutonium components of retired weapons so that the plutonium can be reused. Rocky Flats provides six end components for the B61. Some 22 suppliers contribute to the plant's final product.

The Pinellas Plant, operated by General Electric, manufactures the neutron generators that help initiate nuclear reactions in the B61 bomb and other weapons. Pinellas is near St. Petersburg, Fla. Producing neutron generators for the B61 involves assembly of parts provided by 80 suppliers.

The remaining components for the B61 and other weapons are provided by the Mound facility, operated by Monsanto at Miamisburg, Ohio, and the Y-12 plant at Oak Ridge, Tenn. Y-12, which among other tasks builds most of the uranium and lithium parts for nuclear warheads, currently is operated by Union Carbide as part of a four-plant energy complex, but Union Carbide is giving up its management role in 1984.

The various components for the B61 are shipped to Amarillo, Tex., home of the Pantex plant, where all U.S. nuclear weapons are assembled. Pantex is operated by Mason & Hanger-Silas Mason, a privately held corporation. Pantex also fabricates high explosive parts for the final weapons, repairs existing bombs and warheads, disassembles weapons upon their retirement, and checks on the reliability of the stockpile.

Testing--Most nuclear weapons testing takes place at the Nevada Test Site, which is managed by the Energy Department. EG&G is the major contractor, in large part through the company's Reynolds Electrical & Engineering subsidiary.

The test site occupies about 1,350 square miles. The area is divided into four sections for the four agencies using the site: Lawrence Livermore, Los Alamos, Sandia and the Defense Nuclear Agency. The Nevada Test Site was the location of continental United States atmospheric nuclear tests until they were banned by the Limited Test Ban Treaty in 1963. Since then, the site has been the major location for underground nuclear tests. Through June 1983, the U.S. government had acknowledged undertaking 738 underground tests, including 610 at the Nevada Test Site.

Since 1974, underground tests have been limited to 150 kilotons by the Threshold Test Ban agreement. If the pending Comprehensive Test Ban proposal were agreed to by the United States, the Soviet Union and Great Britain, all underground tests would be banned. Representatives of the laboratories and the Nevada Test Site have vigorously opposed such a ban, and the United States has withdrawn from the negotiations.

The Energy Department also operates an inertial fusion program, which makes use of laboratory techniques for examining some of the same variables that are tested in underground nuclear explosions. Inertial fusion research and development efforts are under way at Lawrence Livermore, Los Alamos, Sandia, the Naval Research Laboratory (a DoD-operated facility), the University of Rochester (N.Y.), and KMS Fusion, a subsidiary of KMS Industries, a company in Ann Arbor, Mich.

Nuclear materials production: The nuclear materials production cycle is illustrated in Figure 5. In recent years, all the uranium used for the nuclear weapons program has been provided by reprocessed fuel from within the nation's defense program. However, beginning in 1984, the increased production of nuclear materials at Savannah River and

Figure 5
Defense Nuclear Materials Production Cycle

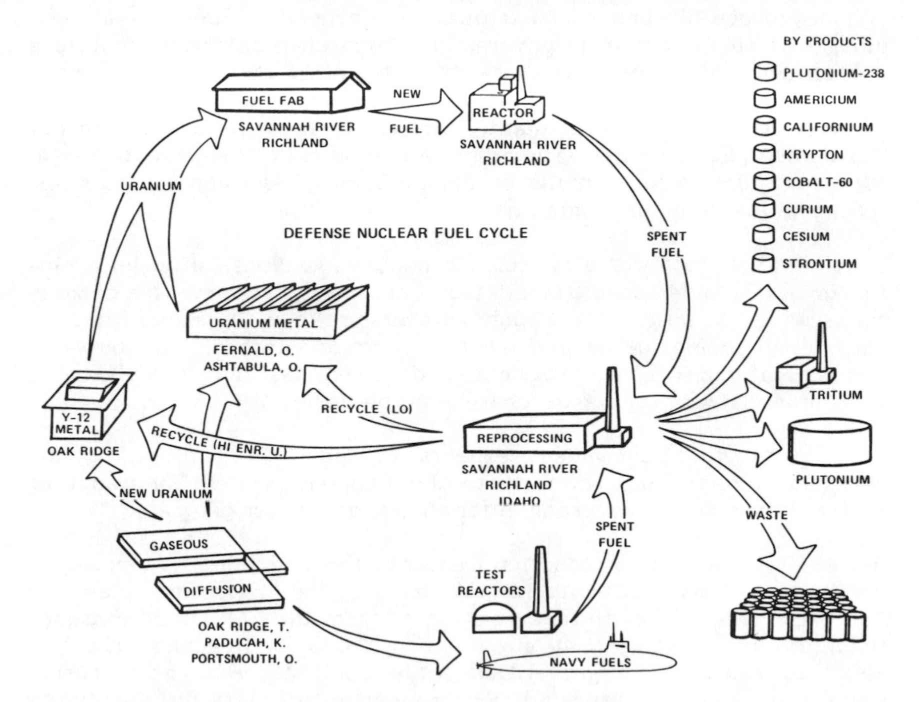

Hanford will require the purchase of low-enriched uranium from outside sources. Uranium supplied to the government is provided in the form of hexa-fluoride gas from plants run by Kerr-McGee and Allied. The gas is processed at three gaseous diffusion plants in Oak Ridge, Tenn., and Paducah, Ky. (both operated by Union Carbide until 1984), and at Portsmouth, Ohio (operated by Goodyear). These plants employ about 11,000 workers.

The Portsmouth plant at one time produced highly enriched uranium for the weapons program, but that program ended in 1964. Today, the highly enriched uranium required by the weapons program is supplied by mining the supply in older weapons as they are retired, and from reprocessing spent fuels from naval nuclear propulsion reactors and research reactors.

Almost all the enriched uranium produced by the gaseous diffusion plants is sent to civilian nuclear power plants. A portion, however, is provided to the naval nuclear power plant program, and, as noted above, a small amount will feed directly into the nuclear weapons production complex in 1984.

The uranium used to power naval nuclear reactors is an important indirect source of nuclear fuel to power the Savannah River reactors (which produce plutonium and tritium for warheads). Spent naval fuel, along with spent fuel from government research reactors, is sent to a processing plant at the Idaho National Engineering Laboratory, where it is reprocessed into highly enriched uranium. From there, it is shipped to the Oak Ridge Y-12 plant, where, according to the Energy Department, it is mixed with other uranium and "converted to metal form for reuse as fuels in the Savannah River production reactors and for use in the weapons program."

No civilian reactor waste is used for nuclear weapons, although a new technology is under development that could use civilian waste cheaply for such a purpose. Many policymakers believe, though, that for purposes of promoting nonproliferation there should be a wall between commercial and weapons programs, and current law does not allow use of commercial reactor waste for weapons purposes.

In FY 1984, the government expects to spend $70 million on the enriched uranium going directly to the weapons program and another $120 million on enriched uranium for the naval reactor program.

At the Feed Materials Production Center in Fernald, Ohio, low-enriched uranium is converted into metal form. The Extrusion plant in Ashtabula, Ohio, takes the uranium ingots from the FMPC and extrudes them into tubes, before returning them to FMPC for finishing. The fuel elements then are used to fuel DoE production reactors. The Extrusion Plant also presses slightly enriched uranium into billets for use at the Hanford N Reactor, which produces plutonium. FMPC is operated by NLO, a subsidiary of NL Industries, while the Extrusion Plant is operated by the RMI Co., a jointly held subsidiary of United States Steel and National Distillers & Chemical.

The Hanford facility is in Richland, Wash., and the Savannah River plant is in Aiken, S.C. The Hanford N Reactor is operated by UNC Resources. Rockwell International provides support services for the Hanford site, and Rockwell is renovating another plant at Hanford for recovering plutonium. Savannah River, which is the most important materials production facility, is operated by Du Pont. Both Savannah River and Hanford produce plutonium for warheads, and Savannah River produces tritium. Spent fuel from the Savannah River and Hanford reactors is reprocessed at those facilities and reenters the nuclear fuel cycle.

Overall, the Energy Department's defense nuclear materials program employs 14,000 workers. The value of the assets at various facilities totals $13.4 billion.

Naval reactors program: The Energy Department also manages the program to develop nuclear reactors for naval ships and submarines.

Work on ballistic missile submarines, such as the Trident, can be considered to contribute directly to the nation's primary nuclear warfare system. Nuclear power plants provided to other ships--notably the Nimitz and other aircraft carriers--provide bases for nuclear weapons platforms such as A-4 and A-6 attack planes. In addition, as noted above, the fuel used in naval reactors is reprocessed into weapons-grade fuel.

The naval reactors program received appropriations of $496 million in FY 1982 and $527 million in FY 1983. The budget for FY 1984, including naval reactor fuels, is $613 million, a substantial increase.

Most of the work on the naval program takes place at the Bettis Atomic Power Laboratory, a Westinghouse Electric-operated facility in West Mifflin, Pa., and at the Knolls Atomic Power Laboratory, operated by General Electric, at Schenectady, N.Y. In addition, some research and reprocessing work is carried out by the Idaho National Engineering Laboratory (INEL) in Idaho Falls, Idaho. INEL is co-managed by EG&G and Exxon, although Exxon will be replaced as contractor by Westinghouse early in 1984.

Leading Nuclear Weapons Contractors

IRRC analyzed prime contract awards for fiscal year 1981 to identify the top nuclear weapons prime contractors. Table 11 presents the 20 public corporations with the most identifiable prime contract awards for work on primary nuclear systems--strategic nuclear weapons and support systems designed primarily to support strategic weapons, and tactical nuclear weapons. The top contractor in FY 1981 was Boeing, with nuclear weapons contract awards totaling at least $1.31 billion.

Excluded from this list are privately held companies and nonprofit institutions that participate in weapons development and production. If these were included, the University of California would be added to the list. Hughes Aircraft, Charles Stark Draper Laboratories and Williams International would be leading candidates for inclusion.

As noted elsewhere, nuclear weapons programs are growing rapidly. It is likely that the top contractors list in 1983 will be led by Rockwell International, primarily because of its B-1B program, but also because of MX and other missile contracts, and increased billings by its Rocky Flats and Hanford facilities.

Any listing of top contractors is highly dependent on definitions. Table 11, for example, excludes the Tomahawk cruise missile, because the missile is being produced in both conventional and nuclear versions, and it is not possible to separate out contract awards. Inclusion of all Tomahawk contracts would put McDonnell Douglas on the list and would increase awards attributable to General Dynamics.

Table 11
Public Corporations with the Most Prime Contracts for Primary Nuclear Warfare Systems, FY 1981*

Company	Prime Contract Awards on Primary Nuclear Systems (in millions of dollars)	Ratio of Primary Awards to sales+
1. Boeing	$1,310	.13
2. Lockheed	914	.15
3. Rockwell International	804	.11
4. General Dynamics	703	.14
5. Martin Marietta	546	.17
6. American Telephone & Telegraph	537**	.01
7. EG&G	399	.55
8. Allied	376	.06
9. Du Pont	374**	.02
10. General Electric	354	.01
11. Union Carbide	275**	.03
12. Singer	165	.06
13. Tenneco	160	.01
14. Northrop	147	.07
15. General Tire & Rubber	136	.06
16. Westinghouse	135	.01
17. TRW	130	.02
18. Honeywell	127	.02
19. Monsanto	107	.02
20. GTE	106	.01

Source: IRRC analysis of Defense and Energy Departments' unclassified contract award listings.

* Investor-owned companies receiving primary nuclear warfare systems prime contract awards from the Departments of Defense and Energy exceeding $100 million in fiscal year 1981.

\+ Based on comparison of U.S. fiscal year awards with company fiscal year sales.

** Based on estimates of value of awards for DoE facilities that was dedicated to defense purposes.

Table 12
Public Corporations
with the Most Prime Contracts in FY 1981
for Primary and Secondary Nuclear Warfare Systems*

Company	Prime Contract Awards on Primary Nuclear Systems (in millions of dollars)	Ratio of Awards to Sales+
1. McDonnell Douglas	$2,851	.39
2. General Dynamics	2,406	.48
3. Boeing	1,916	.19
4. United Technologies	1,407	.10
5. General Electric	1,372	.05
6. Lockheed	1,218	.20
7. Tenneco	1,093	.07
8. Rockwell International	999	.14
9. Litton Industries	897	.18
10. Westinghouse	836	.09

Source: IRRC analysis of Defense and Energy Departments' unclassified contract award listings.

When IRRC includes contracts for dual-capable systems and other nuclear support systems, the top contractor list is considerably different from that presented above. Table 12 presents the top 10 contractors if both primary and secondary awards are included. McDonnell Douglas, General Dynamics and United Technologies lead the list, in large part because of the large dollar expenditures that are going into dual-capable fighter aircraft programs.

Chapter III Footnotes

1. Center for Defense Information, The Defense Monitor, 1983/No. 7, p. 3.
2. Caspar W. Weinberger, "Report of the Secretary of Defense to the Congress," Feb. 1, 1983; included in House Committee on Armed Services, "Defense Department Authorization and Oversight: Hearings," Part 1, Government Printing Office, Washington, 1983, p. 314.
3. For fiscal 1984 DoE defense activities budget, see House Subcommittee on Energy and Water Development, "Energy and Water Development Appropriations for 1984: Hearings," Part 4, p. 59-524. For budget summary, see p. 69 of these hearings.
4. Department of Commerce, Bureau of Industrial Economics, 1983 U.S. Industrial Outlook, Washington, 1983, p. XLI.
5. Unless otherwise noted, the information for the following sections is generated from the Defense Economic Impact Modeling System, a modeling service maintained by Data Resources Inc. for the Department of Defense; the Commerce Department's Bureau of Industrial Economics; and DoD procurement documents including "Program Acquisition Costs by Weapon System" for FY 1983 and FY 1984.
6. Aerospace Industries Association of America Inc. (AIA), Office of Public Affairs, news release, Dec. 15, 1982.
7. Ibid.
8. Fortune, May 2, 1983.
9. AIA, op. cit.
10. Data Resources Inc., Defense Economics Research Report, May 1983.
11. Ibid.
12. Fortune, op. cit.
13. Robert W. DeGrasse, Military Expansion, Economic Decline, Council on Economic Priorities, New York, 1983, p. 130.
14. G.P. Dineen and F.C. Frick, "Electronics and National Defense: A Case Study," in Electronics: The Continuing Revolution, Abelson and Hammond, eds., (1977). Quoted in DeGrasse, op. cit., p. 107.
15. DeGrasse, op. cit., p. 109.
16. Warhead cost estimate from Center for Defense Information, The Defense Monitor, 1982/No. 8, p. 11.
17. House Subcommittee on Energy and Water Development, op. cit., p. 69.
18. House Procurement and Military Nuclear Systems Subcommittee, "Hearings on HR 2496: Department of Energy National Security and Military Applications of Nuclear Energy Authorization Act of 1984," Government Printing Office, Washington, 1983, p. 41.

Chapter IV
The Question of Industry Influence Over Nuclear Weapons Policy

> In the councils of government, we must guard against the acquisition of unwarranted influence, whether sought or unsought, by the military-industrial complex. The potential for the disastrous rise of misplaced power exists and will persist.
>
> --President Dwight D. Eisenhower, 1961[1]

> Defense contractors are active participants and partners in a military-industrial establishment which possesses its own internal, largely self-generating dynamism, whose motive power is the drive for the above-average profit that can be made producing the weapons of war.
>
> --United Auto Workers President Walter Reuther, 1969[2]

> With their ability to dispense money, officials of large corporations may often exercise greater power to influence society than elected or appointed government officials--but without assuming any of the responsibilities and without being subject to public scrutiny.
>
> --Adm. Hyman Rickover, 1982[3]

From the time of President Eisenhower's famous warning on the dangers of the military-industrial complex in his 1961 farewell address, concerns about corporate influence in the shaping of national security policy have persisted. Critics assert that through influence with Congress and with the defense bureaucracies, and through their substantial control over research and development, companies have an undue say over weapons procurement.

At the extreme, this critical view attributes to a shared bureaucratic and corporate self-interest in the war economy the key role in shaping national security policy and in fueling the nuclear arms race. At the other extreme are observers who dismiss any notion of a military-industrial complex. Among them are Secretary of Defense Weinberger, who recently declared that "I have not seen anything resembling industrial influence on or in the military."

Most observers of Defense Department-industry interaction believe that the truth lies somewhere in the middle. It is difficult to argue convincingly that ideological concerns and fear of Soviet militarism--factors that play a major role in shaping American nuclear weapons policy--spring wholly from the fevered imaginations of profit-seeking corporate managers. On the other hand, there is a clear pattern of corporate influence with Congress and the Pentagon on military issues. Given the fact that the government asks corporations to fulfill military requirements for equipment and services, however, such influence may be inevitable and appropriate.

The two sides of corporate influence: While Secretary Weinberger dismisses the notion of a military-industrial complex, he provides a good description of the two aspects of concern embodied in that concept. He told The Los Angeles Times that "the military-industrial complex, in the sense in which Ike used it,...was a warning that forces would combine to perhaps get more of their share of the national resources than was required, or that they would try to exert an unhealthy influence on policy."[4] Critics frequently allege that defense contractors overcharge or pad their work, and the Pentagon has been subject to cycles of scandal and generally ineffective reform. Most recently, attention has been focused on excessive charges for spare parts by such companies as United Technologies, Boeing and Sperry.

While concerns that contractors exploit their uniquely close relationship with the Defense Department to gain excessive sales and profits are important, the crucial issue for the purposes of this report is the question of industry influence in shaping the nation's military posture.

Pentagon critics, such as defense analyst Gordon Adams (formerly of the Council on Economic Priorities), suggest that a tight and self-serving network exists consisting of defense contractors, members of Congress and the Defense Department. Adams labels this network the "iron triangle," and he asserts that the mutuality of interest among the three corners of the triangle forecloses discussions of alternative defense postures.[5]

In that defense contractors do most weapons research and development, industry critics allege that there is a deliberate bias on the part of industry to research and develop systems that will be the easiest to sell and the most profitable. Some observers feel that Congress and the Pentagon are soft-sells when it comes to "sexy hardware"--large, impressive and expensive systems such as ICBMs, aircraft and submarines. "Such systems are highly visible and identifiable as to congressional district," said an assistant defense secretary.[6] Simpler conventional weapons and regular operations and maintenance are slighted, in this analysis.

Most spokesmen for the defense industry and Defense Department agree that the relationship between companies and the military is close, but they insist that a close relationship is essential to national security, and that abuses can be controlled. They feel that critics over-emphasize the extent of cooperation and mutuality of interest between DoD and industry, and under-emphasize systematic and regulatory obstacles to excessive contractor influence. Company officials also note that much of their efforts to win defense contracts is the result of competitive pressures. One spokesman told IRRC that his company does not attempt to influence policy decisions, but that "once a decision is made" on a military requirement, "we go out and scrap and fight as hard as we can" to win the contract. The government encourages this kind of competition in order to bring some benefits of the free market to military procurement.

Industry Influence in Congress

Leverage over defense procurement can mean jobs and economic development for a congressman's district, and there is no claim more potent politically than that of economic development. National defense requirements account for 70 percent of all federal purchases (excluding compensation of employees). Thus, military procurement is an ideal target for parochial concerns of congressmen.

Industry critics say that contractors play on the more parochial congressional interests to win support for their programs. In many areas across the country, defense companies employ more people than any other industry. In the state of Washington, Boeing is the biggest company. In Maine, Bath Iron Works, a division of Congoleum Corp. and a large builder of destroyers and other ships, is the largest employer. General Dynamics is a dominant employer in Connecticut. Military companies are the most important source of employment in California. Even the relatively small Energy Department nuclear weapons program is a major economic factor in some areas. The Sandia National Laboratories, for example, is the largest employer in New Mexico. In all, defense accounts for more than 10 percent of personal income in 11 states.

With this level of defense dependence, members of Congress from these areas and others know that their political careers may depend on their success in bringing defense work home. Contractors know that their presence in certain congressional districts could be the key to a major contract. Speaking about competition with General Electric to produce aircraft jet engines, a representative from United Technologies complained that "we're only big in maybe 20 congressional districts; General Electric is big in 200 congressional districts. That's what we're up against."[7]

With this sort of competition in mind, contractors have emphasized local economic impacts in discussions with congressmen about weapons projects. Major contractors also have tried to distribute their subcontract dollars (which often total more than 40 percent of the prime contract) as widely as possible. They also may direct subcontracts to specific key congressional districts.[8]

Most major defense contractors are active in Washington and in their home communities in exerting pressure on Congress. They also direct appeals to the communities of their major subcontractors. These "grass roots" activities, frequently planned from corporate public affairs offices, include appeals to employees and other community members to write their legislators. Speakers and films promoting certain weapons programs are presented to civic groups and veterans organizations. Companies advertise the military and economic benefits of their products in both the local and the national press.

Contractors insist that these activities are akin to marketing of commercial products, and from a company's perspective, that is certainly true. Corporate spokesmen add that some of the most intense courting of Congress occurs when competitors--such as GE and United Technologies--are seeking the same work. They say that such competition, while fierce, may not affect the nation's defense posture one way or another. Critics, however, find fault with that position. New Yorker columnist Elizabeth Drew wrote that "the flaw in the argument is that it can assume a universe composed of the parties at interest, and that when the parties carve up the universe everyone is served."[9] Drew suggests that lobbying, even in a competitive environment, can bid up the size of the "universe."

Moreover, by the time many defense programs reach Congress, they are identified closely with particular contractors. Thus, in recent years congressional votes on the B-1 have been tied inextricably with the interests of Rockwell International, which has campaigned aggressively for the bomber.

Washington representative offices: Much of the debate over the influence of the defense industry centers on the activities of corporations' Washington representative offices. In 1982, Gordon Adams studied eight top defense contractors and found that those companies had 200 Washington employees working on defense issues, including 48 registered lobbyists.[10] All of the leading Defense Department contractors on nuclear weapons that are described in detail in this study maintain Washington offices.

Sen. David Pryor (D-Ark.), a critic of defense lobbying, has described the changes in the Washington representative office over the years: "While its major function in the 1950s was to provide information and monitor legislation, today's office emphasizes one concern: political pressure. It may be defined as 'government relations' or 'public affairs' but the application of pressure and influence is the key to a contractor's success."[11] In an analysis of defense lobbying, The Wall

Street Journal agreed with this view and indicated that Washington offices "bring the big guns to bear in support of the company's interests."[12] Some companies, however, such as Honeywell and GE, have policies against lobbying on issues of defense policy.

Gordon Adams writes that the Washington offices of defense contractors cover many responsibilities, all of which are directed toward making the company more competitive in the weapons procurement process. They "gather vast amounts of data on government activity, the status of legislation, the work of key members of Congress, procurement policy decisions in the executive branch, plans and programs for research and development, emerging regulation, actions and federal rule-making."[13] Corporations use this information among other purposes to choose government officials to call on, candidates to support with PAC contributions, strategy for "grass-roots" campaigns in the corporations' home areas, and legislative wording to recommend to sympathetic members.

While Adams sees these activities as undue influence in shaping defense debates, the companies emphasize their provision of technical information to members of Congress. Many companies, such as Boeing and GE, say their Washington offices exist in part to respond to congressional (and bureaucratic) inquiries, and many defense analysts consider corporate officials to be indispensable sources of technical information. Members of Congress say it is important for companies to provide reliable--and relatively unbiased--information in order to maintain their credibility.

Political action committees: Defense contractors are among the most active sponsors of corporate political action committees. In the 1981-82 election cycle, five large defense contractors--Tenneco, General Dynamics, Grumman, General Electric and Rockwell International--were among the 10 largest corporate PAC spenders, according to the Federal Election Commission. With total expenditures of $499,651, the Tenneco PAC was the largest among corporations. No company PAC, however, approached the spending of a number of independent, trade association and labor union PACs. The largest spender among all PACs in 1981-2 was the National Congressional Club, a conservative group based in North Carolina, which spent $10.4 million. The largest amount given to federal candidates was the $2.1 million given by the Realtors PAC.[14]

Nevertheless, candidates received more support from corporate PACs--which comprise half of all PACs--than from any other PAC category in 1981-2.

Company PACs are administered with corporate funds. They solicit contributions from company executives, administrative personnel and stockholders and distribute the funds as campaign contributions. Federal law prohibits direct corporate contributions to candidates for

Lobbying and United Technologies

In the interest of expanding their influence in Congress and at the Defense Department, defense contractors try to recruit their lobbyists from the Capitol Hill and Pentagon communities. Usually, they employ long-time veterans with years of experience in the procurement process. In addition to their expertise, these lobbyists must bring with them important contacts that may benefit the company.

The lobbying team at United Technologies might best illustrate this trend. The head of the Washington office is Clark McGregor, a former Minnesota congressman, congressional lobbyist for the Nixon White House, and director of Richard Nixon's 1972 campaign. The Wall Street Journal has called McGregor "the prototypical Washington insider."[15]

In his United Technologies job, McGregor has cultivated close ties to the Republican party. (Some firms emphasize Democratic party connections, and still others attempt to be evenhanded.) Elizabeth Drew wrote in The New Yorker that McGregor played an important role in raising and channeling money from corporate PACs to Republican candidates in the most crucial congressional races in 1982.[16]

McGregor's strong congressional ties are matched by the Pentagon ties of Hugh Witt, McGregor's "right hand man." Witt spent 18 years at the Pentagon as a specialist in logistics and procurement and then several years at the Office of Management and Budget setting up the first Office of Federal Procurement Policy. Witt is "the kind of expert technician that is filling up more and more Washington corporate affairs" offices, according to The Wall Street Journal. McGregor has said of Witt: "Hugh has maintained his friendships at the OMB and they help the company make its case at budget time."[17]

Congress or the presidency. Defense PACs give heavily to members of armed services and defense appropriations committees and subcommittees, and at times they work both sides of the street, giving money to two or more candidates for the same office.

PACs became popular with the business community in the mid-1970s following changes in the Federal Election Campaign Act. Before then, the Corrupt Practices Act prohibited government contractors from making direct or indirect campaign contributions. The law was changed amid considerable pressure from labor unions and business after Common Cause managed to shut down a TRW political action committee in 1972.

In 1974, there were 89 corporate PACs and 600 PACs of all kinds.[18] By 1982, there were 1,310 corporate PACs, out of a total of 2,651, that made contributions to federal candidates.[19]

Of the 19 DoD contractors for nuclear weapons and related equipment studied by IRRC in this report, all but Singer maintained PACs in 1982. The table shows the companies' PAC contributions, along with a breakdown of contributions to defense committee members. The 18 companies gave a total of $2.8 million in 1981-2, including $939,000, or 34 percent of the total, to defense committee members. As with corporate PAC contributions generally, the overwhelming majority of contributions went to incumbents.

Congressional Quarterly reported in 1980: "How highly defense companies prize their relationship with Congress is evident from their campaign giving. Even the most outspoken critics of defense spending receive gifts from defense companies in their home districts."[20]

The degree to which PAC donations influence the actions of members of Congress is a matter of debate. The Washington Post, reporting on a close 1982 House vote that upheld production of the MX missile, asserted that "some Democrats fear being labeled soft on the Soviets, or want to cash in on defense-related campaign contributions." The article quoted Rep. Edward Markey (D-Mass.), a leading opponent of the MX: "People are looking for fundraising sources....Every one of these weapons systems has a constituency. If you want to make them (the defense contractors) happy, you can do so without any peril."[21]

In conjunction with the nuclear weapons freeze campaign, Rep. Dennis Eckart (D-Ohio) sought bipartisan support in 1982 for a boycott by House members of PAC donations from seven of the largest nuclear weapons contractors. Only 10 congressmen, all Democrats, responded. None of the 10 sat on defense committees, and none had received any contributions from PACs of the seven companies.

A lobbyist for a major defense contractor, however, belittled the influence of PAC donations in an interview with IRRC: "Sometimes the people we give money to listen to us and sometimes they don't. There's no guarantee. They're very independent." The lobbyist pointed up an important fact. Few critics allege that PAC contributions "buy" votes; they may buy "access," but there is no guarantee of success.

Trade associations: There are more than 20 defense industry trade associations. Representing a wide spectrum of competing companies, trade associations avoid involvement in marketing and promotion issues. They work primarily at expediting and influencing the flow of

PAC Contributions by Leading Defense Companies in the Nuclear Weapons Industry
(dollar figures in thousands)

Company	1981-82 Contributions to federal candidates	Contributions to members of defense committees*	Percentage given to members of defense committees
Tenneco	$454	$70	15
Litton Industries	219	56	26
United Technologies	204	78	38
Lockheed	185	74	40
Rockwell International	175	82	47
General Dynamics	172	76	44
General Electric+	149	36	24
GTE	140	28	20
McDonnell Douglas	137	70	51
Westinghouse Electric	136	42	31
TRW	136	47	35
Martin Marietta	131	54	41
Boeing	125	49	39
Raytheon	115	52	45
Avco	113	56	50
Northrop	102	52	51
Honeywell	82	9	10
General Tire & Rubber**	25	7	28
Singer	0	0	NA
TOTAL	$2,799	$939	34

Source: Federal Election Commission.

* Defense committee members include voting members, including full committee chairman, on armed services committees and on defense appropriations subcommittees. In addition, members of the defense task force of the House Budget Committee are included.

\+ Excludes a second PAC for Utah International, a GE subsidiary.

** Includes only the PAC for Aerojet-General, a subsidiary of General Tire & Rubber.

information among the Pentagon, Capitol Hill and the various contractors. Most trade associations are involved in direct lobbying, and many have PACs.

The industry, with the help of its trade associations, has had some success in defeating inimical legislation. In the late 1960s and early 1970s, for example, intense lobbying defeated all attempts at strengthening the DoD Renegotiation Board, which was set up to recoup excess profits made by defense contractors. In 1979, Congress killed the Board.

Effectiveness of congressional lobbying: There is considerable disagreement about the effectiveness of corporate lobbying in influencing defense appropriations in Congress. A representative from a major defense trade association told IRRC that there unquestionably have been "instances" where "the Congress has purchased things that have been generated, not out of the needs of the Defense Department, but from political pressures." On the other hand, those pressures relate to more than the companies involved. Even if the companies took no action to facilitate approval of programs that they benefit from, there would be considerable pressure on members of Congress to assist the economic well-being of their districts through defense contracts. Whether corporate lobbyists, with their economic impact studies in hand, play the key role in forming congressional pressures is difficult to determine. "The consensus among those who handle defense legislation," reports Congressional Quarterly, "is that the industry's influence is probably marginal compared to other factors that shape defense spending." Nevertheless, CQ adds, companies "may influence how much of a weapon the government buys, how quickly and for how long."[22]

Industry Influence with the Department of Defense

Webster's dictionary defines synergism as the "cooperative action of discrete agencies such that the total effect is greater than the sum of the effects taken independently." At the core of the concept of a military-industrial complex is the notion that the government and private defense bureaucracies are synergistic, operating together with great effect.

While this view forms the basis of a highly skeptical view of the military-industrial complex, it is shared in a certain sense by most Pentagon supporters. Adm. Thomas Moorer (USN-Ret.), former chairman of the Joint Chiefs of Staff and a director of Fairchild Industries, told IRRC, "If we didn't have such a large military-industrial complex, we would have to build one." Moorer and others within the complex see the relationship between the Pentagon and private industry as a source of strength; they believe that the synergistic effects of this kind of public-private cooperation provide a more dynamic defense apparatus than would a system of government-owned and -operated military industries.

Until World War II, the United States maintained only a small peacetime defense industry, and most of the industry that did exist was owned and operated by the government. As President Eisenhower commented in his farewell address, the "conjunction of an immense military establishment and a large arms industry is new in the American experience."[23]

The Pentagon depends on industry for many functions, including the research, development and planning of new weapons systems and technologies, as well as research on the nature of strategic problems. Harvey Gordon, an assistant to the under secretary of defense for procurement, told IRRC that "outside the function of fighting a war, all of DoD is involved in the acquisition process. We really don't have engineers who engineer or logisticians who 'logistlate.' We have people who determine what is required and where to buy it from."

Critics believe that defense contractors use this close relationship with the bureaucracy to gear the nation's weapons procurement to corporate profit maximization, and that contractors manipulate political partisanships and rivalries among the military services.

'Revolving door': Corporate influence with the defense bureaucracy is most evident in the "revolving door" between the Pentagon and industry, and in the development of new weapons. In addition, industry is in a position to perform certain "favors" for the military.

A large number of individuals within the military-industrial complex travel through this door at various points in their careers. In fiscal 1981, for example, some 1,824 mid- to high-level Defense Department employees and former employees went to work for major defense contractors, and 21 contractor employees moved to DoD.[24] Many high-level employees are among those who move back and forth. Deputy Defense Secretary Paul Thayer, for example, was a Navy pilot before he went to work for Vought Aircraft, now a division of LTV, in 1948. Thayer was chairman of LTV from 1970-83, and chairman of the U.S. Chamber of Commerce from 1982-83, until President Reagan named him to his current position, the second-highest in the Pentagon.

Richard De Lauer was a senior official with TRW from 1960-81, before he was named under secretary of defense for research and engineering in 1981. While at TRW, De Lauer served on the Defense Department's Defense Science Board, probably the department's most important advisory board as far as weapons procurement is concerned.

Navy Secretary John Lehman served as an assistant to Secretary of State Henry Kissinger and as deputy director of the U.S. Arms Control and Disarmament Agency before working as a consultant for Northrop, TRW and Boeing in 1977-81.

The revolving door is not limited to the private corporate participants in the military-industrial complex. Harold Brown, Defense Secretary from 1977-81, was the director of the Lawrence Livermore Laboratory at one time. (Today he serves as a consultant to TRW, among other roles.)

The existence of the revolving door means not only that those passing back and forth have questionable loyalties. Critics say that the lure of high-paying jobs in private industry influences the way military officers and other DoD employees do their jobs while they work for the government.

Adm. Rickover thinks the revolving door is a major factor in defense procurement. He testified in 1982:

> Every time I recommend building ships in [government-owned] Navy shipyards the Defense Department refuses to go along. They protect private industry because that is where the civilian superiors come from and that is where they are going back when they leave government.[25]

Pentagon supporters believe that no significant favoritism goes on. Adm. Moorer suggests that those going through the revolving door either are engineers and technicians, who "don't make decisions," or are higher-level officials who receive too much press and congressional scrutiny to survive in public office if they favor their friends in industry.

Other observers point to former industry officials who take actions contrary to the interests of their former employers. Deputy Defense Secretary Thayer, for example, has approached the Navy budget most skeptically--and recently suggested transferring some $10 billion of the Navy's funds to the Army over the next five years, even though LTV is a major Navy aircraft manufacturer.

Still other observers agree that an old boy network influences defense decisionmaking, but they say such networks are typical of any industry, and are unavoidable. Moreover, these analysts emphasize that the Defense Department is bound to require the services of professionals with backgrounds in the military because that is where the expertise is.

Research and development: In the view of some Pentagon critics, industry plays its most important role in shaping defense posture through its role in developing weapons systems. The Pentagon distributes substantial research and development funds--$18.7 billion in FY 1983. Because of the high technical risk and large expenditures required for otherwise useless "state of the art" research, the government must pick up the tab for most R&D work. Corporations, however, play a major role in shaping R&D programs.

Research and development work is extremely important in gaining military production contracts. When the Pentagon chooses to produce a certain weapon, the firm that performed the research and development usually will be awarded the production contract. Contractors are anxious to get the jump on DoD planning; thus they make a considerable effort to anticipate Pentagon requirements. Defense critic Mary Kaldor describes the process in her book, The Baroque Arsenal:

> To ensure continuous work, all defense companies have planning groups, whose sole function it is to choose suitable successors for the weapons that are currently being produced and who work closely with similar groups in the services. The planning group is supposed to predict what a particular branch of the armed forces might require when current projects come to an end, and the various ways the corporation might meet that requirement. Because of the relationship with the armed forces, particularly during the so-called concept-definition phase, the prediction tends to become a self-fulfilling prophesy. As one corporate vice president said, the government "depends on companies like ours to tell them what they need."[26]

Firms go to considerable lengths to analyze the future plans of the military and to recognize vulnerabilities. Often firms are developing technologies before the Defense Department expresses an interest in them or, at times, even knows about them.

A Raytheon executive has said that military requirements tend to be defined jointly by military and industrial personnel, "and it is not unusual for industry's contribution to be a key factor."[27]

Clark MacGregor of United Technologies has said that at the time a weapons system is being developed, contractor personnel often work side by side with government technicians. MacGregor has suggested that this gives companies a good chance to influence defense contracts.[28]

One defense program in particular provides contractors with assistance in shaping new weapons systems--independent research and development (IR&D). Through this program, the Pentagon reimburses companies for a portion of the cost of research and development efforts that the companies both initiate and control. The reimbursement is negotiated between each contractor and the Defense Department. In FY 1980, companies told the department that they incurred $2.4 billion in IR&D costs. The government reimbursed the companies for $809 million of that total.

IR&D assists companies in pursuing whatever projects they feel are worthy. Contractors say that they are most innovative when they are free to explore promising ideas without government interference.

IR&D reimbursements are not contingent on the government using resulting technologies.

Nevertheless, there has been much criticism of the IR&D program from both inside and outside the military. Many see it as a subsidy for the defense industry from which the government receives little benefit. Critics, including defense analyst Jacques Gansler and Adm. Rickover, point out that the companies retain the patent rights on government-funded IR&D work. They add that under the present negotiation system, there is little if any incentive to control costs. Another problem is that IR&D tends to favor larger, established firms.

In support of the program, one industry representative told IRRC: "The key part of IR&D is the 'I.' It's our brains that develop these technologies. If we are doing it for the government, then the government should pay for it."

Conclusions

What is the extent of industry influence over defense policy and weapons procurement? The answer is not easy. As industry critic Gordon Adams has said, there is no "smoking gun." Even describing the nature of corporate influence is difficult. In certain areas, one can measure particular variables; the amount of PAC contributions, the number of transfers between DoD and private business, the number of lobbyists in Washington can be quantified. These quantifiable variables may be of only limited importance, however. The formal and informal contacts between Pentagon officers and corporate personnel with responsibility for weapons development may play a more important role.

Clearly, industrial political activities and the important corporate role in developing new weapons systems gives the defense industry an important voice in shaping the nation's defense posture. It is also clear that other factors, including ideological considerations and the nature and perception of the Soviet and other foreign threats play important roles as well.

Chapter IV Footnotes

1. The Los Angeles Times, "Servants or Masters," July 10, 1983. (This Times special section provides a good background for debate over the military-industrial complex.)
2. Walter Reuther, "Swords into Plowshares: A Proposal to Promote Orderly Conversion to Defense Production," (1969), p. 13.
3. Adm. H.G. Rickover, testimony, "Economics of Defense Policy: Hearing Before the Joint Economic Committee," Jan. 28, 1982, Government Printing Office, Washington, D.C., p. 7.
4. The Los Angeles Times, op. cit.
5. Gordon Adams, The Iron Triangle: The Politics of Defense Contracting, Council on Economic Priorities, New York, 1981.
6. Congressional Quarterly, Weekly Report, Oct. 25, 1980, p. 3202.
7. The Wall Street Journal, April 1, 1982.
8. Adams, op. cit.
9. Elizabeth Drew, "Politics and Money: I," The New Yorker, Dec. 6, 1982, p. 127.
10. Ibid., p. 137.
11. Sen. David Pryor, "Butter for Big Guns," The New York Times, Jan. 31, 1982.
12. The Wall Street Journal, op. cit.
13. Adams, op. cit., p. 130.
14. Federal Election Commission, "1981-82 PAC Giving Up 51 Percent," April 29, 1983.
15. The Wall Street Journal, op. cit.
16. Drew, op. cit., p. 68-71.
17. Congressional Quarterly, op. cit., p. 3206.
18. Drew, op. cit., p. 60.
19. Federal Election Commission, op. cit.
20. Congressional Quarterly, op. cit., p. 3205.
21. The Washington Post, Aug. 1, 1982.
22. Congressional Quarterly, op. cit., p. 3201-2.
23. The Los Angeles Times, op. cit.
24. Office of the Secretary of Defense (OSD), "FY 1981 Statistical Summary of Reports Received by OSD Pursuant to Section 410, Public Law 91-121."
25. Rickover, op. cit., p. 49.
26. Mary Kaldor, The Baroque Arsenal, Hill and Wang, New York, 1981, p. 69.
27. Adams, op. cit., p. 98.
28. Congressional Quarterly, op. cit., p. 3203.

Chapter V
Military Spending and the Economy

The development of the nuclear bomb and the subsequent nuclear arms buildup have raised the ante of war in terms of dollars as well as destruction. Nuclear weapons do not come cheap, and the United States and the Soviet Union maintain thousands of strategic nuclear weapons and support systems poised to act on a moment's notice. Unlike battlefield nuclear weapons, which at least in Europe may provide an inexpensive alternative to maintaining conventional forces, strategic nuclear weapons are an addition to the nation's arsenal, not a substitute.

As the costs of deterrence have risen, deliberations about the economic impact of military spending have become central to the defense debate in the United States. Although no consensus exists, it is clear that the current arms buildup could have extensive ramifications for the nation's economy.

Economic Effects of the Current Buildup

At the root of much of the criticism surrounding the Reagan administration's military buildup are fears that such a rapid expansion of the defense sector could jeopardize the recovery from the 1981-82 recession. These fears have prompted calls for a slowing of the buildup from unlikely sources, including the Business Roundtable, the President's Council of Economic Advisers, and a group of former high-level government officials: Robert McNamara, Cyrus Vance, Adm. Elmo Zumwalt Jr. and McGeorge Bundy. In 1982, these four men told Congress that high levels of military spending "have undermined the economic foundations of our national security, which are every bit as important as our defense competence...."[1]

Administration and other analysts who support the buildup believe the economy is more resilient. "Fears that the defense budget of this administration will strain the United States economy are unfounded," Defense Secretary Weinberger told Congress in 1983.[2] Other analysts argue that although the size of the buildup is large and its pace is brisk, the economy has absorbed even larger and faster buildups in the past with no serious economic side effects.

Figure 1
Federal Budget Outlays by Function

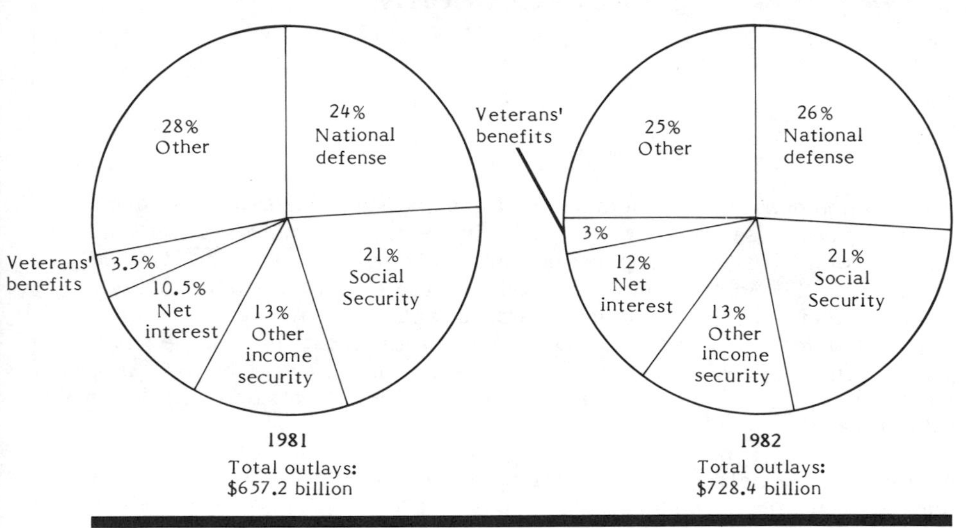

Source: Office of Management and Budget.

Measuring military spending: Part of the reason why opinions about the buildup range so widely is that analysts often do not agree on how to measure its extent.

Each year the federal government calculates the amount of national defense outlays (actual expenditures) and determines defense's slice of the federal budget pie. In 1982, the Office of Management and Budget calculated that national defense made up 26 percent of the federal budget for fiscal year 1982. (See Figure 1.)

Some analysts believe that this measure is misleading, however, in part because it compares defense expenditures, which are primarily purchases of goods and services, with transfer payments such as Social Security, which involve few direct purchases. These analysts prefer to look at defense purchases (roughly equal to defense outlays minus military retirement pay) in relation to the total amount of goods and services purchased by the government in a given year. Using this measure, defense spending equaled 69 percent of federal purchases of goods and services in 1982. Thus, military spending plays a much larger role in the government's purchases of goods and services than it does in the overall budget. (See Figure 2.)

Figure 2
Measures of Defense Spending

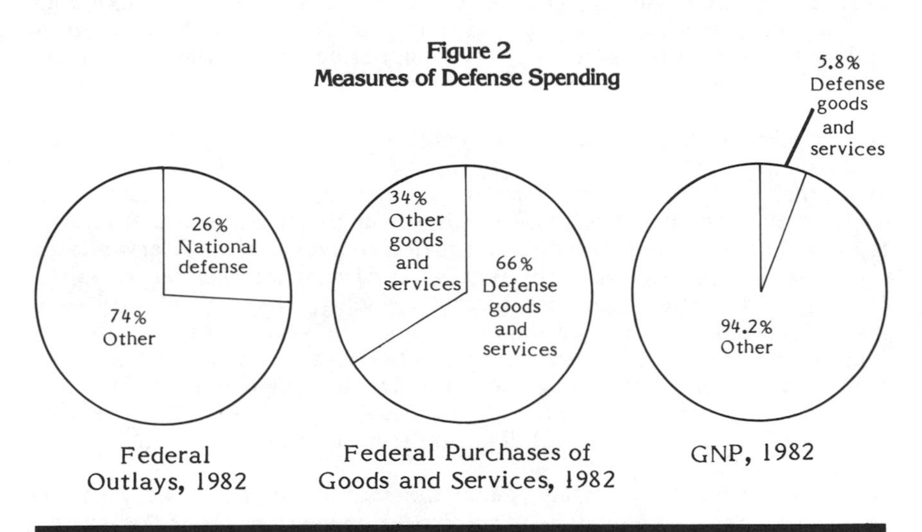

Sources: Office of Management and Budget, Department of Commerce.

Another common measure of military spending uses the yardstick of gross national product (GNP), the market value of the nation's output of goods and services. Defense outlays equaled approximately 6 percent of GNP in 1982. (See Figure 2.) Economists who use this measure tend to conclude that the defense buildup will have a minor role in the economic scene because defense outlays are not estimated to exceed 7 percent of GNP, even at the height of the buildup in 1987. "These figures are fairly low by the standards of the 1950s and early '60s," Defense Secretary Weinberger has said.[3]

Some economists argue that this measure also distorts the size of the buildup. They say that because this buildup takes place in peacetime, it concentrates more on the production of new weapons systems than on the personnel and operations and maintenance needed for combat. In February 1983, then-Congressional Budget Office Director Alice Rivlin told Congress that "because of this emphasis on investment, the defense buildup could have more effect on the goods-producing sectors of the economy than the overall growth rate suggests."

Charles L. Schultze, a senior fellow at the Brookings Institution's Economic Studies program and a former chairman of the Council of Economic Advisers, suggests a different yardstick. He believes it would be useful to look at military spending, less personnel costs as a share of GNP, less services. This measure, called the "goods-producing" GNP absorbed by the military budget, was developed by Gary Wenglowski, head of research for Goldman, Sachs and Co. If this measure is used, the current arms buildup accounts for some 30 percent of the estimated $195 billion increase in "goods-producing" GNP over the next four years. This proportion is substantially higher than that of past wartime buildups. Even during Vietnam, nonpersonnel defense outlays as a share of GNP less services totaled a little more than 10 percent, according to Schultze. He concludes that the buildup will lead to production bottlenecks within some defense industries.[4]

Still other analysts have challenged the way the government calculates defense outlays. Bob DeGrasse of the Council on Economic Priorities argues that the government's definition leaves out military-related expenses such as veterans' benefits (a cost of past wars), interest on the federal debt attributable to military spending, NASA's military programs, foreign military assistance grants and several other military-related programs that he thinks should be considered part of national defense's portion of the budget each year. Making these adjustments, DeGrasse concludes that national defense outlays were 49 percent of the federal budget in 1981, not counting trust funds.[5]

Given his definition, it is not surprising that DeGrasse is wary of the economic effects of the current buildup. However, some of DeGrasse's additions, such as interest on the federal debt attributable to military spending, are very difficult to calculate. Moreover, he includes veterans payments, which are transfers of income, as a part of defense, but he excludes Social Security, also a transfer, as part of the nondefense budget. For all these reasons, DeGrasse's figures are controversial.

Economic risks from the buildup: Definitional disagreements aside, most economists agree that today's large defense expenditures pose risks to the economy. They disagree, however, about the nature and extent of those risks.

Some supporters of the buildup believe that national security depends on the buildup and thus, some economic risk-taking is warranted. "We must not lose sight of the fact that the defense budget is most appropriately measured against the reality of the threat to our national security and our fundamental obligation to protect our basic values and institutions," said Secretary Weinberger in his 1983 report to Congress.

Critics of the buildup agree that defense of the nation is important, but they believe the administration overstates the military threat and understates nonmilitary elements of national security.

A recent report by the Congressional Budget Office concludes that the economic risks of the buildup are minimal. The report says that if economic growth continues to be as sluggish as current predictions indicate, "the administration's proposed defense buildup should neither rekindle inflation nor stunt employment growth over the next few years." It predicts that bottlenecks will occur in some defense sectors that will drive up weapons prices, but they are "unlikely to spawn widespread inflation."[6]

However, the CBO tempers this conclusion with two warnings. One is that if the economy starts to recover rapidly, "the proposed buildup could increase risks of renewed inflation and of crowding out of private borrowing in financial markets." The other warning was voiced by economist Rivlin. In early 1983, she told Congress that the buildup should not be financed by increasing the deficit. Allowing the deficit to grow as a result of defense spending is "the biggest risk that the defense buildup poses for the economy," she said, because deficit financing is likely to slow economic growth or rekindle inflation in the long run.

Most economists agree. Some believe that the only substantial risk that the buildup poses to the economy is that it might increase the deficit. In their view, if the buildup is financed with tax increases or federal spending reductions in nondefense areas, it should have no negative effects on the economy in either the short or the long term. Economist Schultze claims that as long as the nation "is willing to pay for increased defense spending through lowered spending on consumption rather than investment," the buildup will have no deleterious economic effects. "There is nothing inherently inflationary or productivity-lowering about defense spending," he says.[7]

Other analysts see many more risks ahead. They cite evidence that high levels of military spending, however financed, can damage the economy by spurring inflation and weakening productivity in the longer term, if not immediately.

One such analyst is Miroslav Nincic, a political scientist at the University of Michigan and author of a book on the political economy of military growth. He agrees that military spending (or, for that matter, any form of government spending) is able to absorb labor and capital idled by a recession and thus has gained a reputation as a good economic stimulant. However, he contends that while military spending may fill a void during recessions, it actually can jeopardize subsequent recovery by stimulating inflation and driving up interest rates.[8]

Nincic and other analysts claim that the economy already has suffered as a result of the relatively high levels of peacetime military spending sustained by the United States since World War II. If more federal dollars had been put toward civilian industries, especially for research and development and capital equipment, these analysts believe that the current economic picture might look a lot brighter.

Longer-Term Economic Effects

In absolute terms, of course, military expenditures generate some amount of employment, technological progress, and overall economic growth. When compared with the amount of growth that could be generated by other kinds of expenditures, however, military spending does not necessarily come out ahead, especially over time. In fact, many studies have indicated that military spending represents a net loss to society in the longer term. To use economic terminology, the opportunity costs--the value of alternative goods or pursuits forgone by the decision to build military goods--could be great.

Measuring opportunity costs is tricky, however, because it involves predictions. For example, if the American public is more willing to put its tax dollars toward military goods and services than nonmilitary goods and services (which, according to Nincic, is a historical trend), the opportunity costs of spending federal dollars on military goods could be small. But if a cut in federal spending on military goods were replaced by an increase in spending on education or other expenditures that generate more employment than military expenditures do, the opportunity costs--at least in terms of employment--might be great.

More specifically, several analysts have calculated what could be seen as opportunity costs between civilian and military federal spending in the last couple of years. (See Table 1.) These tradeoffs are not made consciously, of course, but Seymour Melman, industrial engineering professor at Columbia University, says that "within a given level of public spending" there are limits to the taxes that people will bear, and "such tradeoffs are being made in effect, though rarely stated openly." [9]

In recent years, a number of economic theorists have advanced predictions regarding the long-term effects of military spending on three major indicators of economic health: employment, productivity and growth, and inflation.

Employment: An estimated 2.4 million civilians worked to produce defense goods in 1981, about 2 percent of total employment. Despite this large number, several recent studies indicate that federal government purchases of nondefense goods could have generated just as many jobs, if not more.

One of these studies was conducted by the Congressional Budget Office. The CBO estimated the number of private and public jobs that would be created by a $10 billion increase in defense spending versus the number of jobs created by the same amount of nondefense spending. It found that both expenditures would create an equal amount of jobs.

Table 1
Social Spending Reductions and Weapons Costs in the FY 1984 Budget
(in millions of dollars)

Domestic Programs		Weapon System	
Program	FY 1984 Budget Reductions Resulting from Cuts in Prior Years*	System	Projected 1984 Cost**
Work Incentive Program	$ 153	3 C-5 Aircraft	$ 180
Community Service Block Grants	274	1 B-1B Bomber	205
Title XX (Social Service Grants)	812	5 E-3A Awacs Aircraft	815
Student Financial Assistance	1,080	5 B-1B Bombers	1,025
Title I (Compensatory Education)	799	13 C-5B Aircraft	787
Child Welfare Services	29	1 F-18 Fighter Jet	34
Medicaid	1,336	F-18 Program	1,600
Health Services Admin.	528	9 C-5B Aircraft	540
AFDC (Child Support)	1,288	F-18 Program	1,600
Child Nutrition	1,392	F-18 Program	1,600
Legal Services Corp.	130	7 F-15 Aircraft	126

* Projected 1984 budget reductions shown here represent the difference in outlays between (1) what the Congressional Budget Office (CBO) projected these programs would have cost in FY 1984 if 1983 spending levels had been increased to keep pace with inflation, and (2) what the programs what have cost in 1984 if no budget cuts had been made in these programs over the past two years and pre-Reagan spending levels had been adjusted to keep pace with inflation. These figures are drawn from the CBO's "Baseline Comparisons for Certain Programs," April 15, 1983. The reductions shown here do not reflect any activity Congress may take in 1983, or the Reagan administration's proposals for further cuts in the FY 1984 budget.

** Weapon system outlays are drawn from the Congressional Budget Office's "Selected Weapons Costs from the President's 1983 Program," March 18, 1982, as projected for FY 1984.

Source: Center on Budget and Policy Priorities, Defense Budget Project Fact Sheet.

However, when CBO narrowed its analysis to defense purchases from private industry (which does not include salaries of DoD's military and civilian employees), it found that $10 billion in defense purchases would create 40,000 fewer jobs than the same amount of nondefense purchases.[10]

The implication of these results is that if all of the $50.5 billion of FY 1981 defense outlays were spent instead on non-military goods, an additional 200,000 jobs could potentially have been created. This figure, however, would barely have chipped away 1 percent of the unemployment rate.

In 1983, CBO's Rivlin told Congress that the employment differences between defense and nondefense spending "are small enough to allow the Congress safely to ignore different effects on overall employment as it chooses between defense and nondefense spending."[11]

Another study, conducted by the Council on Economic Priorities, used data from the Labor Department to calculate the number of jobs created by individual industries. CEP discovered that leading defense industries on the average create fewer jobs per dollar than the average American industry. (See Table 2.)[12]

Additional studies conducted by Chase Econometric Associates and Employment Research Associates found that military spending seems to create fewer job opportunities than other federal programs.[13]

What emerges from the evidence runs against the common notion that defense spending is a good way to generate employment. Thus, the job-creating capabilities of military programs cannot unequivocally be promoted as a side benefit to their military utility.

Rivlin also told Congress that "the defense program is not an employment program....If you are constructing a job creation program... then, clearly, one can employ more people per dollar...."

Analysts have suggested several reasons why military industries might generate fewer jobs than the average nondefense industry. Some point to the fact that defense industries such as electronics and guided missiles are very capital-intensive, and thus have a smaller number of employees per dollar than nondefense industries. Others say that wage and salary levels are higher in the average defense industry than in the average nondefense industry because military industries employ a disproportionate percentage of highly skilled occupations such as aerospace engineers, computer programmers and skilled blue collar workers.

Critics assert that even the jobs that the current buildup creates will not help the nation's unemployed. They say that the new jobs will be concentrated in private industry, where in turn they are concentrated in

Table 2
Jobs Created Per Billion Dollars of Final Demand for Top Defense Industries
(constant 1981 dollars)

Industry	Direct	Indirect	Total
Aircraft	12,318	13,522	25,840
Radio & Communications Equipment	11,556	13,233	24,789
Complete Guided Missiles	7,773	10,481	18,254
Ordnance	12,631	14,722	27,353
Ship Building & Repair	18,051	14,341	32,932
Air Transportation	10,414	11,751	22,165
Business Services, n.e.c.*	24,904	8,006	32,910
Motor Vehicles	6,599	15,587	22,186
Construction of New Military Facilities	NA	NA	NA
Communications, except Radio and TV	9,173	4,232	13,405
Industrial Inorganic & Organic Chemicals	6,857	11,819	18,676
Maintenance & Repair Construction	13,175	11,241	24,416
Wholesale Trade	19,769	6,619	26,388
Petroleum Refining & Related Products	2,412	11,024	13,436
Computers & Peripheral Equipment	10,523	14,046	24,569
Educational Services	53,997	7,202	61,199
Water Transportation	12,617	13,320	25,937
Electric Utilities	6,957	8,716	15,672
Scientific & Controlling Instruments	14,452	13,590	28,042
Median Manufacturing Industry	NA	NA	26,291
Median Non-Manufacturing Industry	NA	NA	30,030

* Not elsewhere classified

Source: Council on Ecomonic Priorities, Military Expansion, Economic Decline, p. 48-49, U.S. Dept. of Labor.

a small number of occupational groups that already have a high employment rate. CEP's DeGrasse says that, "even during December 1982, when overall unemployment was 10.8 percent, unemployment for professional and technical workers was only 3.7 percent. Demand for engineers was so great during the 1980 recession that salaries continued to rise dramatically."

The military buildup also will create, however desirable or undesirable, jobs within the military, which would be available to some unemployed workers.

It is important to remember, though, that cuts in the defense budget also would not necessarily translate into higher levels of employment. If a cut in the defense budget were used instead as a federal transfer payment such as employment insurance, welfare, retirement or veterans benefits, fewer jobs would result because transfer payments, in general, create fewer jobs than defense expenditures. Even critics of the arms race such as CEP's DeGrasse stress the importance of "providing an alternate source of demand when arms expenditures are reduced" in order to maintain or increase employment levels after any cuts in defense spending. The complexity of the employment issue, said former defense official and defense analyst Jacques Gansler, should caution anyone "who would base the defense debate on the jobs issue."[14]

National productivity and growth: The effect of military spending on national productivity and growth can be assessed in several ways. One is to compare the economic performances of countries with different-sized military budgets, but this sort of analysis involves too many variables to yield conclusive results.

A study by the Council on Economic Priorities compared the economic performance of 17 major non-Communist, industrial countries over the last two decades. It found that countries with larger military burdens tended to invest less, and to have lower productivity growth rates. CEP did not find evidence, however, that large military burdens were associated with higher rates of unemployment or inflation. CEP is careful to point out that the study shows correlations, not direct links, between military spending and poorer economic performance.[15]

The Congressional Budget Office report supports CEP's findings. It states that "international comparisons seem to support the notion that high defense spending retards productivity growth." Like CEP, the report recognizes that there are other possible explanations for these intra-country differences. For one, high growth rates may be explained in part by a country's stage of development. More advanced nations are thought to be at the level end of the growth curve.[16] (See Table 3.)

Defense analyst Gansler disputes the notion that productivity growth is hampered by defense spending. He notes that in the United States, productivity growth and the military's share of GNP declined during the 1970s, which discounts any negative relationship between the two.[17]

Another way to assess how military spending affects national productivity and growth is to look at the amount of research and development funds used for military purposes. This analysis also has serious limitations because economists have not determined how

Table 3
Defense Spending and Productivity Growth:
Comparisons over Time and across Countries

Country	1950-1960	1960-1970	1970-1979
UNITED STATES			
Productivity growth	2.3	2.1	1.1
Defense share of GDP	10.3	8.7	6.1
JAPAN			
Productivity growth	NA	9.7	4.5
Defense share of GDP	1.0	0.9	0.9
GERMANY			
Productivity growth	NA	4.6	3.4
Defense share of GDP	3.9	4.2	3.9
FRANCE			
Productivity growth	NA	4.8	3.4
Defense share of GDP	7.2	5.4	3.9
UNITED KINGDOM			
Productivity growth	NA	2.8	2.0
Defense share of GDP	7.9	5.8	4.9
CANADA			
Productivity growth	3.0	2.4	1.3
Defense share of GDP	5.6	3.3	2.0

Note: NA = not available

Source: Congressional Budget Office; Data Resources Inc.; NATO Facts and Figures, (NATO Information Service, Brussels, 1976); Stockholm International Peace Research Institute, World Armaments and Disarmament SIPRI Year Book 1981, (Taylor and Francis Ltd., London, 1981).

research efforts translate into higher productivity. But most do think that research efforts are an important component of productivity.

In the United States, more than 50 percent of all federal dollars spent on research and development and about 38 percent of all public and private R&D money spent on research and development in the last 30 years went to military programs. (See Figure 3.) A survey by the National Science Foundation in 1978 found that 20 percent of the nation's scientists and engineers received substantial support from the Defense Department.[18]

In critics' views, this sort of emphasis on military R&D cannot help but influence the nation's technological and economic direction. Some suggest that the military has taken more than its fair share of the nation's pool of research and development resources and, as a result, has contributed to American industry's decline in many international markets.

Other analysts question whether the military research and development programs necessarily drain civilian ones. The CBO report cites years when increases in DoD spending on R&D have been correlated with increases in private spending on R&D. However, it also says that because U.S. research and development expenditures are now at a much higher level than in the past, there might not be room for increases in both the civilian and military sectors today.

Supporters of defense research and development programs argue that the research conducted for military reasons has benefited private industry and the economy. These analysts often cite computers, helicopters, medical diagnostic equipment and atomic energy as examples of important civilian products that were developed under military research and development contracts. They suggest that these "spin-offs" have offset some of the possible adverse effects that defense R&D spending might have on private-sector productivity.

Critics question the opportunity costs of such spinoffs. Professor Nincic asserts that "the fact that discernible benefits from spillovers have occurred should not be construed to mean that civilian needs and the economy in general derive a <u>net</u> benefit from the concentration of research and development within the defense establishment....There is, on the contrary, every reason to believe that goals are more efficiently and effectively achieved by <u>direct</u> efforts rather than by reliance on spillovers."

Nincic also questions whether spinoffs will continue to occur: "Independent of whether past spillovers strike one as impressive or not, such effects may be becoming less and less significant and frequent. There were many civilian uses of integrated circuits and the helicopter, but non-military applications of killer satellites may be very rare."

Under Secretary of Defense for Research and Engineering Richard DeLauer believes that spillovers could be much greater if American business would take better advantage of available technology. American managers "do not take this (military) technology and bring it along in a way that it's ready for market," he said in a recent interview. In

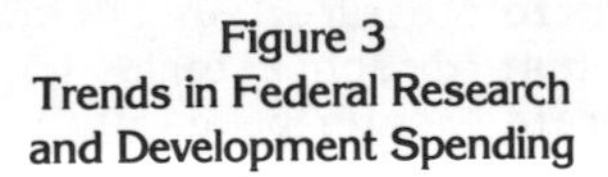

Figure 3
Trends in Federal Research and Development Spending

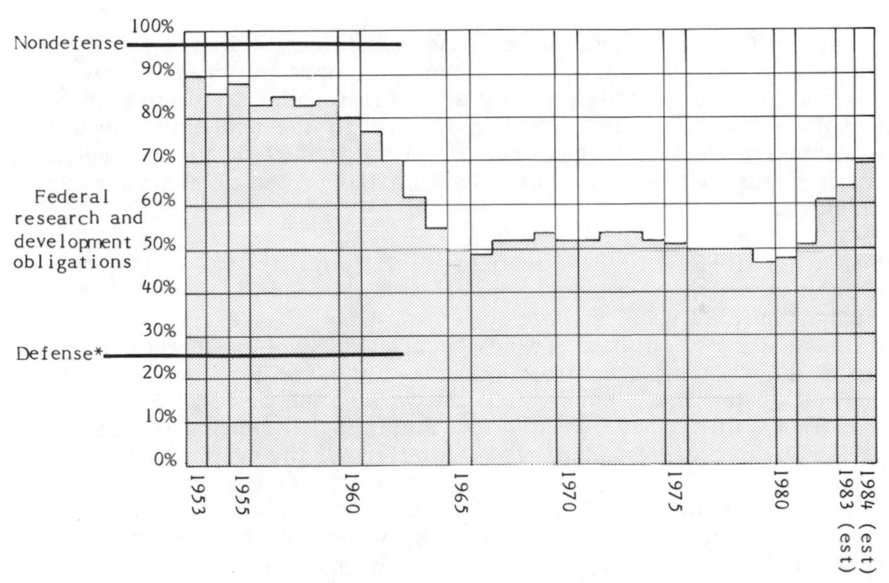

* Includes military-related R&D programs for the Departments of Defense and Energy.

Source: Office of Management and Budget.

contrast to Japanese managers who do develop military technologies into market products, he said, American managers "look for the market to develop before they go develop the product."[19]

However, one important difference between the two countries is that the United States does not have an institution equivalent to Japan's Ministry of International Trade and Industry, which works to promote civilian industrial development in Japan. Thus, Gansler says, in the United States there has not been "sufficient incentive for private industry to make the very expensive, high-risk, long-term investments required" in civilian research and development. In many cases, he says, "the choice is not between defense and civilian stimulation, but between defense and no stimulation."

Gansler's assertion suggests that the decline in U.S. productivity may be caused by inadequate funding for civilian R&D and capital formation, rather than by an overemphasis on the military as such.

However, to the extent that military R&D spending precludes civilian R&D, some tradeoff between the two exists. The extent of this tradeoff may be difficult to measure, but Nincic's point is well-taken: It is hard to dispute that direct efforts in civilian research and development would generate greater productivity growth in the civilian sector than reliance on military spillovers.

Inflation: Critics believe that defense spending contributes to inflation for several reasons. First, they argue, the goods the military buys are unproductive because they end up stored in warehouses or missile silos and do not continue to cycle money through the economy. Thus, the billions of dollars of wages paid for arms production yield fewer and fewer goods. Critics say this drives up the prices of everyday commodities.

Second, critics say, the relatively high inflation rate that exists in some defense industries spreads to other sectors of the economy. Lloyd Dumas, political science professor at the University of Texas, says the military sector's inflation spreads because it "bids up certain resource costs" and "preempts key resources from the civilian economy."[20] In qualitative terms, Columbia University's Melman has argued that corporate executives have assimilated the inflation-causing management philosophy of cost pass-along that characterizes the military industry.[21]

These two arguments have been attacked heavily by other analysts. To the first, analysts point out that many government expenditures (for school buses and museums, for instance) do not increase the supply of goods and services for sale, and thus military expenditures are not the only government expenditures that contribute to inflation. Said economist Schultze: "Government purchases do not add to the market supply in an economic sense of the term. Hence, taxes must be levied. But the military nature of the goods is absolutely irrelevant."

John Tirman of the Union of Concerned Scientists counters that Schultze has failed to prove that defense spending is not inflationary. He "simply equates such spending with other federal expenditures that may be inflationary as well," says Tirman. "Also forgotten in the Schultze (and Reagan) view," he says, "is that the scale of DoD outlays is much larger than that for federal parks."[22]

To the argument that the defense sector inflation spreads to other sectors, analysts who differ say that, if so, the inflation rate should parallel the rate of defense spending over time. The evidence does not bear out this thesis, however. The Congressional Research Service has found that in the last two decades, defense spending as a proportion of GNP has declined while inflation has increased.[23]

Despite these arguments, critics believe that the current buildup in particular has a great potential to cause inflation because rapid

Table 4
Acceleration of Inflation
During Previous Military Buildups
(by calendar year; average annual percent increase)

Start of Buildup	Inflation Rate for Three Prior Years*	Inflation Rate for Three Subsequent Years**
1917	8.7	16.0
1941	1.5	6.2
1950	2.6	3.6
1965	1.4	3.3

* Average annual rate of increase in Consumer Price Index for three years ending in the year when the buildup began.
** Average annual rate of increase in Consumer Price Index for three years following the year the buildup began (for example, in the case of World War II, 1942-1944).

Source: Congressional Budget Office.

increases in defense spending in the past--particularly during the Vietnam war--have set off inflation that spirals upward for decades. A Congressional Budget Office report, although not in full support of the critics, states that during the last four military buildups, including the Vietnam war, prices rose an average of 3.7 percent. "At no time in history has the United States increased defense spending so rapidly [as the current buildup] without encountering at about the same time a substantial increase in inflationary pressures," it said. (See Table 4.)

This argument has been harder to dispute because of the historical precedents. However, the CBO and other analysts discount the similarities between the present buildup and buildups in the past. They claim that because the present buildup is planned, because it represents a smaller percentage of GNP than past buildups, and because it will build gradually and use industrial capacity idled by the recession, it is not likely to spur inflation. "The inflationary impact of the overall spending gap [the deficit], not of the defense budget, is the big economic danger," says Gansler.

The Economic Effects of a Nuclear Weapons Freeze

The flip side to the economic impact of arms production is the impact of arms reductions. All sides in the current arms debate express commitment to ultimate reductions in the nation's nuclear forces, so the economic effects of arms control initiatives also are important.

Two recent reports provide some initial analysis of the economic effects of the proposed nuclear weapons freeze, the proposal that could have the strongest and most immediate effect on the weapons industry and the economy. (The Start agreement and the Intermediate Nuclear Forces agreement, even at their most comprehensive, would have markedly less impact.) Although far from conclusive, both reports suggest that the net effect of a freeze would not be deleterious to the economy.

CRS report: One of these reports, "The Implications of a Nuclear Arms Freeze on the U.S. Economy in the Short Run," was prepared by the Congressional Research Service.[24] It estimates that $14.5 billion could be freed from the 1983 defense budget if a freeze (similar to that proposed by the Nuclear Weapons Freeze Campaign) were implemented. The report then considers three alternative uses for this money: deficit reductions, non-freeze-related expenditures, and nondefense government expenditures. It estimates that the deficit could be reduced by $6.67 billion in 1983 under the first alternative, which in turn might cause a slight decline in interest rates. At the same time, however, the report estimates that real gross national product could go down as much as 1 percent. (For comparison, the report notes that the real GNP dropped 1.7 percent during the 1974-75 recession.) The report says that the effect of the second and third options would vary according to the multiplier effect of each, but such effects were impossible to determine without further data.

Regions that make a high proportion of high-technology products such as guided missiles, aircraft, electronics and communications are likely to have the highest percentage of freeze-related business and, according to the report, they would not be dealt many of the benefits accrued by a freeze. If a freeze took effect today, it said, employment and output in these sectors and regions probably would fall. However, if the economy were in a period of strong recovery and expansion, and if the freeze were accompanied by buildups in conventional weapons, the CRS said that even many of these sectors might feel little, if any, decline in output and employment.

Freeze campaign report: The second report, "Economic Effects of a Bilateral Nuclear Weapons Freeze," was published in February 1983 with support from the Nuclear Weapons Freeze Campaign.[25] The authors estimate that a freeze would save a minimum of $84 billion in defense spending over the next five years, perhaps more than $200 billion over the next decade. The authors are confident that if the money saved by a nuclear weapons freeze were carefully spent, it could go a long way toward restoring social programs, aiding new or ailing civilian industries or workers who might lose their jobs as a result of the freeze. It also might be kept in the Treasury to reduce the deficit. Nevertheless, the authors are quick to point out that even careful expenditures would not serve as a quick fix for the nation's economic problems. "The nuclear freeze would present an opportunity to free up billions of dollars of resources to deal with problems...but these savings in and of themselves cannot turn around the country's basic economic difficulties," they say.

IRRC analysis: IRRC's analysis shows that in FY 1981 DoD awarded contracts worth about $3.2 billion for research, testing and production of freeze systems to the 20 DoD contractors in this study. This sum represented about 10 percent of these firms' total FY 1981 defense contracts.

In FY 1982, DoD awarded contracts worth about $3 billion for production of freeze systems, of which approximately $2 billion went to the companies in this study. This figure does not include research and development contracts, which are not readily available.

These numbers are very conservative. They represent just those contracts that IRRC could positively identify as freeze-related contracts. They also do not include money that is authorized, but not yet spent, for several major weapons programs that would be affected by a freeze. These programs include the the MX missile, the Trident II missile, and much of the B-1B bomber and Tomahawk cruise missile programs. Much larger expenditures have and will come into play as these systems reach production. The B-1B program alone will involve expenditures of $6 billion a year by 1985.

Of course, the Department of Energy contracts also would lose business if a freeze were negotiated. In 1982, the facilities involved in DoE's nuclear weapons programs had budgets totaling $3.6 billion. A portion of this money is used for other purposes, but the majority is directly related to the production of nuclear weapons. Roughly 64 percent of the money went to the 10 contractors covered in this study.

The perhaps surprising conclusion of this analysis is that a freeze would have caused only limited immediate economic hardships if it had been implemented in 1981 or 1982. By 1985, however, most of the weapons systems that would be affected by a freeze should be in full swing and a sudden decision to freeze could have significant economic repercussions.

Conclusions

Judging how much the nation can afford to spend on national security measures requires knowing the costs in both direct and indirect terms. Observers from many points along the political spectrum are concerned, however, that a preoccupation with costs can obscure a straightforward debate on America's legitimate military requirements.

Pentagon critics cite instances where employees, companies and members of Congress have fought hard against cancellation of questionable weapons programs in an effort to protect jobs in their districts. Political scientist Dumas said that "the political importance of the job argument can also be verified by noting that virtually every newspaper account of any curtailment of military activity always contains a statement about job loss, if not in the headline then in the first sentence."

Supporters of increased military spending are afraid that heightened concerns about defense spending's effect on the economy might undercut arguments for bolstering national security to the level they think is necessary.

Many commentators are united in the view that the central task is to set priorities. As the Congressional Budget Office put it, "The choice of appropriate levels of defense spending is essentially a question of priorities, reflecting assessments of the requirements of national security and evaluations of the importance of alternative uses of resources."

As Chapter I demonstrates, assessments of the requirements of national security vary widely. Critics believe that the Reagan administration has recklessly overestimated the nation's military needs. CEP's DeGrasse says that the nation "surely can afford to pay whatever it costs to provide for its security," but "at the same time...America must set limits on military and nonmilitary forms of current consumption. The reason, simply, is to assure that we have enough left to invest in our economic future." Even Gansler, a supporter of a strong defense, has stated, "There is now a growing realization that today's world of rough nuclear parity and sluggish economic growth requires a dramatically different defense posture--one that not only is more credible but also truly affordable in peacetime."

Administration officials argue that their proposed military buildup demands the highest priority. In an article in Aerospace magazine, Defense Secretary Weinberger echoed the call to set priorities. But he also asked: "What can have a higher priority than peace with freedom? The answer is, of course, nothing."

In an economists' ideal world, it would be possible to weigh increments of national security against the value of other national goods in order to set priorities. But the United States is a long way from facing such a clear set of alternatives. One main problem is the lack of consensus about what constitutes sufficient security. Another is the lack of adequate data that can help sort out the complex effects of military expenditures; more research is needed.

What has sifted out from the research done since World War II is that military spending is no panacea for the nation's economic ills. In fact, there are indications that military spending is a contributor to the nation's current economic problems. However, it also is clear that reducing the defense budget also is not a short cut to economic prosperity. As seen above, although a decision to freeze nuclear weapons production in 1981 or 1982 would have caused only limited economic hardships, a freeze implemented in 1985 would have major negative repercussions. In addition, even though an immediate freeze could make more resources available for civilian purposes, it would not guarantee high levels of employment, increased productivity, and low levels of inflation.

Therefore, while critics have successfully countered the notion that war or preparation for war always brings prosperity, many questions about how military spending affects the economy remain.

Chapter V Footnotes

1. The Washington Post, March 1, 1983.
2. Caspar W. Weinberger, Report of the Secretary of Defense to the Congress on the FY 1983 Budget, FY 1984 Authorization Request and FY 1983-87 Defense Programs, p. I-9.
3. Caspar W. Weinberger, "Defense and the Economy," Aerospace, Summer 1982.
4. Charles L. Schultze, "Economic Effects of the Defense Buildup," The Brookings Bulletin, Vol. 18, No. 2, Fall 1981, p. 4.
5. Robert W. DeGrasse Jr., Military Expansion, Economic Decline, Council on Economic Priorities, New York, 1983, p. 211.
6. Congressional Budget Office, Defense Spending and the Economy, February 1983, p. xi, xiii.
7. Schultze, op. cit., p. 2.
8. Miroslav Nincic, The Arms Race: The Political Economy of Military Growth, Praeger Publishers, New York, 1982, p. 50.
9. Seymour Melman, The Permanent War Economy, Simon and Schuster, New York, 1974, p. 120.
10. Congressional Budget Office, op. cit., p. 43.
11. Statement of Alice M. Rivlin, Director, Congressional Budget Office, to House Armed Services Committee, Feb. 16, 1983, p. 863.
12. DeGrasse, op. cit., p. 29-30.
13. Linda LeGrande, "The Impact of Defense Spending on Employment: A Review of the Literature," Congressional Research Service, Oct. 26, 1982.
14. Jacques S. Gansler, "We Can Afford Security," Foreign Policy, No. 51, Summer 1983, p. 72.
15. DeGrasse, op. cit., p. 59-73
16. Congressional Budget Office, op. cit., p. 38-39.
17. Gansler, op. cit., p. 73.
18. National Science Foundation, "National Patterns of Science and Technology Resources 1981," Table 36, p. 43.
19. The Washington Times, July 13, 1983.
20. Lloyd Dumas, "Military Spending and Economic Decay," The Political Economy of Arms Reduction, American Association for the Advancement of Science, 1982, p. 9.
21. Seymour Melman, "Beating 'Swords' into Subways," The New York Times Magazine, Nov. 19, 1978.
22. John Tirman, "The Social Costs of Military Spending," Grantsmanship Center News, May/June 1983, p. 25.
23. Barry Molefsky, "Inflationary Consequences of the Defense Buildup," Congressional Research Service Report #81-213E, Aug. 26, 1982, p. 15-17.
24. Gary L. Guenther, "The Implications of a Nuclear Arms Freeze for the U.S. Economy in the Short Run," Congressional Research Service, Aug. 3, 1982.
25. Dave McFadden and Jim Wake, eds., The Freeze Economy, a joint publication of the National Clearinghouse, Nuclear Weapons Freeze Campaign and the Mid-Peninsula Conversion Project, 1983.

Chapter VI
Coping with Military Cuts: An Analysis of Economic Conversion

If the macroeconomic effects of military spending remain somewhat ambiguous, its microeconomic effects do not. Many plants, companies or even industries rely on military contracts for a large portion of their business. When the contract pickings are good these groups thrive, but when the Pentagon withdraws its hand, the results can be devastating.

The cancellation of the B-1 bomber is a case in point. The prime contractor for the B-1, Rockwell International, had spent more than five years building its B-1 staff and had sunk more than $3.8 billion tax dollars into the controversial aircraft before the government halted production in June 1977. When the cancellation was announced, Rockwell immediately began laying off workers, some with only one day's notice. Within three months, more than 8,000 Rockwell employees--of an average age in the mid- to late 40s--had lost their jobs. Total direct and indirect job loss resulting from the cancellation was estimated to exceed 20,000 jobs.[1]

Large, sudden cancellations like this one are rare, but the B-1 case dramatizes the point that contract cancellations are not easy on anyone--the companies, their employees or the communities in which they work. Neither are other disruptions in a company's business caused by budget cuts, the completion of large contracts or arms control agreements, all of which make up the downside of what many observers call the boom-bust cycle of military spending. The sales, wages and tax revenues that are the bread and butter of companies, employees and communities are pulled out from under them by such disruptions and are not regained easily.

A common interest in avoiding cancellations many times unites contractors, their workers and communities in what has been called one of the most powerful lobbies in the country. Most analysts agree that the pressure this lobby can bring to bear on lawmakers does not facilitate hard-headed assessments of military needs. In fact, there are many well-known politicians who oppose high levels of military spending, and yet support important military programs in their home states. Sen. Alan Cranston (D-Calif.), for instance, supports both the freeze and the B-1B bomber. Thus, the microeconomic effects of military spending can have macroeconomic implications when this lobby influences national defense planning and budgeting.

Many peace activists assert that the defense industry lobby acts as a built-in deterrent to arms control and disarmament proposals because they threaten the industry's business and jobs. "There can be no real hope for American initiatives to end the nuclear arms race so long as millions of Americans and important regions of the country are economically dependent on military contracts," says Seymour Melman, professor of industrial engineering at Columbia University and perhaps the foremost advocate of economic conversion.[2]

Economic Disincentives to Disarm

As Chapter V explains, a freeze on nuclear weapons production could have a significant impact on the economy, especially now that the weapons buildup is well under way. Depending on its implementation, an agreement along the lines proposed by the United States in the Start talks also could have an impact.

The freeze: The freeze proposal would most directly affect companies in the aerospace industry. Rockwell International, probably on its way to becoming the top nuclear weapons contractor, would feel the effect most strongly. The B-1B bomber, and to a much lesser extent the MX missile, are centerpieces of the company's planned production for the 1980s, and a decision to cancel these programs would have a major effect on the company. Other major aerospace companies that would be strongly affected by a freeze include Lockheed (Trident missiles), Martin Marietta (MX and Pershing II missiles) and General Dynamics (ACM and Tomahawk cruise missiles), as well as Boeing, General Electric, McDonnell Douglas, Northrop, General Tire & Rubber, Honeywell, TRW, Morton Thiokol, Hercules and Avco. (See Table 1.) As discussed in Chapter V, a freeze also would adversely affect Energy Department contractors that operate weapons programs.

Start: An agreement along the lines of the U.S. Start proposal could be enacted with virtually no effect on the administration's arms buildup plans because it would not prohibit the production of new weapons systems. It would place ceilings, however, on the numbers of certain categories of weapons such as ballistic missile warheads and strategic bombers. Thus, if the United States completes its military modernization program by 1996, "old" systems would have to be retired rapidly to make room for the planned 100 MX missiles, 1,000 small ICBMs, 100 B-1B bombers, 132 Stealth bombers, 2,880 ALCMs, 400 nuclear-armed SLCMs, 20 Trident submarines and 480 Trident II (D-5) missiles. For example, given the ceilings proposed by the United States, the nation would have to retire all of its Minuteman missiles, even though the Pentagon currently sees no need to retire any of them in this

Table 1
Defense Prime Contract Awards and the Nuclear Weapons Freeze

Company	Percentage of FY 1981 defense prime contracts in freeze-related systems
Avco	17%
Boeing	16
GTE	16
General Dynamics	5
General Electric	4
General Tire & Rubber (Aerojet)	20
Honeywell	4
Litton	6
Lockheed	32
Martin Marietta	39
McDonnell Douglas	5
Northrop	18
Raytheon	4
Rockwell	23
Singer	8
TRW	18
Tenneco	1
Westinghouse	2
United Technologies	none

NOTE: These figures are very conservative. They represent just those contracts that IRRC could positively identify as freeze systems contracts and do not include any classified contracts or subcontracts. They also are low for companies whose freeze programs had not gone into production in FY 1981.

century. Poseidon submarines would have to be retired an average of five and a half years earlier than scheduled, and it is possible that in the late 1990s even some MX missiles would have to go, only 10 years after production. More B-52 bombers than currently planned would be grounded prematurely.

It is difficult to believe that the prospect of discarding effective older systems well before their time while continuing full-scale production of new weapons systems will be a politically sustainable position, especially if budget pressures continue to be strong. The waste involved in this scenario could spur Congress to scrutinize new weapons systems closely, and the systems that are seen as adding momentum to the arms race while adding marginal military utility would likely be cut. So, in the end, even the Start proposal could cut into the administration's nuclear arms production program.

INF: In the nearer term, an agreement limiting intermediate range missiles in Europe would have a relatively minor economic effect, except on Martin Marietta, which manufactures the Pershing II missile. General Dynamics, McDonnell Douglas and Williams International, manufacturers of the ground-launched cruise missiles, could absorb the cancellation with little trouble, especially given overall growth in other cruise missile programs. Even Martin Marietta could accept cancellation without a crisis.

Specific arms reductions: Even if the administration's modernization program is carried out, there is likely to be sharp debate over particular weapons programs. According to the current schedule, B-1B orders will escalate from 1 in 1982 to 48 in 1986. At that point, with 50,000 to 60,000 people working on B-1B production lines, orders are supposed to fall to zero. Pressure to keep the production lines open will be strong, particularly in the absence of planned alternative employment for the workers involved. The termination of the B-1B program as now planned could make the dislocation caused by the B-1A cancellation pale by comparison. B-1B opponents believe that this is exactly what the Air Force and B-1B contractors are counting on, and that these groups would like to build more than 100 of the aircraft. With Start or budget constraints, further production of the B-1B would come at the expense of the Northrop Stealth bomber program or with sped-up retirement of B-52s. If Start led to another agreement that further reduced weapons levels, the conflict could become even more severe.

Economic Conversion

Because many peace activists believe that economic concerns keep many defense companies and their employees from endorsing arms control or reduction proposals, they have proposed economic conversion as a way to counteract this disincentive. Lloyd Dumas, political science professor at the University of Texas, says conversion could make peace possible "by concretely reassuring those who directly fear loss of their own jobs as a result of cutbacks in military spending, as well as the much larger segment of the population who fear that such cutbacks will generate unemployment (or broader economic recession or depression)."[3]

Advocate Melman believes that conversion "would transform the present situation" in the military industry. "There would be ready options for defense factories," he says. "Completion of military contracts could be contemplated without panic. And members of Congress could consider military policy for military reasons, and not for the same spurious spurring the economy arguments that obfuscate the problem today."[4]

Of course, economic conversion is not the only way to defuse these financial concerns. For reasons discussed below, most Defense and Energy Department contractors do not embrace it. They prefer other strategies.

The concept of conversion: Stripped of any political coloring, economic conversion plans are blueprints for the orderly reallocation of capital, labor and other resources from one kind of production to another. One of the main tenets of conversion is to minimize disruption and hardship for the firm and its employees when faced with a major change in business. As such, it can provide some financial insurance against contract cancellations or other unanticipated disruptions. If Rockwell had formulated a conversion plan, at least in theory, it could have weathered the B-1 cancellation without massive layoffs by putting its employees to work on planned alternative projects.

In 1980, the Congressional Budget Office characterized conversion as the means by which a small group that might be injured as a result of a government decision could receive compensation by the larger groups who benefited by the same decision. "If governmental aid for economic conversion were available to mitigate the harm done to injured groups," said the CBO, "decisionmakers might find it easier to press for the general benefit over the particular interest. There might be less tendency to argue the employment effects of defense spending, to protect inefficient industries, or to weaken needed environmental regulations."[5]

To advocates of conversion, the term has taken on a more specific meaning. To most, conversion means a commitment to decreasing military production. To some, conversion is part of a broader strategy of social change toward peace, economic revitalization, full employment and workplace democracy.

Advocates see a crucial role for government planning and support for conversion, but they insist that a share of the responsibility--and the benefits to be derived--rests with the corporations now in defense production. Advocates envision a framework for conversion that requires the cooperation of the company, the workers and the unions as well as support from the community and various government agencies. This framework is contained in a bill, the Defense Economic Adjustment Act, sponsored by Rep. Ted Weiss (D-N.Y.).

Strategies for conversion planning: Economic conversion is nothing new. Its history stretches as far back as the Bible's admonition to beat swords into plowshares.

In World War II, conversion from civilian to military production was a patriotic duty. "You, too, must convert, for conversion is America's job," said a pamphlet published in 1942 by the Office of Emergency Management. "The President's blueprint for victory calls for production of 60,000 planes, 45,000 tanks, 20,000 anti-aircraft guns and 8 million tons of shipping this year," it continued. "The translation of that blueprint into actual weapons to overwhelm the enemy depends upon the manufacturers, the workers, the citizens of America."[6]

And the U.S. industrial base did convert--virtually overnight--to meet the wartime needs. Auto companies learned to produce airplanes, safe and lock companies made tank parts, and even one merry-go-round producer found a way to manufacture military goods.[7] Production levels in the war industries reached all-time highs. In one single month (March 1944), the nation produced 9,117 military aircraft.[8]

As those who lived through it know, however, neither the conversion to war production nor reconversion after the war was always smooth. In fact, at the beginning so many people were out of work, because their plants had closed down to convert, that Congress considered legislation mandating "layoff" wages until facilities reopened. Congress also considered providing additional benefits for workers such as auto salesmen, whose jobs disintegrated during the war and whose skills were not compatible with much of the wartime work.[9]

At the end of the war, many people also found themselves out of work. Walter Reuther, head of the United Auto Workers during that period, told the story of the Willow Run bomber plant (a Ford plant that was famous for its record-breaking production of military aircraft during the war):

> When we got to the end of that tremendous production achievement the Navy sent its brass and the Army sent its brass and we had a big ceremony and I represented, as the spokesman for the UAW, the 20,000-odd workers. The Navy brass and the Army brass thanked the workers for a tremendous production achievement and they gave them the "E" award for excellence. Then they told them: "The plant is expendable and you are all going to be laid off." That was the reward.[10]

Some companies made notable postwar conversion efforts. General Electric, for example, probably had as successful a record as any. GE made ship turbines and aircraft engines during the war, but started planning for reconversion with great care as early as 1941. A 1942 Fortune article describes GE's postwar plans as "a sheaf of blueprints on which the new world is worked out to three decimal points and in which its own position is as clearly defined as the details of one of its turbines."[11]

On the average, other companies in consumer goods industries prospered after the war, in large part because of the demand for consumer goods that had been tabled during wartime. Companies outside of these industries had a much harder time returning to civilian production, however. The aircraft companies, the naval shipyards, and certain specialized companies, which had developed in response to the special technological demands of war, had problems in a peacetime economy. In her book, The Baroque Arsenal, University of Sussex professor Mary Kaldor argues that in the name of national security, the government came to support these industries after the war, which marked the growth of the nation's first large peacetime military industry.[12]

Overall, postwar reconversion was not as planned or organized as conversion to military production had been. Members of the War Production Board were aware of this problem. In a report dated February 1944, they stated:

> With the coming of war a sort of totalitarianism is asserted. The government tells each business what it is to contribute to the war program, just what it is to make....Patriotism exercises a strong compulsion. With peace the opposite becomes true. Each has the right to make what he pleases. Government direction and aid disappear....[13]

The War Production Board, which coordinated the war industrial effort, started planning for reconversion in April 1943, "long before victory was in sight," according to its chairman, Donald Nelson.[14] But its attempts to ease the nation back into a peacetime economy met with some stiff opposition from the army and from industry. Nelson explains that many companies opposed gradual reconversion because they were afraid it might give an advantage to those companies that reconverted first and "would upset established competitive positions and industrial patterns, and would enable new producers, especially small ones, to invade commercial fields which heretofore had been the special preserve of certain long-established corporations," he said.[15] A compromise was reached, and industries were allowed to reconvert in a planned sequence of four installments.

The framework for economic conversion that most advocates endorse today is an attempt to establish an even more organized peacetime conversion plan.

Sen. George McGovern (D-S.D.) introduced the first conversion legislation in 1964, and a version of his bill has been reintroduced in every congressional session since. It has never passed either the House or the Senate. Called the Defense Economic Adjustment Act, it would:

-- establish a Defense Economic Adjustment Council in the executive branch. Its main task would be to encourage and coordinate government-sponsored projects that could create markets for defense companies that wished to convert to civilian production.

-- establish conversion planning groups called "Alternative Use Committees" at each defense-related facility that employed more than 100 persons. These committees, made up of representatives from labor and management, would be responsible for preparing detailed conversion plans for their facilities.

-- extend benefits to employees of a facility undergoing conversion including salary compensation, vested pension credit, health and life insurance coverage, job retraining and reimbursement for relocation where appropriate.

-- establish a Workers Economic Adjustment Reserve Trust Fund, to be funded by defense contractors, that would pay the costs of carrying out the act.

A limited version of this act, the Dodd-McKinley amendment, passed the House in 1979 but failed to get through a House-Senate conference committee. This amendment would have required the Defense Department to notify a company one year before any cutbacks, and would have provided planning grants and economic assistance for communities and laid-off defense workers.

Federal assistance for those injured by government decisions is not without precedent, however. The Trade Act of 1974 covers firms and workers injured as a result of changes in U.S. trade agreements. As the Congressional Budget Office describes the act, it is designed "to compensate both these groups for losses resulting from lowered trade barriers and to assist the losers in making the transition to new jobs or markets. Benefits to firms included technical assistance, loans and loan guarantees, and tax relief. Benefits to workers included readjustment allowances, additional assistance to cover expenses while participating in training and relocation allowances to cover the costs of moving to take jobs in new locations."[16]

<u>Roadblocks to successful conversion</u>: Even those who promote economic conversion are under no illusion that it is an easy task. The reconstruction required of a company that switches from military to civilian production is complex and arduous.

Many analysts argue that economic conversion would be more difficult today than it was after World War II because many defense contractors have little, if any, experience in the civilian marketplace. Further, today's environment provides few, if any, of the incentives to convert that existed after World War II.

Only a handful of firms have attempted conversion in recent years, and their experiences have not been encouraging. Two of the most publicized failures involved aerospace firms. In one, Boeing-Vertol, a subsidiary of The Boeing Co., switched from the production of helicopters to rail vehicles. In the other, Rohr Industries won a bid to make subway cars for the San Francisco Bay Area Rapid Transit System. Both endeavors resulted in cost overruns, high rates of technical failures and lawsuits. Neither company continued in the mass transit business.

Conversion advocates have looked carefully at these and other conversion efforts in order to determine the hurdles that any successful conversion plan must clear. They have identified economic barriers such as occupational, capital equipment and market changes as well as political barriers that must be overcome.

Jobs--Conversion advocates say that all the employees in a defense facility, from the managers and engineers to the administrative workers, would need to adapt their skills and their outlook to work effectively in a civilian marketplace.

Managers, engineers and scientists would need the most attention, according to advocates, because they need to learn the ropes of the cost-minimizing, multi-customer civilian markets, which differ greatly from the performance-maximizing, one-customer defense market. Although many of the skills these occupational groups have would be useful in either environment, many analysts say the importance of reorientation should not be underestimated. Said one Defense department official:

> Often the conversion of industrial facilities to new product lines has been more an issue of corporate management and marketing strengths than it has been a case of plant engineering conversion to new manufacturing processes. The limiting factors may not necessarily be engineering or technical issues but are instead corporate planning and management issues.

Marketing strategies seem especially difficult to adapt. Dumas explains:

> Rather than knowing how to run an effective electronic and print media advertising campaign, how to survey markets for public acceptance of a new product line, how to price a product for penetration into new markets or expansion of existing ones, etc., it becomes critical [for defense managers and engineers] to know the minute detail of the Armed Services Procurement Regulations, to develop good working relationships with key government procurement personnel, and to be able to lobby effectively with members of the Congress.[17]

Dumas also argues that defense managers, scientists and engineers who have been working in the military industry for a substantial amount of time tend to be less willing to adapt to the requirements of civilian production. This "economic stiffening of the joints" also must be overcome, he said.

Technical, administrative and production workers do not need as much reorientation as executives and technologists. Several studies indicate that these workers would be able to step into civilian jobs with very few problems.

Perhaps the most detailed of these studies was commissioned by the Arms Control and Disarmament Agency in 1967. It analyzed 127 skilled technical and production jobs in two California missile plants--Aerojet General in Sacramento and Lockheed Missiles and Space Co. in Sunnyvale. The report found that "the vast majority" of the occupations surveyed could be matched with at least one nondefense occupation. "More than 60 percent of the occupations were found to require no retraining at all...for transfer to their counterparts," it said. "And only about 5 percent were found to require more than three months of retraining."[18]

The study did not consider clerical, service, sales or unskilled jobs because skills in these occupations were "assumed to be readily transferable to their counterparts in the nondefense sector."

A similar study conducted in 1978 by the Mid-Peninsula Conversion Project (MPCP), a nonprofit corporation that promotes conversion, found that almost all of the 162 skilled and semi-skilled aerospace occupations it analyzed could readily be applied to the solar industry. (See Table 2.)

However, the MPCP study recognizes that large numbers of aerospace workers would not be able to find jobs in the solar industry in the near future. The transfer "is not prevented because of skill mismatches, but rather because of other obstacles, such as numbers and ready availability of jobs," said the report.[19]

Capital equipment--Capital equipment seems to be the least of a company's worries when contemplating conversion. Except for highly specialized machine tools and shipbuilding facilities, many analysts agree, most defense industries' capital equipment is of a sufficiently general nature to be used in civilian production.

The notable exception to this general assessment are nuclear warhead production facilities. These facilities have two problems that would make their conversion very difficult. First, they tend to have a large amount of highly specialized equipment. Second, much of their equipment and many of their buildings have been contaminated by radiation. Thus, some parts of nuclear weapons facilities "may have to be

Table 2
International Association of Machinists Jobs at Lockheed Compared with Jobs in the Solar Industry

IAM Job Category	Number at LMSC	Comparable Solar Job Description	Job opportunities in 30-year solar commitment
TECHNICIANS:			
Missile Systems Inspector	118	Inspector of hybrid and industrial solar systems	Small
Space Lab Technician (testing equipment in space conditions)	123	No direct applications	None
Weapons Effect Technician	20	No direct applications	None
Electronic Equipment Technician	18	Wind and hybrid systems	Small
Machine Technician and Inspector	196	Checking/metering parts of precision wind turbines	Small
Electronic Assembly Inspector	82	Assembly controls for hybrid	Small
Electronic Products Assurance Technician	30	Highly specific tasks not applicable	None
SKILLED:			
Machinist (including bench ceramic, general, milling, jig borer, lathe, precision jig, fisture builder, tool and die maker)	289	Wind machines, materials production for solar components, aluminum extrusion, pumps, controls, all parts	Moderate
Missile Electronics Development Mechanic	47	Wind systems controller	Very few
Mechanic	58	Fix all factory machines easily	Small-moderate
Plumber	28	Install active systems	Large
Air Conditioning Mechanic	28	Design and install solar cooling systems	Small
Carpenter	26	Active/passive systems	Large
Painter	16	Passive systems	Small
Electrician	54	Installation of various systems	Large
OPERATIVES (semi-skilled):			
(Note: With minimum retraining, nearly all of the semi-skilled operatives are transferable to assembly and sub-assembly jobs in the solar industry.)			
Electronic/Mechanical Assembly	207	Component assembly	Moderate
Structure Assembly	59	Assembly of solar collectors and wind machines	Large
Machine Operator	19	"Can work in any factory"	Moderate
Processor/Molder/Electroplater	49	None	None

Source: Mid-Peninsula Conversion Project, 1978.

reckoned as a dead loss in planning conversion," said Dumas. The only resource that could be useful in civilian pursuits would be the labor force.[20]

A recent study sponsored by the Energy Department backs up Dumas's assessment. The report looks at the possibility of converting the Department of Energy's Rocky Flats plant. (Rocky Flats' primary responsibility is the production of components for nuclear warheads.) The report estimates that "the cost of cleanup and decontamination at the plant could reach $200 million." Even if a cleanup were undertaken, the report says, "Because little equipment will be left, a number of buildings stripped, and perhaps the utility systems disrupted--there may not be much left at the plant that is highly desirable for others."[21]

Markets--Companies are not likely to plunge into conversion unless potentially profitable markets exist for their products. Finding such products and markets probably represents the greatest hurdle that a company considering conversion would face. The DoE nuclear weapons production complex does not lend itself to many civilian uses, for example. Nuclear power production might be one logical alternative for two of the DoE nuclear warhead facilities--Savannah River and Hanford--but many might question the desirability of this plan.

In the abstract, many more alternative product possibilities come to mind for other nuclear weapons industries. Aerospace companies could make planes and satellites for civilian customers. Shipbuilders could make tankers and other commercial ships. The radio and TV communications, electronic components and computer industries already sell their products to both the military and commercial customers.

When a group of workers at Lucas Aerospace Corp. (an English company) put their heads together, they identified more than 150 civilian products that could be made in Lucas's plants. These products, outlined in a six-volume document called the "corporate plan," include medical equipment, alternative energy sources, transport systems, braking systems, oceanics and telechiric (remote control) equipment, some of which have since been developed.

An abundance of product possibilities, however, does not translate automatically into sales; markets must also exist. And most of the products identified above are not in large demand. As discussed in Chapter III, the commercial shipbuilding industry is so severely depressed that shipyards cannot even make use of current commercial capacity. The commercial aircraft industry is not much better off. Civilian markets for products from the space systems, radio and television communications and electronic components industries are somewhat stronger; analysts predict growth in both the military and civilian segments of these markets.

Nevertheless, some of the largest military contractors, including many covered in this report, have found ways to stake a claim in commercial fields related to their military work. Most have entered new markets by acquiring smaller companies already in the field; some have developed new businesses internally.

For example, Raytheon's microwave ovens, now a part of its appliance business, were a chance spin-off from the company's military radio microwave technology. Raytheon's military sonar and radar systems have been adapted for commercial ships and air traffic control systems. Litton's Ingalls shipyard is finishing up a contract for oil rig construction. Tenneco's Newport News shipyard now has a subsidiary that provides planning, design, construction and repair services for the commercial power generation industry, which evolved out of the shipyard's knowledge of naval nuclear shipbuilding. McDonnell Douglas has a computer subsidiary that manufactures a computer-aided design and manufacturing system and provides computer services to health care institutions. Boeing and Grumman also have taken commercial advantage of their computer expertise, developed initially for aerospace requirements. Other mostly commercial companies have taken advantage of military development contracts. GTE, for example, has developed fiber optics equipment for both civilian and military customers.

There are just as many examples, however, of companies that have not prospered in civilian ventures. Rockwell International was instrumental in developing the world's first integrated circuits for the Minuteman missile, but it has not been able to build a strong business for its nonmilitary semiconductors. In 1982, it decided to hire two outside commercial managers to head up the program. General Dynamics' Secretary John Maguire told IRRC that marketing in new areas is "extremely difficult, just like U.S. Steel saying it is going to build airplanes." Maguire said General Dynamics' Electric Boat division tried 10 different commercial products when its business fell off after World War II, and all failed. Grumman wants to earn half its profit from commercial business, but it has not yet made its goal, in part because of market entry problems. (See box.)

Some conversion advocates say that the government can take a role in creating markets for defense companies in areas of national need; they say the government already supports areas in which defense companies could participate. In an unpublished study conducted in 1979, the Exploratory Project for Economic Alternatives, a research group, identified four federally supported products that defense contractors could manufacture: railroad cars, mass transit vehicles, municipal solid waste processors and solar energy technologies.[22]

However, conversion critics argue that the government could never find enough new markets to support a large scale conversion of the defense

Grumman's Diversification Experience

Grumman has been attempting to diversify for a number of years. In 1976, the company set a goal of earning half its profits from commercial business by 1982. The company has made some progress, but with considerable difficulty, and it abandoned the goal of a 50/50 balance before the 1982 deadline.

Grumman's efforts illustrate, though, that diversification can broaden a company's base while providing no protection for workers. Grumman is the largest private employer on Long Island. A Grumman spokesman told IRRC that the aerospace division employs 21,400 workers, most of whom work on Long Island. Most of Grumman's military aerospace work is done on Long Island, but its diversification efforts have been aimed elsewhere. A cut in military contracts would result in layoffs at Grumman and high levels of unemployment on Long Island, similar to those experienced in the early 1970s, the last time the Defense Department cut back on Grumman's military contracts. Assuming that the skills of the company's aerospace workers could be transferred to other segments of production and that those segments were growing, Long Island workers would be kept employed only if Grumman distributed its work force among its commercial segments in Ohio, Georgia, New York, and elsewhere around the country.

Thus far, the reverse situation has occurred. Military contract dollars remain large, and Long Island remains prosperous. Grumman's diversified commercial businesses, in contrast, have not fared well. The company is curtailing or divesting itself of losing and unpromising operations. It has jettisoned unproductive portions of its computer service, withdrawn from the liquid waste treatment industry, sold a foundry, closed down its Athens, N.Y., truck body manufacturing plant, and sold its bus business.

industry. Advocates dispute this claim. Melman says both the federal government and business have come forward several times with agendas for national civilian economic development on a scale that could provide markets for many military contractors. For example, he says:

> Fortune magazine of March 1969 titled an article "We Can Afford a Better America." It listed and priced work to be done that is well appreciated as public responsibility--in pollution control, mass transit, removing eyesores, suburban

sprawl and inner cities disrepair, crime control, welfare reforms, medical care and education. The annual bill for Fortune's better America was $57 billion a year.[23]

Political barriers--Despite advocates' optimism that the economic barriers to conversion can be overcome, the nuts and bolts of conversion planning will not even begin to be sorted until the political barriers are cleared.

The groups that oppose economic conversion include many defense contractors and, with some notable exceptions, labor unions that represent workers in defense industries. These and other groups question the need for conversion planning.

Many analysts believe that the market should be left to redistribute resources released from reductions in defense spending. These analysts believe that defense workers' higher risk of dislocation is balanced through the market by higher wages and other benefits.

Thus, the debate surrounding conversion planning has not gotten much farther than step one: Is any kind of conversion planning necessary or desirable? Further, there are other aspects of the proposed conversion framework that are potentially volatile politically. First, the pending Weiss bill could be seen as an active promotion of reductions in defense spending. An aide to Rep. Weiss told IRRC that the conversion bill represents "a major shift in the emphasis of the federal government. It focuses the resources of the federal government in a sense on disarmament, in a sense on facilitating the move away from the military--and that's a big shift."

Second, Weiss's bill, because it would require defense facilities of a certain size to formulate conversion plans and to give management and labor equal representation on the alternative use committees, could be interpreted as a threat to management's jurisdiction.

Third, labor unions fear that economic conversion might result in the loss of jobs, at least in the short term. When Sen. McGovern first proposed conversion legislation in 1963, only one national union, the National Farmers Union, formally endorsed the legislation.[24] Since then a few unions--notably the Machinists and the United Auto Workers--have expressed interest in and support for conversion legislation but most are still uncomfortable with the concept.

The corporate view: Corporations prefer to insulate themselves against the loss of contracts in two ways. One is cancellation clauses, a standard feature of many defense contracts, which commit the Defense Department to pay penalty fees when it terminates contracts. Rockwell received penalty fees when the B-1 was canceled. The other common way that corporations insulate themselves against contract losses is diversification. During the 1960s and 1970s, many defense contractors, including many of those profiled in this report, diversified into civilian markets in order to reduce their dependence on military contracts.

In the 1970s--In 1970, a Senate Government Operations subcommittee wrote to the heads of 118 major companies, the mayors of 18 major cities and the leaders of seven labor unions to solicit their opinions on conversion as outlined in the bill sponsored by McGovern. Of the 69 companies that responded, many supported the goals of the legislation but questioned whether it would work in practice. Their doubts paralleled many of the barriers to conversion outlined above.

Some companies said the technology gap between defense-aerospace needs and civilian needs was so great that conversion might be impossible. LTV's chief executive officer James Ling wrote that firms might experience "difficulty in converting a process or product from one that is rigidly controlled to high-performance, high-quality specifications [a defense product] to one that does not require the same specifications, and, in fact, cannot be produced at a profit unless designed to be produced to less stringent specifications [a commercial product]."[25]

Other companies questioned whether businesses could adjust to other differences between defense and commercial markets. "Personally, I happen to question the ability of a company devoted solely to defense-space to succeed in the commercial field," wrote the president of General Tire & Rubber. "They have a tendency to underrate the complexity of the problems and the capabilities of their future competitors." A Lockheed senior economic adviser said: "Everyone is talking about opportunities in enviromental engineering, urban renewal, housing and systems analysis in health and education, but the problem is that there is no central contracting authority. You have to contract with every city, state and county. The market is fragmented. And it takes an awful lot of systems analysis contracts to take the place of a C 5A cargo jet."

Seven companies asserted that the process of systems engineering--overseeing and integrating all parts of a production program--used in many defense industries was ill-suited for social and political problems. "We suspect people have overestimated the virtues of the system sciences (systems analysis, systems engineering and systems management) to problems having large sociological and economic elements," said Boeing. Du Pont wrote: "It must be recognized that when the decision was made to go to the moon, there were no building codes, zoning regulations, existing landowners, jurisdictional disputes among laboring forces, political leaders with attendant constituent interest, and other governmental complications to impede the landing on the moon. In summary, it was an engineering feat with very few 'people' problems as compared with the problems of cities."

Several companies questioned whether conversion plans were necessary at all. General Electric said that the nation's experience after World Wars I and II showed that no conversion commission was needed. Besides, the company doubted that military spending would decline. Even though the Vietnam war was winding down, "there is a backlog of strategic military projects which will absorb the attentions of defense contractors, including General Electric...," it wrote.

After assessing the responses, the Senate subcommittee concluded that "private industry is not interested in initiating any major attempts at meeting critical public needs. Most industries have no plans or projects designed to apply their resources to civilian problems. Furthermore, they indicated an unwillingness to initiate such actions without a firm commitment from the government that their efforts will quickly reap the financial rewards to which they are accustomed."

The subcommittee recognized that multiple political jurisdictions, unclear markets, union practices and public resistance to innovation were legitimate obstacles that make it difficult for defense companies to enter nondefense fields. "But to retreat from entering virtually all the territory in the civilian field on the basis of these obstacles, and to defer to government to overcome them, conflicts with the best traditions of the free enterprise system," it said.

In the 1980s--Two of the 19 Defense Department contractors profiled in this study, General Electric and Boeing, have attempted conversion in the past, but none of the 19 maintains what could be called a conversion plan.

With careful planning, GE sucessfully converted from military to civilian production after World War II. Boeing, however, did not succeed in converting its helicopter subsidiary, Boeing-Vertol, into a viable transit vehicle manufacturing firm. Many analysts blame Boeing's failure on the company's lack of expertise in that area.

Of the companies that agreed to comment on the subject, many told IRRC they believed that diversification sufficiently protected them from adverse impacts of contract cancellations or other reductions in defense spending. In response to shareholder resolutions that asked them to consider formulating conversion plans, TRW, GTE and Rockwell stated in almost identical language that such plans were not necessary because their diversification efforts limit "the adverse impact of reductions in or discontinuance of a particular business or program."

Three companies in this report--Raytheon, Northrop and Singer--have become major subcontractors within the defense industry. This strategy of spreading their business among many contracts allows them to minimize financial risk without entering civilian business.

Seven companies reported that they have formal policies designed to aid laid-off employees. Aerojet said it provided a job bank, and job search, guidance and counseling services that were able to help 90 percent of its displaced workers find jobs on one occasion. Allied said it "traditionally has made every effort to place people within the company or elsewhere." Avco said it gives advance notice and severance pay. Boeing said it redistributes employees to other projects whenever possible. GTE's "manpower planning program" includes provisions to help displaced employees. Honeywell says it gives its laid-off workers first consideration for job openings within the company. Rockwell arranged job fairs and other employment services for its laid-off B-1 workers and said, if need be, it would take similar actions in the future.

None of these programs matches the job security that the pending conversion legislation would mandate. If conversion succeeded, almost all of a company's employees would have a job in the new enterprise. Diversification, to the extent that it is carried out in the same region where defense production occurs, and utilizes skills possessed by defense workers, may provide some employment to workers who lose their defense-related jobs, but this often is not the case. However, if the conversion bill were passed, defense workers would enjoy more job security and/or transition benefits than most other occupations.

Conclusions

At a time when defense is the fastest growing sector of the nation's economy, planning for conversion from military to civilian production might seem superfluous. Companies and communities are increasing their business with the Defense Department, not decreasing it.

Most opponents of conversion would like to minimize the disruption caused by contract cancellations and the like, but they prefer strategies that are closer to most corporations' traditional methods of doing business. They believe that the administration's defense program will go forward, and that the cancellations conversion advocates fear are going to be few. Thus, they question whether setting up alternative use committees at each defense facility is necessary. They also question whether many defense firms could convert successfully to civilian production and whether defense employees should be exempt from what many observers see as the normal risks of the marketplace.

But conversion advocates offer several reasons for formulating conversion plans now.

The first reason is that even today's large arms buildup is not likely to prevent major disruptions of the work and livelihoods of many defense contractors and their employees. For example, it will not prevent the disruption that occurs when a company completes a big contract and has no other similar program in place. As discussed previously, some analysts are predicting that many of the estimated 50,000 to 60,000 jobs that the B-1 program will create will be in jeopardy in 1987 when annual orders for the plane are slated to drop from 48 to zero.

The buildup also will not prevent individual contract cancellations that might occur for any number of reasons. The costs of new weapons systems are predicted to exceed the $1.8 trillion that has been allocated for them over the next five years. Deputy Defense Secretary Thayer, while not naming an amount, has conceded that the "gap indeed is a real one." If the defense budget is not increased to cover such increases, some programs will have to be canceled.[26]

Finally, possibilities for arms control agreements--however remote they may seem at times--cannot be ruled out. The implementation and timing of such agreements will be an important factor in how much they will affect military industries, but adverse economic effects, as discussed earlier, certainly are possible.

The second reason that advocates want conversion planning now is because they want to counteract what they see as the 'built-in deterrent' to arms control and reduction proposals. "The very existence of such [conversion] plans would encourage a realistic view of the feasibility of alternatives to war economy, thus defusing at least some of the fears associated with long dependence on the military dollar," said Melman.[27] Without some way to counter such fears, advocates believe, influential constituencies will continue to make it difficult if not impossible for lawmakers to support cuts in the military's budget.

Thus, advocates conclude, the government has a responsibility to defense workers and companies who would suffer as a result of government decisions, and a responsibility to ensure that the structure of military forces is determined by military and not employment or business reasons.

Chapter VI Footnotes

1. "Community Economic Impact of B-1B Production Cancellation," prepared for the State of California Business and Transportation Agency by the Economics Research Associates, October 1977.
2. Seymour Melman, "Beating 'Swords' into Subways," The New York Times Magazine, Nov. 19, 1978.
3. Lloyd Dumas, "Political Economy of Reversing the Arms Race," The Political Economy of Arms Reduction, American Association for the Advancement of Science, 1982, p. 146.
4. Melman, op. cit.
5. Congressional Budget Office, "Economic Conversion: What Should Be the Government's Role," January 1980, p. 19.
6. Office of Emergency Management, The Arsenal of Democracy Series, "Conversion: America's Job," 1942, p. 31.
7. Ibid., p. 18-22.
8. Donald Nelson, Arsenal of Democracy, the Story of American War Production, Grover Press Inc., New York, 1946, p. 238.
9. Office of Emergency Management, op. cit., p. 24-5.
10. Mary Kaldor, The Baroque Arsenal, Hill and Wang, New York, 1981, p. 213.
11. Fortune, Feb. 11, 1970, p. 101.
12. Kaldor, op. cit., p. 61-4.
13. Nelson, op. cit., p. 391.
14. Nelson, op. cit., p. 391.
15. Ibid., p. 410.
16. Congressional Budget Office, op. cit., p. 31
17. Dumas, "Conversion of the Military Economy: United States," op. cit., p. 30.
18. Arms Control and Disarmament Agency, "The Economic Impact of Reductions in Defense Spending," 1972, p. 24.
19. Dave McFadden, "Solar Options for Military Workers," Mid-Peninsula Conversion Project, Plowshare Press, Fall 1978.
20. Dumas, op. cit., p. 35.
21. "The Social and Economic Impacts of Changing Missions at the Rocky Flats Plant," prepared for Rockwell International and the U.S. Department of Energy by Battelle Columbus Laboratories, June 1982, revised, p. xxiv.
22. Philip Webre, Jobs to People, Exploratory Project for Economic Alternatives, Washington, D.C., 1979, unpublished.
23. Seymour Melman, The Permanent War Economy, Simon and Schuster, New York, 1974, p. 195-6.
24. Ibid., p. 247.
25. National Economic Conversion Commission, Responses to Subcommittee Questionnaire, submitted by the Subcommittee on Executive Reorganization and Government Research to the Senate Committee on Government Operations, September 1970, p. 64.
26. The Los Angeles Times, "U.S. Defense Establishment Wields a Pervasive Power," July 10, 1983.
27. Melman, The Permanent War Economy, op. cit., p. 190.

Conclusions

During the 1980s, the B-1B bomber, the MX missile, the Pershing II missile, the cruise missiles, and the Trident II missile--nearly enough nuclear weapons to replace all the strategic and medium-range systems that have been put in place to date--all will have moved from the drawing board into full-scale production unless some arms control agreement is reached. Many observers recognize this period as an important turning point in the nuclear arms race, from which several paths could be taken.

Even though both the United States and the Soviet Union profess a desire to curb the arms race, there is a high probability that no arms control agreement will be negotiated in the near future. Thus, it is fairly certain that the new generation of nuclear weapons will cease to be paper bargaining chips and the production lines will begin to roll forward. Nevertheless, budget pressures and a heightened public concern about nuclear warfare are going to make it difficult to build all the weapons currently planned.

Thus, the nuclear weapons industry is poised for growth but threatened with disappointment. Nuclear weapons budget increases set in motion in the Carter and Reagan administrations already are boosting the fortunes of a wide variety of military contractors. Aerospace companies in particular are receiving substantially increased nuclear warfare-related orders (most notably Rockwell International, General Dynamics, Boeing, Martin Marietta, McDonnell Douglas and Northrop). But many other electronic, communications, shipbuilding, and computer companies also are benefiting from orders for nuclear weapons and related systems that will exceed $30 billion annually over the next several years, if current plans are unaltered.

Increased military business also means increased defense dependency for companies, workers and communities that could translate into further momentum for the nuclear arms race. A larger military-industrial complex with a greater economic stake in nuclear weapons production will be hard for Pentagon critics--or presidents with a bent for arms control--to slow. After looking closely at Department of Defense contract awards for fiscal year 1981, IRRC found that the production contracts for nuclear weapons systems that would be covered by a freeze along the lines proposed by the Nuclear Weapons Freeze Campaign totaled $2 billion in that year, a small percentage of all Pentagon contracts (not including research and development contracts). However, cancellations or cutbacks in the mid-1980s--when the major strategic programs are in full swing--would be likely to cause major disruptions for military contractors and defense workers, especially in the absence of a booming civilian economy and/or planning for conversion from military to civilian production.

If the military buildup continues to gather steam, it will spur an increase in economic growth as a traditional stimulant, but the spur to employment, productivity and GNP may be small relative to possible alternative uses for the same amount of resources. Some analysts believe that in the long term, high rates of military spending may harm the civilian economy by draining research and development funds. It is not clear, however, that military funds would necessarily be diverted to research and development.

If strategic arms control talks between the United States and the Soviet Union are successful, there could be a reduction in overall numbers of nuclear weapons in both countries. Both the Reagan Start framework and the Soviet Salt framework could provide such an outcome. In both cases, however, the reduction probably would come at the expense of older weapons that would be retired early. Thus, high rates of spending for strategic systems might continue, and the U.S. nuclear weapons industries might not suffer, at least directly. However, if budget pressures persist, it may not be possible politically to build new systems while retiring older weapons years ahead of their time. As a result, even the Start and Salt framework could create roadblocks to sustained procurement of new strategic systems, and such spending might decline.

Under a freeze, as it is outlined by the Nuclear Weapons Freeze Campaign, new weapons systems would not be built and existing nuclear weapons and delivery systems would be maintained. Thus, the freeze holds the possibility for reducing the burden of military spending on the federal budget and on the economy. Military and nuclear weapons industries would not grow as expected, unless spending for conventional forces were increased significantly.

Whether or not agreement on arms control is reached, the U.S. defense industry will continue to have an important voice in the nuclear weapons debate. Although the influence of military contractors should not be seen as the sole determinant of defense policies, neither should it be dismissed as unimportant. As long as the United States relies on a private contractor system to supply large amounts of military goods and services, the private and public military bureaucracies will work in close cooperation. This bureaucratic symbiosis is an inherent attribute of the system. It is necessary to produce effective military systems, but it also means that an influential military-industrial complex will continue to have an important say in shaping military policy.

Company Profiles

Introduction to the Company Profiles

The following profiles present detailed information on 26 publicly held companies that produce nuclear weapons and related equipment. Some 19 of the 26 companies are industry leaders because of their work under Defense Department contracts. Ten companies are the crucial publicly held corporations that manage most of the Energy Department's nuclear weapons and weapons-grade materials complex. Three of these companies--General Electric, Rockwell International and Westinghouse Electric--fall into both categories. (Profiles of these three companies are included with the Defense Department contractors.)

IRRC analyzed fiscal year 1981 prime contract awards to choose the companies included in this study. Reliance on prime contract data has limitations. One is that much of the actual work is passed on to other companies under subcontract. Another is that awards in any given year are for work performed over time periods ranging from less than a year to seven or eight years. Thus, the amounts awarded are not equivalent to actual sales during a given year.

Moreover, arriving at a satisfactory definition of nuclear weapons is very difficult. As described in Chapter I, IRRC developed two operating definitions by using "primary" and "secondary" designations. (See p. 17.) IRRC included some companies that are most important for their work on primary nuclear systems, and a few others (notably Litton Industries and United Technologies) that do substantial work on secondary systems.

Thus, at the margin, it is not possible to say that all companies included in the following profiles are more important than certain corporations that are not profiled. If different definitions of nuclear systems and different methods of accounting for contract awards were used, some companies that are not included here would count as more important nuclear contractors than do some companies that are included. For example, Morton Thiokol and Hercules are major producers of missile propulsion systems. Nonetheless, the two companies are not profiled in this report, in large part because they received minimal prime contract awards for nuclear systems work in fiscal 1981.

Two companies--UNC Resources and Westinghouse--were included among the Energy Department contractors because of more recent (that is, post-1981) responsibilities. UNC operates the N reactor at the Energy Department's Hanford facility near Richland, Wash., which in 1982 was converted to the manufacture of weapons-grade plutonium. In 1983, Westinghouse Electric won a contract to manage the chemical reprocessing plant at the Idaho National Engineering Laboratory (INEL). Westinghouse will begin management of the facility early in 1984, and among its responsibilities will be the reprocessing of spent fuel from naval and research reactors, for later use in the nuclear warhead program.

It is important to note that IRRC prepared profiles on public corporations only. Universities and nonprofit institutions--notably the University of California--are not included, even though they are major participants in the nuclear weapons industry. IRRC also excluded such privately held for-profit companies as Williams International and Hughes Aircraft.

Information sources for contract awards: Defense and Energy Department listings of contract awards provided baseline data for these profiles. Each year, the Pentagon's Directorate on Information and Reports (DIOR) publishes extensive information on contract awards, including a detailed listing, by company, of all unclassified awards of more than $10,000. Most of the major awards can be identified by weapons system. Using this information for fiscal year 1981, IRRC attempted to match awards with primary and secondary nuclear systems, in order to provide comparable information on the companies profiled. In many cases Defense Department press releases on contract awards provided important information to fill in the blanks left by incomplete information in the annual listings. IRRC also used Defense Department press releases to obtain information on important contracts awarded since 1981.

To make the task manageable, IRRC ignored all contract actions less than $100,000, and all contracts that did not total at least $1 million during the year. On most major contracts, a number of awards (or actions) contribute to the total contract amount. (In a few cases, deductions from previous contract awards caused negative contract totals in excess of $1 million. These were included in IRRC's calculations.) Thus, the figures presented in the profiles on nuclear systems contract awards are minimal documentable figures, and they provide a general indication of the level of the corporation's involvement in particular programs.

Administration testimony and filings with congressional committees also provided important information. In addition, both the Defense and Energy Departments publish a number of informational pamphlets and reports that were used in this study.

The second major source of company data was provided by annual reports, 10-K forms and other documents that publicly traded companies are required to file with the Securities and Exchange Commission. In addition, spokesmen for many of the companies provided information in response to IRRC inquiries. Companies that were particularly helpful included AT&T, Avco, Du Pont, EG&G, GTE, General Dynamics, General Electric, Honeywell, Monsanto, Singer, TRW, UNC Resources and Union Carbide.

To ensure the accuracy of the information presented, IRRC offered a representative of each of the 26 companies to be profiled an opportunity to review a draft of that company's profile. Most of the companies reviewed the drafts, and some submitted substantive comments, which IRRC took into account in preparing the final report. IRRC itself is responsible for all information presented in the profiles.

In some areas, it was difficult to obtain reliable information. Few companies provided IRRC with detailed information on their employees and the number of employees involved in defense and nuclear weapons-related production. In the case of the Department of Energy contractors, reliable information is readily available from the government, but IRRC generally could provide only rough estimates of the defense employees working for Defense Department contractors.

Information on company-government relationship: For the Defense Department contractors, the profiles provide information on political action committee (PAC) contributions, Washington operations, and personnel interchange between companies and the Defense Department. As discussed in Chapter IV, it is difficult to evaluate the importance of these factors in providing companies with influence in government policymaking. This information is presented for each company for the reader to consider, without IRRC evaluation.

The PAC information comes from the Federal Election Commission. It gives a breakdown of contributions to voting members of defense committees, including members of the House and Senate Armed Services Committees, the defense appropriations subcommittees, and, on the House side, the defense task force of the Budget Committee. Contributions to the chairmen of the full Appropriations Committees also are included.

Data on personnel interchange between contractors and the Defense Department were derived from annual reports that the Defense Department is required to file with Congress on such transfers.

Defense Department Contractors

Avco

Avco, once a one-line defense contractor, is now a highly diversified company with markets in financial and management services as well as propulsion systems and aerospace technology. In 1982, the company's sales totaled $2.5 billion, up from $2.2 billion in 1981. Net earnings increased from $70 million in 1981 to $72 million in 1982.

Avco divides its business activities into four major segments: financial services, aerospace technology, propulsion systems, and management services. Financial services brought in half of Avco's 1982 revenues; the other three segments generated the rest.

Avco ranks 263rd on the Forbes top sales list. It has its headquarters in Greenwich, Conn.

Government and Defense Business

Defense dependence: Over its 52-year history, Avco has climbed up and down DoD's top 100 contractor list with concurrent changes in the defense proportion of its business.

In World War II, Avco, then the third largest defense contractor, built 33,000 planes, nine aircraft carriers, the battleship South Dakota and jeep bodies. After the war, Avco shifted half its business to commercial markets. By 1963, the company again was high on the Defense Department's list of top contractors, and it had 75 percent of its sales in military contracts. Government sales dropped to 44 percent of Avco's total revenues in the late 1960s but were back up to 80 percent in 1973 and 1974.

In 1982, Avco's government sales totaled $639 million--26 percent of the company's sales. Turbine engines and other components for military planes, tanks and helicopters made up the majority of these sales, and Avco's high technology research in areas such as missile re-entry systems, high energy laser research and advanced composite materials was responsible for almost all the rest. Avco's other sales to the government included management services for the Department of Labor's Job Corps centers and the Army's St. Louis area support center.

Avco was the nation's 28th largest military contractor in 1982, with DoD prime contract awards worth $668 million, up from $493 million in 1981.

Data on Avco
(dollar figures in millions)

	1978	1979	1980	1981	1982
Revenues	$1,520	$1,666	$1,921	$2,178	$2,459
Net earnings	$129	$134	$115	$70	$72
Sales to U.S. government	$208	$195	$257	$373	$639
Government sales as a percentage of total revenues	13%	12%	13%	17%	26%
Defense Department prime contract awards*	$124	$138	$287	$493	$668
Ratio of DoD prime contract awards to total revenues+	.08	.08	.15	.23	.27
Total Avco employees	NA	24,839	25,775	26,055	25,521

* Contract awards for U.S. fiscal year, ending Sept. 30.
+ Ratio of awards during fiscal year to calendar year sales.

Avco's major defense programs are located at six of its 12 divisions and subsidiaries: Avco Aerostructures Division in Tennessee, Avco Lycoming Stratford Division in Connecticut, Avco Lycoming Greer Division in South Carolina, and Avco Everett Research Laboratory Inc. (AERL), Avco Specialty Materials Division and Avco Systems Division in Massachusetts.

Avco Aerostructures manufactures structural components for military aircraft and space vehicles. It is involved in four government programs: the B-1B bomber, the C-5A and C-130 military transport planes and the Space Shuttle. The Avco Lycoming Stratford Division produces turbine engines for various military vehicles including the M-1 Abrams tank (this contract is Avco's largest, with awards of at least $230 million in 1981 alone) and the Cobra attack helicopter. Avco Lycoming Greer manufactures parts for gas turbine engines.

Avco Everett performs high technology research for DoD, DoE and other Avco divisions. Avco Specialty Materials Division develops composite (strong lightweight plastic) and fire protective materials for missiles and other aircraft. Avco Systems Division produces re-entry systems for the MX, Pershing II and Minuteman missiles as well as tactical munitions, electro-optical measurement systems and computer services.

Backlog and research and development: Avco had a government backlog of $1.3 billion in 1982, of which nearly all was in the propulsion systems and aerospace technology segments. Commercial backlog was $0.7 billion, most of which also was in the propulsion systems and aerospace technology segments.

The U.S. government sponsored $192 million worth of Avco's research and development in 1982. Avco sponsored another $26 million. Most of Avco's research is conducted by Avco Everett Research Lab and Avco Systems Division.

Defense employees and facilities: In 1982, Avco employed slightly fewer than half of its 25,521 employees at facilities where a large proportion of the work is defense-related: 5,100 at Avco Lycoming Stratford Division, 3,500 at Avco Aerostructures, 3,000 at Avco Systems, 500 at Avco Everett Research Lab and 180 at Avco Specialty Materials.

Since many employees work on products that have both commercial and military buyers, the company was unable to give IRRC an estimate of the number of employees that work directly on defense contracts. If it is assumed that employment is somewhat proportional to sales, then at least half of these employees work on Avco's defense products.

Avco leases or owns all its facilities except for Avco Lycoming's Stratford, Conn., plant, which the U.S. government owns.

Nuclear Weapons-Related Programs

Avco began its work on strategic weapons systems in 1955, the year Avco Everett Research Laboratory was founded. In its first project, the Lab developed a heat shield that allowed missiles and space vehicles to re-enter the earth's atmosphere without bursting into flames. This technological advance was one principal breakthrough that enabled the development of ICBMs and manned space vehicles.

Avco's Systems Division still researches and develops missile re-entry systems. Avco Everett Research Laboratories, however, has moved to the forefront of another high technology field with potentially far-reaching military applications: the laser.

In FY 1981, Avco's prime contract awards on primary nuclear weapons systems totaled at least $83 million. Contracts on secondary and nuclear warfare-related systems totaled at least $19 million.

Primary systems:

MX missile--In the late 1970s, Avco was one of the first companies to receive contracts for an advanced ICBM, now known as the MX. Avco's Systems Division is developing a major portion of the missile's re-entry system. Late in 1982, Avco's ABRV reentry vehicle, now called the Mark 21, was selected as a replacement for the reentry vehicle that had originally been planned for the MX--General Electric's Mark 12A. Avco's current MX contracts include:

Avco's Nuclear Weapons-Related Contracts
(in millions of dollars)

Primary Systems		Secondary Systems	
FY 1981		FY1981	
MX missile reentry system	$58	Asat space defense system	$14
Minuteman missile	$10	Maui space facility	$5.3
Pershing II missile	$9.6		
C-135 reconnaissance plane	$4.9		
Other current contracts		Other current contracts	
LoAD program		Blue-green laser program	
		Space Shuttle components	
		Boron for F-15 fighter	

-- $238 million to develop the Mark 21 reentry vehicle for the MX. (The company says that the development and production of this reentry vehicle could generate $1.7 billion in revenues for the company by 1990.)

-- $189 million ($49 million in FY 1981) for design, development, testing and evaluation of the MX re-entry system and associated support equipment.

-- $11 million ($7.5 million in 1981) for other work on ABRVs.

-- $8.6 million ($1.7 million in 1981) to fabricate and deliver carbon-carbon (a strong plastic) nosetips for the MX's Mark 12A and Minuteman Mark 12 re-entry vehicles.

Under subcontract to Aerojet-General, the Systems Division also has a small subcontract on the second stage of the MX's propulsion system.

Minuteman missiles--As is true of many MX contractors, Avco has had a substantial role in the Minuteman missile program. The company now provides components for three Minuteman re-entry vehicles: the Mark 11B and 11C for the Minuteman II, and the Mark 12 and Mark 12A which have been backfitted on 300 Minuteman III missiles. Avco also provides equipment used in the Minuteman I for experimental flight tests.

Altogether, Avco has six contracts for Minuteman components that will total $33 million over several years, $10 million of which was awarded in FY 1981. Another contract totaling $8.6 million--including $1.7 million in FY 1981--was for work on both the MX and the Minuteman Mark 12A reentry vehicle.

B-1B bomber--When President Carter canceled the B-1 program in 1977, Avco lost its contract to build the plane's wing sets, which would have been the company's largest defense contract ever. However, Avco is back at work on the B-1B. In 1982, Rockwell International again selected Avco as one of its major B-1B subcontractors. Under an initial subcontract, Avco Aerostructures Division will build the wing sets for the first eight planes. The company expects this subcontract to generate more than $200 million in revenues. Avco says that receiving contracts to build wing sets for all 100 planned B-1Bs would mean about $1 billion in revenues between 1983 and 1990.

Avco also says its B-1B contract could generate about 1,000 jobs by 1986, but the company does not plan to hire many new employees. Avco employees from completed or subsiding commercial aircraft programs are being transferred into Avco's B-1B program.

Also in 1982, Avco Specialty Materials Division received an initial subcontract from Rockwell to supply more than one-half of the boron needed for the first eight B-1Bs. (Boron is a chemical element that is very resistant to high temperatures.)

Pershing II--Avco also is working on the re-entry system for the Pershing II missile. Awards on this contract have totaled $19 million, including $9.6 million in FY 1981.

RC-135 Stratolifter--In FY 1981, Avco received contracts worth $4.9 million to provide photographic equipment for the RC-135 strategic reconnaissance plane.

LoAD--Also in FY 1982, Avco received $10 million to develop components for a low altitude defense system.

Secondary systems:

Lasers and antisatellite systems--Avco Everett Research Lab, among other functions, is one of the nation's premier laser labs. A company spokesman said that Avco Everett has conducted a pulsed laser program for the last six years under five DoD contracts totaling $13 million. In addition, Avco has received $42.2 million to date (including $13.7 million in FY 1981) for work on an antisatellite space defense system.

One of the lab's main projects is to develop a laser in the blue-green spectrum that could be used in a strategic communications system for submerged submarines. According to some sources, blue-green laser technology also could be developed for use as an antisatellite weapon, but Avco is not involved in such a program.

Space tracking--Avco Everett operates and maintains a DARPA space-tracking and identification station on Maui, Hawaii. The purpose of the station, according to the company, is "to identify and correlate space objects both natural and man-made. To that extent, it is involved in the nation's overall strategic defense." DoD awarded Avco at least $5.3 million in contract awards for this center in FY 1981. In FY 1983, Avco received at least $12 million.

Space Shuttle--Avco Aerostructures is building the intertank structures for the Space Shuttle.

F-15 fighter--In 1982, Avco shipped boron to Grumman and McDonnell Douglas for use in the F-14 and F-15 fighter planes. In 1983, Avco will supply all the boron for both companies' needs.

Avco-Government Relationship

Political action committee: In 1979-80, Avco's PAC contributed $61,920 to candidates for federal offices. In 1981-82, it contributed $112,700. The company's contributions to defense committee members increased substantially over the four-year period, from $17,200 (28 percent of total contributions) in 1979-80 to $56,175 (50 percent of total contributions) in 1981-82. Major contributions went to House Speaker Thomas P. O'Neill (D-Mass., $5,000), and several defense committee members: Sen. Jim Sasser (D-Tenn., $5,200), Rep. William Chappell (D-Fla., $5,500) and Rep. John Murtha (D-Pa., $4.500).

In response to IRRC's questions about the structure of its PAC, Avco replied:

> Funds are solicited for Avco's PAC via written and personal appeals to Avco's administrative, executive and professional personnel. In 1981, that number came to approximately 1,500, of whom approximately one-third actually contributed. Individuals with the appropriate interest, dedication and background are selected to serve on the committee by Avco's top executive team. The committee receives voluminous requests from political candidates which are weighed by the committee, other members of Avco's executive team and Avco's Washington office. Factors considered in determining which candidates receive funds include geographic locale (giving emphasis to candidates in areas where Avco has operations), general political orientation of the candidates and, for incumbents, committee assignments and past voting records.

Washington office: Avco maintains a Washington office with one registered lobbyist, six staff people and four support people. Its purpose is "to present Avco's views to the Congress, administrators and government officials, to identify marketing opportunities within government, to monitor legislative and regulatory activities affecting Avco and to advise Avco units of pertinent intelligence and develop appropriate legislative/marketing strategy," a company spokesman told IRRC.

Personnel interchange: Avco hired 37 mid- to high-level DoD employees between 1977 and 1981, of whom 34 were former military officers. Five Avco employees moved to mid- to high-level positions in DoD during the same period.

One member of Avco's board of directors is Amos Jordan, now vice chairman of Georgetown University's Center for Strategic and International Studies in Washington, D.C. He held various senior positions with the Departments of Defense and State from 1974-77, and was first elected to Avco's board in 1977.

Contingency Planning and Prospects

Contingency planning: Avco has made several ventures into commercial markets. In the 1950s, it built an appliance business that it later sold to Philco. In the 1960s, the company acquired a wide range of commercial businesses from credit cards to land development. Although some of these acquisitions were a drain on Avco, some, including the consumer loan and insurance companies that today are responsible for half of Avco's revenues and operating profits, are now among the company's most successful operations. Avco told IRRC that the balance between the company's commercial and government manufacturing business has enabled the company to weather declines in its defense business.

However, Avco is not immune to the effects of defense cuts, as exemplified by its loss of a potential billion-dollar subcontract when the original B-1 bomber was canceled in 1977. That cancellation prompted Avco's chief executive to tell Business Week: "That's the sort of surprise that made me diversify away from defense and into service business years ago."

According to Joanne Lawrence, Avco's communications director, the B-1 bomber contract was canceled at the beginning stages of the program, and thus the effects were minimized because Avco had just begun to gear up for production. Approximately 100 employees, mainly machinists, were laid off. Most were rehired within a few months on a new aircraft program.

This example seems indicative of the company's general policy on canceled projects. The company told IRRC:

In the event of a layoff due to the cancellation of any project, efforts are made, when practicable, to transfer employees to other positions in the company for which they are qualified, or to other divisions of Avco Corp. If a large number of employees are involved in addition to the above, contacts are made with other area companies to assist in finding them employment. As has happened in the past, companies are invited to send representatives to the Avco division to interview potential employees.

Avco's policy calls for advance notice in the event of necessary termination. In the event of a layoff, employees are given severance pay in accordance with a schedule of benefits based on longevity with the company. Wherever possible, every attempt is made to balance employees between declining and growing projects to minimize layoffs. If the timing of a new opportunity is such that employees from a canceled program can be transferred, every effort is made to do so. This was the fortuitous case of the L-1011 cancellation and the B-1B and C-5A wing modification which were started up at the Avco Aerostructures Division. Employees were released during the L-1011 phase-down and picked up on the B-1B and C-5A. If a new opportunity is not available, however, there may be little ability to absorb people, and manpower reductions will be made on a seniority basis as prescribed by union contractual agreements.

Prospects: Arms control agreements or defense budget cuts potentially could affect Avco's largest defense programs: the B-1B and the MX missile.

An Avco spokesman told IRRC that "there is no single alternative" contingency plan to replace MX production, but that "Avco's Systems Division has a primary business objective to broaden its customer/product base in tactical weapon systems, space and advanced technology systems and advanced materials." If the MX were canceled, Avco says, approximately 1,500 employees would be let go to compensate for the loss in revenues. However, the company's 1982 annual report says that "termination clauses in the present contracts are expected to cover most of the expenses incurred by Avco prior to cancellation." If the MX goes into production, the company says, it will receive more than $1 billion in revenues between 1983 and 1990 and would add an estimated 2,500 employees.

Avco has a potential 1,000 jobs and $1 billion in revenues riding on its B-1B subcontract.

Boeing

Boeing, based in Seattle, is best known for its commercial jet transports, such as the 747. It is also one of the nation's leading defense companies, participating in the research, design, development and production of military aircraft, missiles, space vehicles and hydrofoil boats. The company also has expanded its energy and computer service activities. Boeing's total sales for 1982 were $9.0 billion, a 7 percent decrease from 1981. The company's net earnings slipped from a record high of $600 million in 1980 to $473 million in 1981 and $292 million in 1982, a decline attributable to the depressed commercial air transport market. The combination of recession, inflation, high interest rates and escalating fuel costs forced commercial airlines in 1981-2 to reduce sharply their orders for new jet transports.

Boeing employed about 91,000 workers in late 1982. The company ranks 48th on the Forbes 500 top sales list.

Boeing has been particularly hard hit by a loss of overseas orders, as the historically competitive commercial market has become even more competitive. Export sales were 62 percent of Boeing's total sales in 1981, and Boeing was the largest U.S. exporter in that year. The company has relied heavily upon the financial assistance of the Export-Import Bank, which the Reagan administration would like to cut back.

The Boeing Co. is comprised of eight divisions: Boeing Commercial Airplane; Boeing Military Airplane; Boeing Aerospace; Boeing Vertol; Boeing Engineering and Construction; Boeing Computer Services; Boeing Services International; and Boeing Marine Systems. Major production facilities are in Seattle, Wichita, Philadelphia, Granville, Tex., and Kent, Wash.

Commercial transportation is Boeing's mainstay, to a greater degree than with competitors Lockheed and McDonnell Douglas. Approximately 56 percent of the company's total revenues in 1982 resulted from the sale of commercial transport systems, 26 percent from the sale of military transport systems, and 10 percent from missile and space ventures. The remainder was generated by Boeing's other activities, including marine production and computer and ground support services.

Data on Boeing

(dollar figures in millions)

	1978	1979	1980	1981	1982
Total revenues	$5,648	$8,456	$9,786	$10,073	$9,206
Net earnings	$323	$505	$600	$473	$292
Military sales	NA	NA	$1,300	$2,200	$3,200
Military sales as a percentage of total revenues	NA	NA	14%	22%	35%
DoD prime contract awards*	$1,524	$1,514	$2,385	$2,683	$3,239
Ratio of DoD prime awards to total revenues+	.27	.18	.24	.27	.35
Total Boeing employees	81,200	98,300	106,300	105,300	95,700

* U.S. fiscal year, ending Sept. 30.
+ U.S. fiscal year awards compared with calendar year revenues.

Government and Defense Business

Government sales as a proportion of total Boeing sales increased sharply in recent years, from 17 percent in 1980 to 35 percent in 1982. The sale of a wide array of military products and services accounted for most of these government sales. The company played, and continues to play, a major role in the modernization and improvement of existing weapons systems, such as the B-52 Stratofortress bomber, the KC-135 aerial tanker, the Short Range Attack Missile (SRAM), the Minuteman intercontinental ballistic missile (ICBM), the E-4 Advanced Airborne Command Post, and the CH-46 Sea Knight and CH-47 Chinook helicopters.

Among weapons systems under development by Boeing in 1981 were: the offensive and defensive avionics for the B-1 bomber; a standoff missile/torpedo to be used by the Navy in antisubmarine warfare; the Wasp, an air-to-ground antitank weapon; and the Designating Optical Tracker, a component crucial to the development of an antiballistic missile system.

Previously developed systems now in production include the Air-Launched Cruise Missile (ALCM), the Roland air defense system, and the E-3A Airborne Warning and Control Systems (Awacs), which are being built for the U.S. Air Force, the North Atlantic Treaty Organization and Saudi Arabia.

Finally, Boeing is researching development of an air-launched antisatellite system (Asat), possible short- and long-term basing modes for the MX missile, and applications of Stealth radar-evading technology.

Boeing Services International is under contract to manage and maintain a string of Army and Air Force facilities in Spain, Turkey and Greece. This division also operates and maintains Fort Irwin, a special base in California where a broad range of combat environments are created for training purposes.

Boeing Engineering and Construction completed construction of a new plant in Oak Ridge, Tenn., in 1981. Production at the plant is for the government's nuclear fuel enrichment program.

Defense dependence: Boeing's involvement in the production of military goods predates World War II, and its dependence on DoD peaked during the war years. The company was responsible for the design and production of such major systems as the B-17 Flying Fortress and the B-29 Superfortress, two heavy bombers that saw extensive action in Allied campaigns in Europe and the Pacific. Production for the military continued after the war, but realizing the potential vulnerability of a narrow and limited sales base, the company also began to expand into other areas. It developed a line of jet-powered commercial transports and in the mid-1950s introduced the first, the Boeing 707. This trend of expansion and diversification continued into the 1960s, when Boeing began producing gas turbine engines, hydrofoils and missiles. At the same time, the company entered the helicopter industry with its acquisition of Vertol Aircraft Corp.

Direct and close links exist between Boeing's production activities in the commercial and military sectors. The direct military applications of many of Boeing's commercial ventures in air transportation are one kind of link. The airframe of the 707 Jetliner serves as the foundation for both the KC-135 jet tanker and the E-3A Awacs, and the 747 jumbo jet has been transformed into the E-4 Advanced Airborne Command Post and has been promoted as a military cargo plane.

Moreover, Boeing's sales to the military establishment have served as an effective counterweight to losses from sagging sales in the commercial market, and vice versa. Harold Mansfield, a biographer of the company, reported that in the early 1960s, when commercial airlines were slow in accepting the new Boeing jet transports, "it was regarded as fortunate that the large scale production of B-52s..., of KC-135 jet tankers...and Bomarcs (a surface-to-air nuclear-capable missile designed to shoot down enemy aircraft) were bringing enough in to more than offset the commercial airplane loss."[1]

Boeing's situation now is similar to that of the early 1960s. Worldwide recession and high interest rates have brought a sharp decline in commercial orders for new jet transports, and the sales of two new Boeing commercial jet transports--the 757 and the 767--are lagging. Meanwhile, Boeing faces stiff competition in the international market, primarily from the European firm Airbus Industries.

The ratio of Defense prime contract awards won by Boeing to corporate sales was .39 in 1977, slipped to .19 by 1979, and then rose again to .36 in 1982. In FY 1982, Boeing received $3.24 billion in prime DoD contract awards, making the company the sixth largest defense contractor.

Defense employees: Boeing had 101,000 employees at the end of 1981. By late 1982, the number had dropped to 91,000, as a result of lagging commercial sales. In 1981, approximately 77,000 workers, or more than 70 percent of the company's work force, were in the Seattle area. The company was unable to provide IRRC with a division-by-division breakdown of employment figures or with the percentage of its employees currently manufacturing defense products, so it is not possible to determine with any degree of accuracy what percentage of Boeing's work force is engaged in the production of nuclear warfighting systems. The most that a Boeing spokesman would say is that "between 1977 and 1981 Boeing's military employment has been reasonably stable versus historical cyclical norms."

If employment on various Boeing programs is proportionate to sales, about 17,000 employees would have worked on military transport systems, and another 7,000 on missile and space programs, in 1981.

Nuclear Weapons-Related Programs

Boeing's involvement in the nuclear weapons industry spans the entire atomic age. The Boeing B-29 was judged the only bomber capable of delivering the atomic bombs dropped on Hiroshima and Nagasaki in 1945. Since then, the company has been responsible for production of the B-52 Stratofortress bomber, the Minuteman ICBM, and the Air-Launched Cruise Missile. Boeing has been involved in the production of an array of secondary nuclear weapons systems as well.

Boeing's DoD prime contract awards on primary nuclear weapons systems totaled at least $1.3 billion in fiscal 1981, and prime contracts for work on secondary and nuclear warfare-related projects totaled at least $606 million. The ratio of primary nuclear weapons systems prime awards to revenues was .15 in 1981.

Primary systems:

B-52 bomber--One of Boeing's most important contributions to the current strategic forces of the United States has been the development, production and modernization of the B-52 bomber, the mainstay of the strategic bomber force. Work on the B-52, also known as the "Stratofortress," began in 1955, and 744 planes had been delivered to the Air Force by the time production ceased in 1962. Since then, the company has received contracts each year for the maintenance and modernization of the B-52 fleet.

Boeing's Nuclear Weapons-Related Contracts
(in millions of dollars)

Primary Systems

FY 1981	
B-52 modernization	$433
KC-135 and variants	$245
Air-launched cruise missile	$245
MX missile	$153
E-4 command post aircraft	$97
Minuteman missile	$83
ABRES	$14
Ballistic Missile Defense	$7

Other current contracts

B-1 avionics system
Advanced technology bomber
Common strategic rotary launcher

Secondary Systems

FY 1981	
E-3A Awacs aircraft	$325
Inertial Upper Stage	$221
Asat	$39
Space Shuttle	$16
P-3C Orion	$5

The B-52G and B-52H versions of the bomber are undergoing extensive modernization. Both versions are being equipped with modern digital avionics systems, along with state-of-the-art sensors and subsystems. Meanwhile, the Air Force's 171 B-52Gs are being equipped with the Boeing-made ALCMs (see below), and later the Air Force may equip the 96 B-52Hs with ALCMs. The new avionics system will help align, target and launch the ALCMs.

The ALCMs are being mounted externally on the B-52G, six on each of two wing pylons. For now, the B-52G will continue to carry Short-Range Attack Missiles (SRAMs) and gravity bombs as well, although the company expects eventually to fit the bomb bay where these weapons are carried with an internal rotary launcher that would carry an additional eight ALCMs.

The Pentagon awarded at least $433 million in FY 1981 for work on the B-52. The bulk was for work on ALCM-related modernization, and all but $4 million went to the company's Wichita operations. The company says that in all of 1982, it received funding of $238 million for avionics equipment and cruise missile integration on the B-52, for a total of $1.3 billion on these modernization programs to date.

Air-launched cruise missile (ALCM)--Boeing's newest nuclear weapons delivery system is the ALCM, to be deployed on the B-52 and perhaps other airplanes. In a 1980 fly-off competition, the Boeing-developed ALCM (also designated the AGM-86B) outperformed General Dynamics' air-launched version of the Tomahawk cruise missile, and DoD consequently informed Boeing of its desire to procure some 3,400 ALCMs. Subsequently, the Air Force announced that it was cutting short the ALCM production line in favor of early production of an advanced cruise missile (ACM). The ACM will incorporate "Stealth" radar-evading technology and other new technologies. Boeing lost the ACM competition to General Dynamics. As a result of the ACM decision, only 1,750 Boeing ALCMs will be produced.

Boeing began producing ALCMs in 1982, and the production rate is 40 missiles a month. The company built a new factory near Seattle to produce the missiles. It is not clear how the factory and the workers there will be employed after General Dynamics takes over cruise missile production.

Boeing received at least $245 million in prime contract awards in FY 1981 in support of its ALCM project, and was awarded at least $264 million in fiscal 1980.

Short-range attack missile (SRAM)--In the mid-1960s, the Air Force became concerned with the B-52 bomber's ability to penetrate Soviet air defenses and determined that it needed a new "standoff" weapon that could be launched a distance from the target, rather than dropped directly over it. Boeing had begun work on such a standoff weapon in 1963, and the Boeing SRAM (designated the AGM-69A) was chosen by the Air Force as the best way to extend the effective life of the B-52. (Later, of course, cruise missiles became even more important in extending B-52 service life.) The SRAM missiles, first deployed in 1972, have a maximum range of 100 miles. Each B-52G/H can carry 20 SRAMs, and the FB-111 can carry six.

Boeing had delivered 1,500 SRAMs by mid-1975. Orders for an improved version of the missile were canceled when the B-1 bomber was canceled in 1977. Boeing continues to provide maintenance and modernization services on the SRAM, and it received more than $25 million in prime contracts in FY 1981 for work on the Air Force's inventory of SRAMs.

B-1 bomber--Boeing, a participant in the development of the original B-1 before the cancellation in 1977, expects to work on the B-1B that President Reagan has resurrected. Boeing received a $55 million contract in 1981 to develop the offensive avionics as well as components of the B-1's defensive avionics system. The avionics system is an updated version of the systems currently being produced for B-52 modernization. Boeing reports that it received more than $600 million for full-scale development of the B-1B offensive avionics system and production of the first nine sets of hardware in 1982.

Advanced technology bomber--In 1981, DoD appointed Boeing Military Airplane to serve as key subcontractor to work with Northrop on the development of the top-secret radar-evading Stealth advanced technology bomber. The cost of the program has been estimated at $20 to $30 billion for the purchase of some 100 Stealth bombers, according to news reports; the Congressional Budget Office says that current plans are to build 132 of the bombers. Delivery is scheduled to commence in 1991, following the conclusion of the B-1B program, although Northrop would like to get the Stealth in the air as early as 1988. The Northrop/Boeing hegemony over the Stealth development has been challenged by Rockwell and Lockheed. The two newcomers agreed in late 1982 to develop a Stealth version of the B-1 bomber, and their research is being funded by company-controlled research and development funds, unlike the Northrop/Boeing version, which is funded directly by the government.[2]

Common strategic rotary launcher--Boeing is developing the common strategic rotary launcher, which may be used on B-52s, B-1s and advanced technology bombers to launch cruise and other missiles.

Minuteman missile--In October 1958, Boeing received its first ballistic missile contract. Boeing was assigned to assemble and test the country's first solid fuel ICBM, the Minuteman. With time, the company acquired additional responsibilities for the Minuteman project, including the development and maintenance of launch control, transport and security systems. The first Minuteman I was delivered to the Air Force in 1962, and the last Minuteman III was delivered in 1967. Boeing's work with the Minuteman (and to a lesser degree the Titan ICBMs) has continued. Components of both systems, notably those dealing with command, control and communications (C^3) and launch support, have been upgraded repeatedly. DoD awarded Boeing at least $83 million in prime contracts in fiscal 1981 for maintenance and modernization work related to the Minuteman.

MX missile--Boeing's extensive experience with the Minuteman project qualified the company to participate in the development and production of the next generation of American ICBM, the MX. As a result, Boeing has been involved with the MX program since 1976, primarily on evaluation and support for basing plans. The company received about $153 million in prime contract awards in connection with MX-related work in 1981. Boeing's work on MX support systems includes the preliminary design of the missile's transporter and launcher, and the development of a security system and support systems for both the missile and its shelters.

Work also is under way at Boeing Aerospace on the development of an Advanced Ballistic Reentry System (ABRES). The ABRES program focuses attention on technological improvements in the reentry vehicle's shape and material construction to increase the vehicle's accuracy without endangering its survivability. DoD awarded Boeing at least $14 million in FY 1981 for ABRES development work.

KC-135 aerial tanker and variants--Following its decision to purchase the B-52 Stratofortress, the Air Force determined that it needed a new jet tanker for in-flight refueling of its intercontinental bomber force. In 1955, DoD chose a modified Boeing 707, later designated the KC-135, to serve this purpose. Currently, the Air Force is replacing the engines on KC-135s and otherwise modernizing the aircraft. The new engines are more fuel-efficient.

Boeing also produced and continues to do work on the EC-135 strategic reconnaissance aircraft. Boeing Military Airplane received at least $246 million in prime contracts in FY 1981 for work on the KC-135 and its variants. Most of the funds are being used for replacing the KC-135's engines. Boeing states that, with receipt of a 1983 contract for $344 million, the company has received about $600 million in the engine replacement program.

E-4 Advanced Airborne Command Post--Boeing Aerospace is upgrading the Air Force's three E-4As to an E-4B configuration featuring sophisticated command, control and communications hardware. The E-4s are modified Boeing 747s that serve as airborne command platforms from which the country's strategic forces can be directed in times of emergency. The original Air Force order called for three E-4As and one E-4B. Following Boeing's modernization of the E-4A, the Air Force's fleet of Advanced Airborne Command Posts will consist of four in the E-4B configuration. Prime contract awards to Boeing for work related to the Advanced Airborne Command Post totaled at least $97 million during FY 1981.

Hanford complex--Under an Energy Department contract, Boeing Computer Services supports scientific, engineering and business activities at the Hanford nuclear complex in Richland, Wash. (The managers of major facilities at the complex are Rockwell International and UNC Resources.) The contract was renewed for five years in 1983, and awards are expected to exceed $85 million over the period. Boeing has had the contract since 1975.

Ballistic missile defense--Work continued during 1981 on the Designating Optical Tracker (DOT), a project initiated in 1976. The DOT is a component essential to the development of a ballistic missile defense system. The tracker consists of a system of infrared sensors mounted on a delivery vehicle. The DOT would be placed into orbit around the earth and would monitor, detect and track incoming ICBM reentry vehicles. Boeing Aerospace is responsible for constructing the sensor vehicle, attaching the infrared sensors to it, test-launching the complete system, and analyzing the test results.

Boeing's work on ballistic missile defense brought prime awards of at least $7.5 million in fiscal 1981.

Secondary systems:

E-3A Airborne Warning and Control Systems (Awacs)--The Boeing-produced E-3A Awacs monitors the skies for enemy aircraft and provides information and coordination to friendly air forces. Twenty-five of the 34 E-3As ordered by the Air Force in the mid-1970s had been delivered by the end of 1981. The first of 18 upgraded E-3As ordered by NATO was completed in 1981. The improved NATO version offers upgraded computer and communications systems and equipment necessary for tracking ships at sea. The DoD announced in 1981 that it intended to increase its original order of 34 E-3As to 40.

Following the Reagan administration's victory in a protracted congressional fight, Boeing received a letter contract in 1981 to construct five E-3As for delivery to Saudi Arabia.

During the same year, the Air Force commissioned Boeing Aerospace to design, develop and test electronics systems to enhance the command, control and communications capabilities of the older E-3As already in its service. Prime contracts awarded to Boeing in 1981 for work on the Awacs topped $325 million (excluding foreign military sales).

Antisatellite weapon (Asat)--Boeing Aerospace is developing an air-launched antisatellite (Asat) weapon for the Air Force, to be launched from an airborne McDonnell Douglas F-15 Eagle. Boeing is developing the missile's lower stage, the pylon with which the missile would be attached to the delivery aircraft, and the weapon's mission control center. Boeing Aerospace also is responsible for assembling the entire missile. Contracts for Asat work totaled at least $39 million in fiscal 1981.

Inertial Upper Stage (IUS)--Boeing Aerospace's Inertial Upper Stage system is designed to transport satellites from the Space Shuttle and expendable launch vehicles, such as the Titan rocket, to points in space that are beyond the current range of the vehicles. The IUS has direct military application in enhancing the nation's ability to place military satellites into orbit around the earth. The DoD awarded $221 million in prime contracts in FY 1981 for work on the IUS.

P-3C Orion--Boeing also works on the P-3C Orion patrol aircraft, which is equipped to carry the B57 nuclear depth charge. FY 1981 contract awards for this work were $5.1 million.

Boeing-Government Relationship

Political action committee: The Boeing Political Action Committee, established in 1980, donated $125,400 to the campaigns of 164 congressional candidates during 1981 and 1982, before the 1982 mid-term congressional elections. Boeing contributed $65,900 to Democrats' campaigns, $59,500 to Republicans'. Some $48,900 of the total, or 39 percent, was given to members of House or Senate defense committees during 1981-82.

Candidates from Texas, Washington, Kansas and Pennsylvania, states with major Boeing facilities, were awarded a major portion of the total contributions. The eight candidates from the state of Washington were by far the most heavily endowed recipients; contributions included $3,600 each to Sen. Henry Jackson (D) and Rep. Norman Dicks (D), both considered key players on defense issues and strong advocates for Boeing.

Washington office: Boeing's Washington office has three staff divisions. The International Affairs staff monitors international events and maintains contacts with foreign customers. The staff responsible for National Affairs and Strategic Planning gathers information on domestic issues, arranges company-government contacts and provides public relations services. The Congressional Affairs staff monitors legislation affecting the company's activities, keeps members of Congress briefed on Boeing's programs and gathers information on members for later use in making political contributions. Boeing considers information regarding the cost of maintaining its Washington office to be proprietary.

Eight members of the Boeing Washington office staff and three additional individuals are registered as lobbyists for Boeing. The company also enlists the services of four law firms and one consultant group, the Washington Industrial Team. Former Reps. Robert Wilson and Richard Ichord, who until 1981 were members of the House Armed Services Committee, are principals of the Washington Industrial Team.

Personnel interchange: Between 1977 and 1981, Boeing hired 575 mid- to high-level DoD employees, of whom 92 percent were former military officers. Eight Boeing employees transferred to mid- to high-level DoD positions during the same period.

David Packard, chairman of the board of Hewlett-Packard Co., who serves on Boeing's board of directors, was deputy secretary of Defense from 1969-71, and was a member of the President's Commission on Personnel Interchange from 1972-74. Another Pentagon official formerly with Boeing is T. K. Jones, deputy under secretary of Defense for research and engineering.

Contingency Planning and Prospects

Contingency planning: Boeing's attitude toward fluctuations in business is simple. When asked how the company handled the impact of canceled or curtailed projects on employment levels, a Boeing official explained that the company tries "to keep the work force sized to the amount of work to be done--irrespective of whether the work is commercial or military." Boeing redistributes employees to other programs whenever possible. Because the company's commercial sales are lagging and its military workload is expanding, a spokesman says, the "military programs have been absorbing some of the people who otherwise would have been laid off because of the decline in commercial orders." Unfortunately, he told IRRC, "the government's work hasn't increased enough to prevent an overall employment decline of about 10,000 people" in 1982.

When the "racetrack" concept for the development of the MX that Boeing designed and constructed was shelved in 1981, many observers speculated that 900 members of District 751 of the International Association of Machinists and Aerospace Workers would lose their jobs. The company reports that the cancellation resulted in the transfer of several hundred persons to other, ongoing projects, and the laying off of approximately 100 employees. Further, a Boeing spokesman told IRRC, the decision "removed a source of potential employment for quite a few people whose jobs on Boeing's commercial programs were about to expire." The company had thought that this program "would grow and provide a place for some of these people," the spokesman said. "The cancellation ended that thought."

Some of Boeing's commercial projects have taken employees transferred from declining military projects. The Carter administration's cancellation of the B-1 bomber coincided with an expansion of Boeing's commercial business. Hence, many of those involved in the B-1 found refuge in the growing commercial sector.

Expanding military programs similarly have served as reservoirs for employment spillover from other canceled or curtailed military projects. The decision not to go ahead on the production of the B-70 bomber and the winding down of the Bomarc air defense project in the 1960s freed up electronics specialists for work on the new Minuteman missile. A second cancellation of the revived B-1B bomber would have a similar impact. According to a company official, if the B-1 were canceled tomorrow, Boeing "would attempt to place the people on other military programs where their skills would make a worthwhile contribution." The company cautions that not all the displaced employees would be guaranteed jobs: Layoffs undoubtedly would result, and the employees laid off would not necessarily be those directly involved in the B-1 program. A Boeing spokesman told IRRC that "the people who would be laid off undoubtedly would be less skilled employees on a variety of different military and commercial programs who would be dislocated or 'bumped' by the influx of the most senior and highly trained people from the B-1 avionics program."

The largest fluctuation in employment experienced by Boeing occurred in the early 1970s. The company faced a depressed commercial market and a concomitant decline in the government's procurement of military goods accompanying the U.S. withdrawal from Vietnam. The number of people employed by Boeing in the Seattle area alone dropped from 101,000 to 37,000.

The Boeing Vertol conversion effort--Perhaps Boeing's most notable effort to respond to declining military sales in the 1970s was the conversion of a portion of the Boeing Vertol division's production from helicopters to streetcars and subway vehicles. The Boeing Vertol division, based in Philadelphia, suffered as helicopter orders dwindled with the wind-down of the Vietnam war. At the war's height, the division employed 13,500; by 1978, the work force had declined to 4,300.

In 1971, Boeing began planning for conversion to civilian transportation production. Company analysts and engineers saw a likely upswing in demand for urban mass transit rail vehicles--particularly light-rail vehicles, or streetcars. During this period, energy concerns and subsidies from the federal Urban Mass Transportation Administration made this field promising. The company had hoped to set a standard for electric trolleys, which had not been produced in the United States for 25 years.

Boeing Vertol received orders for 275 streetcars from Boston and San Francisco, and 200 rapid-transit cars from Chicago. The first cars were delivered to Boston in 1976, and initially they received good reviews. By 1978, one-third of the division's employees were at work on the transit vehicles.[3]

Despite early success, problems developed. In its effort to gain a quick lead in what promised to be a renewed domestic industry, the company set unrealistically early delivery dates and rushed the new vehicles into production without full field testing, according to Columbia University engineering professor Seymour Melman. Moreover, Melman noted, "even though many of these managers and engineers had their main experience in the cost- and subsidy-maximizing military industry, formal professional retraining for civilian designing, producing and selling was not considered. And importing skilled transit-vehicle designers from abroad was unthinkable."[4]

Experience soon proved that the attractive transit equipment produced by Boeing Vertol was prone to breakdown. In addition to many smaller problems, the Boston streetcars derailed frequently, and the complex doors failed often, as did cooling motors. The new cars required inordinate maintenance efforts to keep them operational, and Boeing Vertol was forced to spend a great deal to modify the cars. In 1979, with continuing problems, the company agreed to pay the Boston transit authority $40 million as a final settlement, and Boeing Vertol terminated its streetcar program.

Diversification efforts--Boeing's purchase of Vertol was itself an attempt to diversify within the aerospace industry to helicopter production. More recently, the company has tried development and construction of desalination plants; management of low cost housing projects for the federal government; irrigation and farming of what had been wasteland; and the design and construction of giant windmills.

The success of these efforts has varied. A Boeing spokesman says the desalination program "has grown substantially but its focus has changed from removal of salt to removal of other impurities from water." The company successfully completed several low cost housing projects, he wrote to IRRC, "but then dropped out of the field because we didn't believe that our contribution really was meaningful." On the other hand, the windmill program is proceeding because company officials "believe that our technological skill is such that we are making a meaningful contribution."

A more important and successful diversification effort was the formation of Boeing Services International to provide services on a contract basis at government installations in the United States and abroad.

Prospects: Boeing remains overwhelmingly dependent on the aerospace market, but this market in turn is dominated by commercial rather than military sales. The company's prime alternative to any foreseeable decline in military business presumably would be civilian aircraft production. As noted earlier, while Boeing remains one of the strongest--if not the strongest--of competitors in the commercial jet transport market, the market for sale of such aircraft is suffering. A drastic decline in Boeing's military business could not be greatly softened by a pick-up in commercial work in the present environment unless the government, as part of a conversion effort, aided Boeing in increasing its international market share, or otherwise assisted the company.

On the other hand, if the recession in the jet transport market is reversed in the recovery, and if Boeing does well in the international marketplace, it is reasonable to assume that many workers and facilities engaged in military projects--particularly those involved in aircraft programs--could be moved to civilian work, since the company already shifts workers back and forth as market conditions demand.

A nuclear freeze would cut Boeing's business severely. In particular, a strong agreement to end further production of nuclear weapons would threaten $800 million or more in contract work, measured by 1981 levels, on Air-Launched Cruise Missiles, modification of B-52s to carry the ALCMs, MX missiles, and the B-1 bomber. Boeing's expected work on the new Stealth bomber presumably would come to a halt as well. Maintenance work on the B-52, Minuteman, SRAM and other programs would continue.

Boeing programs, including the MX and B-1, are threatened by budget cuts as well as by negotiated agreements. Cancellation of the B-1, however, very likely would rebound to Boeing's favor in the absence of a freeze, because of Boeing's relatively small involvement with the B-1 and its relatively large involvement in producing two competitors of the B-1--the modernized B-52 and the Stealth bombers.

Boeing Footnotes

1. Harold Mansfield, Vision: The Story of Boeing, Duell, Sloan and Pearce, New York, 1966, p. 245.
2. The New York Times, Oct. 6, 1982.
3. Seymour Melman, "Beating Swords into Subways," The New York Times Magazine, Nov. 19, 1978.
4. Ibid.

GTE

GTE is the parent company of more than 60 subsidiaries, including 16 domestic telephone companies that together constitute the largest independent (non-Bell) telephone system in the country. When AT&T splits apart in 1984, GTE still will be number two, but its size relative to AT&T will expand from one-tenth to one-half.

Telephone operations account for the majority of GTE's sales--65 percent in 1982. The other third of its business is divided into three groups --the communications products group, the electrical products group and the telenet communications group, which operates a public network for data communications.

GTE ranked 31st on the Forbes list of the nation's top industrial companies in 1982. Revenues and sales were $12.1 billion, up 9 percent from 1981. Net income increased 16 percent, from $691 million to $805 million. GTE is based in Connecticut.

Government and Defense Business

Defense dependence: Although GTE is one of the largest Defense Department contractors, only a small portion of its total sales go to the military. As the table shows, the ratio of GTE's DoD prime contract awards to its revenues and sales in 1982 was under 5 percent. This ratio has been growing steadily, however, since 1979.

GTE's military products are mostly communications-related systems and components such as command, control and communications (C^3), satellite and electronic warfare systems. In 1981, The Countermeasures Handbook ranked GTE as the nation's fifth largest electronic warfare producer, with estimated electronic warfare sales of $165 million.[1] The company's major nuclear warfare-related contracts are outlined below. Other major military contracts include: a $190 million contract awarded in 1980 for electronic switching equipment for the Air Force, Army and Marine Corps; an $81 million Army contract awarded in 1981 for message and circuit switches, spare parts and related equipment; and an $8.6 million contract received from the Defense Logistics Agency in 1981 for electron tubes.

The communications products group performs most of GTE's military-related work. This group increased its government backlog from $360 million at the end of 1981 to about $570 million at the end of 1982.

Data on GTE
(dollar figures in millions)

	1978	1979	1980	1981	1982
Revenues and sales	$7,736	$8,898	$9,979	$11,026	$12,066
Net income applicable to common stock	$551	$638	$589	$691	$805
Communications products group sales	$1,759	$2,052	$2,110	$2,238	$2,514
Department of Defense billings	$219	$219	$290	$406	NA
DoD billings as a percentage of total revenues and sales	2.8%	2.5%	2.9%	3.7%	NA
DoD prime contract awards*	$195	$227	$310	$426	$567.1
Ratio of DoD prime contract awards to total revenues and sales+	.03	.03	.03	.04	.05
Defense employees	NA	NA	NA	6,000	6,600
Total GTE employees	NA	NA	NA	204,000	196,000

* U.S. fiscal year, ending Sept. 30.
+ U.S. fiscal year awards compared with calendar year sales.

GTE's total backlog of government orders was approximately $387 billion in 1981 and $559 billion in 1982.

Defense employees: A company representative told IRRC that approximately 6,500 of GTE's 198,000 employees work on defense programs.

Research and development: The government sponsored 11.3 percent of GTE's 1982 research and development costs. None of GTE's facilities is government owned.

Nuclear Weapons-Related Programs

GTE received prime contract awards worth at least $106 million for primary nuclear warfare systems in FY 1981, which represents about 1 percent of the company's 1981 sales. GTE's prime contract awards for secondary systems totaled at least $6.9 million.

Primary systems:

MX missile program involvement--GTE is one of the prime contractors for the MX. Until recently, the company has had primary responsibility for developing the sophisticated command, control and communications (C^3) system necessary for a mobile missile. Under a five-year contract that began in 1980, GTE would have supplied "several thousand miles of optical fiber cable, radio networks and data processing equipment to provide continuous control of the (MX)

GTE's Nuclear Weapons-Related Contracts
(in millions of dollars)

Primary Systems		Secondary Systems	
FY 1981		FY1981	
MX missile	$80	Radar system for strategic and attack submarines	$6.9
Minuteman missile	$15		
BMD radar	$11		
Other current contracts		Other current contracts	
Project ELF		Low frequency communications	
		GLCM components	

system's mobile missiles and to monitor their operational readiness," said the company's 1980 annual report. However, now that the MX will be based in silos, its C^3 system must be altered. GTE reports that its MX contract is being reconfigured.

The new MX C^3 system is still likely to be an optical communications system. GTE says these systems "convert voices, television pictures and data messages into light pulses or waves which travel through thin, flexible strands of ultra-pure glass known as optical fibers." An important feature of this fiber optics equipment is its relative imperviousness to many effects of nuclear explosions that would disrupt other communications systems. It also reacts to commands, reports missile status quickly and is difficult to tap covertly. GTE is a leader in developing and installing optical communications systems for both civilian and defense purposes.

GTE won two smaller MX contracts in 1981. A $4.5 million contract involves incorporating Martin Marietta's launch support equipment and other instrumentation into GTE's fiber optics network. A $3.7 million contract provided for development of a fiber optics system to allow communication between flight safety and other equipment on the MX. GTE completed this project in 1982. In all, GTE's MX missile contracts in FY 1981 totaled $80 million.

A spokesman for GTE estimated that the company's MX research and development contracts represented 0.5 percent of its 1982 sales, about $60 million. He also told IRRC that approximately 560 GTE employees work on MX projects at the company's facility in Westborough, Mass., near Boston.

GTE has hired three subcontractors on its MX contracts, one of which is a subsidiary of United Technologies. GTE gave this subsidiary a $60 million subcontract to produce a digital equipment computer for the MX's C^3 system that would survive the blast, heat and radiation effects of a nuclear explosion.

Minuteman missile--GTE's work on the MX, like that of many MX associate contractors, was preceded by similar work on the Minuteman missile system. GTE Sylvania produced the ground electronics systems for the MX and still works on the missile's C^3 system. The company says that in calendar 1981 it received contracts worth $12 million for such work. (IRRC figures for FY 1981 were slightly higher--$15 million.) In 1982, the company says, it received additional contracts worth another $12 million. In 1983, GTE has been awarded at least one additional Minuteman contract worth $26 million.

Ballistic missile defense--GTE received FY 1981 contracts worth $11.1 million from the Ballistic Missile Defense System Command to upgrade a radar system (Altair) in the Marshall Islands.

Project ELF--In mid-1982, GTE received a $2.2 million contract for Project ELF, an extremely low frequency electromagnetic radiation antenna that the Navy hopes will be able to send messages to ballistic missile submarines at the depths at which they usually travel. The Navy has operated a 28-mile ELF test facility in Wisconsin. Plans now call for the development of a 56-mile-long ELF corridor in Michigan's upper peninsula.

In FY 1982, GTE also received $7 million to upgrade the ELF transmitter at Clam Lake, Wis.

Secondary systems:

Radar--In FY 1981, GTE received contracts worth $6.9 million for work on the electronic warfare radio receiver (designated AN/WLR-8) that it believed to be used on Trident submarines. It also is used on surface ships and other submarines. In FY 1983, GTE received additional contracts worth $10 million for WLR-8 components and spare parts.

Low frequency communications--GTE is designing low frequency and very low frequency equipment that will be used to sustain strategic communications between submarines, aircraft, surface ships and shore stations under a $750,000 contract awarded early in 1983.[2]

Ground-launched cruise missile--GTE is a subcontractor on the GLCM's communications system. Its contract is worth $73 million.

GTE-Government Relationship

GTE's loose ties to defense-related government agencies reflect the relatively small role that military contracts play in its overall business. GTE maintains a government relations office in Washington, D.C., that deals with defense issues but focuses on other government matters. In 1982, two firms registered as GTE lobbyists, but neither listed defense issues as an area of legislative interest.

Political action committee: GTE's PAC contributions to defense committee members were also small, relative to other major defense contractors, in the 1979-80 and 1981-82 election cycles. Such contributions made up 19 percent of GTE's $62,500 in 1979-80 contributions and 20 percent of its $140,120 in 1981-82 contributions. Nevertheless, some of GTE's largest contributions went to defense committee members. In 1979-80, GTE gave $3,000 to Sen. Daniel K. Inouye (D-Hawaii) and $2,500 to Sen. Warren G. Magnuson (D-Wash.), members of the defense appropriations subcommittee. In 1981-82, three of GTE's larger contributions went to defense committee members: Sen. Howard Cannon (D-Nev., $3,000) and Sen. Henry Jackson (D-Wash., $2,500), members of the Senate Armed Services Committee, and Rep. James Jones (D-Okla., $2,000), chairman of the House Budget Committee.

Contingency Planning and Prospects

Contingency planning: GTE believes contingency planning for any single contract is unnecessary. Instead, as it asserted in its 1983 proxy statement, the company believes that its diversification limits "the adverse impact of reductions in or discontinuance of a particular business or program." In addition, GTE said it is "continually involved in the development of new businesses to replace programs which are completed or discontinued" for "commercial as well as government work." The company acknowledged that no amount of planning could ensure that particular businesses would not be hurt by changing conditions, but it asserted that "in all such cases, positive steps are taken to assist the employees and thus the communities concerned." GTE said that these steps include "arranging job relocations within GTE and working with other companies and governmental agencies to maximize employment opportunities."

GTE Secretary Joel Mellis told IRRC that the company has a human resource department that would assist any displaced GTE employee. This department carries out what the company calls its manpower planning programs. Mellis said the company does not make this policy available to the public, but any displaced employee would have access to it.

Prospects: Although GTE is not overwhelmingly dependent on defense work, its largest defense contract is for the MX missile. If the MX were canceled, the company could lose about 0.5 percent of its business, and 560 employees could lose their jobs. However, these effects might be mitigated if GTE were able to apply its C^3 fiber optics technology to other weapons systems (ballistic missile defense systems are one possibility) and MX employees were placed elsewhere in the firm.

Mellis told IRRC that if the company's MX contract were canceled, GTE's sales and earnings would not be materially affected, and the company would pursue "other defense-related projects." Displaced employees could find new job opportunities "in many of our high technology communications activities," he said.

A freeze also could affect GTE's MX contracts but would not directly affect any of its other military contracts.

GTE Footnotes

1. Electronic Countermeasures Handbook, 1981, p. 38.
2. Aviation Week and Space Technology, April 4, 1983, p. 71.

General Dynamics

General Dynamics is the nation's largest defense contractor, producing major weapons systems for air, sea and ground use, including F-16 fighter aircraft, Tomahawk cruise missiles, Trident nuclear submarines, SSN 688 attack submarines, and M-1 tanks. In the view of many critics, General Dynamics' track record in these diverse defense fields is mixed. The company's success in producing the relatively inexpensive F-16 on time has been coupled with huge cost overruns and delays in delivery for both submarines. More recently, however, General Dynamics has delivered submarines ahead of schedule and under budget.

Largely because of the acquisition in 1982 of Chrysler's tank division, General Dynamics' net sales increased from $5.06 billion in 1981 to $6.15 billion in 1982, and net earnings increased 9 percent to $160 million. The company ranks 78th on the Forbes 500 top sales list and employs more than 91,000 people. It is based in St. Louis.

General Dynamics' business includes production of military aircraft, tactical missiles, gun systems, space systems, tanks, submarines and electronics. Commercial lines of business include construction of surface ships and aircraft subassemblies, along with mining of coal and the production of building materials and lime.

Aerospace overshadows General Dynamics' original business, shipbuilding. In 1982, government aerospace accounted for 50 percent of sales and 110 percent of operating earnings (due to shipbuilding losses). The Fort Worth division, which produces the F-16 and its progeny, accounted for two-thirds of the sales compiled by government aerospace. Two other aerospace divisions, Convair and Pomona, build cruise missiles, tactical missiles and space vehicles. Almost all of General Dynamics' aerospace production is of military products, although the Convair division also works on NASA programs and as a subcontractor on the DC-10 and 767 commercial airliner programs.

Shipbuilding generated 19 percent of sales and a pretax operating loss in 1982. Most of the company's shipbuilding efforts are devoted to the Trident and attack submarines produced for the government by the Electric Boat Division in Groton, Conn., although the company's Quincy, Mass., shipyard continues to do some commercial work. Defense shipbuilding work accounted for 94 percent of General Dynamics' shipbuilding sales in 1982, up from 84 percent in 1980.

In March 1982, General Dynamics purchased Chrysler Defense and named it the Land Systems Division; the principal land system that this

Data on General Dynamics
(dollar figures in millions)

	1978	1979	1980	1981	1982
Total sales	$3,205	$4,060	$4,645	$5,063	$6,154
Military aircraft sales	NA	NA	$1,744	$1,978	$1,946
Government shipbuilding sales	NA	NA	$1,105	$1,027	$1,110
Tactical missiles and gun system sales	NA	NA	$667	$747	$949
Net income	($48)*	$185	$195	$124	$161
Sales to the U.S. government	NA	$2,720	$3,497	$3,987	$5,375
Government sales as percentage of total sales	NA	67%	75%	79%	88%
Defense Department prime contract awards+	$4,153	$3,492	$3,518	$3,402	$5,891
Ratio of DoD prime awards to sales^	1.30	.86	.76	.67	.96
Total General Dynamics employees	69,000	73,000	76,100	74,000	85,100

* Loss.
\+ Awards for U.S. fiscal year, ending Sept. 30.
^ U.S. fiscal year contract awards compared to calendar year sales.

division produces is the M-1 tank. The division accounted for 18 percent of sales and 10 percent of operating earnings in 1982.

Government and Defense Business

General Dynamics was the largest recipient of Defense Department prime contract awards in U.S. fiscal year 1982, with awards totaling $5.89 billion, the most ever to a single company in one year. The company's awards were up sharply from $3.40 billion in 1981. A large portion of the increase was due to the company's acquisition of the Chrysler tank unit, but substantial increases in awards for fighter aircraft and Trident submarines were important factors.

The percentage of net sales that go to the U.S. government (virtually all of which are for defense) has risen steadily from 69 percent in 1979 to 88 percent in 1982. General Dynamics' growing reliance on its federal customer is even more striking because it has occurred in the context of a greater than 20 percent jump in net sales over the same period. A company spokesman told IRRC that the increased defense share reflects three factors: 1) the addition of the tank division; 2) the sale of the company's telecommunications business; and 3) the growth of the Trident and F-16 programs. Military aircraft alone (principally the F-16) generated 32 percent of sales in 1982, military shipbuilding 18 percent, tanks 18 percent and tactical missiles and gun systems 15 percent. The Defense Department in turn has resold some of General Dynamics' hardware abroad (again primarily the F-16).

Defense dependence: One way to trace General Dynamics' extreme dependence on defense contracts is to study the effects that its much-publicized disputes with the Navy have had on the company's overall economic performance. In 1978 General Dynamics and the Navy settled $838 million in claims arising from design changes, cost overruns and quality control problems in the first Trident submarine. General Dynamics took a $359 million pretax writeoff, leading Chairman and Chief Executive Officer David S. Lewis to comment, "We lost more money on that settlement than Electric Boat has made in its entire history."[1] Electric Boat subsequently became embroiled in what the company called "a number of long-running and debilitating controversies" with the Navy over the cost of SSN-688 attack submarines that were finally settled in 1981 with the announcement that the company would absorb a $45 million loss.

These temporary reverses have not deterred the company from positioning itself even more prominently in the defense trade. Indeed, General Dynamics claims to have been inspired by its Trident experience when it purchased Chrysler's tank division. Lewis wrote to shareholders: "We were struck by the very similar positions in time of the M-1 and the Trident....Each had technical problems and delays and yet the two systems are coming into service at about the same time amid high praise and support...." Nor was Dynamics deterred by the $336 million price financed by short-term debt at near-prime rates; Director Henry Crown told Business Week, "The price was no great bargain, but the tank business fits our picture well...."[2] Shortly after the Chrysler purchase, General Dynamics sold off several struggling commercial telecommunications operations, a combination of events the company describes as a "major restructuring."

Yet the rewards of General Dynamics' strategy are becoming apparent, as the "General Dynamics: Striking It Rich Off Defense" headline on Business Week's May 3, 1982, cover proclaims. The principal source of optimism is General Dynamics' extraordinary funded backlog, which stood at $6.5 billion at the end of 1981 and since has grown to $15.1 billion. The company's prospective good fortune derives from having a variety of expensive weapons systems in production at a time of rapid increase in defense spending. General Dynamics, Business Week concluded, has "widely diversified and long-running contracts with the Army, Navy and Air Force that will keep it busy through the rest of this decade and possibly until the turn of the century."

Defense employees: Corporate Secretary John Maguire estimates that 87 percent of the company's 91,000 employees work on defense projects. Of these, 26,200 defense workers are employed at the Electric Boat Division's two submarine facilities, 20,600 at Groton, Conn., and 5,600 at Quonset Point, R.I. Many of these employees belong to unions such as the Metal Trades Council of New London, Conn., the International Association of Machinists and Aerospace Workers, the International Union of Marine and Shipbuilding Workers of America and the Marine Draftsmen's Association. As noted earlier, about 6,000 San Diego employees work on the cruise missile. The Land Systems Division employs 9,300 people. In all, 88 percent of General Dynamics' hourly employees are unionized.

Nuclear Weapons-Related Programs

General Dynamics has been among the most important contractors for nuclear weapons delivery systems and launch platforms since the 1950s. Electric Boat produced the first two U.S. submarines to be armed with ballistic missiles. The submarines--the George Washington and the Patrick Henry--carried ballistic missiles from their launchings in 1959 until they were decommissioned in 1980. General Dynamics' Convair division built America's first generation of ICBMs, the Atlas missiles, which were deployed beginning in 1959.

In FY 1981 the Defense Department awarded General Dynamics at least $703 million in prime contracts for work on primary nuclear weapons systems, and at least $1.70 billion in prime contract awards for work on secondary and nuclear-related systems. The secondary category includes $147 million in Tomahawk cruise missile contract awards. It is unclear which of these awards are for work on nuclear variants of the Tomahawk.

Preliminary analysis of FY 1983 prime contract awards indicates that General Dynamics received awards for primary systems totaling more than $1.5 billion and awards for secondary systems of more than $2 billion in that year. The increase in primary work is due mainly to increased awards for the Trident submarine.

Primary systems:

Trident submarine--The Navy's Trident program has both shipbuilding and missile components. General Dynamics' Electric Boat Division is the sole producer of the Trident submarine, a 560 foot underwater platform for launching 24 strategic nuclear missiles. The submarine carries the Trident I missile, an updated version of the current Poseidon missile. Lockheed is the prime contractor for the Trident missile, which also is being fitted on Poseidon submarines. By 1989 the Trident II missile is expected to replace the Trident I on the new submarine. General Dynamics has embarked on an "extensive design effort" to accommodate the Trident submarine to the Trident II missile.

The first Trident, commissioned in November 1981, is the Ohio, which General Dynamics proudly calls "the Free World's most powerful

General Dynamics' Nuclear Weapons-Related Contracts
(in millions of dollars)

Primary Systems		Secondary Systems	
FY 1981		FY 1981	
Trident submarine	$680	F-16 fighter	$1,324
Modification of SSBN equipment	$21	Tomahawk cruise missile	$167
Advanced ballistic reentry system	$1	Miscellaneous attack submarine work	$40
		SSN 688 attack submarine	$38
		Atlas rocket	$27
		F-111 fighter and derivatives	$25
		P-3 patrol aircraft	$5
		S-3 ASW aircraft	$2
Other current contracts		Other current contracts	
Advanced cruise missile		Standard Missile 2	
FB-111			
Small ICBM (Midgetman)			

weapon system and the most invulnerable leg of our nation's land-sea-air strategic deterrent forces." It is the first of at least 14 Tridents the Navy plans to buy. (The Congressional Budget Office assumes in its analyses that 20 Tridents will be bought by the United States.)[3] The Navy has ordered 10 so far from Electric Boat, enabling General Dynamics to boast a multi-billion-dollar backlog. Congress appropriated $1.2 billion for the Trident program in 1981; at least $680 million was awarded to General Dynamics, $407 million of it in one contract for construction of the eighth submarine. A $523 million award in early 1982 secured the future of the ninth Trident, which will be the first to carry Trident II missiles. The procurement budget for the Trident submarine was $2.15 billion in FY 1983, and was proposed at $2.71 billion for FY 1984. In FY 1983, General Dynamics received at least $1.4 billion in Trident awards. The Navy plans to buy Trident subs at the rate of one per year.

General Dynamics also has a stake in the export of the Trident submarine and missile system to Great Britain. Britain plans to install Trident II missiles on four new submarines not due to be built until the 1990s. Although Britain plans to build both the Trident-type submarines and the missiles at home, the technology and expertise of America's

Trident contractors will certainly be used. Electric Boat already has undertaken a "major engineering program" to assist Britain in designing its Trident submarine.

Cruise missile--For the last 10 years, General Dynamics has been working on cruise missile design and development. The company's Tomahawk cruise missile, which has both nuclear and conventional versions, can be launched from the ground, sea and air, and has received a great deal of attention. Perhaps most notably, the Tomahawk ground-launched cruise missile (GLCM) will be based in Europe as part of the NATO theater nuclear force modernization. General Dynamics is the systems manager and airframe manufacturer on the GLCM and other versions of the Tomahawk. (More information on the Tomahawk is included below under secondary systems.)

In April 1983, the Air Force awarded General Dynamics the contract to develop and build the advanced cruise missile (ACM). This new, important program will result in production of an advanced "Stealth" version of the cruise missile, with improved ability to penetrate enemy radar detection. General Dynamics won the contract over competitors Boeing and Lockheed. Boeing's loss is substantial because the Air Force is cutting short producton of the Boeing ALCM in order to move into early production of the ACM. (General Dynamics lost its bid to produce the ALCM in a 1980 "fly-off" with Boeing.)

The ACM is expected to be a multi-billion-dollar program. The Air Force, however, has kept figures on the program--including contract value and production quantities—classified. Some analysts project production at 1,500 to 3,000 missiles.

The ACM may use a new Williams International engine made of plastic parts. According to Defense Electronics, the range of the new missile might reach 6,000 miles, compared with 1,500 miles for the current ALCM. With that range, the U.S. could launch the missile from within the continental United States to targets within the Soviet Union, adding a new dimension to the arms race. As Defense Electronics stated, "Such a capability would eliminate the need to forward-base ground-launched cruise missiles in Europe."[4]

Guidance for the ACM may be provided by a small Navstar GPS receiver, giving the missile an extraordinary 16-meter accuracy.

FB-111--General Dynamics manufactured the FB-111 strategic bombers. Some 63 of these medium-range aircraft are assigned to the nation's strategic forces. The FB-111, a variant of the F-111 fighter, carries nuclear short-range attack missiles (SRAMs) and nuclear gravity bombs. (FY 1981 contract awards for the F-111 and its variants are combined; they are included below in IRRC's secondary systems category.)

Midgetman--The New York Times has reported that General Dynamics is one of a handful of companies that are putting together a bid for the contract to develop the small (or Midgetman) ICBM, as recommended by the Scowcroft Commission as a follow-on to the MX.[5]

Secondary systems:

Tomahawk cruise missile--The most controversial of the current generation of Tomahawk cruise missiles being built by General Dynamics is the nuclear GLCM that the company is developing for the Air Force. Four hundred sixty-four of these weapons were slated for deployment in NATO countries beginning in late 1983. The Air Force plans to procure 560 GLCMs in all; Congress appropriated $505 million to buy 54 in 1982 and $562 million to buy 84 in 1983.

The Navy sea-launched cruise missile program is both larger and farther along in production. Non-nuclear sea-launched Tomahawks are now being built for deployment on SSN 688 attack submarines and reactivated battleships. The Navy plans to equip more than 100 ships with 4,000 Tomahawks for conventional antiship and land-attack missions. While the current SLCMs are conventional, General Dynamics is developing a nuclear land-attack SLCM that will be deployed on attack submarines beginning in 1984.[6]

General Dynamics also is developing three other cruise-related missiles, including an air-launched conventional version.

In March 1982, General Dynamics reached an agreement with McDonnell Douglas to exchange necessary data and technical knowledge on all variants of the Tomahawk. General Dynamics states in its 1982 Form 10-K that "This reciprocal exchange of data and technology establishes a fully competitive production environment, while also broadening the cruise missile industrial base."

Tomahawk contract awards to General Dynamics totaled at least $167 million in FY 1981, $223 million in FY 1982 and $392 million in FY 1983. The 1983 figure includes $168 million for the European ground-launched cruise missile project. (Note: Because FY 1981 awards for nuclear-armed Tomahawks could not be separated from those for conventional versions, all Tomahawk awards are included in the "secondary" category in IRRC's accounting of nuclear-related awards.) The backlog on Tomahawk work was $1.4 billion at the end of 1981. The company's cruise missile sales are likely to increase, as the budget for the two versions produced by General Dynamics grows.

As a Navy official told Business Week: "Cruise missiles could emerge as the most cost-effective method of delivering high-firepower weapons through the rest of the century. And no company is in a better position to profit from this than General Dynamics."[7]

In a January 1983 letter to the Securities and Exchange Commission, a law firm representing General Dynamics said that the company's investment in special tools and equipment to support cruise missile production would have to be written off at a loss of $65 million if a shareholder resolution asking the company to cease involvement with the cruise missile were implemented. A company spokesman told IRRC that approximately 6,000 General Dynamics employees work on the cruise missile, and that about 6,000 more workers are employed on the program by General Dynamics subcontractors and suppliers.

SSN 688 submarine--The SSN 688 submarine is a fast attack vessel that is armed with tactical nuclear missiles--and soon to be equipped with cruise missiles--and is designed to sink both surface ships and submarines. Unlike its status as sole supplier for the Trident, General Dynamics shares responsibility for the SSN 688 with Tenneco's Newport News Division. Until late in 1981, it looked as if the raging dispute between the Naval Sea System Command and General Dynamics over delays and cost overruns in building the SSN 688 might make Newport News the sole builder of attack submarines. In March the Navy abruptly canceled bidding on three additional SSN 688s and awarded the contracts to Newport News. But in October 1981 General Dynamics agreed to forgo its claims against the Navy to recover the extra costs; the Navy in return awarded it a $232 million contract for a fourth submarine and invited the company to bid on three more. During all of fiscal 1981 (which ended before that award was announced), General Dynamics received at least $38 million in SSN 688 awards. General Dynamics to date has produced 13 of the attack submarines. Although as many as 56 SSN 688s have been projected, the growing cost of the vessels may prompt the Navy eventually to trim its acquisition plans.

For the last three years, as part of its SSN-688 work, General Dynamics has been developing a method of launching Tomahawk cruise missiles vertically as well as from torpedo tubes (the current method). Early in 1982 the Navy awarded the company a $24 million contract to begin detailed engineering development work on this project, which ultimately could greatly expand the attack capability of the submarine. Further awards in FY 1983 for this work totaled at least $35 million.

The Trident and attack submarine programs together produced 20 percent of the company's 1980 sales but a net operating loss for Electric Boat. The company expects that the sales share for submarines will remain stable in the near term and that Electric Boat's profitability will pick up.

F-16--The nuclear-capable F-16 "Falcon," first developed as a light-weight fighter to succeed the costly and complex F-15, performs both conventional ground attack missions and nuclear strikes. It has proven to be a "huge sales success" with American and Allied air forces.[8] At least $1.32 billion in Air Force F-16 contracts, excluding foreign military sales (FMS), went to General Dynamics' Fort Worth division in 1981. Recently the Air Force upped its planned F-16 purchases from 1,388 to 1,985, and in 1982 General Dynamics received a multi-year order for 480 F-16s, to be built between 1983 and 1987. Awards for non-FMS F-16s totaled at least $1.46 billion in FY 1983.

The F-16, manufactured in Texas and in Europe, has been bought in quantity by a number of foreign air forces. Some 388 have been sold to Belgium, Denmark, the Netherlands and Norway, 75 to Israel and 40 to Egypt. The F-16 Falcon also appears to be a main feature of the Reagan administration's plans for military exports to Third World countries: Venezuela will buy 24, South Korea 36, and Pakistan 40.

Two new models of the F-16 are in the works. Fort Worth is developing for the Air Force the F-16 C/D, an aircraft carrying advanced radar and fire control equipment and the new Advanced Medium Range Air-to-Air missile (Amraam). The F-16XL, affording greater range and weapons capability by virtue of a wing modification, is now being test-flown.

F-111--As noted above, General Dynamics produced the F-111 fighter and its variants, the FB-111 strategic bomber and the EF-111 electronic warfare aircraft. The F-111 fighter is a nuclear-capable tactical aircraft that can carry the B43 and B61 nuclear gravity bombs, and the B57 nuclear depth charge. Contract awards for work on all F-111 variants totaled at least $25 million in FY 1981; awards in FY 1983 were at least $54 million.

Other aircraft--General Dynamics also does work on other nuclear-capable aircraft, including, in FY 1981, the S-3 Viking antisubmarine aircraft, the P-3 Orion patrol aircraft and the F-106 Delta Dart fighter. The Delta Dart originally was produced by General Dynamics.

Space systems--Convair produces the Atlas launch vehicle (which was developed for the original Atlas ICBM) and the Centaur high-energy upper-stage booster used by the Defense Department and NASA to launch satellites and spacecraft. Satellites propelled by the Atlas/Centaur combination may perform communication or navigation functions related to nuclear weapons. In 1981 General Dynamics rockets launched five NASA and DoD spacecraft. Atlas/Centaur contracts awarded in 1981 were at least $27 million. Convair has orders for five new Atlas boosters and for modifications on four existing ones, all to be used for Air Force space flights. The Navy plans to order several Atlas/Centaurs during the 1980s. In 1982 Centaur was selected as the high energy upper state launch vehicle for the space shuttle, an initial award valued at more than $200 million and expected to last into the 1990s.

Standard Missile 2 (SM-2)--General Dynamics' extended range Standard Missile 2 will be produced in both conventional and nuclear versions. The nuclear SM-2 will be deployed at sea on such ships as the Aegis cruisers, and will replace the old Terrier nuclear-armed missile. (The Terrier also was produced by General Dynamics.) The new anti-aircraft weapon is being developed to destroy a number of targets, most notably nuclear-armed Soviet cruise missiles.[9] The Defense Department plans to build 500 of the missiles, which will use the W81 warhead. Initial deployment is planned for FY 1987.

General Dynamics-Government Relationship

Political action committee: General Dynamics uses the same techniques of political contributions and lobbying for selling its products in Washington as other large defense contractors. Its PAC directs contributions to congressmen in Missouri, Texas, California, Connecticut and Rhode Island districts where company installations are located. Substantial assistance also is given to the campaigns of members of the Armed Services and Appropriations Committees.

In 1979-80, General Dynamics' PAC gave $140,000 to the campaigns of 137 congressional candidates. Some 34 percent of the total went to members of defense committees. In 1981-82, General Dynamics gave $172,440 to 150 congressional candidates, including $76,470 (or 44 percent) to defense committee members. Major contributions included $7,300 to Sen. John Chafee (R-R.I.); $5,000 to Sen. John Tower (R-Tex.), now chairman of the Senate Armed Services Committee; $5,200 to Sen. Pete Wilson (D-Calif.); $6,500 to Rep. Duncan L. Hunter (R-Calif.); and $6,650 to Rep. Bill Lowery (R-Calif.).

Washington office: The company maintains a Washington office near the Pentagon. Its staff members monitor legislation, publicize the company's defense activities, and scout foreign sales opportunities. General Dynamics is assisted in these tasks by the Washington Industrial Team which represents many large defense contractors. Two of Washington Industrial Team's principals are Richard Ichord and Robert Wilson, former congressmen who until 1981 were senior members of the House Armed Services Committee and two of the representatives most favored by General Dynamics' PAC. A company spokesman said, however, that the Washington Industrial Team is not used much by General Dynamics. The spokesman also said that the company itself does not lobby, but relies on industry associations like the Aerospace Industries Association.

Corporate Secretary Maguire told IRRC that most of the representative office's dealings with members of Congress are in response to inquiries. He added that the company's Washington activities "are closer to the marketing done by commercial firms" than to lobbying on public policy issues. Maguire said that "lobbying on defense policy issues" is handled by trade associations.

Personnel interchange: In 1977-81, 276 mid- to upper-level defense officials left the government to join General Dynamics, while four company officials moved in the reverse direction. Maguire said that the company turns to former government defense employees because it needs their expertise. He said, "We need people with experience in these areas, and where else do you get experienced people?"

Contingency Planning and Prospects

Contingency planning: With defense sales growing to more than 80 percent of its business, commercial sales stagnant, and the nearly simultaneous sale of a struggling commercial telecommunications operation and purchase of a struggling but potentially lucrative military tank supplier, General Dynamics definitely seems to have turned away from a strategy of balancing commercial and military operations. "It sounds to me like they see a big swing back to defense (spending) and decided to go all the way with the government sector," former General Dynamics vice president and board member, James M. Beggs, told Business Week. But the same story quotes Herbert Rogers, head of the booming Fort Worth division, as saying: "The defense world has become extremely complex, and you do worry about your lack of control over your own destiny. The Air Force is happy with the way our program has been managed. Yet no one knows who will be in power next (in Washington) and what they will do to it."

As a partial measure to ease its extreme dependence on defense contracts, General Dynamics is working to increase direct export sales. For the last three years, export sales have amounted to less than 10 percent of total sales. General Dynamics' primary export success has been with the F-16s sold through the Air Force.

The alternative strategy of planning to convert military installations to civilian use has not been embraced by the company, as was evident in the company's opposition to a 1979 shareholder resolution requesting it to develop conversion plans. Corporate Secretary Maguire said the company will pursue good commercial opportunities, but that the defense share has increased recently because "this is a business we know, that we do well in." Maguire said the company sold its telecommunications business because it was not large enough to have a "critical mass." General Dynamics "did not have other operations that fed into that market," unlike giant competitors like AT&T and GTE, said Maguire. He added that marketing in new areas is "extremely difficult, just like U.S. Steel saying it is going to build airplanes." Maguire said that Electric Boat tried 10 commercial projects ranging from pleasure craft to steel vessels when its business fell off after World War II. All 10 projects failed. In 1955, the company set a goal of a 50-50 balance between commercial and military work, but the goal was never reached.

Prospects: If the Reagan military buildup goes ahead as planned, General Dynamics is well-positioned. With strong aircraft, missile and submarine programs, the company should benefit substantially from increased nuclear weapons production. Given the company's military dependence, however, a major reduction in military spending in all probability would leave the company in a difficult position. And in the long term, given General Dynamics' heavy reliance on two programs in particular--the Trident and the F-16--there are dangers of substantial disruption even if military spending continues to escalate.

An arms agreement along the lines discussed by the Reagan administration in the Start talks would have little effect on General Dynamics in the near and medium term. Agreement along the lines suggested by the Soviets could have a greater impact, particularly since the USSR would like to limit cruise missiles. A nuclear freeze would have a substantial impact by ending the cruise missile program; in addition, although a freeze as described by the proposal's proponents would not directly affect production of delivery vehicles such as Trident submarines, it is likely that an agreement that ended new production of Trident missiles also would have an impact on the submarine program.

Assuming that there are not major cost escalation problems, and in the absence of meaningful arms control agreements, the Trident program is not likely to run into serious political difficulty in the next several years. Many Pentagon critics in Congress and elsewhere believe that the Trident program is a better buy than the B-1 or the MX, so the Trident has faced less opposition. Trident supporters point out that the submarines are and will continue to be difficult to detect, and are therefore relatively invulnerable. The MX missile, in contrast, is thought to be vulnerable to a Soviet first strike. In suggesting less expensive alternatives to the administration's current strategic plan, the Congressional Budget Office has focused on expanding the Trident force faster than is currently planned. CBO estimates that Electric Boat could produce Trident submarines at the rate of two a year, as opposed to the current rate of one a year. Thus, the Trident also is less vulnerable than other strategic systems to budget reduction pressures.

General Dynamics Footnotes

1. The New York Times, April 23, 1981.
2. Business Week, May 3, 1982, p. 105-6.
3. Congressional Budget Office, "Modernizing U.S. Strategic Offensive Forces: The Administration's Program and Alternatives," Washington, 1983.
4. Defense Electronics, May 1983, p. 65.
5. The New York Times, Sept. 7, 1983.
6. Congressional Budget Office, op. cit., p. 80.
7. Business Week, op. cit.
8. Business Week, op. cit.
9. Aviation Week & Space Technology, Dec. 6, 1982.

General Electric

General Electric is a diversified, high-technology manufacturer and the nation's leading producer of electrical products. The company has major market positions in electronics, power systems, aerospace, transportation systems, engineered materials, financial services, medical equipment, consumer goods and natural resources.

GE's roots go back to 1878, when Thomas Edison and a Wall Street lawyer named Grosvenor Lowrey joined forces to develop a commercial market for Edison's incandescent lamp. They formed the Edison Electric Light Co., the first of several companies later joined to become General Electric.

In its early years, the company's most important products were the electrical generation and distribution systems required to electrify people's homes so that they could use Edison's new light bulbs. From this precedent grew the electric utility companies as well as today's General Electric Co.

The company's involvement in military production also goes back to the turn of the century, when GE electric motors were first developed and used to operate shipboard gun turrets. But the company played its most important military role in World War II when its headquarters offices, then in Schenectady, N.Y., were, in the words of one writer, "the nerve center of one of the world's biggest and most complex war machines."[1]

The government called upon GE to meet a variety of its wartime needs. For example, when Great Britain's Sir Frank Whittle came up with the idea for a new kind of aircraft engine, the British islands were besieged and its factories overloaded with defense production. The Allies turned to General Electric for the development and manufacture of reliable high-speed turbines. Thus, GE came to develop and manufacture the first U.S. aircraft jet engine, based on the Whittle design.

GE made a major contribution to the U.S. World War II effort after a rapid conversion from civilian to military production. During the war, GE produced $4 billion in war equipment, including giant turbines for ships, aircraft engines and instrumentation and related equipment--and mass spectrometers for the Manhattan Project. Its work for the Manhattan Project established GE as an early participant in the emerging nuclear power industry and in the U.S. nuclear weapons program.

Data on General Electric
(dollar figures in millions)

	1978	1979	1980	1981	1982
Sales	$19,654	$22,461	$24,959	$27,240	$26,500
Net earnings	$1,230	$1,409	$1,514	$1,652	$1,817
DoD prime contract awards*	$1,786	$2,043	$2,202	$2,955	$3,654
Ratio of DoD prime contract awards to total sales+	.09	.09	.09	.11	.14
Total GE employees	401,000	405,000	402,000	402,000	367,000

* U.S. fiscal year, ending Sept. 30.
\+ U.S. fiscal year awards compared with calendar year sales.

World War II quadrupled GE's business, and it joined the ranks of billion dollar companies. With preparation and planning for a post-war return to predominantly commercial production, the company maintained its position.

General Electric is now the 14th largest company in the country, according to the Forbes ranking of sales leaders. The company had sales of $26.5 billion in 1982, down 2.7 percent from $27.2 billion in 1981. GE had total assets of $21.7 billion and 367,000 employees in 1982.

The company breaks down its business activities into seven major segments: services and materials; consumer products; industrial products; power systems; technical systems; natural resources; and aircraft engines.

Government and Defense Business

Defense dependence: General Electric reports that in 1982 approximately one-sixth of its external sales, or between $4 billion and $5 billion, were to the U.S. government. In 1981, the company reported government sales at one-eighth of external sales. Most of these sales were aerospace products and services, aircraft engines and related products and services, and Navy ship propulsion equipment, and most were to the military.

GE said in its 1982 annual report that "higher defense spending and the transition of advanced research and prototype work into production produced a very strong increase" in 1982 aerospace sales. The company also said that the government's decisions to go ahead with B-1B and C-5 aircraft programs "add to the current healthy GE position in the military market."

GE has done or is doing work on a wide variety of military programs, including propulsion systems for nuclear submarines, the B-1 and advanced technology bombers, and components for the MX, Minuteman and Trident strategic missiles. The company also provides the engines for tactical fighters and attack aircraft such as McDonnell Douglas's F/A-18 and Fairchild's A-10, KC-10 tankers and various helicopters. GE's aircraft engine segment, which accounts for much of its defense business, increased its revenues and earnings in 1981, despite a drop in commercial shipments. The company reported that "increased engine shipments in 1982 for new military aircraft and the rapid buildup in commercial re-engining programs offset the decline in maturing military applications and continuing erosion of commercial airline markets for new aircraft."

In 1982, GE was the fourth largest military contractor, with prime contract awards of $3.65 billion from the Defense Department during U.S. fiscal year 1982, ending Sept. 30. This was an increase of 24 percent over 1981, and was two-thirds more than the 1980 figure. GE alone accounted for more than 3 percent of total contracts awarded by DoD in 1982.

In addition to DoD awards, GE received $254 million in FY 1982 Energy Department contract awards for its operation of two facilities primarily concerned with military production. The ratio of the combined DoD and DoE awards to total GE sales was .15 in 1982.

Defense employees: GE employed about 367,000 employees worldwide in 1982. Of these, the aerospace group employed some 28,000 and the aircraft engine group about 30,000. Both of these groups have a significant volume in commercial, nondefense businesses.

Nuclear Weapons-Related Programs

General Electric's involvement in the development of nuclear technology predates World War II. In 1940, scientists at the General Electric Research Laboratory successfully isolated small amounts of uranium 235. As the Manhattan Project secretly developed the atomic bomb between 1942 and 1945, GE became an important supplier of process equipment and power supply apparatus. GE provided the electrical power systems for each of three plants at Oak Ridge, Tenn., that were experimenting with methods for isolating large amounts of uranium 235. In addition, the company's General Engineering Laboratory provided various instruments for the plants, including hundreds of mass spectrometers, used to identify elements of nature by their distinctive color spectrum signatures.[2]

General Electric also provided the principal electrical apparatus for the Hanford Engineer Works in Washington state, which was established to produce plutonium. In 1946, the War Department gave General Electric the responsibility for management of Hanford, which was to participate in an extensive program of atomic energy research and development. GE's fee for operating this U.S. government facility was $1 a year. GE managed Hanford until 1966.

GE's early work in nuclear research and development led the company into important roles in the production of nuclear reactors to generate electricity, in nuclear medicine and other civilian technologies and in the U.S. nuclear weapons program. In addition, the company undertook a leading role in the design and development of nuclear propulsion systems for Navy ships and submarines, including today's Trident submarines.

General Electric's work on nuclear weapons and related systems is performed under contracts to the Defense Department and the Energy Department. IRRC identified contract awards totaling $354 million for primary nuclear warfare systems in fiscal 1981, including both DoD and DoE awards. Total awards for secondary and nuclear-related systems (including some awards for primary systems that could not be separated out from secondary work) totaled at least $1.02 billion.

Primary systems:

Pinellas plant--General Electric manufactures electronic components for use in the U.S. nuclear weapons program at the government-owned Pinellas plant in St. Petersburg, Fla. The facility was constructed by GE in 1956 and has been operated by the company under contract with the Department of Energy (and its predecessor agencies) since that time. In 1982, the facility employed 1,741 workers, according to the department. GE says the work force is now more than 1,800, up from 1,380 in 1978. The staff in 1982 included 309 scientists, 270 other professionals and 234 technicians.

The Energy Department's operating costs at Pinellas in fiscal 1982 were $75 million, according to DoE, and the amount spent for plant operations that year was $117 million. DoE contract awards to GE for Pinellas were $72 million in 1981 and $96 million in FY 1982. GE's management fee for the plant was $3.5 million in 1982, up from $1.6 million in 1978.

The principal role of the Pinellas plant is the development and production of neutron generators, which prime the initiation of the chain reactions within nuclear bombs. GE developed the first neutron generator under contract to the government in the early 1950s.

The Energy Department describes Pinellas's responsibilities as follows:

> Originally built for developing and producing neutron generators for nuclear weapons initiation, Pinellas's mission now encompasses production of a wide range of weapons com-

General Electric's Nuclear Weapons-Related Contracts
(in millions of dollars)

Primary Systems		Secondary Systems	
FY 1981		FY1981	
Minuteman missile	$92	F/A-18 fighter	$339
Trident missiles	$83	Attack submarines	$218
Pinellas plant (management)	$72	Knolls Laboratory (management)	$136
Trident submarine	$59	DSCS III	$84
MX missile	$20	F-111 fighter	$46
Spacetrack radars	$15	P-3C patrol aircraft	$32
B-52 bomber	$7	Miscellaneous sonars	$25
B-1 bomber	$3	S-3 ASW aircraft	$23
Other current contracts		BQQ-5 sonar	$23
Trident submarine propulsion systems		F-4 fighter	$20
FB-111 bomber		F-16 fighter	$15
OTH-B radars		E-3A Awacs aircraft	$13
Seek Igloo radars		Global Positioning System	$13
Air Force Satellite Communications System			

ponents....The technology and skills at the plant focus on the development and manufacture of highly complex, miniaturized, neutron generators and electrical assemblies; medium-power radioisotope thermoelectric generators and thermoelectric converters; electrical connectors that arrest lightning discharges; and specialty neutron generation and neutron measurement devices for nuclear weapons testing....

GE has operated the plant under five-year contracts. The most recent such contract expired at the end of September 1983. Negotiations on a new contract were under way, but no agreement has been reached.

In a 1979 report for shareholders on Pinellas, GE said that the primary radionuclides used at the facility are tritium gas, used in neutron generators, and plutonium oxide, contained in thimble-sized triple metal sealed capsules. All nuclear materials are shipped in containers approved by the Departments of Energy and Transportation. Tritium and tritium-contaminated waste materials are transported to and from the plants in approved DoE vehicles. GE reports that there have been no accidents and no loss of items during transportation of radioactive materials to and from the Pinellas plant, and that there have been no radioactive discharges to the environment that have approached the limits set by the federal radiation exposure standard. GE states that no employee has been exposed to radiation over 1 rem at Pinellas.

Intercontinental ballistic missiles--GE has produced the re-entry vehicles (RVs) for several U.S. ICBMs, including the Titan II and Minuteman III, the mainstays of the current land-based ICBM force.

One of the company's most important nuclear weapons-related programs has been the production of the Mark 12A reentry vehicle. The Mark 12A production line closed in 1982, after the reentry vehicle was produced for 300 of the existing Minuteman III missiles. The warhead for the Mark 12A carries an explosive yield of 335 kilotons, or 27 times that of the bomb that destroyed Hiroshima. Each Minuteman carries three of the independently targetable warheads. The Mark 12A-equipped Minuteman is a counterforce weapon with accuracy of 900 to 1,000 feet. Development of improvements in the Minuteman's guidance system could result in an improved accuracy of up to 500 feet, says Aviation Week.

GE had won a contract in 1980 to adapt the Mark 12A RV to the MX missile. Each MX would carry 10 Mark 12As. Subsequently, however, the Pentagon dropped the Mark 12A in its MX plans in favor of Avco's Mark 21, now in development. GE in 1982 merged its Reentry Systems Division into the Space Systems division, because the outlook for reentry business did not justify retaining the divisional status. During 1982, GE reduced its reentry systems work force from 1,600 to 1,100.[3] GE's reentry work is done in Philadelphia.

Despite GE's loss to Avco on the reentry vehicle contract, the company continues to do other work on the MX. GE in 1982 was awarded a $150 million development contract for the arming and fuzing system for the Mark 21. GE's other earlier work on the Minuteman had included production of certain electronic components under subcontract.

IRRC identified prime contract awards for Minuteman work totaling $92 million in FY 1981. Awards for MX work totaled at least $20 million.

Submarine-launched ballistic missiles--General Electric contributes to the nation's sea-based strategic forces in work on both submarines and missiles. The company makes the fire control systems for sea-launched ballistic missiles, including the Poseidon and Trident I (also designated C-4) missiles. GE also is developing advanced fire control concepts for the Trident II (D-5) missile, which some experts believe to be the most important new nuclear weapon on the horizon. If all works as planned, the D-5 will be the first submarine-launched missile with the ability to destroy hardened missile silos in the Soviet

Union. In addition to the fire control system, GE works on the guidance system for the Trident missile. DoD contract awards for Trident missile work totaled at least $83 million in FY 1981. Awards in FY 1982 totaled at least $43 million, and FY 1983 awards through March totaled at least $38 million.

In addition, the Navy may use the Mark 6 stellar inertial guidance system with the D-5, which may provide an accuracy of 400 feet. General Electric also is participating in the development of this guidance system.

Finally, GE was the principal subcontractor to Lockheed on the Mark 500 Evader Maneuverable RV (MaRV). The advanced test program for this MaRV was designed to ensure that it is compatible with the Trident I (C-4) SLBM, although if it is deployed, it will likely be with the Trident II (D-5) missile, or perhaps with the Minuteman (with which it is also compatible). The Mark 500 is designed to be capable of evasive maneuvers during reentry. While the Navy does not plan to proceed with engineering development or deployment of the Mark 500, the advanced test program was undertaken to ensure that it could be put into production rapidly if the Soviets resort to an ABM system at some point.

Ballistic missile submarines--General Electric is a major producer of propulsion systems for nuclear-powered submarines, primarily through its management of the Knolls Atomic Power Laboratory for the Department of Energy. Knolls is based in Niskayuna, N.Y., two miles east of Schenectady. The Knolls complex also includes facilities in West Milton, N.Y., and at Windsor, Conn.

Knolls and the Westinghouse-run Bettis Laboratory design and develop naval reactor cores and nuclear propulsion plants for submarines, aircraft carriers and other ships. According to DoE, Knolls "has the responsibility of developing the reactor plant required for the Trident ballistic missile submarines."

The fiscal 1983 operating budget for Knolls is $205 million, including $149 million for the DoE naval reactor development program and another $56 million from the Navy's research budget. DoE contract awards to the lab were $136 million in FY 1981 and $153 million in FY 1982. (Note: Because a breakdown by weapons systems for the DoE Knolls awards is not available, IRRC grouped all DoE contract awards to Knolls under the "secondary" category in determining total awards for nuclear weapons-related work. For more information on propulsion systems for secondary systems, see below.) Defense Department contract awards to Knolls for Trident submarine research and development work totaled $59 million in FY 1981.

At the end of FY 1982, Knolls employed about 3,070 workers, including 1,389 engineers and scientists, 562 other professionals and 182 technicians.

Besides research and development on reactor cores, Knolls is responsible for the training of officers and enlisted personnel for the nuclear fleet. About 1,900 personnel are trained each year.

GE has managed Knolls since 1946, and the current five-year contract was renewed in September 1983.

B-1 bomber--GE also has been an important factor in the third leg of the nation's strategic triad--the strategic bomber force. GE's most important current work on strategic bombers is its manufacture of the F101 turbofan engine for the B-1B bomber. The F101 is "an improved, slightly higher thrust version" of the engine that GE had designed for the original B-1 prototypes, Aviation Week says. The Air Force plans to spend $20 billion to buy 100 B-1B bombers; $1.8 billion of that is budgeted for the GE engine. Many observers believe that the total cost of the 100 bombers will far exceed $20 billion.

GE received contract awards for B-1 work totaling $3.2 million in fiscal 1981, before Reagan revived the B-1 program. In FY 1982, GE received awards totaling at least $261 million for the engines, and since the beginning of 1983, the Air Force has announced further awards to GE for the B-1 engines totaling at least $310 million. The company's B-1 engine work is performed in Evendale, Ohio (near Cincinnati).

Finally, GE is producing the engine thrust control subsystem and other engine instruments for the B-1 at its Binghamton, N.Y., plant.

B-52 and FB-111 bombers--General Electric has also provided components for the B-52 and FB-111 bombers, which make up the current U.S. strategic bomber fleet. GE produced at least two electronic warfare components for the B-52, as well as flight radar simulators for the bomber. The company produced a radar system for the FB-111. Contract awards for B-52 work totaled $7.3 million in FY 1981. More recently, GE received a November 1982 award of $8.4 million for a B-52 ECM subsystem. Awards for FB-111 work are included in DoD listings with awards for other variants of the F-111, and are included in the secondary listings below.

Advanced technology (Stealth) bomber--In October 1981, General Electric was selected as part of the team to proceed with initial research and development on the advanced technology bomber, popularly known as Stealth. Northrop was selected as the prime contractor, and other team members include LTV and Boeing. This secret and top-priority Air Force project is developing a bomber that features a variety of shapes and uses special materials in order to minimize its visibility to enemy radar. GE is developing the engine for this new bomber.

Ballistic Missile Early Warning System--General Electric has been among the most important contributors to U.S. land-based strategic and tactical radar systems. Among radar systems primarily developed for defense against nuclear attack was the FPS-50, part of the Ballistic Missile Early Warning System (BMEWS). GE was an important subcontractor on the very large FPS-50 radars, located in Greenland and Alaska, which have been in operation since 1962. As the BMEWS name suggests, the radars were built to detect a ballistic missile attack on North America. The radars "are reported to have proved extremely reliable," according to Jane's.

Over-the-Horizon Backscatter radars--GE is the prime contractor for an important new addition to the North American strategic defense system, the Over-the-Horizon Backscatter (OTH-B) radars. These radars, designed to provide long-range early warning of bombers approaching North America, were approved for production by the Air Force in 1982. OTH-B radars can detect aircraft at 500 to 1,800 nautical miles by bouncing short wave radio signals off the ionosphere.

GE developed a prototype OTH-B in Maine under a 1975 contract for $39 million. Judging the prototype a success in detecting aircraft over a 180 degree radius off the eastern seaboard, the Air Force awarded GE a $67 million development and production contract for the system in FY 1982. The system will be located in Maine and in an as yet undesignated west coast location. The Air Force also plans to look for a southern site. In March 1983, GE received further contract awards of $112 million for the first OTH-B system in Maine, bringing the cost of the Maine OTH-B to $179 million. The OTH-B system is being produced at GE's Syracuse plant and is scheduled for completion by 1987.

Seek Igloo radars--In fiscal 1982, GE also received Air Force approval for production of the company's Seek Igloo FPS-117 radar system. Seek Igloo, also produced in Syracuse, is scheduled to replace old Distant Early Warning (Dew) Line radars in Alaska. The Dew line, one of the earliest strategic early warning systems, is composed of a string of radar in the northern tier of Alaska, Canada and Greenland. GE received contract awards of $24 million in FY 1982 and $39 million through March in fiscal 1983 for work on Seek Igloo.

Spacetrack radars--GE also has been a participant in the Air Force's Spacetrack system program. Spacetrack is the Air Force's worldwide detection, identification, tracking and reporting system, which records data on all space objects. Four GE-produced radar at two sites--Shemya Air Force Base in Alaska, and a site in Turkey, comprise half of the Spacetrack system. The Shemya radars, however, are being replaced by the Raytheon-produced Cobra Dane radar. GE received contract awards totaling $15 million for Spacetrack work in FY 1981, including $12 million to operate the facility in Turkey.

Air Force Satellite Communications System--GE also is the prime contractor for the Air Force Satellite Communications System (Afsatcom), a system designed for a range of Air Force communications needs, but developed primarily to assist strategic communications. IRRC could verify no contract awards to GE for Afsatcom in FY 1981, although the system was budgeted at $30 million that year.

Other--General Electric's historic production for primary nuclear warfare systems has included:

-- Manufacture of a floating power plant for the Kwajalein test site in the south Pacific, used in support of the Ballistic Missile Defense (BMD) program.

-- Manufacture of the engines for the Boeing E-4B National Emergency Airborne Command Posts. The E-4Bs, modified versions of the 747, will carry leaders and C^3I systems in the case of nuclear attack.

-- Various work for the Defense Nuclear Agency, including support for an underground nuclear test under a 1983 contract award for $4.6 million.

-- Production of the radar system for the old Safeguard anti-ballistic missile system. (The Safeguard system has been deactivated.)

Secondary systems:

F/A-18--General Electric produces engines and other systems for a range of tactical aircraft that are equipped to carry nuclear and conventional weapons. The company's most important program in this category is production of the F404 engines for the McDonnell Douglas F/A-18 aircraft. The F/A-18 is now the second largest U.S. aircraft program. The carrier-based plane is equipped to carry non-GE equipment such as antisubmarine nuclear depth charges and the B61 nuclear bomb.

In addition to building the engine for the F/A-18, GE produces components for the F/A-18 flight control electronic system.

GE received FY 1981 contract awards of at least $339 million for work on F/A-18 components, mostly the engine. FY 1982 awards for F/A-18 work totaled at least $397 million, and IRRC identified contract awards of $370 million for F/A-18 work in the first half of fiscal 1983. GE manufactures the F/A-18 engine at its West Lynn, Mass., facility.

F-4 and F-16--In Cincinnati, Ohio, GE manufactures the J-79 engine for certain nuclear-capable F-4 and F-16 fighters. In addition, the company produces an ammunition loading system, training devices (including flight simulators) and engine instruments for the F-16, and automatic pilot mechanisms, gyroscopes and other equipment for the F-4.

F-111--As noted above, GE makes contributions to several versions of the F-111, including the FB-111 strategic bomber. GE produces equipment for various tactical (but nuclear-capable) versions of the F-111 as well. GE-produced F-111 equipment includes the APQ-161 radar; ALQ-131 ECM pod; automatic pilot mechanisms and de-icing mechanisms. FY 1981 awards for F-111 work totaled at least $46 million.

P-3C and S-3--GE's Utica plant produces radar and data processing systems for the nuclear-capable P-3C ASW and patrol aircraft. Contract awards for such production totaled at least $32 million in fiscal 1981. The company also continues to produce spare engines at its Cincinnati plant for the nuclear-capable S-3 patrol aircraft; contract awards totaled at least $23 million in FY 1981. Both the P-3C and the S-3 are Navy aircraft produced by Lockheed.

Other work on nuclear-capable aircraft--GE also manufactures for the Navy the engine of the nuclear-capable SH-3 helicopter. This engine is also used in other helicopters. (The breakdown of contract awards specifically for the SH-3 is not available.)

The company's other, less important and less substantial work on nuclear-capable aircraft includes production of various components for the AV-8B, F-15 and A-4, as well as flight radar simulators for the A-6E.

Other nuclear warfare-related aircraft systems--GE manufactures engines and other equipment for a variety of aircraft that are designed to play a role in nuclear (as well as conventional) warfare. For example, GE produces the engines and a sonar system for the SH-60 helicopters, which are part of the Lamps III ASW system. FY 1981 contract awards for this work totaled at least $18 million.

General Electric also has a limited participation in the Awacs program, through production of components for the E-3A Awacs air surveillance aircraft, which has both strategic and tactical roles. E-3A contract awards totaled at least $13 million for GE in FY 1981.

(Because these systems provide support for a wide range of defense functions, IRRC has considered the space and satellite systems discussed here as secondary systems. Nevertheless, it should be recognized that strategic warfare concerns appear to be the most important motivation for some of these programs, notably DSCS and Milstar.)

Defense Satellite Communications System III--GE is the prime contractor for the Defense Satellite Communications System III (DSCS III). DSCS is a satellite system that provides for voice and data communication virtually anywhere on earth through satellite relay. The system supports both tactical and strategic national security requirements including world-wide command and control, crisis management, intelligence data relay, diplomatic traffic and early warning detection and reporting. Part of the DSCS III satellite is devoted to the Air Force Satellite Communications (Afsatcom) system, which links together strategic forces. General Electric is involved in the production of a number of NASA and Defense Department military space systems such as this that could play important roles in strategic warfare.

Currently, the system consists of four DSCS II satellites, produced by TRW, and two spares. GE is developing the DSCS III satellites, which can carry more channels and are designed for longer life, increased flexibility and enhanced anti-jam protection. The satellites can be launched by the Titan III booster or carried into space on the Space Shuttle. In either case, the Boeing Inertial Upper Stage (IUS) rocket is used to boost the satellite into synchronous orbit 22,300 miles above the earth. Three satellites at this high orbit should provide global coverage.

The first DSCS III, which is being used for testing, was launched in October 1982. DoD plans to order 12 satellites for service through the mid-1990s. DSCS III will begin full operation in 1985, according to the Air Force.

GE received prime contract awards for DSCS III totaling at least $84 million in FY 1981, $110 million in FY 1982 and $125 million through the early part of FY 1983. GE works on DSCS at its Valley Forge Space Center near Philadelphia.

Military Strategic Tactical & Relay satellite (Milstar)--GE expressed interest in participating in two parts of the new Milstar satellite program. This communications satellite system, announced by President Reagan in his October 1981 speech outlining his strategic program, is designed to serve both strategic and tactical forces by providing a worldwide, highly jam-resistant, survivable communications systems that are less vulnerable to the effects of nuclear explosions. Milstar operates at an extremely high frequency, and the Defense Department considers it a pivotal program in its work to strengthen and refine space systems that can survive jamming and nuclear attack.

General Electric initially expressed interest in becoming a prime contractor for the payload section of Milstar with Rockwell and Raytheon as subcontractors, but the team was dissolved in 1982. Nevertheless, GE is teamed with Lockheed in a successful bid to become a contractor on the spacecraft "bus." GE also is working with Raytheon on ground terminals for the program.

Other space systems--GE has worked and provides support on other military and related satellite and space programs, including Starcom and the Atlas booster. The Atlas is used in two space launch vehicles that in turn are used for commercial, military and NASA purposes. GE also works on the Global Positioning System, for which the company received awards of $13 million in FY 1981.

Attack submarine--GE has at least two major responsibilities in the programs to build the SSN-688 and other attack submarines. The SSN-688 is the major attack submarine now in production. It is equipped to carry several nuclear weapons, including the new cruise missiles.

First, Knolls and GE's other Schenectady facilities are responsible for the nuclear propulsion plant for many attack submarines, including the SSN-688. DoD contract awards for this work totaled at least $218 million in FY 1981. Awards in the early part of FY 1983 totaled $279 million.

GE also works on marine turbines and power plant components for attack submarines in its Fitchburg and Lynn, Mass., plants. DoD contract awards for this work totaled at least $15 million in FY 1981. In April 1983, GE received DoD contract awards totaling $32 million for steam turbines for the SSN-688 program.

Finally, the company works on electronic systems for attack submarines. Most important in fiscal 1981, GE received $23 million in awards for transducers used in the SSN-688's BQQ-5 sonar. Work on the transducers took place in Syracuse, N.Y.

General Electric-Government Relationship

Political action committees: GE sponsors two political action committees, including the Utah International PAC, which is affiliated with a subsidiary that is being sold. Together, the two PACs made GE the eighth largest corporate PAC spender in the 1982 campaign, with total contributions of $290,038, according to the FEC. The company ranked 110th among all PAC sponsors.

General Electric's main PAC contributed $133,400 to 284 federal candidates in 1979-80, and $149,125 to 288 candidates in 1981-82. In 1981-82, GE contributed about 24 percent of the total to members of committees and subcommittees concerned with the military and its budget.

GE's aggregate contributions have gone to a wide range of members, and the vast majority have supported incumbents. The PAC dollars have split about evenly between Democrats and Republicans (with some shift toward the Republican side in 1982). Recipients of major support in 1981-82 included Senate Minority Leader Robert Byrd (D-W.Va., $1,500); House Defense Appropriations Subcommittee Chairman Joseph Addabbo (D-N.Y., $1,000); House Budget Committee Chairman James Jones (D-Okla., $2,000); House Republican leader Robert Michel (R-Ill., $1,000); Speaker of the House Thomas P. O'Neill (D-Mass., $1,000); and House Ways and Means Committee Chairman Daniel Rostenkowski (D-Ill., $1,000).

O'Neill reportedly has been an important supporter of GE programs that involve jobs in Massachusetts. For example, Business Week reports that O'Neill has worked to protect "every penny" of the budget for the controversial F/A-18 fighter.[4] (As noted above, the F/A-18 engine is manufactured at GE's Lynn, Mass., facilities.)

Washington office: General Electric has 15 employees registered as lobbyists in Washington. They do work on "the broad range" of GE's interests, according to a company spokesman, but their primary purpose, as described by the company, is to monitor developments in Washington and handle requests for information, while providing policy-makers with information that the company believes is important.

General Electric officials long have stated in strong terms that the company makes no effort to try to form fundamental U.S. defense or foreign policy. At the company's 1974 annual meeting, then-Chairman Reginald Jones said with reference to the B-1 bomber that GE "has been responsive to the Air Force and the Congress in terms of supplying information, facts, but that is just as far as it has gone in terms of what some might characterize as lobbying."

Nevertheless, GE is described by other sources as a fierce fighter in Washington for using its products in military systems, once the broader decision to produce these systems has been made. In 1981, Aviation Week stated that GE was participating in an "intense lobbying effort" to support use of the Mark 12A reentry vehicle in the MX missile. The Washington Post reported that GE was "lobbying on Capitol Hill" for its reentry vehicle.

Personnel interchange: GE hired 120 mid- to high-level Pentagon employees, and 12 GE employees moved to mid- or high-level positions in the Pentagon, in the period 1977-81.

General Electric is known for producing executives later hired for top positions in other corporations. GE alumni also fill a number of important government positions, most notably the Presidency. Ronald Reagan's path from actor to politician included a long stint as spokesman for GE's products and political views.

Scientists and technologists from GE have filled a number of important positions within the defense bureaucracy over the years.

Contingency Planning and Prospects

Contingency planning: General Electric probably has as successful a record for conversion between military and commercial production as any company in America. Fortune magazine described the company's World War II shift from commercial colossus to leading defense contractor in a 1942 article:

> General Electric is not only making more different war products than any other company but is also undergoing more radical changes in less than two years than it has in 20 previous years. By the end of 1942, GE will have tripled what it used to regard as its "normal" volume. Beyond that, it is completely altering the composition of its volume. Last year, for example, it made some $100 million worth of household appliances; by the end of 1942 practically all of them will be replaced by lethal appliances.

Eventually, as noted earlier, GE quadrupled its business to more than $1 billion a year. Of course, conversion to military production is quite different from the reverse, given an assured market (the government) and the urgency of purpose. However, GE successfully reconverted back to civilian production after the war, in the process consolidating its new high level of production. GE's planning for reconversion began in 1941. In Fortune's 1942 article, GE's postwar plans are referred to as "a sheaf of blueprints on which the new world is worked out to three decimal points, and in which its own position is as clearly defined as the details of one of its turbines." Then-GE president Charles E. Wilson vowed that GE would stay a billion-dollar company, and he set up the conversion planning process that it needed to do so.

In 1970, GE Chairman Fred J. Borch wrote to a Senate committee that for GE, "the movement of manpower and technology back and forth between our commercial and defense activities is a constant effort, as we shift resources to meet the changing needs of the times....So, for General Electric, 'conversion' is a constant process." While Borch agreed that wind-down of the Vietnam war would present difficulties to the company, he predicted it would weather the situation well, which it did.

In 1970, GE's corporate policy was to maintain an 80 percent commercial/20 percent military breakdown in its business. With the end of the war, and with GE's new ventures into other areas, the military portion fell to about half that level, although it now appears to be up to about 15 percent. GE's DoD contracts fell from $1.5 billion in FY 1969 to $1.2 billion in FY 1974.

In 1977, GE suffered the loss of the B-1 program, which at that time brought $100 million a year in engine development work to the company. Because the company's programs on other military and commercial engines were stable or growing, the loss had only a modest impact on employees.

Prospects: General Electric's diversified defense operations generally hold bright promise over the next few years, unless major cancellations or arms control agreements result in major reductions in defense procurement. The company's military aircraft engine sales are going well in general, and the B-1 and F/A-18 contracts should be important sources of revenue and earnings for at least five years. Military requirements for satellite and other space systems show no signs of waning, and GE is well positioned in the market. The company's loss of the Mark 12A contract for the MX is a blow, and it has resulted in consolidation of space and missile operations, but GE should continue to be a major participant in strategic missile programs.

Despite increased reliance on military contracts in recent years, GE's commercial business still towers over its defense activities. The company's earnings and future sales would suffer only marginally relative to the entire company, even in the wake of a nuclear freeze and cancellation of a major contract like the F/A-18. A freeze might affect GE primarily through loss of B-1 and likely ATB (Stealth) engine contracts. Such actions probably would result also in significant layoffs, and would damage the economies of Lynn, Mass., and Cincinnati, Ohio, along with other cities dependent on such contracts.

A nuclear freeze would also drastically reduce the activities of the Pinellas plant, and eventually could be expected to reduce the defense activities of the Knolls Laboratory. This reduction would have a minor effect on the company's earnings, but it could be expected to result in substantial local layoffs. However, a large portion of the workers at these facilities are highly skilled and might be readily employable elsewhere.

General Electric Footnotes

1. Fortune, March 1942; reprinted by Fortune, Feb. 11, 1980, p. 101.
2. See John Anderson Miller, Men and Volts at War, McGraw-Hill, New York, 1947.
3. Aviation Week and Space Technology, April 26, 1982, p. 27
4. Business Week, March 28, 1983, p. 40.
5. Fortune, ibid.

General Tire & Rubber (Aerojet-General)

General Tire & Rubber, which is one of the five largest American tire makers, is considered to be the most diversified firm in the rubber industry. The company offers more than 15,000 products and a wide variety of services, including chemicals and plastics, radio and TV broadcasting, airline transportation, soft drink bottling and aerospace/ defense systems.

General Tire had net sales of $2.06 billion in 1982, down from $2.18 billion in 1981. Net income fell 84 percent to $19 million in 1982, primarily because of the depressed auto, heavy equipment, housing and construction industries. The company has about 32,000 employees. It is based in Akron, Ohio.

Government and Defense Business

Almost all of General Tire's sales to the government are through one of its two main subsidiaries, Aerojet-General Corp. of La Jolla, Calif. In 1982, Aerojet's sales to the government totaled $537 million, which represented 99 percent of General Tire's government sales and 26 percent of total sales. Aerojet has been the most profitable of General Tire's divisions.

Aerojet-General is an aerospace and defense product company that produces missile and space propulsion systems. The company has produced such systems for a wide variety of missiles, including the Sidewinder, Hawk, Harpoon and Standard conventionally armed tactical missiles and the Polaris, Minuteman, Titan and MX strategic nuclear-armed missiles. Aerojet also develops and produces sensing systems for U.S. satellites and ordnance systems. In 1982, the company's major defense programs included the second stage rocket motor for the MX missile, ammunition for the A-10 aircraft and sensor systems for defense space activities.

Aerojet has also been involved with the U.S. space program since the first unmanned test flights. The company did work on both the Gemini and Apollo missions, and it now supplies the Orbital Manuevering Subsystem (OMS) engines for the Space Shuttle.

The company also works as a subcontractor for a number of other defense contractors including Rockwell International (Space Shuttle),

Data on General Tire & Rubber
(dollar figures in millions)

	1978	1979	1980	1981	1982
GTR net sales	$2,576	$1,985	$1,866	$2,175	$2,062
GTR net income	NA	$80	$41	$111	$19
Aerospace and defense net sales	NA	$280	$349	$459	$564
Aerospace and defense sales as a percentage of total sales	NA	14%	19%	21%	27%
General Tire & Rubber's government sales	NA	NA	$339	$441	$541
Government sales as a percentage of total sales	NA	NA	18%	20%	26%
Aerojet's government sales	NA	$252	$335	$438	$537
DoD prime contract awards*	$213	$220	$318	$322	$625
Ratio of DoD prime contract awards to total sales+	.08	.11	.17	.15	.30
Total Aerojet employees	NA	NA	NA	8,500	6,200

* U.S. fiscal year, ending Sept. 30.
\+ U.S. fiscal year awards compared with calendar year sales.

McDonnell Douglas (Delta Space Launch Vehicle), Raytheon (Hawk missile) and Martin Marietta (Titan missile).

Aerojet-General is made up of five divisions, all located in California, that collaborate on a number of projects: Aerojet ElectroSystems Co., Aerojet TechSystems Co., Aerojet Ordnance Co., Aerojet Strategic Propulsion Co. and Aerojet Tactical Systems Co. Aerojet used to have an industrial products group and an engineering, fabrication and construction group, but in 1981 the company decided to dispose of all its nondefense units. General Tire said this decision was made because "it would be advantageous to concentrate Aerojet's efforts in the aerospace, defense and technological areas in which it has demonstrated particular expertise over so many years and which are indicating increasing demands in the period ahead."

General Tire purchased a major interest in Aerojet in 1943, a year after the propulsion company began. Aerojet has been consistently profitable since that time. Sales in 1982 were $564 million, up from $458 million in 1981. Aerojet employed 6,200 people in 1982.

Aerojet propelled General Tire to the 30th spot on DoD's top contractor list in 1982. Of the $625 million in prime contracts awarded to General Tire, all but $.05 million went to Aerojet.

General Tire & Rubber's Nuclear Weapons-Related Contracts
(in millions of dollars)

Primary Systems		Secondary Systems	
FY 1981		FY1981	
MX missile	$66	Titan booster	$7.5
Titan missile	$51		
Minuteman missile	$16	Other current contracts	
Polaris missile	$2.9	Defense Meteorological Satellite Program	

Nuclear Weapons-Related Programs

Aerojet-General has been involved in the production of nuclear weapons since the first generation of ICBMs was built in the early 1960s. To date, the company has developed and produced rocket propulsion for the Titan, Polaris, Minuteman and MX missiles. Over the years, these programs have involved billions of dollars and thousands of employees. The company does not release figures on its accumulated income from specific systems or the number of employees that have worked on each system.

In FY 1981, Aerojet received prime contracts for primary nuclear weapons systems worth at least $136 million. Its contracts for secondary systems totaled at least $7.5 million.

Primary systems:

MX missile--Aerojet-General is the contractor for the MX's second stage propulsion system.

In 1978, Aerojet received a contract for the MX's propulsion system worth $152.3 million. Supplementary additions to this contract have brought the total to $242.5 million. More than a dozen companies serve as subcontractors to Aerojet on this contract, including Avco and McDonnell Douglas.

In FY 1981, Aerojet received MX contracts worth at least $66 million. In FY 1983, Aerojet received a contract worth $241 million for completion of full scale engineering development of the MX's second stage propulsion. Aerojet expects to manufacture the second stage propulsion system when the MX goes into production.

Minuteman missile--Aerojet-General designed and produced the second stage propulsion system for both the Minuteman II and Minuteman III. In all, the company has produced more than 3,000 Minuteman motors. Although the Minuteman production lines have closed, Aerojet continues to refurbish the missiles.

In FY 1981, Aerojet's Minuteman contracts totaled $16 million. Under these contracts, Aerojet will provide various components for the missiles, including propulsion and propellant equipment.

In FY 1983, Aerojet received a contract worth $27 million to overhaul 57 Minuteman rocket motors.

Titan missile--Aerojet-General designed and produced the first and second stage propulsion systems for the Titan I and Titan II ICBMs in the late 1950s and early 1960s. The Titan I was retired from active service in 1964. The Titan II soon will be replaced by the MX missile. In 1981 and 1982, Aerojet-General continued to refurbish the propulsion systems in the Titan II. Aerojet's FY 1981 contracts for the Titan ICBMs totaled $52 million.

Polaris missile--Aerojet-General developed and produced the first stage propulsion system for the Polaris. Its involvement with the system has decreased with the decommissioning of the missile. In 1981, Aerojet had one Polaris contract worth $2.9 million for maintenance, repair and alteration.

Secondary systems:

Titan III launch vehicle--Aerojet also designed and produced the first and second stage propulsion system for the Titan III, a variant of the Titan ICBM that is used to launch satellites. It was used extensively before the reusable Space Shuttle was developed. Now it will be maintained as a backup for the shuttle.

In FY 1981, Aerojet's Titan III contracts totaled at least $7.5 million. In FY 1982 and FY 1983, Aerojet received contracts worth at least $55 million for Titan III rocket engines, spare parts or launch support.

Defense Meteorological Satellite Program--In FY 1983, Aerojet received a contract worth $9.5 million for four microwave temperature sounders that will be used on one of the DMSP satellites.

Aerojet-Government Relationship

Political action committees: Aerojet-General's Aeropac is one of three General Tire political action committees. Aeropac started giving campaign contributions in the 1979-80 election cycle, when its contributions totaled $2,500.

In the 1981-82 election period, Aeropac contributed $24,709 to 38 candidates, a ten-fold increase. Twenty-eight percent of these contributions went to members of congressional defense-related committees. Aeropac's largest contributions were $2,000 each to Sens. Howard Cannon (D-Nev.), the ranking minority member of the Senate Armed Services Committee, Robert Byrd (D-W.Va.), the Senate minority leader, and Pete Wilson (R-Calif.), then a candidate for the Senate.

Washington office: Aerojet-General told IRRC that the sole purpose of its Washington office is to handle contract matters with the Pentagon. While Aerojet itself does not have a registered lobbyist, General Tire & Rubber has two: Charles Crutchfield of Charlotte, N.C., and the firm of Califano, Ross and Heineman.

Personnel interchange: Aerojet hired 28 mid- to high-level DoD employees between 1977 and 1981. One Aerojet employee moved to a mid- to high-level position in the Pentagon during the same period.

Contingency Planning and Prospects

Aerojet-General has experienced some cutbacks in weapons contracts in its 40-year history. A company spokesman told IRRC that when major cutbacks result in layoffs, the company has no legal obligation to its employees, but feels a strong moral obligation toward them. When cutbacks occur, he said, the company provides a job bank as well as job search, guidance and counseling services. In one instance, Aerojet was able to place 90 percent of its laid-off workers with other firms.

Such a success rate may be due in part to the make-up of Aerojet's work force. Aerojet's spokesman told IRRC that the company employs a very large percentage of highly skilled technicians who sometimes can be transferred among its five divisions as contracts demand. He also said that Aerojet retrains its workers when necessary.

The cancellation of the MX missile would definitely result in a major layoff of Aerojet employees. The company says that figures on the number of employees that would be affected cannot be determined because there is extensive overlap among programs. Aerojet says that if the MX were to be canceled, it would once again assist employees in finding new work.

Honeywell

Honeywell is one of the most homogeneous defense contractors. From its beginnings as a thermostat manufacturer in the 1920s, the company has followed a straight path of expansion in the controls field. Today, Honeywell still makes thermostats and other residential and industrial control systems. To this business base, it has added aerospace and defense control products such as inertial guidance systems for planes, missiles and submarines and, most recently, computers. The information systems segment, which includes computers, now is Honeywell's largest line of business. It accounted for about 31 percent of the company's 1982 sales.

Honeywell's total revenues were $5.5 billion in 1982, up from $5.4 billion in 1981. Net income rose from $259 million to $271 million, which the company says reflects the gain on the sale of two computer firms--Cii Honeywell Bull, a French firm, and GE Information Services Co. Not counting these gains, Honeywell's operating profits decreased from $499 million in 1981 to $427 million in 1982. Honeywell ranks 97th on the Forbes list of top manufacturing companies. The company is based in Minneapolis.

Government and Defense Business

Honeywell entered the military business before World War II when it started producing precision optical equipment for submarine periscopes and artillery. During the war, the company made aircraft control products including the first automatic pilots. Since the war, Honeywell has grown to be one of the largest manufacturers of military products. In 1982, it ranked 16th on DoD's list of top defense contractors.

The Pentagon is Honeywell's largest government customer, but the company's government business is not limited to defense products. Honeywell also works with federal and local government agencies and NASA. The company says it has been involved "in nearly all space missions since the mid-'60s."

For the military, Honeywell manufactures guidance systems and controls for a range of military vehicles from spacecraft to ships. Its other military products include military computers and related products, torpedoes and other antisubmarine warfare equipment, aircraft dispenser and guided weapons, including cluster bombs similar to the ones used in Vietnam, ammunition for the A-10 attack aircraft and the

Data on Honeywell
(dollar figures in millions)

	1978	1979	1980	1981	1982
Revenues	$3,548	$4,210	$4,925	$5,351	$5,490
Operating profits	$384	$471	$517	$499	$427
U.S. government contract revenues	$586	$672	$832	$949	$1,044
Ratio of U.S. government contract revenues to total revenues	.17	.16	.17	.18	.19
Revenues from aerospace and defense contracts with U.S. government	$389	$484	$613	$696	$771
Aerospace and defense revenues from U.S. government as percentage of total revenues	11%	11%	12%	13%	14%
Defense Department contract awards*	$545	$658	$687	$838	$1,217
Ratio of DoD contract awards to total revenues+	.15	.16	.14	.16	.22
Total Honeywell employees	86,328	94,620	97,202	96,923	94,062

* U.S. fiscal year, ending Sept. 30.
+ U.S. fiscal year awards compared with calendar year revenues.

M-1 tank, and chemical defense systems designed to protect soldiers from the effects of chemical weapons.

Honeywell's nuclear weapons-related contracts are described below. Other major contracts awarded in 1982 include:

-- a 10-year, $603 million contract for shipboard computers,
-- several contracts worth a total of $94 million for classified electronics,
-- $72 million for an anti-tank ammunition (GAU-8/A) that is designed for A-10 attack aircraft,
-- several contracts worth a total of $28 million for infrared reconnaissance equipment,
-- $9.2 million for parts for the Rockeye II cluster bomb.

In all, Honeywell received government contracts worth $1,044 million in 1982. Its aerospace and defense segment accounted for 74 percent of these sales, information systems accounted for 21 percent, and control systems and products accounted for the remaining 5 percent.

From DoD, Honeywell received FY 1982 prime contract awards worth $1,217 million for projects that will be carried out over the next several years. From NASA, Honeywell received FY 1982 prime contracts worth $28 million.

Backlog and research and development: Honeywell's backlog of orders totaled $3.4 billion at the end of 1982, of which 32 percent were government defense orders and 4 percent were other government orders. The company's 1982 research and development costs totaled $751 million, of which 31 percent was funded by the government.

Defense employees: Honeywell estimates that 17 percent of its 94,062 employees worked on defense projects in 1982. An additional 2 percent worked on other government projects. A spokesman for Honeywell told IRRC that these estimates were based on sales figures because the ratio between sales and number of employees is fairly close.

Nuclear Weapons-Related Programs

Of Honeywell's $838 million in FY 1981 DoD prime contract awards, at least $127 million went toward components--mostly control systems and computers--for primary nuclear weapons systems, and at least $9 million went toward components for secondary systems.

Primary systems:

MX missile--As early as the 1960s, Honeywell received contracts to develop a guidance system for a new mobile land-based intercontinental ballistic missile, now known as the MX.[1] In 1980, Honeywell received its largest MX contract, under which it developed the part of the missile's reentry guidance and control systems that measures and records acceleration, called the specific force integrating receiver (SFIR). Honeywell received $34 million for this contract, which was completed in February 1983.

Before 1980, Honeywell had received two smaller (also completed) contracts for similar research and development work on MX guidance and control. These contracts had a total combined value of $8.2 million.[2]

In FY 1981, Honeywell received prime contracts worth at least $12 million for work on the MX's command and control systems--the "nerves" of the missile. The company received another $19 million for MX guidance parts. In FY 1982, Honeywell received a $13 million prime contract for work on the MX and computers for the Army.

In addition to its prime contracts from DoD, Honeywell has MX subcontracts from Rockwell International and Avco. Under the Rockwell subcontract, worth $12.4 million, Honeywell is testing hardware changes for the MX's guidance and control computer housing

Honeywell's Nuclear Weapons-Related Contracts
(in millions of dollars)

Primary Systems		Secondary Systems	
FY 1981		FY1981	
B-52 bomber	$88	Nuclear capable fighter components	$2
MX missile	$12	AN/BQR-21 sonar	$7
Trident missile	$11		
Poseidon missile	$1	Other currect contracts	
Minuteman missile	$6	VHSIC program	
BMD program	$6	Cruise missile components	
ABRES	$3	Asroc rocket	
		WWMCCS program	

system. Under the smaller Avco subcontract, Honeywell is working on automatic test equipment for the missile.[3]

Most of Honeywell's MX work takes place at its St. Petersburg, Fla., facility (SFIR and the computer housing system) and its St. Louis Park, Minn., facility (automatic test equipment).

B-52 bomber--Honeywell has worked on several components for the B-52 bomber. Its largest contract is for inertial navigation systems, called SPN/GEANS (pronounced spin-jeans), for the plane. In 1978, the Air Force ordered 700 of these systems for the B-52 fleet. They originally were designed for the B-1 bomber, but after the B-1 cancellation the Air Force decided to use them on B-52s. SPN/GEANS will give the B-52s the highly accurate navigational data necessary to launch Air-Launched Cruise Missles. This contract will be completed in 1984.[4]

In FY 1981, Honeywell received $88 million in prime contract awards for the B-52. These included one award worth $79 million for work on the plane's airframe structural components, one worth $5 million for navigational instruments, and two miscellaneous contracts worth a total of $4.2 million. In FY 1982, Honeywell received an additional $24 million in B-52 prime contracts, mostly for inertial navigation modification kits. In FY 1983, Honeywell received another $90 million for similar work.

Components for the Trident, Poseidon and Minuteman missiles--In FY 1981, Honeywell received $11 million to work on the Trident missile guidance system's memory and $1.2 million to upgrade Trident's predecessor, the Poseidon missile. Also in FY 1981, Honeywell received prime contract awards worth $6 million to repair the Minuteman missile's inertial guidance system.

Ballistic missile defense--Honeywell received several prime contracts worth a total of $3.4 million in FY 1980 and $6 million in FY 1981 for research on ballistic missile defense systems. In 1982, Martin Marietta selected Honeywell to produce an inertial navigation system for its Sentry antiballistic system's interceptor missile.[5]

Advanced ballistic reentry system (ABRES)--In FY 1981, Honeywell received prime contract awards worth $3 million for the ABRES program.

Secondary systems:

Sonar--Honeywell produces components for a passive sonar system (designated AN/BQR-21) used on strategic and attack submarines to detect and track other nuclear submarines. Honeywell's prime contract awards for these components totaled at least $6.8 million in FY 1981.

Nuclear-capable fighter plane components--In FY 1981, Honeywell received at least $2 million for miscellaneous work on nuclear-capable F-15, F-16, F-101, F-104 and F-106 fighter planes.

Antisubmarine rocket (Asroc)--Honeywell has been the prime contractor for the Asroc antisubmarine weapon since 1956.[6] The Asroc is the primary antisubmarine weapon for U.S. destroyers and other ships. It can be armed with a one-kiloton nuclear depth charge or a non-nuclear torpedo.

Very high-speed integrated circuits (VHSIC)--Along with Texas Instruments, Hughes Aircraft, TRW, IBM and Westinghouse, Honeywell is involved in the development of a new integrated circuit that will form the base of the next generation of military electronics. This very high-speed integrated circuit (VHSIC) will have applications for all kinds of military systems, especially electronic warfare, communications and radar. In 1982, the company's Solid State Development Center continued its work on submicron circuitry for the VHSIC program.

Cruise missiles--Honeywell says it has worked on the radar altimeter (an instrument for measuring altitude) for the tactical version of the sea-launched cruise missile. In 1983, Honeywell received a contract worth $6 million to conduct research on an advanced inertial navigation system for cruise missiles and airplanes.

Worldwide Military Command and Control System (WWMCCS)--In FY 1983, Honeywell has received two contracts worth a total of $18 million for staff support and computer support for WWMCCS.

Honeywell-Government Relationship

Political action committee: Honeywell's political action committee contributed $63,966 to congressional candidates in the 1979-80 election cycle and $81,600 in the 1981-82 cycle. Eight percent of the 1979-80 contributions and 11 percent of the 1981-82 contributions went to incumbent candidates holding positions on House and Senate committees and subcommittees concerned with the military and its budget.[7]

In 1981-82, Honeywell's largest contributions went mainly to candidates from Minnesota, Honeywell's home state. The PAC also gave $4,000 to Sen. Harrison Schmitt (R-N.M.), then chairman of the space subcommittee and a member of the defense appropriations subcommittee, and $3,500 to Sen. Pete Wilson (R-Calif.).

Washington office: Honeywell employs one registered lobbyist and one other Honeywell professional at its Washington, D.C., office. Corporate Secretary Sigurd Ueland Jr. says the responsibilities of this office are to gather information, follow legislation and keep in contact with trade associations, as well as to lobby. He stressed that Honeywell has a written policy against lobbying "for or against specific levels of government spending or for specific products." For example, he said, Honeywell would not take a position on a particular weapons system such as the MX missile.

Personnel interchange: Honeywell hired 103 mid- to high-level DoD employees between 1977 and 1981. Twenty Honeywell employees moved to similiar positions in DoD during the same period.

Contingency Planning and Prospects

Contingency planning: In its 1982 Form 10K, Honeywell said that although its government business is significant, its "dependence upon individual programs is minimized by the large variety of products and services it provides." Ueland told IRRC that this statement typifies the company's approach to contingency planning. He said Honeywell is very careful not to develop a dependence on any individual program.

Ueland said the company also tries to minimize the effects of layoffs on its employees. In the past, he said, it has worked to place laid-off employees in other jobs within Honeywell. He said laid-off employees are given first consideration for openings within the company. Honeywell also has offered early retirement options to some employees to reduce the number of layoffs and has organized job fairs for those who have not found jobs within the company or retired early.

In 1982, Honeywell pared its information systems work force by 6 percent (1,150 people), and about 100 other employees accepted

Honeywell's early retirement option. While this policy cost Honeywell more dollars than a simple work force reduction, the company stressed that the opportunity to retain some of its newer employees and the maintenance of company morale were worth the expense.[8]

Prospects: Because Honeywell's inertial guidance and control systems can be used on a large number of weapons systems, its business is flexible and could adapt to many military force structures. Ueland told IRRC that if the MX were canceled, Honeywell would be in a position to receive contracts for guidance systems for the proposed small ICBM. He noted that Honeywell could even gain on this cancellation because it is likely that the number of small missiles built would exceed the number of MX missiles that would have been built, and thus more inertial navigation systems would be needed. If a freeze on nuclear weapons were negotiated, he said, Honeywell certainly would lose some business in the short run (Honeywell's freeze-related contracts equaled approximately 3 percent of its FY 1981 DoD awards), but the company is confident that it is in a position to refurbish the inertial guidance systems on the existing Minuteman missiles. In the case of a total arms control package, Ueland said, Honeywell's missile guidance business probably would be affected adversely, but the company as a whole would not be.

Honeywell Footnotes

1. Gold, et al., MisGuided Expenditure, Council on Economic Priorities, New York, 1981, p. 176.
2. Ibid., footnotes to Table A.
3. Ibid., Table C.
4. Aviation Week and Space Technology, "Honeywell Breaks into the Inertial Market," p. 83-85.
5. Aviation Week and Space Technology, "Tests Find New Uses for Laser Gyros," Sept. 9, 1982, p. 281.
6. Ronald T. Pretty, ed., Jane's Weapons Systems 1982-83, Jane's Publishing Co. Ltd., London, 1982, p. 140-1.
7. Honeywell reported somewhat different PAC totals from those IRRC received from the Federal Election Commission. For the sake of consistency, the FEC figures are included in the text. Honeywell says it contributed a total of $74,875 to federal candidates in 1979-80 and a total of $99,000 in 1981-82.
8. The New York Times, "The Rise in Worker Buyouts," Feb. 23, 1983.

Litton

When two former Hughes Aircraft executives purchased Electro Dynamics Corp. in 1953, it was a small electronics firm. Under their direction, the company--renamed Litton Industries--quickly grew, mainly through acquisition, into one of the first large high technology conglomerates. Still a major conglomerate, Litton Industries had sales of almost $5 billion in its fiscal year ending July 31, 1982. Net earnings were $315 million, slightly above 1981 earnings of $312 million. In 1978, Litton lost money after it paid the Navy $333 million to settle a contract dispute, but otherwise the company has increased its earnings each year since 1977. Commercial and industrial earnings fell in 1982 because of the recession, but earnings in defense electronics and resource exploration rose enough to compensate. Litton is based in Beverly Hills, Calif. In 1982, the company ranked 111th on the Forbes top sales list.

Litton Industries has five major business segments: advanced electronic systems (11 divisions), business systems (7 divisions), electronic and electrical products (20 divisions), industrial systems and services (26 divisions), and marine engineering and production (2 divisions--Ingalls Shipbuilding and Ingalls Industrial Products in Pascagoula, Miss.). The industrial systems and services segment brought in 29 percent of Litton's sales in 1982, and the other four segments each contributed between 15 and 20 percent.

Early in 1983, Litton acquired Itek Corp., a company known for its defense electronic equipment and industrial graphics. (See box.)

Government and Defense Business

Contracts from the U.S. government have represented about 30 percent of Litton's sales over the last six years, 27 percent in 1982. The company's advanced electronic systems segment and the marine engineering and production segment perform the bulk of its government--mostly military--work, but the electronic and electrical products divisions also receive some defense contracts.

In 1982, 54 percent of Litton's advanced electronic systems sales and 74 percent of marine engineering and production sales were to the U.S. government. Another 13 percent of Litton's advanced electronic systems sales went to Saudi Arabia, where Litton is building an air defense system under a 1979 contract worth a total of $1.6 billion. Inertial guidance and navigation systems are the leading products for several

Itek Corp.

Itek Corp., acquired by Litton early in 1983, is a technology company with a foot in two fields: defense electronics and industrial graphics. Sales in 1981 totaled $312 million, and net income totaled $4 million. The company is based in Lexington, Mass.

As part of Litton Industries, Itek will expand the company's defense business. Itek is expected to receive more than $1 billion in defense sales through 1987, primarily for electronic devices designed to warn pilots of enemy radar signals and approaching missiles.

Itek also is a leading supplier of photographic equipment used on military satellites. In the 1950s, the company produced an optical, telescopic camera that tracked Sputnik for the Pentagon. It also produced the cameras used on the Voyager and Apollo flights.

In FY 1981, Itek received DoD prime contracts worth $94 million. Under some of these contracts, Itek will provide electronics equipment for the SH-60 Seahawk helicopter and the F-105 nuclear-capable fighter plane. In FY 1982, Itek's DoD contract awards totaled $82 million. Major awards included electronics equipment for the F-16 fighter plane and the A-7 attack plane.

of Litton's advanced electronic systems divisions (Guidance and Control Division, Litton Systems Canada, LITEF and Litton Italia). These systems are designed to help aircraft stay closer to their planned flight routes and, as a result, reduce fuel consumption and increase safety. Over the last 20 years, Litton has sold more than 17,000 inertial guidance and navigation systems to both commercial and military customers, and it has orders for thousands more.

Other advanced electronic systems divisions produce a variety of defense electronic equipment including electronic surveillance systems for reconnaissance aircraft (the RF-4C Phantom and the E-2 Hawkeye); electronic warfare components and information command and control systems for tactical aircraft; and fire control, communications, data processing and computer systems for planes, artillery equipment and ships.

Since the late 1950s, Litton's Ingalls Shipbuilding has built a variety of Navy ships, from nuclear-powered attack submarines to destroyers,

Data on Litton
(dollar figures in millions)

	1978	1979	1980	1981	1982
Total sales	$3,653	$4,088	$4,246	$4,943	$4,942
Net earnings	($91)*	$189	$291	$311	$315
U.S. government sales	$1,059	$1,063	$1,147	$1,236	$1,334
U.S. government sales as a percentage of total sales	29%	26%	27%	25%	27%
DoD prime contract awards+	$1,557	$832	$652	$1,385	$1,317
Ratio of DoD prime contract awards to total sales^	.43	.20	.15	.28	.27
Backlog as of July 31, 1982	$2,506	$4,331	$4,507	$4,403	$5,264
Total Litton employees	90,400	77,700	75,400	76,700	75,000

* Loss.
+ U.S. fisal year, ending Sept. 30.
^ U.S. fiscal year awards compared with calendar year sales.

guided missile cruisers, and other auxiliary ships. Ingalls is one of the nine private U.S. shipyards considered capable of warship construction. The yard also builds offshore oil rigs and rail cars, and it overhauls and modernizes older warships.

Military products from the electronic and electrical products divisions include components for electronic countermeasures systems, high power radars, and fire control systems. This segment also supplies the large electric motors that form part of the propulsion systems for Trident submarines and Navy escort ships (patrol frigates).

Defense dependence: Litton has been a major defense contractor for more than 20 years. In 1982, Litton ranked 15th on the DoD's top contractor list, with $1.3 billion in prime contract awards.

Like so many defense contractors, Litton wants to take advantage of the recent increase in government military spending, and the company has charted defense electronics and shipbuilding as potential growth areas. Because electronic systems are important additions to new and existing weapons systems, growth for Litton in this field seems assured. Shipbuilding is less certain. Ingalls is one of the few shipyards in the United States with enough work to keep it busy through the 1980s, but orders for the 1990s are still in the bidding stage.[1] In 1982 Litton received a contract to design an amphibious assault ship and completed a proposal for the design and production of the Navy's next generation of destroyers, the DDG 51. These actions put the company in a good position to receive production contracts for the new ships.

Backlog: Litton's backlog was $5.3 billion in 1982. Defense contract backlog, both domestic and foreign, was approximately $4.4 billion. Backlog for the advanced electronic systems segment was worth $2.5 billion in 1982, and the marine engineering and production segment had a backlog of almost $2 billion.

Defense employees: In 1982, the advanced electronic systems segment employed 15,900 people, and the marine engineering and services segment employed 13,000, for a total of 28,900 employees in Litton's major defense-related segments. If employment is roughly proportional to sales, roughly 8,000 of Litton's employees in these segments worked on government projects in 1982.

Nuclear Weapons-Related Programs

Litton's prime contract awards for nuclear weapons-related systems totaled at least $897 million in FY 1981. Awards for primary nuclear weapons-related systems were $4 million. Awards for secondary systems totaled $893 million. Most of the nuclear weapons-related contracts were for inertial guidance systems and ships.

Primary systems:

Electronic countermeasures for the B-52 bomber--In FY 1981, a Litton division in San Carlos, Calif., received contract awards worth $3.9 million for work on the B-52 bomber's electronic countermeasures systems. In FY 1983, Litton has received an additional $13 million for similar work on the B-52.

Advanced ballistic missile re-entry vehicle--Litton is one of six subcontractors helping Lockheed develop and test an advanced re-entry vehicle--the part of the ballistic missile that carries the warhead to the target--for the Navy's nuclear missiles. This re-entry vehicle, called the Mark 500, will be capable of evasive maneuvers after it enters the earth's atmosphere. Although no plans exist to produce the Mark 500, the testing program is under way to ensure that such an advanced vehicle could be produced rapidly if existing U.S. reentry vehicles could not penetrate any ballistic missile defense system that the Soviet Union might deploy.[2]

Ballistic missile defense--In FY 1983, Litton received a contract worth $5.7 million to begin to assemble the materials needed for the Lode (Large Optics Demonstration Experiment) advanced mirror program, which could be used in a space-based ballistic missile defense system.

B-1B components--In FY 1981, Litton received a small contract ($11,000) for B-1B bomber components.

Litton's Nuclear Weapons-Related Contracts
(in millions of dollars)

Primary Systems		Secondary Systems	
FY 1981		FY 1981	
B-52 ECM system	$3.9	Guided missile cruisers	$743
B-1B components	*	Cruise missile guidance	$78
		AN/ALQ-131 and ALQ-119 ECM systems	$32
		Navigation and communications equipment for nuclear-capable aircraft	$20
		Destroyers	$14
		Advanced data processing at nuclear weapons-related agency	$4
		F-106 components	$2
Other current contracts		Other current contracts	
ABRES		IRS for M109 howitzer	
Ballistic missile defense lasers		Submarine motor components	
		EF-111A EW components	

*under $1 million

Secondary systems:

Litton's Ingalls Shipyard has been involved in nuclear warfare-related production for many years. In the 1960s and 1970s the yard produced 10 nuclear-capable attack submarines that are still in service. Litton's current work on secondary systems at Ingalls and other divisions includes:

Cruise missiles--Litton's Guidance and Control Division in Woodland Hills, Calif., and Litton Systems Canada are working together to produce inertial navigation systems for all versions of the cruise missile--air-launched, sea-launched and ground-launched. Developed by Litton's Woodland Hills Research Center, these systems will be essential to the cruise missile's accuracy.

In 1979, Litton was awarded a $1 billion contract to construct 5,500 cruise missile guidance systems. In 1980, the company produced the first 225 systems for the air-launched cruise missile (ALCM). In FY 1981, Litton received $78 million in awards for more work on the ALCM and for a computer for the sea- and ground-launched versions of the missile. This contract is expected to be completed within about two years. In FY 1983, Litton has received contracts worth $83 million to produce related cruise missile components.

Also in FY 1983, Ingalls Shipbuilding received contracts worth $9.3 million to begin production of a vertical launch system. This system will be used to launch cruise missiles and other weapons from surface ships and submarines. The first two launch systems will be placed on the battleship Iowa and the destroyer USS Comte DeGrasse.

Guided missile cruisers (CG-47 Ticonderoga class)--Ingalls Shipbuilding and Congoleum Corp.'s Bath Iron Works in Maine are building the Navy's new class of guided missile cruisers. (Cruisers are designed to protect aircraft carrier battle groups from air or sea attacks.) The Navy wants 24 of these 9,000 ton ships, and Litton will build at least the first nine. The first two ships--Ticonderoga and Yorktown--have been completed. They are armed with antisubmarine rockets (Asrocs), some of which have nuclear warheads. The vertical launch system will replace the Asroc launcher on future ships.

Litton received prime contract awards of at least $559 million in 1980 for the production of the first four guided missile cruisers. In FY 1981, Litton's prime contract awards for the ships totaled $743 million, of which $664 million was for initial work on the fifth and sixth ships. In 1982, the company also received a $111 million contract for the fifth ship's electronic systems. In FY 1983, Litton received a contract worth $926 for the construction of the seventh, eighth and ninth ships. Also in FY 1983, Litton received a contract worth $111 million for machinery and electronic equipment for the fifth ship and a contract worth $239 million to acquire long lead time materials for the cruisers.

Destroyers (DDG-993 Kidd class)--Early in 1976, Iran ordered six destroyers from Litton, similar in construction to the Ticonderoga class of guided missile cruisers described above. In 1976, Iran reduced its order from six to four ships, in part because Litton had increased the price from $116 million to $333 million per ship.[3] When the Shah's government fell in 1979, the rest of the order was canceled. At the suggestion of the Carter administration, Congress approved the purchase of these ships and other weapons originally sold to Iran. As part of the U.S. fleet, these destroyers carry Asrocs, which can be fitted with nuclear warheads.

Destroyers (DD963 Spruance class)--Over the last 12 years, Litton has built the entire class of 31 Spruance class destroyers for the Navy. The last ship was christened in March 1982. The largest destroyers ever built, these ships carry Asrocs and other weaponry. They also will be backfitted with vertical launch systems.

Litton received the initial contracts for the Spruance fleet in 1970. In 1979, the company received a $231 million contract for the last ship. However, Litton's involvement in this program has not ended. In FY 1981, the company received contracts worth at least $14 million for this program, some for the overhaul of four older ships, and some for the destroyers' electronic systems.

Navigation and communication equipment for nuclear-capable aircraft--Litton's prime contract awards for these systems totaled at least $20 million in FY 1981, of which $10 million went to the Navy's most sophisticated antisubmarine warfare aircraft, the nuclear-capable P-3 Orion. Awards for the F-111 and the F-4 fighter planes were $4 million and $2 million, respectively. Smaller awards went to components for the A-6 attack plane and the F-15 fighter planes.

In 1982, the company received at least $17 million for electronic systems for the F-111, $25 million for an electronic countermeasures system for the F/A-18, and at least $80 million for various electronic equipment for a variety of nuclear-capable planes, including the P-3C, A-10 and the F-16.

Jamming systems for nuclear-capable planes--Litton works on two jamming systems, the AN/ALQ-131 and AN/ALQ-119, that are designed for a number of aircraft including the nuclear-capable F-4, F-15, F-16 and F-111 fighter planes, as well as the A-7 and A-10 attack aircraft. Litton received prime contract awards worth $32 million for these two jammers in FY 1981. Jamming systems protect aircraft by preventing radar and other tracking systems from locating them accurately.

Other--In FY 1981, Litton received contracts worth $2 million for components for the nuclear-capable F-106 Delta Dart, an older plane soon to be replaced by F-15s, and $4 million for advanced data processing at a satellite facility where most work applies to nuclear weapons-related systems.

Other nuclear weapons-related projects mentioned in the company's annual report include:

- Large electric motors that form part of the propulsion systems for Trident submarines and the Navy's escort ships (patrol frigates).

- Cockpit displays (LED) for the nuclear-capable F-16 aircraft (produced under subcontract to General Dynamics).

- Electronic warfare components for the EF-111A.

- Inertial reference system for the nuclear-capable M-109 howitzer artillery gun.

Litton-Government Relationship

Litton's relationship with the government has been rockier than that of most defense contractors. Although the disputes themselves have been similar to other government-defense contractor disputes, Litton seems to have been less successful in settling them amicably. Two cases, in particular, have stretched out over years. One, which concerned costs for three Litton nuclear-powered submarines, erupted in the early 1970s and has yet to be settled. The second, which concerned cost overruns on a different contract, ended in 1978 after six years of feuding. Litton paid a negotiated settlement of $333 million (before taxes) to settle this dispute.

Litton also has become embroiled in some labor disputes that could affect the company's status as a defense contractor. The disputes have been serious enough to motivate several Litton unions to publicize them in hopes of bringing about what the unions see as necessary reforms in Litton's labor practices. In support of the unions' efforts, Rep. Paul Simon (D-Ill.) and 100 cosponsors have introduced legislation that seeks to bar firms with repeated labor law violations from receiving government contracts. The bill has cleared a House subcommittee. Ingalls Shipbuilding is among the Litton divisions that the National Labor Relations Board has charged with labor law violations.

Political action committee: Litton's PAC (Lepac) contributed a total of $409,560 to candidates for federal offices over the last four years: $191,010 in 1979-80 and $218,550 in 1981-82. In 1979-80, Lepac gave 14 percent of its contributions to members of defense-related committees. In 1981-82, almost 26 percent went to such members.

Major contributions in 1979-80 went to Ronald Reagan ($5,050); Daniel Quayle (R-Ind., $4,500), candidate for the Senate; and Bobbi Fielder (R-Calif., $3,000) and John Hiler (R-Ind., $1,500), candidates for the House. In 1981-82, major contributions went to Sen. John Stennis (D-Miss., $10,000), then chairman of the Senate Armed Services Committee, Rep. William Chappell (D-Fla., $4,500), member of the House defense appropriations subcommittee, and several Republicans. More than three-quarters of Lepac's 1981-82 contributions went to Republicans.

Washington office: Litton declined to provide IRRC with information on the company's lobbyists, or on its Washington office. According to other sources, Litton employs three Washington counsels or consultants: Howney & Simon; Miller and Chevalier, Chartered; and Patton, Boggs and Blow. Litton's Washington office is represented by at least three staff members.

Personnel interchange: Litton's chief executive officer and one of the company's directors have backgrounds in the military. Chief executive officer Fred O'Green formerly worked at the Naval Ordnance Lab and was once the technical director of all space programs at Lockheed Missiles and Space Co. Director Thomas B. Hayward is a retired Navy admiral who served as chief of naval operations from July 1978 to early 1982. (Roy Ash, who founded Litton with Charles Thornton, left Litton to head the Office of Management and Budget in the Nixon administration.)

Litton hired 115 mid- to high-level DoD employees between 1977 and 1982, of whom 97 percent were former military officers. Fourteen Litton employees moved to mid- to high-level positions in the DoD during the same period.

Contingency Planning and Prospects

As a highly diversified company with a mix of governmental and commercial business, Litton is not as vulnerable to swings in military programs as many other defense companies. While the company is somewhat protected, however, its divisions that work primarily under defense contracts are not. Ingalls Shipbuilding may be particularly vulnerable because it depends on a small number of large contracts to stay in business. Litton does not appear to maintain contingency plans to assist workers in primarily defense-related divisions in the event of contract cancellations. Further, Litton is now scouting for more defense contracts and, if it is successful, the defense dependency of certain divisions is likely to increase.

The cruise missile and ballistic missile re-entry vehicle contracts would be the only Litton contracts significantly affected by a freeze or other arms control agreements. If the cruise missile were canceled, the company would lose roughly 6 percent of its prime military contracts, judging from 1981 awards. If employment is roughly proportional to sales, the company also would have to lay off some 500 employees.

Major reductions in defense spending could affect all of Litton's nuclear weapons-related programs. Litton's guided missile cruiser contracts seem the most vulnerable to defense budget cuts. And, if Ingalls does not receive contracts to build some of the next generation of destroyers or the new amphibious assault ship, the yard could find itself without work in the 1990s unless commercial shipbuilding picks up substantially.

Litton Footnotes

1. Business Week, June 28, 1982, p. 133.
2. Ronald T. Pretty, ed., Jane's Weapons Systems 1982-83, Jane's Publishing Co. Ltd., London, 1982, p. 12.
3. Tom Gervasi, Arsenal of Democracy, Grove Press, New York, 1981, p. 261.

Lockheed

Lockheed, long a leader in the aerospace industry, develops and produces space systems, aircraft and missiles, as well as electronic subsystems and ground support systems. Lockheed also is involved in shipbuilding and ship repair. The corporation is composed of 14 subsidiaries, and it divides its business into four major categories: aircraft and related services; missiles, space and electronics; aerospace support; and shipbuilding.

Lockheed reported $5.51 billion in sales from continuing operations in fiscal year 1981, up 8 percent from 1981. Net earnings in 1982 were $207 million, compared with a loss of $289 million in 1981. The loss in 1981 was due to a $396 million write-off caused by the cancellation of a major program, the L-1011 Tri-Star, a wide-bodied commercial jet transport. The company said it canceled the Tri-Star in part because of the depressed state of the commercial aircraft market.

Lockheed devotes most of its energies to aerospace production. The sale of missiles, space and electronics systems, aircraft and related services, and aerospace support systems accounted for about 95 percent of the company's sales from continuing operations in FY 1981. Shipbuilding and repair ventures, and other activities, were responsible for 5 percent.

Lockheed was the 90th largest U.S. company on the Forbes 500 list of sales leaders for 1982.

Government and Defense Business

Lockheed relies heavily upon business from the U.S. and foreign governments in its sales efforts. Sales to the U.S. government alone totaled $4.55 billion and accounted for 81 percent of the company's sales from continuing operations in 1981. Sales to foreign governments amounted to $859 million in 1981, accounting for another 15 percent of total sales. Commercial sales, valued at $200 million, constituted a small percentage of Lockheed's continuing operations. Most of the company's government sales are of military products and services.

Major current defense production programs include: the C-130 Hercules and C-5B Galaxy aircraft, used by the military as a cargo and personnel transport; the P-3C Orion antisubmarine warfare aircraft; the TR-1 tactical and SR-71 strategic reconnaissance aircraft; the CP-140 maritime patrol aircraft; the Trident I sea-launched ballistic missile;

Data on Lockheed
(dollar figures in millions)

	1978	1979	1980	1981	1982
Total sales	$3,485	$4,058	$5,396	$6,233	$5,613
Sales from continuing operations	$3,191	3,532	4,445	5,176	$5,613
Net earnings	$65	$57	$28	($289)*	$207
Sales to the U.S. government	$1,968	$2,317	$3,161	3,852	$4,554
Government sales as a percentage of total sales	56%	57%	59%	62%	81%
Government sales as a percentage of sales from continuing operations	70%	66%	71%	74%	81%
DoD prime contract awards+	$2,226	$1,797	$2,037	$2,657	$3,499
Ratio of DoD prime contract awards to total sales^	.64	.44	.38	.43	.62
Total Lockheed employees	61,500	66,500	74,600	71,300	70,200

* Loss.
\+ U.S. fiscal year, ending Sept. 30.
^ U.S. fiscal year contract awards compared with calendar year sales.

the MK-86 weapon control system used in conjunction with conventional missiles aboard some of the Navy's newest combat ships; the LSD amphibious assault vessel; submarine tenders; overhauling and servicing of destroyers; and various naval command and communications systems, including a guidance system for the Harpoon antiship missile and the Tomahawk cruise missile.

In 1982, Lockheed won a protracted and controversial battle with Boeing to produce a new cargo transport aircraft. The result is the company's $7.8 billion C-5B program.

Lockheed also modifies and maintains existing systems, including cargo aircraft, that it produced originally for the military. Lockheed maintains the Navy's Poseidon and Trident sea-launched ballistic missile force as well as the British Navy's Polaris submarine-launched ballistic missile arsenal, and it is installing advanced avionics and radar systems in the Navy's S-3 Viking and P-3C Orion antisubmarine warfare aircraft.

Lockheed is developing several new weapons systems, most notably the Trident II (D-5) sea-launched ballistic missile. In addition, in 1981 the company conducted developmental work on various advanced radar systems, on a space laser defense system, and on battlefield targeting systems.

Subsidiaries of Lockheed provide ground support and management at the Johnson Space Center in Houston, Tex., the Goddard Space Flight Center in Maryland, both run by NASA, and the Army missile range in White Sands, N.M. In 1983, Lockheed won the contract to provide support services for future Space Shuttle missions.

The majority of government production is carried out by five of Lockheed's subsidiaries. Lockheed-Georgia Co., based in Marietta, Ga., is responsible for building and modifying cargo transports. Lockheed-California Co., whose headquarters is in Burbank, works on the remaining aircraft programs. All ballistic missile contracts are handled by Lockheed Missile and Space Co., in Sunnyvale, Calif., and shipbuilding and repair are the responsibility of Lockheed Shipbuilding and Construction Co., based in Seattle. Lockheed Electronics Co., in New Jersey, manages the production of electronic subsystems.

Since World War II, Lockheed consistently has ranked among the top 10 DoD prime contractors. The first Lockheed aircraft to go to war was the Hudson, a bomber version of a commercial transport that was exported to Britain in 1939. The company delivered more than 10,000 P-38 Lightning fighter planes to the U.S. government during the war years. It was also during World War II that Lockheed began producing airplanes designed to haul large cargo loads.

The company's volume of business again expanded rapidly as a result of the Korean war, which Anthony Sampson has described as "above all, a Lockheed war."[1] Lockheed cargo planes were used extensively to transport men and materiel across the Pacific, and the P-80 Shooting Star, the first American jet fighter, which Lockheed designed and manufactured, flew approximately 40 percent of all combat missions over Korea. In a move that subsequently came to be viewed as a turning point in the company's growth, in 1950 Lockheed acquired its Marietta, Ga., facilities, where it initially assembled Boeing-designed B-47 bombers for use in the Korean war.

The company continued to grow through the 1960s, a period during which Sampson says the "Pentagon...was [Lockheed's] mainstay."[2] Much of this growth resulted from sales of weapons systems to foreign governments, and many of these sales were arranged with the assistance of the Pentagon. By 1968, Lockheed had become the world's largest arms company.

Lockheed was ranked as the Defense Department's fifth largest prime contractor in 1982. The company received $3.50 billion in prime contract awards in FY 1982, up 32 percent from the 1981 level of $2.66 billion. In 1982, the ratio of DoD prime contract awards to sales was .62, compared with only .46 in 1980, only two years earlier.

Defense employees: Lockheed employed about 70,200 persons at the end of 1982, down from 71,300 a year earlier. The 1981 employees included 25,300 in southern California, 22,000 in northern California,

12,900 in Georgia and 11,000 in various other locations in the United States and abroad.

Lockheed Chairman Roy Anderson said in 1982 that Lockheed is "90 percent military to 10 percent civilian."[3] If those percentages apply to the work force as well as to sales, roughly 64,000 employees work on military-related programs. Lockheed Missile and Space, the company's largest division, accounted for 47 percent of the corporation's 1981 sales, and 40 percent of the division's work in 1981 was on nuclear armed missiles.

Nuclear Weapons-Related Programs

Lockheed formally entered the nuclear arms industry in 1954 with the establishment of its missile division. Shortly thereafter, Lockheed emerged as the prime contractor and program manager for the Navy's Submarine Launched Ballistic Missile (SLBM) project.

The first SLBM, the Polaris A-1, was fired successfully from a submerged submarine in July 1960. Lockheed's Missile and Space subsidiary delivered a more advanced SLBM, the Polaris A-2, to the Navy in 1962. Two years later, the Navy introduced another upgraded version of the Polaris, designated A-3.

Lockheed has served as the prime contractor for the subsequent generations of American SLBMs as well. Lockheed's Poseidon C-3 SLBM became operational in 1970. DoD awarded Lockheed Missile and Space contracts for the development of the Trident C-4 in 1974, and the company began delivery of the missile five years later. Lockheed has maintained and modernized the missiles over the years.

Lockheed also is responsible for the production of secondary nuclear weapons systems, notably the nuclear-capable P-3 Orion and S-3 Viking aircraft used in antisubmarine warfare.

In FY 1981, DoD awarded Lockheed at least $914 million in prime contracts for work on primary nuclear weapons, and at least $304 million in prime contracts for work on secondary and nuclear-related systems. In addition, the company received awards worth at least $93 million for military space systems, portions of which fall within IRRC's definition of primary and secondary systems. However, DoD listings were not specific, and Lockheed declined to provide IRRC with further information. The company also performs a substantial amount of classified work.

Primary systems:

Trident Sea-Launched Ballistic Missile--The Trident SLBM is the Navy's newest ballistic missile. Delivery of the Trident I, also known

Lockheed's Nuclear Weapons-Related Contracts
(in millions of dollars)

Primary Systems

FY 1981	
Trident (C-4 and D-5) missiles	$800
Polaris (maintenance and other work for British Polaris force)	$62
Ballistic missile defense	$50

Other current contracts
- Advanced strategic bomber
- U-2 reconnaissance aircraft maintenance
- SR-71 reconnaissance aircraft
- EC-130

Secondary Systems

FY1981	
P-3 patrol aircraft	$210
Precision location strike system	$40
S-3 ASW aircraft	$27
F-104 fighter	$14
Tomahawk cruise missile	$4

Other current contracts
- Milstar
- TR-1 reconnaissance
- Space Shuttle

as the C-4, started in 1979. By 1984, according to DoD plans, 12 Poseidon class submarines will have been modified to carry the Trident I. The Navy's new nuclear powered ballistic missile submarine (SSBN), also designated Trident, is armed with the C-4 SLBM. The first Trident SSBN, the USS Ohio, completed sea trials in September 1982 and began patrol operations shortly thereafter. A second Trident submarine now is also on patrol.

The C-4 is a long-range SLBM, with a maximum range of 4,600 miles. The Poseidon C-3, predecessor to the Trident I, has a maximum range of 2,875 miles. The Trident I allows U.S. submarines to operate farther from the Soviet Union, thereby dramatically increasing the area of the ocean in which they can patrol and yet remain within striking distance of targets in the Soviet homeland. This in turn complicates the Soviet Union's antisubmarine warfare efforts and provides the sea-based leg of the U.S. triad with an additional measure of security.

The Trident I is capable of delivering a large payload. Whereas the tip of the Poseidon SLBM houses 10 independently targetable 40 kiloton warheads, each C-4 can deliver eight 100 kiloton warheads, roughly double the aggregate explosive power of the C-3. An improved guidance system makes the Trident I much more accurate than the earlier model Poseidon. The Trident missile program (including both the

Trident I and Trident II missiles) was Lockheed's largest contract winner in FY 1981, when DoD awarded the company at least $800 million in prime contracts related to Trident. Of that figure, $611 million went toward the purchase of 72 additional C-4 missiles, bringing the total number of Tridents procured by the Navy from Lockheed at the end of FY 1981 to 450.

Congress has strongly supported the C-4 program, approving the administration's full request for $724 million to procure 52 of the missiles in FY 1984.

Lockheed Missile and Space is developing the more advanced Trident II, or D-5, SLBM. The D-5 will offer an extended range of about 6,000 miles and will be capable of delivering an even greater payload. The most significant improvement, however, will be in the D-5's guidance system. The Trident II is expected to be accurate enough to give the United States a sea-based counterforce weapon, capable of destroying hard targets such as land-based ICBM silos and command bunkers. Deployment of the D-5 aboard Trident SSBNs is expected by 1989. The FY 1984 research and development authorization for the D-5 is $1.51 billion.

Lockheed is DoD's prime contractor for the Mark 500 Evader Maneuverable Reentry Vehicle (MARV), which General Electric also is working on. The Mark 500 is designed to elude ballistic missile defense systems by performing evasive maneuvers during its reentry into the earth's atmosphere. DoD has not ordered full-scale production of the Mark 500; instead, it has authorized the development of the MARV to ensure that full-scale production can be initiated rapidly if the need arises. If produced, the Mark 500 most likely will be mounted on the Trident II. Lockheed also manufactures the Mark 4 reentry vehicle on the Trident I SLBM.

Polaris Sea-Launched Ballistic Missile--The Lockheed Polaris SLBM was the country's first generation sea-launched ballistic missile. Lockheed manufactured three versions of the Polaris. The most advanced model, the A-3, was deployed in 1964, and was removed recently from the Navy's arsenal. During 1982, the Navy deactivated two of its 10 Polaris SSBNs and converted the remaining eight into attack submarines.

British Polaris and Trident SLBMs--The A-3 SLBM does remain in service elsewhere. In the mid-1960s Britain acquired 64 Polaris SLBMs, which have served as the backbone of the independent British nuclear force ever since. Lockheed Missile and Space Co. maintains and modernizes the British Polaris arsenal; it received at least $62 million in British Polaris-related prime contract awards in FY 1981.

The British government will continue to be a Lockheed customer. The Polaris SLBM is approaching the end of its operational life, and Britain announced in July 1980 that it would replace the aging A-3s with either Trident I (C-4) or Trident II (D-5) missiles. Subsequently, the British government chose the Trident I, and then reversed itself and expressed its willingness to buy the more advanced and expensive Trident II SLBM. Only the missiles themselves will be purchased from the United States; the British will build the warheads and the submarines on which the Trident II SLBM will be deployed.

The original C-4 program would have called for an outlay of $11.5 billion to cover the cost of constructing four new nuclear-powered ballistic missile submarines and the necessary shore support facilities, and of procuring 100 C-4 missiles. The missiles were projected to cost the British government $2.5 billion, of which $2.3 billion would have gone to Lockheed. The current D-5 program is expected to cost $14 billion overall. Of that, Lockheed will receive $3.2 billion for the actual missiles.

Advanced strategic bomber--While Lockheed has worked on "Stealth" radar-evading technology for more than 10 years, the Air Force selected Northrop to develop the Stealth advanced technology bomber, scheduled for deployment early in the 1990s. However, Lockheed has joined with Rockwell International, producer of the B-1B bomber, to challenge Northrop's Stealth program. The two aerospace giants signed a 10-year memorandum of agreement in 1982 that called for the development of a Stealth version of Rockwell's B-1B. The companies will use new materials designed to absorb emissions and new engine designs intended to minimize aircraft visibility on radar screens. These innovations will be incorporated into the existing B-1B design, thereby eliminating the necessity of constructing an entirely new bomber. DoD publicly is neither encouraging nor discouraging Rockwell and Lockheed. The department expects to spend $20 billion for procurement of a Stealth bomber.

Ballistic missile defense system--Lockheed plays an important role in efforts to develop a space-based, chemical laser weapon for shooting down hostile ICBMs in mid-flight. Under the auspices of DoD's large optics demonstration experiment (Lode), Lockheed is managing a mirror system to direct and control laser beams. The company also is the manager of DoD's Talon Gold project. The Talon Gold mission is to develop a system to detect, track and aim laser beams at hostile ICBMs.

DoD awarded at least $50 million in prime contracts to Lockheed during FY 1981 for research and development related to ballistic missile defense. DoD appointed the company to the position of prime contractor of the Talon Gold program in 1981, and of the Lode program in June 1982.

EC-130--Lockheed produces a modified version of the C-130 Hercules for the Navy. The aircraft, designated EC-130, is a strategic communications platform used to communicate with submerged ballistic missile submarines as part of the Navy's Take Charge and Move Out (Tacamo) program. The EC-130 transmits signals that are highly jam-resistant. Lockheed received a $13 million contract for one of the aircraft in 1981 as well as smaller contracts for the repair and maintenance of existing EC-130s.

The Navy has begun a search for its next generation Tacamo aircraft, currently designated ECX. In an unsolicited bid, Lockheed offered 22 improved EC-130s to meet the Navy's future needs. The company has only one competitor: Boeing has proposed that the Navy procure 15 of its E-3 aircraft, as modified, at a cost of $1 billion. Lockheed asserts that purchase of its version would cost only $820 million.

High Altitude Reconnaissance Aircraft--Lockheed manufactured the famous U-2, the strategic reconnaissance aircraft that CIA pilot Francis Gary Powers was flying when he was shot down over the Soviet Union in 1960. More than 40 U-2s remain in service today, and Lockheed continues to overhaul and upgrade the aircraft. Lockheed is now producing a larger, improved version of the U-2 to perform tactical reconnaissance missions. The Air Force plans eventually to purchase 35 of the upgraded aircraft, designated TR-1.

Lockheed produces a second high altitude reconnaissance aircraft, the SR-71 Blackbird. Unlike the U-2 and TR-1, whose top speeds are approximately 500 miles per hour, the SR-71 is a supersonic aircraft capable of flying three times the speed of sound, making it the world's fastest aircraft. Thirty-four SR-71s remain in service with the Air Force today, and Lockheed maintains and upgrades them.

Both the TR-1 and the SR-71 perform valuable reconnaissance missions in times of peace, and in conventional or nuclear war. The aircraft can fly relatively undetected at extremely high altitudes, in excess of 80,000 feet. From this vantage point, high resolution cameras and delicate sensors map large tracts of the earth's surface.

Secondary systems:

P-3 Orion--As the producer of the P-3 Orion land-based maritime patrol aircraft, Lockheed contributes substantially to the Navy's antisubmarine warfare program. The P-3 is used to detect, track and, in times of war, destroy enemy high performance submarines. Lockheed delivered the first Orion to the Navy in 1962, and by 1982 the company had sold 209 to the Navy and 321 to foreign governments.

A complex system of advanced sensors, avionics and computer equipment enables the Orion to detect submerged ballistic missile and attack submarines. The P-3 carries a mixed array of weapons, including torpedoes, air-to-ground missiles, antiship missiles, mines and depth charges, including the B-57 nuclear warhead. The Orion can remain aloft for up to 16 hours.

Prime contracts awarded by DoD to Lockheed for new P-3 Orions (excluding foreign military sales) and for the maintenance of the Navy's existing fleet totaled at least $210 million in FY 1981.

S-3 Viking--Lockheed has provided the Navy with another antisubmarine warfare aircraft, the S-3 Viking. Unlike the P-3 Orion, the Viking is based on aircraft carriers. Lockheed completed delivery of 187 S-3s in 1978. The company has since suggested to the Navy that it produce a modified version of the S-3. The proposed ES-3A Tactical Airborne Signal Exploitation System (Tases) would provide the U.S. Navy with an enhanced carrier-based electronic warfare and early warning capability.

The S-3 is equipped with sensor, avionic and computer equipment comparable to those systems built into the P-3 Orion. The S-3 carries fewer weapons, however, and is not equipped with missiles or mines, although it can be armed with the B-57 nuclear depth charge.

Lockheed received at least $27 million in prime contract awards for maintaining and upgrading the Navy's fleet of S-3 Vikings in FY 1981, including a contract with initial funding of $14 million for the development of an improved avionics system to be installed in as many as 160 S-3s starting in 1987.

F-104 Starfighter--The member nations of NATO were concerned with the issue of weapon standardization from the time of the alliance's inception. By the mid-1950s, it became clear that NATO needed a new jet fighter, and the nations involved agreed to choose a single plane. The contract promised to be large. Lockheed's entrant, the F-104 Starfighter, beat out aircraft built by Grumman, Northrop and the French company Dassault, and was chosen as the NATO fighter in the late 1950s.

Although primarily an interceptor, the F-104 is capable of delivering nuclear warheads and therefore figures in any discussion of European theatre nuclear weapons. Most of the Lockheed supersonic fighters are stationed in NATO countries, and none is retained by the Air Force.

The Air Force operates a training base in Arizona where West German Air Force pilots learn to fly the Starfighter. Lockheed received contracts totaling at least $14 million in FY 1981 for the maintenance and repair of these Starfighters.

Military Strategic Tactical and Relay Satellite (Milstar)--Early in 1983, Lockheed won the Air Force contract for full-scale engineering development of the space and mission control segments of the Milstar communications satellites. This communications satellite system, announced by President Reagan in his October 1981 speech outlining his strategic program, is designed to serve both strategic and tactical forces by providing a worldwide, highly jam-resistant, survivable communications system that is highly invulnerable to such nuclear effects as electro-magnetic pulse (EMP). Milstar will operate at an extremely high frequency, and DoD considers it a pivotal program in its work to strengthen and refine space systems that can survive jamming and nuclear attack.

Submarine tender--In 1981, Lockheed fulfilled a contract awarded in 1977 when it delivered the last of three AS-39 submarine tenders to the U.S. Navy. The first was authorized in 1972. These ships provide mobile base facilities for maintenance and support of nuclear attack submarines.

Space Shuttle--Lockheed Missile and Space manufactures major components for the Space Shuttle, most notably the insulating tiles that protect the shuttle's outer skin from the extreme temperatures generated during reentry into the earth's atmosphere. (Recently, Lockheed also won the NASA contract to provide support services for shuttle missions.)

DoD has awarded several smaller contracts to Lockheed for work on shuttle-related systems, ranging from providing biotechnological and other scientific equipment for future experiments in space to performing feasibility studies on an orbiting space station designed to retrieve and repair orbiting spacecraft. It is difficult to determine from DoD records alone how much funding the DoD has granted Lockheed for Space Shuttle programs. Lockheed was unable to provide IRRC with a more comprehensive breakdown of Space Shuttle contracts.

Precision location strike system (PLSS)--Lockheed is developing and producing the precision location strike system (PLSS) for F-16 and other aircraft. The PLSS is designed to identify and to locate enemy radar emplacements and to coordinate air strikes on them. The company received at least $40 million in fiscal 1981 contract awards for the PLSS.

C-5 Galaxy--Although the C-5 Galaxy transport is used only for non-nuclear purposes now, Lockheed is conducting research for the Air Force into the feasibility of modifications that would enable the transport to carry and deliver air-launched cruise missiles. A B-52 Stratofortress converted to ALCM carrier configuration would be able to transport 20 of the missiles. The proposed B-1 would not carry many more than that. A C-5, in contrast, would be able to deliver 80 or more ALCMs, and therefore has been proposed by opponents of the B-1 as a more cost-effective alternative to the new bomber. The Air Force, in having Lockheed look at the possibility of converting C-5s, is keeping all options open.[4]

Lockheed-Government Relationship

Political action committee: The Lockheed PAC contributed $99,000 in 1979-80 and $184,000 in 1981-82 to congressional candidates. Some 31 percent of the 1979-80 total and 40 percent of the 1981-82 total went to 69 members of congressional defense committees.

The Lockheed PAC's major contributions during 1980-81 include: $3,000 to Senate minority leader Robert Byrd (D-W.Va.), $6,000 to Sen. Howard Cannon (D-Nev.), $4,000 to Sen. John Stennis (D-Miss.), $5,000 to Rep. William Chappell (D-Fla.), and $3,250 to Rep. John Murtha (D-Pa.). All but Byrd were members of defense committees.

Washington office: Lockheed maintains several offices in Washington, D.C. Their activities include foreign sales marketing; market intelligence gathering; dissemination of technical information; customer coordination; lobbying and responding to congressional inquiries. Three individuals and four law and consulting firms, including the Washington law office of Patton, Boggs and Blow, were registered in fall 1981 as lobbyists for the various subsidiaries of Lockheed and for the parent corporation.

Personnel interchange: According to DoD records, 392 mid- to upper-level DoD personnel transferred to Lockheed in 1977-81. Another 18 transferred from Lockheed to the DoD.

At least four of Lockheed's board members have had military or government experience. Lawrence O. Kitchen, president of the corporation, served for 12 years as an aeronautical engineer and staff assistant to the assistant chief for logistics planning and policy on the Navy's Bureau of Aeronautics. Robert A. Fuhrman has been a member of the Advisory Committee to the Defense Science Board and has served on the Production Panel for Navy and Marine Corps acquisition. Edward W. Carter entered the Navy as an ensign and exited as a rear admiral. For two years he was a staff member for Naval Operations, and more recently he held the position of Deputy Commander with the Naval Sea Systems Command.

Contracting controversy: Lockheed has been the center of controversy several times during the last 15 years. In 1969-71, the company wavered on the brink of bankruptcy. It experienced severe cost overruns on its C-5A Galaxy air transport almost from the program's inception in 1965. Increases of nearly 100 percent in the plane's unit cost taxed Lockheed's resources. The Pentagon tried unsuccessfully to conceal the overruns, which by 1969 amounted to $1.36 billion.[5] The company experienced concomitant overruns and complications in other defense programs. Lockheed engines produced for the Boeing short range attack missile also were above cost, and the company had difficulty with other defense programs. Finally, its financial resources were stretched by its L-1011 Tri-Star commercial jet program.[6]

As the company teetered on the brink of bankruptcy between 1969 and 1971, several government assistance plans were proposed and fiercely debated. In 1971, Congress narrowly approved a $250 million emergency federal loan guarantee. The guarantee proved sufficient to tide Lockheed over.

Lockheed's overseas operations led to further difficulty in 1975, when it was disclosed that Lockheed executives had made questionable payments to officials of foreign governments in efforts to secure contracts for the company. The scandal rocked the governments of West Germany, Japan and Italy and tarnished the Netherlands royal family. The payments scandal led to the resignation of two top Lockheed officials.

Contingency Planning and Prospects

Contingency planning: As a business strategy, Lockheed appears to rely not so much on contingency planning and diversification as on intensive lobbying to ensure the continuation of its defense programs. In fact, while perhaps the company is becoming more diversified within the military sector, it is also increasingly dependent on military business overall, particularly with its withdrawal from the civilian aircraft market.

Lockheed's approach to the vagaries of the defense business is illustrated by its behavior during the recent effort to find a new cargo plane. The company's monopoly on cargo planes was threatened in 1981 when McDonnell Douglas won a design competition for a new strategic military cargo plane. Despite serious design problems in the past with the Lockheed C-5A, Lockheed challenged the competition results with an updated version of the C-5. Lockheed ultimately won, even though there was strong support within the Air Force for McDonnell Douglas, and even though Boeing made a late but attractive bid to build a new cargo plane for less than Lockheed wanted. Many analysts believe that Lockheed won on the basis of its political pull with the civilian leadership of the Pentagon and within Congress. If Lockheed had not won the bidding with its C-5B, it would have been forced to lay off many of the 12,900 persons employed by Lockheed-Georgia and close down the C-5 production line. Instead of planning for alternative production to keep the workers there employed, the company went to work in Washington and eventually prevailed.

Similarly, in 1981, when DoD announced a five-year suspension of P-3C Orion procurement, Lockheed lobbied against the decision, claiming that it would place Lockheed-California in "great jeopardy."[7] The Pentagon reversed its decision and ordered six P-3Cs a year, enough to keep production lines rolling and to promote continued sales of the aircraft to foreign governments.

In 1980, Lockheed successfully fought a citizens' initiative in Santa Cruz County, Calif., that called for the closing of a Lockheed plant in the county that produces components for the Trident missile. The initiative proposed to allow a five-year period for Lockheed to convert its plant and retrain its 370 workers to produce non-nuclear-weapons-related goods. Campaigning under the slogan, "Politics Shouldn't Cost People's Jobs," Lockheed spent $214,000 on the campaign against the initiative, more than five times the amount spent by initiative supporters, and won with 63 percent of the vote.

Lockheed's plans for diversification are limited. The New York Times reports that Chairman Anderson's highest priority is to use funds that otherwise would have gone to the Tri-Star program to "diversify in our core businesses," and to expand military space, SLBM and Stealth aircraft business. [8]

Prospects: Lockheed's overwhelming dependence on the military and its agreement to run the $9 billion C-5B program on a fixed-cost basis spell problems for the company if budget considerations force a general cutback in military production, or if the C-5B runs into the same cost and performance problems as the C-5A. However, as far as its nuclear weapons programs are concerned, the company can be relatively confident. Of all the current nuclear weapons development programs, the Trident I and II SLBM programs appear to be the most secure, and Trident programs represented 30 percent of total DoD contract awards to Lockheed in FY 1981. A nuclear freeze, of course, would affect the Trident programs, particularly development of the Trident II or D-5 missile, which critics believe will be destabilizing. Nevertheless, the Trident II appears to be less vulnerable to attack, at least on the budgetary front, than other nuclear weapons systems.

Lockheed's increasing commitment to space-based lasers and ballistic missile defense work could well fall victim to arms control concerns, although the current administration supports such work enthusiastically. Finally, Lockheed's antisubmarine warfare aircraft program appears somewhat vulnerable to budgetary concerns (and might well be cut if tensions with the Soviet Union are reduced). In particular, the P-3 Orion may be cut back at some point, given that DoD already has indicated skepticism about current procurement levels.

Footnotes

1. Anthony Sampson, The Arms Bazaar, The Viking Press, New York, 1977, p. 99.
2. Ibid., p. 218.
3. The New York Times, Oct. 17, 1982.
4. The New York Times, Sept. 15, 1982.
5. The Washington Post, Sept. 28, 1982.
6. Gordon Adams, The Iron Triangle, Council on Economic Priorities, New York, 1981.
7. The New York Times, Oct. 17, 1982.
8. Ibid.

Martin Marietta

Martin Marietta was formed in 1961 when the Glenn L. Martin Co., an aircraft manufacturer, merged with the American Marietta Co., a chemical and cement conglomerate. Martin Marietta maintains a diversified line of products and divides its business into five segments: cement, aggregates, chemicals, aluminum and aerospace.

Martin Marietta was the 178th largest corporation in 1982, when it had sales of $3.53 billion, 7 percent more than the previous year. Net earnings of $92 million in 1982 was less than half the company's 1981 income.

Most analysts attribute the lackluster 1982 performance of Martin Marietta to depressed commercial markets for cement and aluminum products. In addition, Martin Marietta's prolonged and expensive battle to fight off a hostile takeover bid by Bendix Corp. damaged the company's performance.

The rapid expansion of the company's aerospace business, which has more than tripled in the last five years, contrasts sharply with the sluggish performance of the company's other segments. Sales of aerospace products alone totaled $2.31 billion and accounted for 65 percent of the corporation's total sales for 1982. Martin Marietta aerospace operations accounted for 43 percent of the company's earnings before interest and taxes in 1981. Because of non-aerospace losses in 1982, aerospace earnings that year exceed those for the company overall. Most observers expect the trend of aerospace expansion to continue.

The prospect of obtaining Martin Marietta's aerospace operations motivated Bendix to attempt an unfriendly takeover of Martin Marietta during the fall of 1982. Martin Marietta resisted, and ultimately retained its independence. But the victory was costly. To fight the takeover, Martin Marietta countered Bendix's tender offer with one of its own. Bendix wound up owning 70 percent of Martin Marietta, while Martin Marietta won 50 percent of Bendix. An impasse between the two companies was resolved when Allied Corp. agreed to purchase Bendix, including shares owned by Martin Marietta. Bendix's shares in Martin Marietta were split between Allied and Martin Marietta, leaving control lodged in the latter company. Since then, Allied has sold its interest in Martin Marietta.

Martin Marietta was forced to borrow heavily in order to purchase the Bendix stock, increasing its debt load by $900 million. At the same

Data on Martin Marietta
(dollar figures in millions)

	1978	1979	1980	1981	1982
Net sales	$1,758	$2,061	$2,619	$3,294	$3,527
Net earnings	$136	$178	$188	$200	$92
Aerospace government sales	$670	$780	$1,120	$1,780	$2,190
Aerospace government sales as a percentage of total sales	38%	38%	43%	54%	62%
Sales of missiles and weapons systems*	$281	$330	$576	$1,021	$1,199
DoD prime contract awards+	$539	$519	$809	$1,287	$2,008
Ratio of DoD prime contract awards to total sales^	.31	.25	.31	.39	.57
Total Martin Marietta employees	28,000	30,200	34,650	41,200	40,900

* Excludes space systems and launch vehicles.
\+ U.S. fiscal year, ending Sept. 30.
^ U.S. fiscal year contract awards compared with calendar year sales.

time, shareholder equity was cut in half. Martin Marietta's finances were so strained by the battle that Allied Chairman Edward Hennessy predicted "it will take Marietta seven years to straighten out its balance sheet."[1] To help reduce its debt load, the company has tried to sell some of its nondefense properties.

Martin Marietta's corporate headquarters is in Bethesda, Md. The company's principal facilities are spread throughout 36 states and 11 foreign nations. The bulk of Marietta's aerospace research, development and production is carried out at its complexes in Denver, Orlando, Fla., and, to a lesser extent, Baltimore. The aerospace division also provides services at Vandenburg and McConnell Air Force Bases, and at Cape Canaveral.

Government and Defense Business

The overwhelming majority of Martin Marietta's aerospace business is with the U.S. government. DoD and NASA are Marietta's chief government customers.

A wide range of conventional and nuclear weapons systems are under development or in production at Martin Marietta facilities. They include: the MX and Pershing II missiles; the conventional Patriot surface-to-air defense missile, which may be armed with a nuclear explosive in the future; ADATS, an air-defense/antitank system; and Hellfire, a conventionally armed air-to-surface attack missile which is being developed by Rockwell International. Marietta also is prime contractor for the conventionally armed Copperhead missile program.

Martin Marietta is developing an intercept missile prototype for use in an antiballistic missile system. In addition, the company is developing a missile launch system for the Navy.

Marietta also is developing and producing a series of navigation, target acquisition and fire control systems.

NASA has chosen Martin Marietta as a major contractor for its space programs. The Titan III space launch vehicle has successfully placed payloads into orbit around the earth for NASA and DoD, and it is used now as a complementary back-up system to the Space Shuttle. Martin Marietta also is an important contractor for the Space Shuttle program, providing some of the spacecraft's systems, as well as ground and launch services.

Defense dependence: The Martin Co. delivered its first military aircraft, the TT trainer and MB-1 bomber, to the U.S. government during World War I. Martin B-2 bombers, produced during the early 1920s, were used in a test conducted in June 1921 that convinced the U.S. military that airplanes could be used successfully to destroy naval forces. The event was regarded as a revolutionary display of the potential of air power, for it prompted the Navy to develop aircraft carriers.

At the beginning of the Depression, in 1929, Martin Co. moved from Cleveland, where it was founded, to new and expanded facilities in Baltimore. A Martin biographer notes that "government contracts [enabled] the Martin Co. to remain quite immune to the effects of the stock market crash."[2] A succession of Martin military aircraft rolled off the new Baltimore assembly line during the 1930s. The B-26 Marauder, used extensively in the Pacific theater during World War II, became the best known Martin-manufactured military aircraft. More than 5,000 of the bombers were produced, and together they flew approximately 110,000 sorties, dropping 150,000 tons of bombs.

Government assistance in the form of military contracts came to the company's rescue once again in the 1950s. Early in 1952, the company teetered on the edge of bankruptcy: "Only the fact that the Martin Co. was producing material necessary to the national welfare in time of war (Korea)...prevented the bankruptcy proceedings," says its biographer.[3] The procurement of large numbers of the Martin Marlin "flying patrol boats" and the Air Force's encouragement of the rapid development and production of the Martin B-57 tactical bomber greatly assisted the company in its efforts to remain solvent.

The merger between Martin and American Marietta in 1961 provided a more diversified base for the company. Nevertheless, Martin Marietta's military business remained its largest concern, and the company consistently has ranked among the top 25 defense contractors. With the new strain placed on the company by the costs of defeating Bendix's takeover attempt, Martin Marietta is likely to become even more dependent on defense sales as it sells some non-aerospace assets.

DoD assigned $2.01 billion in prime contract awards to Martin Marietta in FY 1981, compared with $1.29 billion in fiscal 1980. The government's increased reliance on the company propelled Martin Marietta from its position as the 20th largest DoD contractor in 1979 to the 10th largest just three years later.

Defense employees: Martin Marietta employed 40,900 persons in 1982. Almost all Martin Marietta employees who are engaged in research, development and production for DoD are in the company's aerospace division. Martin Marietta said in 1980 that at that time there were 20,600 aerospace employees, 60 percent of the company's total work force.

The New York Times reported that as of late 1982, Martin Marietta had 2,400 employees at its Denver complex, and 800 more at Vandenberg Air Force Base, working on the MX missile program.[4]

The number of Martin Marietta workers who devote their efforts to defense production can be expected to rise in the short term if production funds for the MX and Pershing II missile programs are approved by Congress. The continued expansion of the Space Shuttle program likewise will result in increased levels of employment at Martin Marietta.

Nuclear Weapons-Related Programs

The Martin Co. began producing nuclear weapons and related systems soon after World War II. The Air Force tested the first Martin-manufactured nuclear-capable weapon, the Matador (later renamed Mace) ground-launched tactical cruise missile, in 1950, and entered it into its arsenal four years later. Since then, Martin Marietta has worked on the Titan I and II ICBMs, the Pershing Ia and II intermediate range ballistic missiles (IRBMs), the MX ICBM, ballistic missile defense systems, and space transportation systems, including the Space Shuttle and Titan III launch vehicles.

The Defense Department awarded Martin Marietta at least $546 million in prime contracts for work on primary nuclear weapons systems and at least $207 million in prime contracts for secondary system-related programs in FY 1981. The ratio of awards for primary nuclear weapons systems to sales was .17 in 1981; the ratio of all identifiable nuclear-related awards to sales was .23.

Martin Marietta's Nuclear Weapons-Related Contracts
(in millions of dollars)

Primary Systems		Secondary Systems	
FY 1981		FY 1981	
MX missile	$359	Titan rocket booster	$107
Pershing missiles	$143	Space Shuttle	$69
Titan missile	$40	Vertical launch system	$24
Ballistic missile defense	$4	F-111 fighter	$7
Other current contracts		Other current contracts	
B-1B		Lantirn navigation and targeting system	
Advanced cruise missile technology			

Primary systems:

MX missile--If continued, the Air Force's MX intercontinental ballistic missile program promises to be Martin Marietta's most lucrative current nuclear weapons program. Prime contracts awarded by DoD to Martin Marietta aerospace topped $359 million in FY 1981 alone.

At the same time, the MX may to be Martin Marietta's most vulnerable nuclear weapons program. Work on an MX advanced ICBM began more than 10 years ago. Since then, support for the project has ebbed and flowed. The Reagan administration's nuclear weapons modernization program calls for the procurement of 100 MX ICBMs, with initial deployment starting in 1986. According to administration and Pentagon officials, the MX is an essential component of the country's nuclear weapons modernization program aimed at overcoming the increasing vulnerability of the land-based leg of the nation's strategic triad, but developing an invulnerable and politically acceptable MX basing mode has been a vexing problem for Reagan.

As a major associate MX contractor charged with assembly, systems test and support, ground transportation and handling duties, Martin Marietta stands to lose much if the MX program is canceled or postponed.

Midgetman--The New York Times reports that Martin Marietta is one of several companies preparing bids to develop the proposed small intercontinental ballistic missile, nicknamed Midgetman.[5] All the various companies interested in the new missile are expected to receive support during the next year, as the Pentagon weighs various approaches to the Midgetman, planned as a follow-on to the MX. Some $604 million in the FY 1984 budget is allocated to the small ICBM. The Pentagon would like to begin deploying the missile in 1992.

Pershing Mobile Intermediate Range Ballistic Missile (IRBM)--The Martin Marietta Pershing missile is the Army's most capable IRBM. The company began developing the original Pershing in 1958, and the Army deployed the weapon in Europe six years later. The Pershing 1a, an improved version of the missile system that began development in 1969, has a maximum range of 460 miles and can deliver a 40, 200, or 400 kiloton warhead. A total of 180 of the missiles currently are deployed in West Germany, although Martin Marietta has produced 575. The U.S. Army is equipped with 108 Pershing 1a launchers, and an additional 72 are controlled by West German armed forces.

Some 108 of the Pershing 1a missiles and launchers are slated to be withdrawn and replaced by the more advanced Pershing II starting in December 1983. The Pershing II is similar to its predecessor, the 1a, in name and little else. The Pershing II has a range of 1,100 miles, more than twice that of the older missile. The extended range puts Moscow and much of the western portion of the Soviet Union within reach of European based American missiles. The newer Pershing is also the first U.S. ballistic missile capable of being guided to its target during the final stages of its flight. The incorporation of a radar system that homes in on the target theoretically makes the Pershing II 10 times more accurate than its predecessor, making it possible to destroy hardened military targets. Because the missile is so accurate, the W85 warhead to be carried by the Pershing II is small--10 to 20 kilotons--in comparison with the 1a warhead's yield.

Martin Marietta and the Army had trouble getting the Pershing II off the ground. The missile turned out to be more complex, and therefore more expensive, than expected. Difficulties encountered in the production of Pershing II prototypes resulted in delays in the missile's testing schedule. Tests originally planned for April 1982 were conducted the following July. The propulsion system of the first Pershing II malfunctioned in that first test, and the missile's on-board batteries failed in the second test. The missile's motors fired successfully on the third attempt, but loss of hydraulic pressure caused a malfunction of the missile's reentry vehicle. The sophisticated terminal guidance system was unable to make the proper adjustments during the reentry vehicle's descent through the atmosphere, and the Pershing II's mock warhead did not land near its target.

Some of the Pershing II's problems result from a development speedup to meet the December 1983 NATO deadline, one year earlier than originally planned. In order to meet the new deadline, DoD reduced the number of test launchings from 28 to 18, and the Army gave Martin

Marietta permission to begin full scale production of the Pershing II in June 1982, even though the missile had not been tested. This move has turned out to be costly. When the first test firing failed, a new motor had to be manufactured for the prototype test missile, as well as for all the production missiles already built by Martin Marietta.

While arms control negotiations over U.S. and Soviet missiles based in Europe have not reached agreement, opposition in Europe is strong and there may yet be some chance that the Pershing II program will not be totally implemented.

The 1984 authorization budget for Pershing II missiles is $431 million. Total program costs have been estimated at $3 billion.

Martin Marietta won at least $143 million in prime contracts for both Pershing missiles in FY 1981, including $118 million for a Pershing II R&D contract. Most of the other awards apparently were for Pershing Ia maintenance.

Titan ICBM--Martin Marietta began developing the Titan ICBM more than 20 years ago. The Air Force deployed the Titan I, the country's first generation ICBM and Martin Marietta's first ballistic missile, in 1962. Martin Marietta delivered an improved Titan II the following year. About 40 Titan IIs remain in service today. The military considers the aging liquid fueled missile obsolete, and the phased deactivation of Titan II began late in 1982. The Titan II is armed with the General Electric Mark 6, 9-megaton nuclear warhead, the largest yield warhead in the U.S. arsenal.

Martin Marietta has received annual government contracts for the maintenance and modernization of the nation's Titan II ICBMs. For FY 1981, DoD prime contract awards for such work were at least $40 million.

Other--DoD has chosen Martin Marietta to serve as an associate contractor for the development of a Low Altitude Defense System (LoAD), designed to detect and destroy incoming enemy ballistic missiles. Martin Marietta has been assigned to develop the actual missile that would intercept warheads reentering the earth's atmosphere. DoD presented Martin Marietta Orlando with $3.6 million in prime contract awards during FY 1981 for research into and development of a prototype antiballistic interceptor.

Martin Marietta also produces horizontal and vertical stabilizers for the B-1B bomber under subcontract to Rockwell International.[6] In addition, the company has participated in recent years in the development of advanced cruise missile technology, working on a rocket/ramjet propulsion system for the advanced strategic air-launched missile.

Secondary systems:

Titan III Space Launch Vehicle--Martin Marietta aerospace's third largest nuclear weapons-related program in FY 1981, in terms of prime contract awards, was the Titan III space launch vehicle. DoD awarded the company at least $107 million for Titan IIIs. The newest version, the Titan 34D, was launched successfully for the first time in late 1982, when the Martin Marietta launch vehicle, assisted by a Boeing Inertial Upper Stage (IUS), placed two defense satellite communications systems (DSCS)--a TRW DSCS-2 and a General Electric DSCS-3--into a synchronous orbit around the earth. According to DoD, the Titan will continue to offer the Air Force an "expandable launch vehicle back-up capability to guarantee the launch of critical USAF and DoD operational payloads in the event the Space Shuttle is delayed."[7]

Space Shuttle--Martin Marietta aerospace is heavily involved in the Space Shuttle program. DoD awarded the company at least $70 million in prime contracts for work on the shuttle during FY 1981. The company also received contracts from NASA. The aerospace division manufactures the giant external tanks that have the large amounts of fuel needed to launch the shuttle. The external tank used on the sixth shuttle flight was an improved version, weighing 6,000 pounds less than the original tanks. The improvement enables the shuttle to carry heavier payloads aloft at a reduced cost.

Martin Marietta also is developing a manned maneuvering unit for individual astronaut propulsion. The unit would allow astronauts to leave the shuttle cabin to perform missions in space. Under another contract, Martin Marietta aerospace continued as a manager of DoD's shuttle operations at the Vandenberg Air Force Base launch complex. The company's duties range from testing computer control systems to designing launch facilities and navigational systems for the shuttle.

Other space systems--Additional Martin Marietta space programs include work on acquisition, tracking and targeting systems to be used by space-based high energy weapons and investigations into the technology necessary for enhancing spacecraft survivability, including work on radiation hardened space processors, robotics, and advanced automation.

F-111--DoD awarded International Laser Systems Inc., a Marietta subsidiary that produces laser-related products, at least $7 million during FY 1981 for integration of upgraded optical sighting and ranging equipment into the Air Force's fleet of F-111 nuclear-capable fighter aircraft.

Vertical launch system (VLS)--Martin Marietta is developing the Navy's vertical launch system (VLS). The VLS is designed to be mounted on the deck of all types of surface ships, and to store and launch a wide range of missiles, including the Tomahawk nuclear-capable cruise missile and the Asroc antisubmarine missile. The VLS is scheduled for installation aboard Ticonderoga-class cruisers and Spruance-class destroyers starting in 1985. A production award for VLS was awarded to Martin Marietta's Baltimore division in 1982, after five years of development. The company received at least $24 million in VLS contract awards in fiscal 1981.

Other systems--Martin Marietta Orlando is responsible for development of the Low Altitude Navigation, Targeting Infra-Red Night (Lantirn) navigation and target acquisition system, which is being developed for the A-10 and nuclear-capable F-16 aircraft. Fiscal 1981 awards for this totaled at least $44 million. (These awards were not included in the total for secondary systems, since a large portion is unrelated to nuclear warfighting.) International Laser Systems is responsible for the laser designator for Lantirn.

Martin Marietta-Government Relationship

Political action committee: Martin Marietta's Political Action Committee made contributions to congressional candidates of $72,500 in 1979-80 and $131,500 in 1981-82. In the 1981-82 period, 40 of 111 members of defense committees received a total of $56,700 from the company's PAC, or 43 percent of the total. Republican candidates consistently edged out their Democratic counterparts in terms of both the number of individuals supported and dollars spent by Martin Marietta's PAC.

The Martin Marietta PAC allocated a large portion of its 1981-82 donations to candidates from Florida, including a $12,000 contribution to Rep. William Chappell (D). Other notable contributions to individuals included: $2,500 to Sen. Barry Goldwater (R-Ariz.), now chairman of the Senate Armed Services subcommittee on military construction and stockpiles; $2,000 to Sen. John Stennis (D-Miss.), former chairman of the Senate Armed Services Committee; $5,000 to Rep. William Dickinson (R-Ala.); and $2,500 to Sen. Harrison Schmitt (R-N.M.), then a member of the defense appropriations subcommittee and chairman of the space subcommitte. The Martin Marietta PAC contributed $1,000 in 1981-82 to George Mitchell (D) and $2,000 to David Emery (R), opponents in the 1982 Maine senatorial race.

Martin Marietta's PAC consists of a three member board--including President Thomas Pownall--that meets monthly to determine which candidates will receive donations.

Washington office: According to the Defense Contract Audit Agency, the funds devoted to Martin Marietta's Washington office cover expenses incurred for market research, customer relations, dissemination of technical data, information gathering, and preparation of sensitive bid proposals. Five Marietta executives including President Pownall and Vice President James D. Simpson are, or have been in the recent past, registered as lobbyists on the company's behalf. Herbert S. Matthews and the firm of Cederberg and Associates lobby in Washington for the company.

Personnel interchange: DoD reportedly considered selecting Pownall to succeed outgoing Deputy Defense Secretary Frank C. Carlucci late in 1982 but ultimately chose Paul Thayer of LTV. Other top-ranking Martin Marietta executives have had prior government experience. Melvin R. Laird, a former U.S. Representative (R-Wis.) and Secretary of Defense who is now senior counselor to The Reader's Digest Association, was elected to the board of directors late in 1981. Former Air Force Secretary Eugene Zuckert also sits on the board.

Martin Marietta hired 455 mid- to high-level DoD employees between 1971 and 1981. Some 13 Martin Marietta employees transferred to mid- to high-level positions in the DoD during the same period.

Contingency Planning and Prospects

Martin Marietta is likely to remain dependent on DoD for much if not most of its business. However, despite the sale of some nondefense assets, the company is likely to remain somewhat diversified, providing a degree of insulation against down cycles in both military and commercial markets.

Of the companies covered in this study, Martin Marietta is among the most dependent on contracts for nuclear weapons systems. A significant portion of Martin Marietta's business is generated from such politically vulnerable nuclear weapons as the MX and Pershing II. Reportedly, however, the company has recognized that these missiles remain somewhat vulnerable, and therefore company officials have discounted the two programs for long-range planning. Analyst Larry Lytton of Drexel Burnham Lambert told The Washington Post late in 1982: "In terms of looking at the two missile programs, with them, (Martin Marietta will have) 20 percent growth over the next few years. Without them, it will maybe be 12 percent."[8]

At this point, it appears certain that Pershing II missiles will be deployed in Europe, although it is possible that arms negotiators will reach some agreement that would block full deployment. The MX program remains more vulnerable, especially given budget pressures facing Congress. A sudden cancellation of the MX would harm Martin Marietta, one of its lead contractors, and might lead to layoffs of some employees. It is estimated that the company will receive $500 million in each of the next several years for assembling MX missiles. On the other hand, if an MX cancellation led to a speed-up of the Midgetman small ICBM, the damage to Martin Marietta could be minimized. The company is considered a leading candidate for Midgetman development, in part because of its role in developing the Pershing II intermediate range missile.

Martin Marietta officials declined to comment on any contingency plans that the company may have for relocating workers previously employed in curtailed or canceled defense projects.

Martin Marietta Footnotes

1. The Wall Street Journal, Sept. 27, 1982.
2. Henry Still, To Ride the Wind, Julian Messner Inc., New York, 1964, p. 173.
3. Ibid.
4. The New York Times, Nov. 29, 1982.
5. The New York Times, Sept. 7, 1983.
6. Council on Economic Priorities Newsletter, February 1982, p. 6.
7. Department of Defense, Program Acquisition Costs by Weapon System, Government Printing Office, Washington, D.C., 1982, p. 154.
8. The Washington Post, Dec. 5, 1982.

ADDENDUM: In December 1983, Martin Marietta won the contract to replace Union Carbide as manager of the Energy Department's $2 billion-a-year Oak Ridge complex in Tennessee and Kentucky. The complex includes the Y-12 nuclear weapons facility. Martin Marietta estimated that the contract could result in a fee of $6 million to $19 million a year. The company's contract runs until 1989.

For more information on the Oak Ridge complex, see the profile of Union Carbide on pages 353-5.

McDonnell Douglas

McDonnell Douglas is perhaps the world's most prominent manufacturer of combat aircraft. Since the original McDonnell Co. got started a few years before World War II, tens of thousands of fighter and attack planes have rolled off its assembly line. Just counting the company's major programs since 1960--the F-4 Phantom, the A-4 Skyhawk and the F-15 Eagle--MDC has manufactured more than 9,000 military planes. Orders for MDC's new planes--the F/A-18 Hornet, the KC-10 Extender and the AV-8B Harrier--number more than 1,000.

McDonnell Douglas, of course, also produces commercial planes. Its DC series of aircraft (including the controversial DC-10) was started at Douglas Aircraft Co. in the early 1930s. Since Douglas merged with McDonnell Co. in 1967, however, the combined company's commercial aerospace segment has recorded losses in all but two years.

McDonnell Douglas also manufactures missile and space systems, including the Tomahawk cruise missile, and a small amount of non-aerospace products.

Although McDonnell Douglas's sales declined slightly from $7.4 billion in 1981 to $7.3 billion in 1982, the company claimed the year as a "considerable achievement," considering that its commercial aircraft sales decreased 42 percent ($1 billion). Earnings increased 22 percent to $214.7 million, but if write-offs for commercial aircraft losses had not been counted, the increase would have been 14 percent instead. The company ranked 65th on the 1982 Forbes top sales list. It is based in St. Louis.

Government and Defense Business

Defense dependence: The only McDonnell Douglas Corp. (MDC) products that are not sold to the government are commercial aircraft and non-aerospace services. The rest--66 percent in 1982--went to the military and NASA. Over the last five years, MDC's sales to the government have averaged about 62 percent of its total sales, and commercial aircraft sales have averaged about 30 percent.

A look at the company's backlog indicates that MDC's government business will remain at the same level or higher in the near future. Orders for military aircraft, space systems and missiles made up 88 percent of MDC's $10 billion backlog in 1982, and the company reported another $6.6 billion in government orders that had been received but not yet funded.

Data on McDonnell Douglas
(dollar figures in millions)

	1978	1979	1980	1981	1982
Total sales	$4,130	$5,278	$6,066	$7,385	$7,331
Net earnings	$161	$199	$145	$177	$215
Military aircraft sales	$2,287	$2,337	$2,694	$3,600	$4,088
Space systems and missile sales	$720	$790	$830	$952	$1,299
Sales to U.S. government	$2,864	$3,002	$3,410	$4,362	$4,857
Government sales as a percentage of total sales	69%	57%	56%	59%	66%
DoD prime contract awards*	$2,863	$3,229	$3,247	$4,409	$5,630
Ratio of DoD prime contract awards to total sales+	.69	.61	.54	.60	.77
Firm government backlog at year end	NA	NA	NA	$7,321	$8,984
Additional government backlog at year end^	NA	NA	NA	$5,357	$6,617
Total McDonnell Douglas employees	70,547	82,736	82,550	74,264	72,451

* U.S. fiscal year, ending Sept. 30.
+ U.S. fiscal year awards compared with calendar year sales.
^ Includes government orders not yet funded and orders being negotiated as continuations of authorized programs.

Not only are military sales an important part of MDC's business, but the company is one of the nation's most important military contractors. For the last 10 years, it has been one of a handful of companies that has ranked among the top 10 recipients of military prime contract awards. In FY 1976, 1977 and 1981, McDonnell Douglas received more contract awards than any other company. In FY 1982, it received awards worth $5.6 billion, second only to General Dynamics. This amount equaled close to 5 percent of the Pentagon's total awards in 1982.

The company's major military aircraft programs include the F-15 Eagle fighter plane; the AV-8B Harrier, a vertical and short take-off and landing plane; the KC-10 Extender, a military tanker cargo aircraft (patterned after the company's DC-10 commercial aircraft); and the new F/A-18 Hornet fighter-attack plane. MDC's most important missile programs are the Harpoon anti-ship missile and the Tomahawk cruise missile. In addition, MDC serves as the main contractor for one of the Pentagon's two main ballistic missile defense programs.

MDC also has been a major NASA contractor. In the early days of the space program, McDonnell Co. designed and built the first manned space vehicles, the Mercury and Gemini capsules. Today, MDC produces the Delta space launch vehicle that NASA uses to launch communications, weather and scientific satellites. After 1983, NASA will launch all its satellites from the reusable Shuttle, but MDC may sell the non-reusable Delta directly to commercial customers. MDC also makes the Payload Assist Module (PAM), a booster used to move satellites from the launch vehicle--either the Delta or the Space Shuttle--into their designated orbits.

Defense employees and facilities: All of MDC's 30 million square feet of floor space is either owned or leased by the company. About a third of it is in Missouri, and a little under half is in California. In St. Louis, production facilities spread around the city support all the company's business segments but primarily are devoted to military aircraft manufacture. MDC's facilities in Long Beach and Torrance, Calif., and Tulsa, Okla., produce both military and commercial aircraft. Missiles and space systems are manufactured in Huntington Beach, Calif.; St. Louis County, Mo.; and Titusville, Fla. McDonnell Douglas also operates a plant in Ontario, Canada, that manufactures aircraft components, which later are assembled in the United States.

At the end of 1982, MDC employed 72,451 persons, roughly 2,000 fewer than in 1981. A company spokesman told IRRC that all employees work on defense projects except those in non-aerospace operations and most of Douglas Aircraft's employees.

Nuclear Weapons-Related Programs

Contracts for nuclear weapons-related programs are nothing new at McDonnell Douglas. In the 1950s, the original McDonnell Co. was the prime contractor for the nuclear-tipped Thor, an intermediate-range ballistic missile that the United States deployed in Britain from 1956 through 1963. About the same time, Douglas Aircraft produced the Nike series of strategic air defense systems and the Honest John battlefield missiles, both of which are nuclear-capable and were first deployed in Europe the early 1950s. Neither system is now part of the U.S. arsenal, but the conventional versions of the latest Nike missile, the Nike Hercules, and the Honest John are used by several NATO nations and other U.S. allies.[1] After McDonnell and Douglas merged, the company produced the nuclear-armed Genie missile, an air-launched missile designed to destroy aircraft. Although MDC no longer produces this missile, about 400 Genies are still in service with five Air Force squadrons.[2]

More recently, MDC has become a major contractor for two primary nuclear weapons-related programs, the Tomahawk cruise missile program and the Ballistic Missile Defense program. In addition, the company makes a variety of planes, missiles and space systems that are designed primarily for conventional roles, yet are capable of delivering nuclear weapons or would be important in fighting a nuclear war.

McDonnell Douglas's Nuclear Weapons-Related Contracts
(in millions of dollars)

Primary Systems		Secondary Systems	
FY 1981		FY 1981	
BMD program	$56	F/A-18 fighter	$1,120
ABRES program	$5	F-15 fighter	$780
Titan II missile	$3	AV-8B aircraft	$295
		Tomahawk cruise missile	$155
		KC-10 tanker aircraft	$134
		F-4 aircraft	$121
		Navstar components	$3
		A-4 aircraft	$2.4
Other current contracts		Other current contracts	
B-1B ejection seats		F-16,F-111,P-3C components	
		Space Shuttle components	
		Laser strategic communications	
		Manned space station	

In FY 1981, MDC received prime contract awards for primary nuclear weapons systems worth $63 million. Awards for secondary nuclear weapons-related systems totaled $2.79 billion, including the Tomahawk cruise missile.

Primary systems:

Ballistic missile defense (BMD)--As mentioned above, MDC is the prime contractor for one of the Pentagon's two main ballistic missile defense programs, the systems technology program. The purpose of this program is to take the technologies developed by the other main BMD program, the advanced technology program, and make them into complete BMD systems. At present, the systems technology program has two major projects: the low altitude defense system (LoAD) and the layered defense system.[3]

In 1981, MDC was named the prime contractor for the LoAD system, a relatively short range system that would destroy attacking warheads inside the atmosphere. In June 1982, the company received a contract worth $302 million to develop a LoAD system that could be used to defend the MX and Minuteman missiles. Martin Marietta and Raytheon are two of the subcontractors for the latter contract.[4]

For the layered defense system, MDC has a smaller contract worth $35 million. The layered defense system would consist of two tiers. The first tier would destroy attacking warheads before they entered the Earth's atmosphere. The second tier would be a backup system, similar to a LoAD system, that would stop any warheads that the first tier missed. Under its contract, MDC is developing an infrared sensor system, called the forward acquisition system (FAS), that would detect and track attacking missiles as part of the first tier.[5]

In FY 1981, MDC's total prime contract awards for ballistic missile defense totaled $56 million. In FY 1982, in addition to the $302 million contract for LoAD, the company received $47 million in BMD awards. In FY 1983, the company has received awards worth at least $17 million for this program.

Advanced Ballistic Reentry System (ABRES)--In FY 1981, MDC received prime contract awards worth at least $5 million for ABRES research and development. The ABRES program studies and develops reentry technology designed for existing or future ballistic missiles.

Titan II ICBM--In FY 1981, MDC received contracts worth $3 million for work on the Titan II, the oldest ICBM in the country's land-based arsenal, which soon will be retired. Along with Minuteman missiles, about 40 Titan IIs make up the nation's current ICBM force.

B-1B bomber--MDC makes ejection seats for the B-1B bomber.

Secondary systems:

Cruise missile--McDonnell Douglas's importance in the cruise missile program grew in 1982 when the Navy named MDC the second manufacturer for the Tomahawk cruise missile. Previously, MDC had built the guidance systems for the five versions of the Tomahawk, and General Dynamics had manufactured the missile airframes. Now the companies will compete each year for missile production contracts. In 1982, MDC received contract awards worth $13.3 million to manufacture an initial 10 missiles. It started to expand its facilities in Titusville, Fla., where the first MDC-produced Tomahawk is planned to come off the line early in 1984.

MDC will continue to develop and produce the Tomahawks' guidance systems. In 1981, MDC received initial orders for guidance systems for four of the five Tomahawk variants--the three sea-lauched missiles and the ground-launched missile. All the Tomahawks, with the exception of the anti-ship version, use the terrain contour matching (Tercom) guidance system. Tercom provides the continuous guidance necessary to make the slow, low-flying cruise missile a highly accurate weapon. By comparing aberrations in the contour of the terrain with a series of maps stored in its memory, Tercom reportedly will keep the missile within 200 feet of its target. The anti-ship Tomahawk has a guidance package similar to the one used on MDC's Harpoon missile.

Also in 1981, the company started to produce the launch-control equipment that would be used on any ground-launched cruise missiles based in Europe. The company also reports that it has developed several mission planning centers to provide the data needed for the maps stored in the Tercom guidance system's memory.

In all, MDC received at least $155 million in prime contract awards for cruise missile work in FY 1981, which is equal to about 4 percent of the company's government sales and about 2 percent of its total sales. In FY 1982 MDC received at least $94 million in cruise missile prime contract awards, and in 1983 it has received at least eight contracts worth more than $110 million. MDC says its cruise missile program now has a "multi-billion-dollar" sales potential.

The St. Louis Post-Dispatch has reported that 1,000 to 1,500 MDC employees work on cruise missile guidance systems in St. Louis, and that the Tomahawk program in Titusville will hire another 850 employees. An MDC spokesman told IRRC that these figures were roughly accurate.

Nuclear-capable aircraft:

F/A-18 Hornet--The F/A-18 fighter and attack plane is MDC's newest aircraft program. Although it will serve primarily as a carrier-based, conventionally armed fighter plane, it is one of the many nuclear-capable planes in the nation's arsenal.

The Pentagon plans to buy 1,377 Hornets over the next several years, the largest number of aircraft procured in any one program. However, performance problems and cost overruns have caused some heated controversy over the plane, and although Congress approved orders for 84 F/A-18s in 1984 and another 84 in 1985, future orders may be reduced.

In FY 1981, DoD awarded MDC $1.1 billion in development contracts for the F/A-18. In FY 1982, MDC received more than $600 million. In FY 1983, MDC received more than $1.7 billion, a large portion of which went toward the production of 79 F/A-18s. MDC delivered 25 F/A-18s (including 11 development aircraft) to the U.S. military in 1981 and 54 in 1982. Northrop, General Electric and Hughes Aircraft also are major subcontractors for the Hornet program.

Foreign orders for the F/A-18 also have been large. In 1982, the Australian government ordered 75 planes at a cost of $2.79 billion. Canada ordered 138 planes, and Spain ordered 84.

F-15 Eagle--MDC's F-15 is another nuclear-capable fighter plane. It can carry the Genie nuclear bomb. DoD also has chosen the Eagle to serve as the launching platform for the anti-satellite weapon (Asat) currently being tested. The F-15 will launch the Asat in the atmosphere, and a two-stage rocket then will boost it into space, where it will track and destroy satellites.[6] This Asat system is supposed to be tested late in 1983 or early in 1984.

In FY 1981, DoD awarded McDonnell Douglas at least $780 million for work on the USAF F-15, excluding foreign military sales. In FY 1982, MDC received $89 million in F-15 prime contract awards, and in FY 1983 it has received at least $609 million. By the end of 1982, MDC had delivered 776 F-15s to the Air Force. The FY 1983 budget calls for 39 more planes.

F-4 Phantom--Until a few years ago, the F-4 Phantom was MDC's largest combat aircraft program. Since 1969, the company has produced more than 5,000 Phantoms for air forces around the world. The F-4 has flown in the Middle East and Vietnam wars, and still is used by the Air Force, the Navy and the Marines. However, the F/A-18 and the F-16 soon will replace some of the older F-4 planes.

As with the F/A-18 and the F-15, the Navy F-4 is assigned to both conventional and nuclear strike roles. The Marine Corps F-4, however, is not nuclear-capable.

In FY 1981, MDC received $121 million in prime contract awards to maintain and modernize the F-4. In FY 1982, no awards appeared in IRRC's sources for this plane. In FY 1983, MDC received $166 million for repairs and improvements.

AV-8B Harrier II--The AV-8B Harrier is an attack plane that MDC is building for the Marine Corps that can take off and land on short aircraft carrier runways. The AV-8B, like the F/A-18, is nuclear-capable.

In FY 1981, MDC received $295 million in prime contract awards for AV-8B development. In FY 1982, the company received at least $593 million, most of which was for the production of the first 12 aircraft. In FY 1983, MDC has received additional AV-8B prime contract awards worth $554 million toward the production of these aircraft. The Navy plans to procure 32 more Harriers in 1984, but this plane also has had some performance problems, and Congress may not approve the full order.

A-4 Skyhawk--During its original development in 1956, the A-4 Skyhawk explicitly was designed, along with its tactical missions, as a nuclear bomber that could reach the Soviet Union from naval carriers positioned offshore its borders.[7]

Before the production of the Skyhawk ceased in 1979, MDC had built more than 3,000 A-4s for the United States and many foreign countries. In FY 1981, MDC received $2.4 million for miscellaneous work on the plane.

KC-10 Extender--This strategic tanker is a modified version of MDC's DC-10. If B-52 and FB-111 strategic bombers are to reach their target ranges as quickly as possible, they must be refueled in the air. The KC-135 and the KC-10 are the nation's two aerial refueling tanker aircraft.

MDC received $134 million in FY 1981 contract awards for the KC-10. In FY 1983, MDC received more than $2.8 billion toward the production of 44 planes.

Other nuclear-capable planes--MDC has received small contracts for miscellaneous work on several nuclear-capable planes produced by other companies: General Dynamics' F-16 and F-111 and Lockheed's P-3C Patrol Aircraft. Recently, the company also received small contracts for Boeing's KC-135 strategic refueling plane.

Space systems:

--In FY 1981, MDC received contracts worth $3 million for research and development on the Navstar global positioning system. (See section on Rockwell for details.) In addition, the company is the prime contractor for the Payload Assist Module (PAM) booster that will be used to place Navstar satellites in orbit. Awards for this system in FY 1983 totaled at least $6 million.

--In FY 1981, MDC received contracts worth $4 million to conduct research on materials that could harden satellites against attack.

--In July 1981, MDC received a contract to develop and test a secure, high-capacity laser communications system for space satellites.

--The company has manufactured the Space Shuttle's aft solid rocket booster structures and propulsion subsystems.

--MDC is one of eight companies under contract to study the feasibility of a manned space station.[8] (See section on TRW for details.)

McDonnell Douglas-Government Relationship

Political action committee: The McDonnell Douglas Corp. Good Government Fund, the company's PAC, doubled its contributions to congressional candidates in 1981-82. In 1979-80, it gave $68,000 to 115 congressional candidates; in 1981-82, it gave $136,675 to 140 candidates. The fund's contributions to candidates who serve on defense-related committees more than doubled--from $30,850 to 41 defense committee members in 1979-80 to $69,875 to 61 members in 1981-82. The proportion of MDC's contributions to defense committee members rose from 45 percent of its total contributions in 1979-80 to 51 percent in 1981-82.

Many of MDC's largest contributions went to defense committee members, three of whom represent districts in Missouri and Illinois in which large numbers of MDC workers reside. In 1979-80, Rep. Bill D. Burlison (D-Mo.), then a member of the House subcommittee on defense appropriations, received $4,000, MDC's largest contribution. Reps. Joseph P. Addabbo (D-N.Y.), chairman of the House defense appropriations subcommittee, and Melvin Price (D-Ill.), chairman of the House Armed Services Committee, each received $2,000. In 1981-82, Sen. Howard W. Cannon (D-Nev.), a member of the Senate Armed Services Committee, received $5,000, Addabbo received $4,000, and Rep. Ike Skelton (D-Mo.), a member of the House Armed Services Committee, received $5,000. Other large contributions went to Sens. John Danforth (R-Mo., $3,000) and Richard Lugar (R-Ind., $3,500).

Washington office: McDonnell Douglas maintains an office in Washington, D.C., that conducts lobbying activities, responds to inquiries and matters pertaining to export licensing, and provides technical information to the government. The office also plays a role in the international marketing of MDC commercial aircraft.

The Washington Industrial Team currently is registered as MDC's lobbyist. Clark M. Clifford of the Clifford and Warnke law firm and five other individuals have been MDC lobbyists in the recent past, but are not currently registered.

Personnel interchange: MDC hired 202 mid- to high-level Pentagon employees, and seven MDC employees moved to mid- to high-level positions in DoD, from 1977 to 1981.

Several of MDC's officers and directors have military backgrounds. Sanford N. McDonnell, MDC chairman and chief executive officer, was a sergeant during World War II who did lab work on the atomic bomb project at Los Alamos, N.M. James S. McDonnell, MDC's vice president for marketing, spent three years at the Air Force's special weapons center in New Mexico before he started to work at the company in 1963. Robert Johnson, another MDC vice president and president of McDonnell Douglas Astronautics division, left the company in 1969 to become the assistant secretary of the Army and a consultant to the DoD research and development board. He returned to MDC in 1973. William H. Branch, former adviser to the Defense Science Board's task force on antiballistic missile systems, became McDonnell Douglas's director of advanced defense systems in 1973.[9]

Contingency Planning and Prospects

Diversification has been a long-lived issue at McDonnell Douglas. In 1978, Business Week reported that MDC founder and former chairman James S. McDonnell has always worried that a single, big military contract cancellation or the loss of a key design competition could wreck the company and has taken steps to reduce such vulnerability.[10] However, the company's first and largest acquisition--Douglas Aircraft --has not brought the buffer that was envisioned. In fact, the unprofitability of MDC's commercial aircraft segment probably has caused the company to rely on its government contracts even more.

Since the merger with Douglas, MDC has entered several other non-defense businesses. The largest is in the computer field: data processing, systems design, programming and other services. MDC also has a commercial financing and leasing program. Recently, MDC has entered the energy field. It designed Solar One, a 10-megawatt solar power plant built in California's Mojave Desert, which started operation in 1981. Also in 1981, MDC purchased facilities in Oak Ridge, Tenn., where it plans to conduct research into fusion energy. However, MDC's non-defense business still remains limited. In 1978, Chairman McDonnell said all MDC's non-defense businesses were comparatively small and would be for some time to come.[11] Business Week said in 1978 that MDC "continues to limit new ventures to natural outgrowths of the company's existing aerospace, electronics and related high-technology operation. McDonnell Douglas is not--and never has been--interested in acquiring companies in general industrial fields, although such deals are brought regularly to its attention."

Thus, McDonnell Douglas's operations remain sensitive to fluctuations in government military spending. In its 1982 10K form the company states: "The loss of a major portion of U.S. government business could have a material, adverse effect on MDC."

Despite this vulnerability, MDC has not taken the financial lumps that other large aerospace companies such as Lockheed, Grumman and General Dynamics have. Although some financial analysts attribute fluctuations in MDC's income and earnings largely to changes in government military spending, such fluctuations have not swung downward precariously. As Business Week explained it: "By luck or design, MDC has benefited from projects with extraordinarily long production lives--enabling it to reap the profits of the learning curve far more effectively than any other military contractor."

Contingency planning: Contingency planning has not been part of MDC's efforts to protect itself from military contract cancellations. In 1981, when shareholders introduced two resolutions asking in part that MDC disclose its alternative employment plans for workers on the F/A-18 and other projects, the company said it had "no such plans." Instead, the company stated that it "has historically, and with demonstrable success, sought new business opportunities for the benefit of its employees and stockholders, and that the economic conversion planning or plans envisioned by the proponents are neither practical nor necessary." In other words, the company believes that diversification is preferable to conversion to protect MDC shareholders and workers.

In the past, diversification has not protected all of MDC's workers from layoffs. McDonnell Douglas officials told IRRC that in 1979 approximately 1,500 blue collar workers were laid off in the St. Louis area--600 because of the phasing out of F-4 production, 800 as a result of reduced F-15 production and about 100 because of a normal slowdown in F-18 production. According to these officials, the company remains in contact with workers who have been laid off and by March 1981 had been successful in rehiring more than 1,000 of them--in most cases for jobs in St. Louis. The company believes that the full-scale production of the F/A-18 and the expansion of its nonaerospace subsidiaries will continue to help smooth out fluctuations in defense-related employment.

Prospects: If the United States and the Soviet Union negotiated a freeze on nuclear weapons production or a substantial arms control agreement, MDC's cruise missile might be cut back substantially. These contracts totaled $155 million in FY 1981 and at least $204 million in FY 1982 and 1983. In addition, MDC's $302 million contract to develop a LoAD system to defend MX or Minuteman missiles also might be affected.

However, a decrease in the production of nuclear weapons might mean a corresponding increase in conventional weapons production, possibly including some MDC planes and missiles. In this scenario, MDC employees might be able to switch from nuclear weapons-related programs to conventional weapons programs within the company. If MDC were not able to gain such contracts, though, it is doubtful that MDC's commercial aerospace or nonaerospace businesses would be in a position to absorb laid-off employees.

MDC probably is more vulnerable to cuts in its military aircraft programs than to reductions caused by arms control agreements. If Congress cut back the F/A-18 or the AV-8B programs, even while increasing defense spending overall, MDC probably would experience a substantial loss of future income. Although now it appears that orders will not be changed, several congressional hurdles still must be cleared.

McDonnell Douglas Footnotes

1. Ronald D. Pretty, ed., Jane's Weapons Systems, 1982-83, Jane's Publishing Co. Ltd., London, 1982, p. 80, 379.
2. Ibid., p. 185; Taylor, Missiles of the World, p. 42.
3. Pretty, op. cit., p. 18-19.
4. Ibid., p. 20.
5. Ibid., p. 19.
6. Aviation Week and Space Technology, May 2, 1983, p. 14.
7. Tom Gervasi, Arsenal of Democracy, Grove Press Inc., New York, N.Y., 1981, p. 114.
8. Space World, November 1982, p. 16.
9. Gordon Adams, The Iron Triangle, Council on Economic Priorities, New York, p. 348, 351, 353.
10. Business Week, "Where Management Style Sets the Strategy," Oct. 23, 1978, p. 10.

Northrop

Northrop is only one-half the size of competitors McDonnell Douglas or Lockheed, but it is considered one of the best-performing aerospace companies. Net sales were $2.5 billion in 1982, up from $2 billion in 1981. Net income declined to $5 million from $48 million, in part because in 1982 Northrop wrote off the $258 million it invested in its new plane, the F-20 Tigershark.

Northrop began 1983 with a backlog of nearly $2.8 billion in orders, 20 percent higher than the year before and higher than the level of any previous year. The U.S. government made about 83 percent of the orders, some of which were placed on behalf of foreign governments.

Northrop's business is divided into four segments--aircraft, services, electronics and construction--but the emphasis is on aircraft. Aircraft design, development and production has been Northrop's primary undertaking since the company was formed in 1939. Aircraft sales accounted for more than half the company's revenues in 1982. The services and electronics segments each accounted for about one-fifth of revenues; the construction segment is minor.

Northrop ranks 261st on the Forbes 500 top sales list, and it employs 35,500 people. The company is based in Los Angeles.

Government and Defense Business

Northrop for years has had a large percentage of its business in defense, but it belies the image of a big defense contractor. The company has gained a reputation for efficient production, on-time deliveries and independence from government subsidies.

Northrop estimates that 80 percent of its business is in defense. In 1982, the U.S. government bought $1.9 billion worth of goods from Northrop, equal to about 75 percent of the company's net sales. This amount includes $444 million in foreign military sales also channeled through the government. It does not include direct foreign sales, another $381 million.

In FY 1982, Northrop received DoD prime contract awards worth $1.6 billion, up from $623 million in 1981. Northrop ranked 12th on DoD's list of top contractors.

Major defense programs: Northrop's largest defense program is the F/A-18 Hornet. McDonnell Douglas is the prime contractor for the

Data on Northrop
(dollar figures in millions)

	1978	1979	1980	1981	1982
Sales	$1,830	$1,583	$1,655	$1,991	$2,473
Net income (earnings)	$88	$90	$86	$48	$5
Sales to government (domestic agencies)	$505	$586	$715	$970	$1,429
Sales to government (domestic sales and foreign military sales	$1,451	$1,119	$1,187	$1,522	$1,873
Domestic government sales as a percentage of total sales	28%	37%	43%	49%	58%
All government sales as a percentage of total sales	79%	71%	72%	76%	76%
DoD prime contract awards*	$586	$800	$1,227	$623	$1,598
Ratio of DoD contract awards to to total sales+	.32	.51	.74	.31	.66
Backlog	$1,196	$2,100	$2,229	$2,306	$2,775
Total Northrop employees	31,200	28,800	30,200	31,400	35,500

* U.S. fiscal year, ending Sept. 30.
+ U.S. fiscal year awards compared with calendar year sales.

plane, but Northrop, which designed the original F-18 prototype, is the major subcontractor.

Northrop's other military aircraft programs include the Advanced Technology Bomber (Stealth), the F-20 Tigershark, the F-5 fighter jet and target aircraft.

The company's Electronics Systems Group produces navigation and guidance systems, electronic countermeasures, and other defense electronics for aircraft and other weapons systems. One of its biggest sellers is gyroscopes. Northrop reports that in 1981, it delivered more than 21,000 of these systems for some 100 military and commercial programs in the United States and 20 other nations. Northrop's gyroscopes will form part of many major new weapons systems including the MX, the F-16, the air-launched cruise missile and the Patriot missile system.

Another major product is electronic countermeasures (ECM) sets. Northrop's ECM sales have increased from $45 million in 1977 to $182 million in 1981. This huge increase reflects the fact that ECM systems have become standard equipment on all ships, submarines and planes. Northrop was the fourth largest U.S. electronics warfare contractor in 1981, behind E-Systems Inc., Loral Corp. and Raytheon.[1] Current contracts include orders for ECM systems for the B-52, the F-15 Eagle and, most recently, the B-1B.

The Northrop services group's main contract is with Saudi Arabia. Under this contract, called the Peace Hawk Program, Northrop is training Saudi pilots to use and maintain F-5 and F-15 fighter planes. Revenues from this program have exceeded $2 billion since it started in 1977. In 1982, Saudi Arabia gave the company a $666 million, three-year extension to the contract. Peace Hawk "makes Northrop practically part of the Royal Saudi Air Force, at least temporarily," said Fortune magazine in 1978.

Northrop's services division also provides management and technical support services for military and other governmental agencies.

Defense employees and facilities: Northrop's vice president for public affairs, Les Daly, told IRRC that the number of employees involved in defense is roughly proportional to the amount of Northrop's defense business. Thus, approximately 75 percent of Northrop's employees (26,600) work on defense projects.

Nuclear Weapons-Related Programs

Northrop considers itself "a major contributor to the nation's strategic buildup." As a subcontractor, the company has contributed to the development and production of many nuclear weapons delivery systems: the MX, B-1B, B-52, ALCM and others. As a prime contractor, Northrop is designing the top-secret Stealth advanced technology bomber.

Northrop's prime contracts on primary nuclear weapons systems totaled at least $147 million in FY 1981. Contracts on secondary and related systems totaled at least $104 million.

Primary systems:

MX ICBM--Northrop has been involved in the development of the MX's guidance system since 1975. At present, Northrop's Electronics Division in Hawthorne, Calif., is developing inertial measurement units (IMUs) for the missile, key elements in its re-entry guidance system. At the end of 1982, Northrop had delivered six of these guidance platforms and was testing 23 others.

In FY 1981, Northrop received contract awards for the MX's IMUs worth $97 million. The company says this contract had totaled $366 million through February 1983. Later in 1983, Northrop received an additional contract worth $397 million for full-scale development of the units. Receipts over the life of the project are estimated at $1 billion.

Northrop's precision products division is one of the subcontractors on the IMU contract. In addition, it produces gyroscopes that are used in the guidance "brain" of the MX. Awards for the MX gyroscopes totaled

Northrop's Nuclear Weapons-Related Contracts
(in millions of dollars)

Primary Systems		Secondary Systems	
FY 1981		FY 1981	
MX missile	$111	F-15 ECM system	$101
B-52 ECM	$33	E-3A Awacs aircraft	$1.3
Minuteman missile	$2.5	P-3 aircraft	$1.2
Other current contracts		Other current contracts	
B-1B ECM (subcontract)		F/A-18 aircraft (subcontract)	
Stealth bomber		Target aircraft	
SLBM components		F-16 aircraft	
ALCM components		Space Shuttle	
		Cruise missile components	

$14 million for FY 1981. The gyroscope contract could generate $100 million in sales if all 100 MX missiles are produced.

Advanced technology bomber--Late in 1981, Northrop's stock jumped in response to reports that the company had received a contract to develop the radar-evading bomber called Stealth. The selection of such a small company for such a large project came as a surprise to many observers, but it is believed that the company had been working seriously toward a Stealth program for at least five years. Larger contractors like Boeing and General Electric are lined up as subcontractors to the smaller Northrop for this weapons system.

No official cost estimates for the plane have been verified, but speculation has run rampant. Business Week put the Stealth project's total cost at $30 billion in 1981 dollars.[2] Defense industry analyst Paul Nisbet estimated Northrop's 1982 sales at $150 million for the Stealth. He predicted total sales would reach $3.4 billion by 1987.[3]

Northrop would like to get the Stealth flying as soon as possible, perhaps even by 1988, in hopes that Congress will bypass the B-1B in favor of the Stealth. The Air Force, however, has been reluctant to provide funds required to speed up the program. So far, the Pentagon views the B-1B and Stealth as complementary, and favors building some of each.

On the other hand, Rockwell, the prime contractor for the B-1B, would like its plane to supersede the Stealth. It recently joined with Lockheed in a 10-year agreement to develop a new radar-evading version of the B-1 that could compete with the Northrop plane. The two are likely to compete head-to-head in a high-stakes competition later in the decade. Boeing, as a major subcontractor on the Northrop version, can be expected to weigh in on Northrop's side.[4]

B-52 bomber--Northrop has supplied the major portion of the B-52 bomber's electronic countermeasures (ECM) equipment for the last 20 years.

In FY 1981, Northrop received prime contracts worth at least $33 million to upgrade the B-52's ECM equipment. Northrop's Defense Systems Division in Rolling Meadows, Ill., will do this work.

In FY 1983, Northrop received contracts worth $26 million for various ECM systems for the B-52.

B-1B bomber--Under subcontract to the AIL Division of Eaton Corp., Northrop is developing a major portion of the B-1B's ECM. The potential value of this project is estimated at $500 million. In mid-1982, Eaton awarded contracts totaling $89 million to Northrop for development and initial production of the ECM equipment.

Under a $5 million subcontract that Northrop received from Boeing in 1982, the company is producing systems designed to monitor performance of the B-1B's navigation and weapons operations.

Minuteman missile--In FY 1981, Northrop's Norwood, Mass., facility received a contract worth $2.5 million for work on Minuteman missile automatic pilot mechanisms.

Air-launched cruise missile--Under a small subcontract from Boeing, Northrop is producing rate and acceleration sensors for the air-launched cruise missile.

Sub-launched ballistic missiles--In its Orange County, Calif., facility, Northrop tests equipment for the Polaris, Poseidon and Trident missile systems.

Secondary and nuclear-capable systems:

F/A-18 fighter/attack aircraft--Northrop produces the center and aft fuselage and the twin vertical stabilizers of the nuclear-capable F/A-18, along with all associated subsystems. The company delivered 57 sets of equipment to prime contractor McDonnell Douglas in 1982; 94 deliveries are scheduled for 1983. Work on the Northrop components is performed in El Segundo, Calif.

The U.S. government expects to buy 1,366 F/A-18s. However, the plane has been plagued by performance problems, its cost has escalated, and there has been some talk in Congress about cutting back the number of planes ordered.

Northrop's contract acquisitions for the F/A-18 totaled $522 million in 1981 and $739 million in 1982.

F-15 fighter--Northrop has manufactured more than 800 ECM systems for the F-15 Eagle. The program has had a value of more than $700 million to the company.

In FY 1981, Northrop received F-15 ECM contracts worth at least $101 million. In FY 1982, Northrop received a contract worth $6.4 million for F-15 electronic warfare equipment. In FY 1983, Northrop received contracts worth more than $120 million for F-15 ECM modifications, support and spare parts.

Target aircraft--Northrop's target aircraft (MQM-74C and BQM-74C) are used to train pilots of F-15, F-4 and F-16 aircraft to shoot down missiles, including the air-launched cruise missiles which the drones can simulate. Orders for 3,000 of the BQM-74Cs alone are expected through the 1980s.

In FY 1982, Northrop received contracts worth $42 million to furnish 350 BQM-74C drones to the Navy. It also received a contract for work on a new engine for the BQM-74C. Northrop says this new engine "will further increase its capability to simulate the maneuvers of high-speed cruise missiles."

E-3A Awacs--Northrop produces the navigation system for the E-3A Airborne Warning and Control System surveillance aircraft (Awacs). Its contract calls for the delivery of 64 systems at a cost of $72 million, $1.3 million of which was awarded in FY 1981.

P-3 Orion--Radio navigation equipment is Northrop's contribution to the P-3 Orion Navy patrol plane. In FY 1981, Northrop received P-3 contracts worth $1.2 million.

Cruise missiles--Northrop produces gyroscope packages for the ALCM and guidance units for the Tomahawk cruise missile. Northrop says that more than 1,000 of these guidance units have been delivered under contracts worth more than $50 million.

F-16 fighter--Northrop produces gyroscopes for this fighter plane. The company says it manufactures 300 F-16 gyros per month.

Space Shuttle--Northrop says that nearly 400 of its engineers, scientists and technicians support space shuttle missions. The company also supplies navigation and guidance components for the shuttle.

Northrop-Government Relationship

Political action committee: Northrop's PAC (Nepac) contributed a total of $61,657 in 1979-80 and $101,565 in 1981-82 to candidates for federal offices. Northrop increased its contributions to defense committee members over the four-year period, from $24,425 in 1979-80 (40 percent of its total contributions) to $52,250 in 1981-82 (51 percent of its total contributions).

In 1981-82, major contributions went to Rep. Joseph P. Addabbo (D-N.Y., $2,500), chairman of the House defense appropriations subcommittee; Rep. Norman Dicks (D-Wash., $2,500), a member of the House defense appropriations subcommittee; and Sen. Howard Cannon (D-Nev., $5,000), a member of the Senate Armed Services Committee. Nepac's largest contribution to a non-defense committee member ($2,300) went to David Emery of Maine, who ran for a House seat.

Northrop spokesman Daly provided the following information on Northrop's PAC: All contributions to the PAC are confidential. The corporate secretary organizes a group of employee volunteers to explain the PAC and solicit contributions from fellow employees. Solicitations are not done on an employer-to-employee basis, but among peers. The PAC receives solicitations from candidates and makes contributions based on a candidate's or incumbent's voting record, position, interest in defense and geographic affiliation.

Washington office: Northrop's Washington office exists to provide information on Northrop's programs to the government, and to collect information from the government that is pertinent to the company's interests, according to Daly.

Six lobbyists registered on behalf of Northrop in 1981, including Manatt, Phelps, Rotherberg and Tunney of Los Angeles (a law firm that includes Democratic Party Chairman Charles Manatt and former Democratic Sen. John Tunney of California); the Washington Industrial Team (a firm that includes former Reps. Richard Ichord and Robert Wilson, both members of the House Armed Services Committee until 1981); and former Rep. Jim Lloyd. The legislative interests of these lobbyists ranged from a general concern with "defense issues," to specific interests in "F/A-18 and F-5 series aircraft, plus other Northrop Corp. programs."

Daly said the defense industry's lobby differs little from those of other industries. He feels that it is not easy to determine the effectiveness of lobbying, and that the system of defense contracting is so big, with so many groups involved, that it is unassailable by any one special interest group. Although he said he was sure that lobbying had its good and bad consequences for individual companies, he described defense contracting in general as "a pristine kind of system."

Although Northrop has tried to avoid defense contracting inefficiencies, government dependency and cost overruns, the company has not been immune from domestic and foreign payments controversies. In 1972, Northrop was fined for making an illegal contribution of $150,000 to President Nixon's re-election campaign. Northrop's President Tom Jones pleaded guilty to the charges, and he paid the fine from his own pocket. In the mid- to late 1970s, Northrop was questioned by the Securities and Exchange Commission on the legality of some sale commissions the company paid overseas, and by the Defense Department on some of the consultant and entertainment fees that it charged on government contracts. Northrop has since revised its policies in both areas.

Personnel interchange: Several Northrop board members have worked in the Defense Department: William Ballhaus served on the Technical Advisory Panel on Aerospace in the Office of the Secretary of Defense. Ivan Getting was the assistant for development planning to the Air Force deputy chief of staff for development. Richard Horner has served in various military positions, including assistant secretary of the Air Force for research and development.

Northrop hired 381 mid- to high-level DoD employees between 1977 and 1981, of whom 87 percent were former military officers. Eight Northrop employees transferred to mid- to high-level positions in DoD during the same period.

Contingency Planning and Prospects

Contingency planning: At any one time in the 1950s and early 1960s, Northrop relied on two or three defense projects for a large portion of business. The cancellation of a major contract--the Flying Wing aircraft in 1953--put the company near bankruptcy. When the current Northrop chairman, Jones, became president of the company in 1959, he worked to reduce Northrop's vulnerability to such cancellations. By 1961, the company had become a major subcontractor on 70 projects. Nevertheless, the cancellation of the Skybolt air-to-ground missile was a sharp blow in 1962. Northrop lost 25 percent of its business, and 3,300 employees were laid off. But the company recovered so fast from this jolt that a Forbes article asked, "Need defense companies be as vulnerable to contract cancellations as most of them have been?"[5]

Winning subcontracts--not diversification--brought Northrop out of the Skybolt disaster, and it has been the company's formula for survival in the defense industry. As a major defense subcontractor, Northrop has increased its earnings year by year, despite the ups and downs of the defense marketplace. Northrop did not begin major commercial business until 1966, and even then, the company chose businesses that made use of its aerospace expertise. The production of gyroscopes for a wide range of commercial and military contractors is one example; electronics is another.

Northrop maintains no structured contingency plans, according to spokesman Daly. He said that time and energy spent on making a project work and focusing on technologies that are likely to be adaptable to more than one product are more important ways of protecting the company's business and employees.

Daly could not recall times other than the Skybolt cancellation when Northrop laid off large numbers of employees. Forbes has remarked that Northrop's employee turnover is relatively low, and cited this as one reason the company is able to operate more efficiently than other defense contractors: "With a small but steady rise in sales, Northrop does not have to fire or rehire masses of people every few years."[6]

However, Northrop now is adding to its staff. The company "is in the most active hiring mode of any defense company in Southern California, including Rockwell on the B-1B," said one aerospace recruiter.[7] Northrop added between 3,500 and 5,000 employees in 1983.

Prospects: A freeze on nuclear weapons or other arms control agreements could affect Northop's MX and Stealth contracts. Defense budget cuts might include the F/A-18 Hornet.

When asked about the impact of possible cancellation of programs like the MX and the Stealth, Daly said the impact would depend on how much advance notice was given, and at what point the program was canceled. Although cancellations are very painful and dramatic, Daly said, they are also fairly rare.

Because at least 700 employees were added specifically for Northrop's work on the MX missile, a comparable number probably could be laid off from Northrop's facility in Hawthorne, Calif., if a cancellation did occur. However, Northrop says that its IMU technology could be used on other guidance systems "where high levels of accuracy are demanded," and thus the company might be able to apply it to the advanced cruise missile or other ballistic missiles.

Given the size of Northrop's F/A-18 involvement--more than $500 million in 1982--cancellation or severe reduction of orders would have a substantial impact on the company. Assuming a fairly close relationship between sales and employment relative to other Northrop programs, roughly 8,000 Northrop employees are at work on the F/A-18 program.

Northrop would lose substantial potential future income if the Stealth project were abandoned, but because the project is classified it is difficult to estimate the extent of the impact.

If the Reagan administration's plans for the U.S. strategic buildup continue to go forward, and if Northrop begins to have success in marketing its new F-20 Tigershark overseas, the company's defense business should increase substantially in coming years.

Northrop Footnotes

1. Countermeasures Handbook 1981, p. 38.
2. Business Week, April 19, 1982, p. 20.
3. The New York Times, Aug. 4, 1982.
4. The New York Times, Oct. 6, 1982, p. A19.
5. Forbes, Aug. 1, 1963, p. 32.
6. Ibid., p. 33.
7. Business Week, April 19, 1982, p. 73.

Raytheon

Raytheon, the first company to heat food with microwaves, to bounce a laser off the moon, and to develop guided missiles, is a technology-based company with half its business in electronics, and half in aircraft products, energy services, major appliances and other lines. Until 1982, Raytheon had posted 11 consecutive years of growth in its sales and earnings. In 1982, however, sales declined from $5.6 billion to $5.5 billion. Net income declined from $324 to $319 million. Raytheon attributed the reversal to the effect of the economy on its commercial businesses. The company's government business increased in both sales and earnings.

Raytheon ranked 96th in the Forbes top sales list in 1982, and it employed 72,000 people in its 10 divisions and 12 major operating subsidiaries spread over 26 states and six foreign countries. Raytheon is based in Lexington, Mass.

Government and Defense Business

Defense dependence: Through the late 1970s, between 30 and 40 percent of Raytheon's net sales went to DoD. In 1982, Raytheon's government sales--mostly to the military--equaled almost 40 percent of total sales, more than $2 billion. Goods with a value of $199 million purchased by the United States on behalf of foreign governments are included in these figures.

The backbone of Raytheon's military work is electronic systems used on a number of conventional and nuclear-related weapons, including missile, fire control, air traffic control, sonar, communications and electronic countermeasure systems for all the services. The company also makes utility and training aircraft, some of which is used by the military.

Except for the utility and training aircraft, which are built by Beech Aircraft Corp., a Raytheon subsidiary, Raytheon's electronic divisions are responsible for all these products. Non-military sales to the government included electronic components, minicomputers, communications systems, marine and medical electronics equipment and air traffic control systems.

In 1982, Raytheon was the ninth largest defense contractor, with awards of $2.3 billion, almost 2 percent of total DoD awards in that year.

Data on Raytheon
(dollar figures in millions)

	1978	1979	1980	1981	1982
Sales	$3,787	$4,354	$5,002	$5,636	$5,513
Net income	$187	$240	$282	$324	$319
Sales to government	NA	$1,500	$1,649	$1,946	$2,160
Government sales as a percentage of net sales	NA	34%	33%	35%	39%
Government sales, not including including foreign military sales	NA	$1,321	$1,378	$1,627	$1,961
Government-funded backlog	$1,660	$1,504	$1,977	$2,156	$3,178
DoD prime contract awards*	$1,307	$1,249	$1,745	$1,826	$2,262
Ratio of DoD prime contract awards to total sales+	.35	.29	.35	.32	.41
Total Raytheon employees	73,900	77,800	77,900	76,500	72,000

* U.S. fiscal year, ending Sept. 30.
\+ U.S. fiscal year awards compared with calendar year sales.

Major conventional military programs: Raytheon invented the guided missile that, in 1950, was the first to hit a flying target, and the company has been a leader in the surface-to-air missile field ever since. In 1956, Raytheon came out with an anti-aircraft missile named the Hawk (Homing-All-The-Way Killer), a version of which is still produced today. The Hawk missile and associated air defense system has been sold to 20 nations, including NATO countries and U.S. allies in Asia. Sales from the Hawk program already have exceeded $6 billion, and orders continue to come in. In the first quarter of 1982, the kingdom of Saudi Arabia gave Raytheon a $605 million contract for continued work on its Hawk air defense system.

In 1981, Raytheon began production of an air defense system to replace the Hawk and the Nike Hercules system. The company hopes to build a worldwide market for this new system, called the Patriot. Boston Magazine estimated that Raytheon would receive more than $6 billion by the time the Patriot is completed.[1]

Raytheon entered the air-to-air missile market with the Sparrow and Sidewinder missiles. Both these missiles, like the Hawk, have been produced for decades and are sold worldwide. Forbes has estimated that at one time, 80 percent of the air-to-air missiles arming U.S. fighter planes were made by Raytheon.[2]

Radar is another field in which Raytheon has played a key role. In World War II, Raytheon scientists were instrumental in the development of the first radar systems. Raytheon also is one of the nation's largest producers of electronic warfare systems.

Defense employees and facilities: If employment is roughly proportionate to sales, approximately 29,000 of Raytheon's 72,000 employees worked on military projects in 1982. Raytheon declined to answer any questions pertaining to this report, including an estimate of its employees that work on defense projects.

Six percent of Raytheon's 26 million square feet of property is owned by the government.

Nuclear Weapons-Related Programs

In FY 1981, Raytheon received at least $84 million in prime contract awards for primary nuclear warfare systems and components. This amount represented about 1.5 percent of Raytheon's total sales in 1981. The company received prime contract awards for secondary nuclear weapons-related systems worth at least $140 million.

Primary systems:

Trident missile--In FY 1981, Raytheon received prime contract awards of at least $67 million to produce parts of the guidance system for the Trident submarine's nuclear missile, the Trident I. In FY 1983, the company received an additional $25 million for this project. Raytheon has participated in the Navy's ballistic missile program for the last 20 years and has made guidance computers and displays for the Polaris and Poseidon ballistic missile submarines, in addition to its work for the Trident.

Strategic radar systems--Raytheon has developed three of the world's largest radar systems: Pave Paws, Cobra Dane and Cobra Judy. As part of the country's strategic missile warning system, all three of these systems use "phased array" technology to watch for Soviet ballistic missile tests and attacks. "Phased array" means that thousands of small radar antennas--the radar's eyes--are steered electronically by two large computers.

Pave Paws watches for surprise nuclear attacks from Soviet submarines. It also is used to track hundreds of satellites and other objects in space simultaneously. Pave Paws "can spot any object approaching the U.S.--provided it is coming at an altitude of above 3 degrees angle from the radar--and then can pick it up as far away as 3,000 miles," a Pentagon spokesman told Business Week.[3] It is 105 feet tall and is housed in a triangular-shaped, 76,732-square-foot building. Pave Paws facilities are located at Otis Air Force Base in Massachusetts and Beale Air Force Base in California, and are under construction at Robins Air Force Base in Georgia at a cost of $100 million.

Cobra Dane, located on Shemya Island in the Aleutians, monitors Soviet ballistic missile flights to the Kamchatka peninsula and Pacific Ocean.

Raytheon's Nuclear Weapons-Related Contracts
(in millions of dollars)

Primary Systems		Secondary Systems	
FY 1981		FY 1981	
Trident missile components	$67	AN/SPS-49 radar	$45
B-52 bomber ECM	$7.2	F-111 plane	$40
Cobra Dane radar	$5.3	AN-BQQ-5 sonar	$28
AN/BQR-19 sonar	$4.0	F-4 components	$11
		AN/SLQ-32	$7.2
		ECM and other work on A-6 aircraft	$7
		Nike Hercules components	$1.6
Other current contracts		Other current contracts	
Cobra Judy radar		Tomahawk cruise missile launcher	
Pave Paws radar		High frequency communications equipment	
OTH-B radar		Milstar satellite system	
B-1B bomber			
LoAD system			

This radar is approximately 100 feet tall and is housed in a 57,000-square-foot building.

Cobra Judy, the newest and first shipborne phased-array radar system, is mounted on the Observation Island, an old Navy freighter. It is designed to complement Cobra Dane's abilities. Cobra Dane can track missiles during initial and intermediate launch phases, and Cobra Judy is designed to monitor a missile's final flight stages. Raytheon received prime contract awards of at least $5.3 million for operation of Cobra Dane radar in FY 1981. In FY 1983, Raytheon received at least $3 million for the operation and maintenance of Cobra Judy.

Raytheon also builds components for the "over-the-horizon backscatter" (OTH-B), an early warning system that can detect objects even over the horizon.

B-1B bomber--In August 1982, Eaton awarded Raytheon's Sedco subsidiary a $94 million subcontract to develop defensive subsystems for the B-1B bomber.

B-52 bomber--In FY 1981, Raytheon received contracts worth $7.2 million for the B-52's electronics countermeasure systems.

Trident submarine sonar and silencing facility--In FY 1981, Raytheon also received contracts worth $4 million for a sonar system (designated AN/BQR-19) used on Trident ballistic missile submarines. In 1982, the company received another $4 million for this system.

Raytheon says it is involved with a magnetic measurement and silencing facility for Trident submarines located in Bangor, Wash. (The less noise a submarine emits, the less chance it has of being detected.)

Low altitude defense systems (LoAD)--Raytheon's 1981 annual report mentioned that the company is one of several companies working to design a system that could defend land-based nuclear missiles--the LoAD system.

Secondary systems:

Electronic warfare--In FY 1981, Raytheon received at least $54 million for electronic countermeasure systems and other work for nuclear-capable aircraft and ships, including $40 million for the F-111. In FY 1983, Raytheon received a $60 million contract for an ECM pod (designated AN/ALQ-119) used on the F-4, F-16, F-111 and A-10 aircraft.

Raytheon's shipboard electronic countermeasure system includes one model--the AN/SLQ-32--that is used on more than 240 Navy ships to protect them from missile attacks. Prime contract awards for this system were at least $7.2 million in FY 1981. In FY 1983, Raytheon received additional contracts worth $79 million for the SLQ-32. Since 1960, Raytheon has sold more than 2,000 of these jammers. Total awards to date on the AN/SLQ-32 system exceed $340 million.

Sonar for attack submarines--In addition to the Trident submarine, Raytheon has provided sonar systems for many of the Navy's nuclear attack submarines. In 1981, Raytheon received a contract worth $28 million for the sonar system that is the primary sensor for the most recent class of nuclear attack submarines, the SSN-688 Los Angeles class. This sonar system is designated the AN/BQQ-5.

Long range radar--Raytheon is producing a new, long-range surveillance radar (designated AN/SPS-49) that is used on a variety of Navy vessels, including the nuclear-capable guided missile cruisers (CG 47 class). In FY 1981, Raytheon received prime contract awards worth at least $45 million for this radar. In FY 1983, the company received additional contracts worth $51 million.

Fire control systems--In FY 1983, Raytheon received contracts worth $14 million to develop the computer software for fire control systems that would control the launch of Tomahawk cruise missiles and torpedoes from attack submarines.

Milstar--Near the end of FY 1983, Raytheon received contracts worth $44 million for the development of Milstar (Military Strategic Tactical and Relay System) terminals.

High frequency communications equipment--In FY 1982, Raytheon received $5 million to upgrade EHF (extra high frequency) and SHF (super high frequency) communications equipment. In FY 1983, the company received an additional $6 million for SHF satellite communication sets to be used for shipboard satellite communications. EHF and SHF equipment is harder to jam than communications equipment in other frequency ranges, and is used for strategic satellite communications.

F-4 components--In FY 1981, Raytheon received awards for at least $11 million for components for the nuclear-capable F-4 Phantom aircraft.

Nike Hercules components--In FY 1981, Raytheon also received contracts worth $1.6 million for components for the nuclear-capable Nike Hercules artillery gun.

Raytheon-Government Relationship

Political action committee: Raytheon's PAC contributions to candidates for federal offices increased more than three-fold from $36,000 in 1979-80 to $115,479 in 1981-82. Contributions to defense committee members increased over the four-year period from $11,075 in 1979-80 to $52,079 in 1981-82.

In 1981-82, major contributions went to several members of defense-related committees: Reps. Nicholas Mavroules (D-Mass., $6,354), William Chappell (D-Fla., $3,000) and John Murtha (D-Pa., $2,500), and Sens. Howard Cannon (D-Nev., $2,500) and John Stennis (D-Miss., $2,500). Non-defense committee members who received $2,500 or more were Reps. Margaret Heckler (R-Mass., $3,200) and Silvio Conte (R-Mass., $3,200) and Sen. Howard Baker (R-Tenn., $5,000).

Washington office: Raytheon maintains a Washington office, but the company would not provide IRRC with information on its structure and purpose. Defense Contract Audit Agency (DCAA) documents, obtained by Common Cause through a Freedom of Information Act request, say that Raytheon's Washington office is headed by a corporate vice president, and that the Washington office staff consists of a manager of government programs with a staff of eight field representatives and a manager of international programs. The functions of the office, as described by Raytheon in the documents, were to:

> provide a properly located, balanced, and qualified team to (i) ensure adequate coverage of the government market,

(ii) provide focal points for government customer contact by company personnel, (iii) create and/or maintain customer relations and acceptance of company capabilities and image, (iv) collect and disseminate information concerning market opportunities, customer reactions, and competitive activities, and (v) support directly the marketing effort of the divisions in specific programs as required.[4]

The DCAA audited Raytheon's lobbying expenses in 1974 and 1975, and it questioned costs charged to government contracts, including some $2,000 for goose hunts organized for DoD employees and unidentified guests and fees paid to several consultants. The documents do not say what actions were taken as a result of the audit.

The Washington Industrial Team was registered as Raytheon's lobbyist in 1981. Among agents listed were former U.S. Reps. Richard Ichord and Robert Wilson. Both have served on the House Armed Services Committee and have received small contributions from Raytheon's PAC.

Personnel interchange: At least two of Raytheon's officers have backgrounds in government work: The company's president, D. Brainerd Holmes, was director of manned space flight for NASA before he joined Raytheon in 1963. Everette Harper, vice president for corporate operations, was once counsel to the Senate Armed Services Committee.

Raytheon hired 137 mid- to high-level DoD employees between 1977 and 1981, of whom 88 percent were former military officers. Seven Raytheon employees moved to mid- to high-level DoD positions during the same period.

Contingency Planning and Prospects

Contingency planning: Ten years ago, Raytheon was able to get off the defense business roller coaster and keep sales and earnings on a steady rise. From the end of World War II through the early 1970s, however, Raytheon's sales followed the cyclic track of defense spending. Business peaked during World War II and again during the Korean War and plummeted after each. The company did not move to diversify until the early 1960s; government sales remained at 80 percent of its income until 1968 and then fell to 37 percent in 1969.

Raytheon moved carefully into commercial business in the early 1960s. The company avoided straying far from its technological base. As a result, Raytheon has been more successful than most contractors in redirecting its defense technology into profitable civilian goods. For example, microwave ovens were a spinoff from the company's military radio microwaves, and military sonar and radar systems have been adapted for civilian ships and air traffic control systems.

A number of factors aid the company's current steady position. First, unlike some defense contractors, Raytheon is not dependent on the depressed commercial aircraft business. Second, the defense products produced by Raytheon, especially electronics equipment, are in high demand and are used on a wide range of weapons systems, which reduces the company's vulnerability when any one program is canceled. And third, weapons markets outside the United States bring Raytheon a substantial amount of revenues.

But there have been some setbacks. In 1970, Raytheon laid off 13 percent of its work force--7,000 people--in response to decreases in government spending. In 1972, Raytheon lost a big source of growth when Congress substantially reduced the Safeguard ABM (antiballistic missile) program for which Raytheon would have supplied the radar. And in 1982, Raytheon lost the bid for a major missile program, the Advanced Medium Range Air-to-Air Missile (Amraam), to Hughes Aircraft. Forbes called this loss "a potential $6 billion disappointment,"[5] but the company said that "although a disappointment, that decision will not significantly affect our sales or margins over the next several years as Amraam production will not begin until the last half of the decade." Raytheon has since been named a major subcontractor for the missile.

Prospects: Raytheon did not provide information on the nature of the 1970 cutbacks, the company's general policy on handling canceled projects, or the potential impact of arms control agreements on the company's business and employees. It is clear, however, that any cutbacks in defense contracts would have a substantial impact on the state of Massachusetts, where Raytheon is the third largest employer.

Raytheon's Trident missile and B-1B contracts would be affected by a freeze on nuclear weapons. However, because Raytheon is a components producer of electronic systems that now are an important part of almost every miltary system, no defense reductions short of deep cuts in the overall military budget are likely to affect the company's business seriously.

Raytheon Footnotes

1. Boston Magazine, "The Missile Merchants of Lexington," May 1982, p. 114.
2. Forbes, June 1, 1969, p. 31.
3. Business Week, May 24, 1982, p. 94.
4. Advisory Report on Review of Washington Area Office Expenses for Calendar Years 1974 and 1975; Defense Contract Audit Agency Report #2740-05-6-0131 S-1, July 1, 1977.
5. Forbes, March 1, 1982, p. 138.

Rockwell International

Rockwell International, a diversified conglomerate, grew out of a merger in the late 1960s between Rockwell Standard, primarily an automotive axle and brake manufacturer, and North American Aviation, a large aerospace firm. Today, aerospace is Rockwell's largest line of business (38 percent of 1982 sales), followed by electronics (27 percent), automotive components (18 percent), and general industries (16 percent).

In 1982, Rockwell's sales and earnings rose for the seventh consecutive year. Sales increased 5 percent from $7 billion in 1981 to $7.4 billion in 1982. Earnings rose 4 percent to $332 million. Automotive and general industry sales suffered from the recession, but electronics and aerospace sales increased substantially.

The company is based in Pittsburgh. It ranks 62nd on the Forbes list of the nation's top industrial companies.

Government and Defense Business

The federal government is Rockwell's largest customer. Its purchases made up 52 percent ($3.8 billion) of Rockwell's 1982 sales, up from 42 percent in 1981. The company attributed this increase primarily to its contract for the B-1B bomber.

Almost all of the government's purchases from Rockwell consist of aerospace and electronics products. In 1982, more than 90 percent of the company's government sales came from these two business segments. Conversely, more than 90 percent of Rockwell's aerospace sales and 53 percent of its electronics sales went to the government in 1982, and a substantial portion of these were to DoD.

Space systems and rocket engines, aerostructures and military aircraft are among the aerospace products that Rockwell sells to the government. In 1981, Rockwell received more prime contract awards than any other firm from NASA ($1.5 billion). Most of these contracts pertained to the Space Shuttle program, for which Rockwell is the prime contractor.[1] Rockwell is also the prime contractor for the B-1B bomber and a satellite navigation system called Navstar, and it is one of the larger contractors for the MX missile.

Rockwell's electronics divisions produce components for many major weapons systems including the MX missile, the B-1B bomber, the Navy's

Data on Rockwell International
(dollar figures in millions)

	1978	1979	1980	1981	1982
Total sales	$5,309	$6,176	$6,907	$7,040	$7,395
Net earnings	$177	$261	$280	$319	$332
Sales to U.S. government	NA	$2,304	$2,580	$2,940	$3,816
Government sales as a percentage of total sales	36%	36%	37%	42%	52%
DoD prime contract awards*	$890	$684	$969	$1,126	$2,691
Ratio of DoD prime contract awards to total sales+	.17	.11	.14	.16	.36
DoE contract awards	NA	NA	NA	$363	$479
Ratio of DoD and DoE prime contract awards to total sales	NA	NA	NA	.21	.43
Rocky Flats and Hanford operating costs	NA	NA	NA	$443	$524
Rocky Flats and Hanford management fees before taxes	NA	NA	NA	$9.5	$9.6
Government backlog (funded and unfunded)	NA	NA	NA	$4,130	$4,980
Total Rockwell employees	114,208	114,452	108,199	103,455	100,271

* U.S. fiscal year, ending Sept. 30.
\+ U.S. fiscal year awards compared with calendar year sales.

ballistic missile and attack submarines, and satellite communications systems. Rockwell says this segment "has an important role in almost every major element of President Reagan's initiatives to improve the nation's defenses ranging from submarines, missiles and aircraft, to vital command, control and communications systems."

Apart from aerospace and electronics, Rockwell manages two DoE facilities that produce nuclear weapons materials and components--Rocky Flats in Golden, Colo., and Hanford in Richland, Wash.

Defense dependence: During World War II Rockwell produced armor for U.S. tanks, but it did not become a major defense contractor until it merged with North American Aviation. At that time, North American was a well-known aerospace military contractor in financial trouble. After 20 years of success in the aerospace field, two of North American's major contracts (one of which at the time was the proposed successor to the B-52 bomber, the B-70) were canceled. In addition, the company's credibility was seriously questioned after one of its Apollo space capsules burned on the launch pad in 1967, killing three astronauts. North American viewed a merger with Rockwell as a way to reduce its dependence on the Department of Defense; Rockwell wanted to reduce its dependence on the automotive industry and to apply its commercial know-how to North American's research projects. Since 1968, the combined North American Rockwell (since re-named

Rockwell International) has consistently ranked among the DoD's leading contractors.

"No company has benefited more so far from the policies of the Reagan administration than Rockwell," said a 1981 article in The New York Times.[2] While defense budget cuts could change this assessment, there is no doubt that Rockwell's defense business is increasing in absolute terms and as a percentage of its total sales. In 1982, Rockwell ranked eighth on the DoD's list of top contractors, with $2.7 billion in prime contract awards, up from $1.1 billion in 1981. The ratio of Rockwell's prime contract awards to its total sales, which had averaged about .15 over the last five years, jumped to .36 in 1982 and will increase if Congress continues to fund the B-1B and the MX.

Not surprisingly, Rockwell's large backlog is dominated by government orders. In 1982, $5 billion of its $6.4 billion backlog was made up of government orders, both funded and unfunded. The backlog for the B-1B program alone was $1.4 billion, of which $1 billion was unfunded.

Rockwell's research and development activities also concentrate on space and defense technology. The company says its research and development programs include "the Space Shuttle and the B-1B programs and...other programs such as those related to strategic and tactical missiles, satellites, defense electronics and nuclear energy." Rockwell reported that 16 percent of its $1.4 billion in 1982 research and development costs were covered by the company itself; presumably most of the remaining 84 percent was funded by the government.

Of Rockwell's 45.9 million square feet of floor space, approximately 16 percent is government-owned. Rockwell's aerospace divisions occupied more than 90 percent of the government-owned space in 1982.

Defense employees: Because Rockwell considers its employment figures proprietary information, it would not provide IRRC with an estimate of how many of its employees work on DoD projects. However, the company is required to disclose the number of employees that work at its DoE facilities: approximately 5,000 at Rocky Flats and 4,200 at Hanford in 1982.

If employment is roughly proportional to sales, then approximately 36,000 of Rockwell's 100,271 employees worked on DoD projects in 1982.

Nuclear Weapons-Related Programs

Rockwell's involvement with nuclear weapons-related systems began after the merger with North American Aviation. North American worked on the guidance system for the Minuteman missile and was the prime contractor for two strategic weapons--the B-70 supersonic bomber and the Navaho intercontinental missile--that were canceled before they reached the production stage.

A list of Rockwell's current nuclear warfare-related programs includes many new military systems: the B-1B bomber, and components for the MX missile, the Trident submarine and the Navstar and Afsatcom satellite systems.

In FY 1981, the company received at least $325 million in DoD prime contract awards for primary nuclear weapons-related activities, which represents about 4 percent of the company's 1981 sales. Rockwell's prime contract awards for secondary systems in FY 1981 totaled at least $193 million.

Rockwell became involved in the Department of Energy's nuclear weapons program in 1975 when it replaced Dow Chemical as operator of the Rocky Flats facility. Not long afterward, Rockwell took on some of the management responsibilities at DoE's Hanford plant. The government pays Rockwell a management fee for its work at each facility and reimburses all operating costs. In 1982, Rockwell's management fee (before taxes and certain corporate expenses) for both facilities was $9.6 million, and the company was reimbursed $524 million for operating costs. Although Rockwell would not provide IRRC with separate figures for Rocky Flats and Hanford, DoE reports that in FY 1982 Rockwell received $478.9 million in prime contract awards--$208.3 million for Hanford and $270.6 million for Rocky Flats--which represent an estimate of operating costs and fees through the end of fiscal 1983.

Rockwell is one of three finalists for the job of operating DoE's Oak Ridge, Tenn., facility, when Union Carbide quits management of the complex in 1984. Oak Ridge, among other activities, manufactures components for nuclear weapons. The final selection was to be made in early December 1983.

Primary systems:

Rockwell's involvement in primary systems falls into two categories. One is nuclear weapons components and materials, which are produced, respectively, at Rocky Flats and Hanford, where Rockwell is a manager under contract with DoE. The other is production of nuclear weapons delivery and related systems, including the B-1B and the MX missile, under contract with DoD.

Rocky Flats--Rockwell had more than 20 years of experience in the commercial nuclear reactor business when it became manager of the 6,500-acre Rocky Flats complex in 1975. Rocky Flats is one of several DoE plants where nuclear warhead components are made. The facility receives plutonium, uranium, beryllium and stainless steel from other plants, including Hanford (see below), and fabricates them into com-

Rockwell International's Nuclear Weapons-Related Contracts
(in millions of dollars)

Primary Systems

FY 1981	
Rocky Flats nuclear components facility	
Hanford nuclear materials facility	
MX missile	$246
Afsatcom satellites system	$41
Minuteman missile	$30
B-1B bomber	$5.1
BMD program	$1.9
Trident program	$1.2

Other current contracts
- Poseidon program
- ABRV program
- Tacamo program
- VLF communications equipment
- Blue-green laser program
- Alpha project

Secondary Systems

FY1981	
Navstar navigation satellites	$90
F-111 aircraft	$56
Teal Ruby experiment	$24
Atlas booster	$14
Space Shuttle	$5.3
Electronics for nuclear-capable aircraft	$4.0

Other current contracts
- Manned space station program

ponents for nuclear weapons such as parts of the hydrogen bomb's plutonium "triggers." These components are then shipped to the Pantex plant in Texas where they are assembled into completed weapons. In addition, Rocky Flats reconditions and recycles plutonium taken from older warheads that have been withdrawn from the U.S. stockpile and supports the development of new systems. A small amount of nuclear energy and alternative energy research also takes place at Rocky Flats.

In a report entitled "Review of Nuclear Related Facilities Managed by the Corporation," Rockwell said it bid for the contract because of "the company's commitment to use its technological and management expertise, as appropriate, in support of vital national interests." Although debate over the safety and health of the communities near Rocky Flats has gone on for several years, government and private groups that assess Rocky Flats agree that the facility's safety record has improved considerably under Rockwell's management. According to the company, its success at Rocky Flats was a major factor in its selection as a manager for the Hanford plant in 1977.

While Rockwell told IRRC that it employed approximately 5,000 people at Rocky Flats in 1982, the company would not break down this number by occupational field, as DoE does. The most recent DoE figures on employment at Rocky Flats are for FY 1981. In that year, the staff at Rocky Flats numbered 4,714. Of these, 578 were scientists and engineers, 1,052 were other professionals, 496 were technicians and 2,588 were lower-level workers.

Rockwell renewed its Rocky Flats contract in 1981 for five years, ending Dec. 31, 1985.

Hanford--Hanford, which manufactured plutonium for the Manhattan Project during World War II, is now one of several nuclear materials production plants. Run jointly by Rockwell and UNC Industries, Hanford supplies nuclear materials to components-producers such as Rocky Flats. Rockwell is in charge of three main activities at Hanford: chemical processing, waste management and site support services.

Rockwell's chemical processing responsibilities include purifying and preparing plutonium for defense and industrial programs, processing irradiated nuclear fuels and recovering and purifying irradiated uranium for reuse as reactor fuel. In addition, Rockwell is upgrading and renovating a facility for the recovery of plutonium, the Purex plant. Although nearly all of Hanford's plutonium production reactors were shut down in the early 1970s because the government had a surplus of weapons-grade plutonium, now more plutonium is needed. The Purex plant will join the Savannah River plant (run by Du Pont) as a weapons-grade plutonium supplier.

The company's waste management duties include storing the nuclear waste that has accumulated over 30 years of Hanford's operations and conducting research on new methods of handling it. The possibilities of solidifying nuclear wastes and/or placing them in geologic formations of flood basalts are under study.

Finally, Rockwell provides support services such as security forces, fire protection, transportation, central stores and electrical distribution at the site.

In late 1983, DoE decided that Hanford would be the site for the first special isotope separation (sometimes called laser isotope separation) demonstration facility. The SIS process, now under research and development at Lawrence Livermore and Los Alamos, uses laser technology to purify and enrich low-grade plutonium. The advantage of SIS is that it can convert the plutonium into weapons grade material faster and more cheaply than the traditional process. The disadvantage is that it could provide a cheap way to make weapons-grade plutonium from the waste from civilian nuclear reactors. Critics are concerned that the development of this process could increase the proliferation of nuclear weapons.

As stated above, Rockwell employed approximately 4,200 people at Hanford in 1982. Again, Rockwell would not break down this number by occupational field. The most recent DoE figures for employment at Hanford also are for FY 1981, and they include both Rockwell and UNC Industries employees because DoE does not distinguish between the two groups. The staff numbered 5,523, including 185 scientists, 748 engineers, 1,463 other professionals, 307 technicians and 2,784 lower-level workers.

Rockwell's Hanford contract will be up for another five-year renewal in 1987.

B-1B long-range combat aircraft--In January 1982, Rockwell began production of the B-1B long-range combat aircraft, a new version of the B-1 strategic bomber that President Carter canceled in 1977. To some observers, the B-1B contract represents, in part, Rockwell's long struggle to keep the B-1 program alive.

The B-1B, like the B-1, is designed to serve as a manned strategic bomber capable of reaching targets within the Soviet Union. Unlike the B-1, the B-1B is designed so that it could be used as a cruise missile carrier in addition to being a conventional bomber, and a support plane in theater land and sea battles. Critics of the B-1B claim that the plane will be obsolete before it gets off the ground; supporters say the plane is needed to fill the gap perceived between the older B-52 strategic planes and the new, radar-evading bomber, popularly called Stealth, now on the drawing board at Northrop. Under current plans, the first B-1B will be in service by 1986, and the first Stealth plane will be ready in the mid-1990s.

The B-1B is no doubt Rockwell's largest and most important program. Fortune magazine has said that even if the rest of Rockwell's business stood still, the B-1B alone "could produce an average sales growth of 14 percent annually and increase in earnings at a 13 percent clip through 1988."[3] If the full proposed fleet of 100 B-1Bs is produced over the next seven years, Rockwell expects to receive about half of the estimated $20.5 billion (in 1981 dollars) production costs, and to net 3 to 4 percent of that $10 billion.[4] In FY 1983, Rockwell received contracts worth more than $2.7 billion to start up the B-1B production lines.

Some observers think that B-1B costs have been underestimated. In June 1982, the General Accounting Office disclosed internal Defense Department estimates that exceeded the publicly stated $20.5 billion price tag by $1 to $4 billion. Air Force officials, however, said they would stand by the $20.5 billion figure.[5]

As of April 1983, Rockwell had hired approximately 12,000 new employees for the B-1B program. About 44 percent of them had worked for Rockwell previously, most of them on the B-1 program. Rockwell expects to employ a total of more than 20,000 of the estimated 55,000 people who will work on the B-1B at the program's peak in 1986-87. The company's four main B-1B facilities are in El Segundo and Palmdale, Calif; Columbus, Ohio; and Tulsa, Okla.[6]

Rockwell recently enlisted the help of Lockheed to design a Stealth version of the B-1B. Rockwell and Lockheed hope the Air Force will want to build their version instead of, or at least in addition to, Northrop's plane. At the same time, Northrop is trying to accelerate the development of its plane in order to circumvent the need for the B-1B, and thus increase orders for its Stealth planes.

MX missile--Rockwell has been one of the largest associate contractors for the MX missile program since it began in the mid-1970s. The company's Rocketdyne division is developing one propulsion stage of the prototype MX under a contract worth $439 million. Rockwell's electronics divisions (including the Autonetics division) are developing the missile's flight computer and part of the guidance and control system under a contract worth about $525 million.

Rockwell received contracts worth at least $246 million in FY 1981 and $600 million in FY 1983 for these two projects.

Although Rockwell could receive a substantial chunk of the $26 billion MX production contract if the missile is approved by Congress, it does not appear to be anxious about the MX's plight. Late in 1982, Rockwell's president told The Wall Street Journal that the company would "lose a business opportunity if it (MX) doesn't go into production. But that could mean we get some enhancement (projects) of the Minuteman (missile) somewhere down the road."[7]

Minuteman missile--Rockwell is the prime contractor for the Minuteman II and Minuteman III inertial guidance systems. (Inertial guidance systems are among the most accurate navigation systems now produced.) The company received at least $30 million in prime contract awards for components and services for these systems in FY 1981. In FY 1983, the company had received additional Minuteman contracts worth $50 million.

Afsatcom (Air Force Satellite Communications System)--Afsatcom is a military space-based satellite system. The Air Force Office of Public Information says Afsatcom "satisfies high priority Department of Defense communications requirements necessary to command and control U.S. nuclear forces around the world." TRW makes the satellites for this system, and Rockwell produces the terminals. Rockwell received Afsatcom prime contract awards worth at least $42 million in FY 1981.

Trident missile and submarine--In FY 1981, Rockwell received a research and development contract worth $1.2 million for the Trident missile. In FY 1983, Rockwell received contracts worth more than $26 million for the Trident program. The company says it is the leading inertial guidance system supplier for Trident submarines and all other nuclear-powered attack and ballistic missile submarines in the U.S. fleet, most of which are nuclear-capable.

Poseidon ballistic missile submarine--Over the last four years, Rockwell has received at least $57 million in prime contract awards for navigation and other components for the Poseidon ballistic missile submarine. Rockwell is the prime contractor for the submarine's inertial navigation system.

Ballistic missile defense--Rockwell participates in the ballistic missile defense research and development program. It received $1.9 million in FY 1981 and $5.6 million in 1982 for this research.

Advanced ballistic reentry vehicle--Rockwell is one of six major subcontractors assisting Lockheed in developing a new ballistic missile re-entry vehicle--the part of the ballistic missile that carries the warhead to the target--for the Navy. This re-entry vehicle, called the Mark 500, will be capable of evasive maneuvers after it enters the earth's atmosphere. Although no plans exist to produce it, the Mark 500 is being developed to ensure that it could be produced rapidly if Soviet advances in air defense or antiballistic missiles rendered present U.S. re-entry vehicles ineffective.[8]

Tacamo communication system--In FY 1982 and 1983, Rockwell has received at least $54 million for the Tacamo strategic aircraft to submarine communication system, including $13 million to harden the Tacamo aircraft from the effects of electromagnetic pulse (EMP), one of the effects of a nuclear explosion.

Very low frequency transmitters--In September 1982, DoD announced that a Rockwell subsidiary, Rockwell Collins, would sell four very low frequency (VLF) airborne transmitters to France for use on French ballistic missile submarines and other strategic nuclear forces. The contract is worth $97 million.

Blue-green laser communications--Rockwell will develop a receiver for a U.S. strategic submarine blue-green laser communications program under a $3 million contract awarded in October 1982.

Alpha project--Rockwell's Rocketdyne division is developing the Alpha laser along with TRW.

Secondary systems:

Navstar Global Positioning System--Navstar is a space-based radio navigation network that, when completed, will allow users to determine their position within tens of feet, their speed within fractions of a mile per hour, and the time within a millionth of a second.[9] Users may include civilian aircraft and conventionally armed weapons systems as well as land- and sea-launched ballistic missiles. Navstar will also conduct geodetic surveys that determine the earth's gravitational pull, an important variable in a ballistic missile's flight path. The Air Force Office of Public Affairs calls Navstar "an excellent example of the unique capability of space to enhance the conduct of traditional military missions."[10] The Nation explains that with Navstar, "pilots will be able to drop their bombs more accurately than before; planes will be able to rendezvous and refuel in complete radio silence; helicopters will be able to land on a dime even in the dark; infantry officers will be able to call in accurate artillery strikes without the need for close-in observers."[11]

To date, Rockwell has built several experimental Navstar satellites. Under a $1.2 billion contract awarded in mid-1983, Rockwell will build 28 operational satellites and related equipment over a five-year period. Any 18 of these satellites will be in orbit at one time; the other 10 will serve as spares.

In FY 1981, Rockwell received contracts worth $90 million for Navstar research and development. In 1982, the company received another $19 million for the program. In addition to the large production contract, Rockwell received other FY 1983 contracts worth $44 million to procure materials to build the first satellites.

Space Shuttle--As mentioned above, Rockwell is the prime contractor for the Space Shuttle. It builds the orbiter and main engines for the spacecraft and assists NASA in the integration and operation of the overall space transportation system.

Although the Shuttle is a NASA project, it also is seen as a vital element in the military space program. The Shuttle carried its first military payload in the summer of 1982, and it will replace older, non-reusable rockets as the primary vehicle for lofting military cargos into orbit, including reconnaissance and communications satellites that monitor Soviet strategic forces. DoD awarded Rockwell at least $5.3 million in FY 1981 prime contract awards for the Space Shuttle program.

F-111--Rockwell received prime contract awards worth at least $55.5 million for navigation components, radar equipment and other support work for the F-111 fighter plane in FY 1981, some of which will be applied to the nuclear-capable FB-111.

Electronics for nuclear-capable aircraft--In FY 1981, Rockwell received a number of contracts to produce electronics for the nuclear-capable F-4 Phantom fighter and the AV-8B Harrier light attack aircraft.

Teal Ruby experiment--The Teal Ruby experiment, which will test new satellite sensors that could detect enemy bombers by the heat they emit into the atmosphere, is another Rockwell project. The company was awarded an initial $25 million development contract for the sensor in 1977, and current estimates for the full program, yet to be awarded, stand at $110 million. In FY 1981, Rockwell received Teal Ruby contracts worth $24 million. The Space Shuttle will place a satellite carrying Teal Ruby in orbit sometime in late 1983 or early 1984.

Atlas space vehicle--In FY 1981, Rockwell received contracts worth $14 million for this military satellite booster.

Manned space station--Rockwell is one of eight aerospace companies funded by NASA and the DoD to examine possible scientific, commercial and military uses of a large, orbiting, manned space station. All eight firms will deliver reports in April 1984.

Rockwell International-Government Relationship

Rockwell's lobbying activities have been more visible and aggressive than those of most military contractors. The best-known example was a campaign called "Operation Common Sense," which the company was reported to have initiated in 1973 to rally public and congressional support for the B-1 bomber, the Space Shuttle, and the improved Minuteman missile guidance system. Operation Common Sense placed ads in many national magazines and newspapers, organized a speakers series featuring advocates of the B-1, and organized a letter campaign directed at Congress that generated more than 80,000 letters from Rockwell's employees, shareholders and subcontractors.[12]

A recent controversy between Rockwell and the government concerned mischarging on the company's Space Shuttle contract. (Mischarging is the act of charging the labor and parts used on a fixed price contract to a cost plus contract in order to preserve profits.) That dispute was settled in late 1982 when Rockwell paid a civil penalty of $500,000 and agreed to install a computerized time-keeping system. In August 1983, however, two investigations into additional mischarging began and have not yet been settled.[13]

Political action committee: Rockwell's PAC contributed $51,700 to 96 congressional candidates in the 1979-80 election cycle, split among almost equal numbers of Democrats and Republicans. Of this total, 37 percent ($19,050) went to 26 members of House and Senate defense committees.

In the 1981-82 election cycle, the amount and number of Rockwell's contributions increased substantially. It gave a total of $174,733 to 74 Democratic and 133 Republican congressional candidates. The amount given to members of defense-related committees more than tripled: In 1981-82, $81,633 went to 67 defense committee members.

Rockwell's largest contributions in 1981-82 went to Rep. William Chappell Jr. (D-Fla., $10,000), the second-ranking member of the House defense appropriations subcommittee; Pete Wilson ($8,000), a candidate for a California Senate seat; and Sens. Lowell Weicker (R-Conn., $8,000) and Harrison Schmitt (R-N.M., $7,000), members of the Senate defense appropriations subcommittee. Contributions of $5,000 each went to Sens. Howard Cannon (D-Nev.), a member of the Senate Armed Services Committee, and John Heinz (R-Pa.).

Washington office: Rockwell maintains several offices in the Washington, D.C., area. In 1982, two firms registered as Rockwell lobbyists. One--Hansell, Post, Brandon and Dorsey--said its legislative interest was "...strategic bomber programs." The other—Patton, Boggs and Blow--is interested in "defense appropriations bills: favor funding of President's defense program, including the B-1." In 1981, the Washington Industrial Team registered as Rockwell's lobbyist. Former Reps. Richard Ichord and Robert Wilson, who were members of the House Armed Services Committee until 1981, are employed by this firm. The Team's legislative interest was stated as "general legislative matters dealing with defense issues."

Personnel interchange: Rockwell hired 148 mid- to high-level DoD employees between 1977 and 1981. Four Rockwell employees moved to mid- to high-level positions in the DoD during the same period.

Contingency Planning and Prospects

Contingency planning: The cancellation of the B-1 bomber was the largest defense cancellation of the 1970s. Within two months after President Carter announced this decision in September 1977, Rockwell had laid off more than 8,000 employees. Rockwell's B-1 subcontractors also were forced to reduce their work forces, bringing the total number laid off to an estimated 16,000.

Although critics felt Rockwell should have had contingency plans ready to minimize the shock of the loss of this major contract, some observers were impressed with the way the company aided its employees. Rockwell placed ads in major newspapers urging other companies to hire B-1 workers. It organized job fairs and resume services. It hired 1,000 workers on other Rockwell programs and lent about 500 more to other companies.[14]

Rockwell believes it handled the B-1 cancellation well. In 1981, a company spokesman told IRRC that "Given the suddenness of the (B-1) cancellation, the company got high marks for its help to affected employees." It is not clear how many people actually found jobs as a result of Rockwell's efforts. An economic consultant's report predicted in September 1977 that of the 6,037 employees laid off by that date, only 1,000 would find jobs by the end of that month. This estimate was based on a survey of jobs available from other aerospace industry employers in California. The consultant predicted that of some 17 percent of all the laid-off workers who would find jobs, 68 percent would be engineering and professional technicians and 32 percent would be machine-ship and other hourly employees.[15]

On the financial side, Rockwell's other businesses were able to cushion the shock of the cancellation while its aerospace divisions scrambled for new business. "I've often said that if we had been solely an aerospace company back in 1977 when the B-1 was canceled, we would have been in trouble," Rockwell's chairman and chief executive officer told The New York Times.[16]

Despite the trauma, the jolt of the B-1 cancellation has not caused Rockwell to shy away from defense contracts, and the company has stated invariably that it has no plans to reduce its defense work. The company also has not changed its view on contingency planning. In response to a 1981 shareholder resolution that asked Rockwell to establish an MX contingency planning committee, the company said that such a committee was unnecessary because its diversification limited "the adverse impact of reductions in or discontinuance of a particular business or program, whether it be governmental or commercial." Equally important, Rockwell said, it continually is developing new business "to replace programs which are phased out or discontinued." Rockwell said that in cases where layoffs still occur it could take the same kind of "positive steps" it took when the B-1 was canceled.

On another front, shareholders, community groups and politicians in Colorado have asked Rockwell to consider converting the Rocky Flats facility to commercial production because they are concerned about the health and safety risks that Rocky Flats poses to the surrounding communities. These concerns have spurred DoE to sponsor a three-year study to assess alternative uses of the Rocky Flats plant. The socio-economic part of this study, completed in 1982, concluded that closing Rocky Flats would have minimal economic and social impact on its employees and the surrounding community, given the small size of the plant, its highly skilled work force, and other opportunities available in the Denver area. This conclusion does not necessarily mean, though, that the conversion of Rocky Flats is at hand. The report also said that despite critics' arguments to the contrary, the health and safety risks posed by the plant were minimal. It concluded: "The only benefit that one may identify as resulting from the mission shift will be the elimination of a potential health hazard perceived by a relatively small group of people."[17] DoE has not acted on the study. Rockwell has no plans to terminate its contract at either Rocky Flats or Hanford.

Prospects: If a freeze on nuclear weapons were implemented, Rockwell's work on the Trident missile, the MX and the B-1B most likely would be affected. Roughly $252 million (about 3 percent) of Rockwell's total DoD prime contract awards went to these projects in FY 1981, not including the large B-1B production contracts awarded in FY 1982. The company's Rocky Flats and Hanford management fees might also be reduced, because a freeze would put a halt to some of the activities at the two sites, especially the Purex plant renovation.

Assuming employment is roughly proportional to sales, about 3 percent of Rockwell's employees could find themselves without jobs if a freeze were implemented.

Budget cuts could affect many of the same nuclear weapons programs as a freeze. If the B-1B program were canceled, Rockwell would experience many of the same problems it had in September 1977.

Rockwell's past attempts to apply its defense technology to commercial products have not been particularly successful. Although the company was instrumental in developing the world's first integrated circuits (for the Minuteman missile), it has not been able to build a strong market for its commercial semiconductors. In the early 1970s, the company attempted to sell electronic calculators and digital watches, but it abandoned this effort after losses of more than $35 million. In September 1978, Rockwell discontinued its domestic Admiral television business because it too was running at a loss. Rockwell is now making another attempt, which it feels will be more successful, to enter the commercial semiconductor business.[18]

Rockwell has had more success diversifying within the defense sector. Its acquisition of Collins Radio in 1973 helped the company to enter the increasingly important defense electronics industry. Although it might seem surprising that Rockwell would choose to develop technologies that compete with its aerospace products (electronics can be used to upgrade the capabilities of older planes effectively and inexpensively, thus reducing the demand for new planes), a Rockwell spokesman told Business Week that the company feels that if technology "is going to wipe us out in some areas, we'd better be at the front end of it in others."[19]

Rockwell Footnotes

1. Aerospace Facts and Figures 1982/83, compiled by Aerospace Industries Association of America Inc. and published by Aviation Week and Space Technology, p. 149.
2. The New York Times, "Builder of the B-1 Bomber," Oct. 11, 1981.
3. Fortune, Nov. 2, 1981, p. 108-12.
4. The Wall Street Journal, Oct. 5, 1981.
5. Aviation Week and Space Technology, June 28, 1982, p. 30.
6. Aviation Week and Space Technology, March 21, 1983, p. 51.
7. The Wall Street Journal, Dec. 9, 1982.
8. Ronald Pretty, ed., Jane's Weapons Systems 1982-83, Jane's Publishing Co. Ltd., London, 1982, p. 12.
9. U.S. Air Force Office of Public Affairs, Fact Sheet, "Navstar Global Positioning System," p. 2.
10. U.S. Air Force Office of Public Affairs, Fact Sheet, "Our Role in Space," p. 5.
11. The Nation, April 9, 1983, p. 445.
12. Fortune, op. cit..
13. The Wall Street Journal, Aug. 1, 1983, p. 8.
14. Fortune, op. cit..
15. Economic Research Associates, "Community Economic Impact of the B-1 Bomber Production Cancellation," prepared for the State of California Business and Transportation Agency, November 1977.
16. The New York Times, op. cit.
17. Battelle Columbus Laboratories, "The Social and Economic Impacts of Changing Missions at the Rocky Flats Plant," prepared for Rockwell International and the U.S. Department of Energy.
18. Business Week, Sept. 9, 1982, p. 58-9.
19. Business Week, Nov. 29, 1982, p. 76.

Singer

Singer's original sewing machine factory, established in 1873 in Elizabeth, N.J., and closed in 1983, was one of the last remnants of Singer's long domination of the sewing machine world. Social and economic factors produced a steep decline in U.S. sewing machine sales in the last 10 years, and with the increase in foreign competition, Singer, which sold two of every three sewing machines worldwide in the early 1900s, found itself in trouble in the 1970s. The company now seems to be recovering, in large part because of its work for the U.S. military.

In 1982, however, Singer's sales of high technology systems could not counterbalance the drop in the company's consumer activities. Net sales fell from $2.7 billion in 1981 to $2.5 billion in 1982. Net income fell from a positive balance of $38 million in 1981 to a deficit of almost $3 million in 1982. The company attributed these results to the impact on the company of the worldwide recession and of peso devaluations in Mexico.

Singer divides its business into four major categories: products and services for the government (mainly high technology aerospace products), products manufactured for the consumer (motor products, furniture, controls and meter products), sewing products for North America and Europe, and sewing products and consumer durables for Asia, Africa and Latin America. Singer is based in Stamford, Conn.

Government and Defense Business

"Singer is a company in transition," Singer's chairman and chief executive officer, Joseph B. Flavin, stated recently. "While we may still be known as 'the sewing machine company' to the average consumer, there is increasing recognition of our new high technology aerospace orientation among the investment community and the financial news media as well." The company is changing fast: Only five years ago, consumer sewing products were still Singer's mainstay, but in 1982 the company's government products and services group--which does mainly defense work--accounted for about 40 percent of net sales. In 1981, this group contributed 31 percent of Singer's total net sales, approximately three-quarters of which came under prime contracts and subcontracts funded by the U.S. government. The remaining quarter consisted of commercial sales of aerospace and marine products and sales from Singer's small education division.

The company's high technology aerospace operations are located in five divisions: Link Flight Simulation Division in Binghamton, N.Y.; Link

Data on Singer
(dollar figures in millions)

	1978	1979	1980	1981	1982
Revenues (sales)	$2,469	$2,598	$2,787	$2,834	$2,523
Net income (earnings)	$63	($92)*	$38	$38	($3)*
Sales to government	$528	$604	$760	$885	$983
Aerospace and marine systems sales (mainly defense)	$462	$520	$663	$781	$892
U.S. government contract business relating to aerospace and marine operations as a percentage of net sales	NA	NA	NA	22%	27%
DoD prime contract awards+	$282	$346	$422	$564	$549
Ratio of DoD prime contract awards to net sales^	.11	.13	.16	.21	.22
Total Singer employees	81,000	77,000	71,000	66,000	58,000

* Loss
+ U.S. fiscal year, ending Sept. 30.
^ U.S. fiscal year awards compared with calendar year revenues.

Simulation Systems Division in Silver Spring, Md.; Kearfott Division in Little Falls, N.J.; Librascope Division in Glendale, Calif.; and HRB-Singer Co., a Singer subsidiary in State College, Pa.

Each of these divisions has a specialty. Link Flight Simulation and Link Simulation Systems (under one roof until January 1981) make simulation systems, mostly for pilot training. More and more military and civilian pilots are receiving some of their training with simulators as the simulators are refined to provide more and more realistic flight rehearsals and as rising jet fuel prices make in-flight training more expensive. Link Flight Simulation specializes in a wide variety of aircraft and spacecraft simulators, and Link Simulation Systems concentrates on non-flight simulator applications. The original Link Division, once a part of General Precision Equipment Corp., was a pioneer of flight simulation systems. Link has developed simulators for more than 100 aircraft, including the Army Cobra helicopter, the Space Shuttle, the B-52 bomber, the F-111 fighter/bomber, the F-16 fighter, the Navy Seahawk helicopter, the P-3 and S-3 antisubmarine aircraft, the Trident submarine, and most major commercial aircraft. In addition, the division has designed simulators for nuclear and fossil fuel power plants, and it has 20 nuclear power plant simulation systems under construction.

The Kearfott Division's specialty is guidance and navigation systems, including a state-of-the-art ring gyro inertial guidance system for the conventionally armed Tomahawk II medium range air-to-surface missile. This system will provide guidance, navigation and control to the missile throughout its flight. The Trident II missile, the Space Shuttle and the F-16, A-7 and P-3 aircraft also carry Kearfott systems. The division produces computers for the F-111, and it is developing an inertial guidance system and avionics equipment for the B-1B bomber.

Librascope Division "has supplied more fire control equipment to the U.S. Navy than any other producer," says William F. Schmied, Singer's president and chief operating officer. Its repertoire also includes command and control tactical communications systems, and acoustic countermeasure devices. Among its major contracts are weapons control equipment for nuclear-attack and strategic submarines, including the Trident.

HRB-Singer Inc. develops and produces tactical and strategic electronic intelligence systems, about which the company says very little "because of the highly classified nature" of its work. Generally, HRB-Singer develops and produces the computer hardware and software required to unscramble electromagnetic signals from radar, satellites, missiles and other sources, and to translate the signals into intelligible information.

Defense dependence: Singer's shift from sewing machines to high technology is reflected directly in its Pentagon contracts. In 1968, Singer did not receive enough military contract awards to qualify as a major defense contractor, but by 1970 it had jumped to number 38 on the DoD's top contractors list, and it has remained at about that position since. In 1982, the company ranked 36th on the DoD list, with $549 million in awards.

The ratio of Singer's military prime contract awards to its total sales was 15 percent in 1980, 19 percent in 1981 and 27 percent in 1982. Given Singer's emphasis on its defense divisions as a principal growth area, this percentage is likely to increase substantially in the near future.

Backlogs for the U.S. government have doubled in the last five years, from $470 million at the end of 1977 to more than $1 billion at the end of 1982.

None of Singer's defense facilities is owned by the government. The government funded approximately $260 million of research and development at Singer in 1981, and the company independently sponsored about $25 million.

Defense employees: For competitive reasons, Singer does not disclose the number of employees in any of its high technology aerospace divisions. Link Flight and Kearfott Divisions are the largest, followed by Link Simulation Systems, Librascope and HRB-Singer Inc. If employment is proportional to sales, roughly 22 percent of the company's 58,000 employees worked on defense projects in 1982.

Singer's Nuclear Weapons-Related Contracts
(in millions of dollars)

Primary Systems		Secondary Systems	
FY 1981		FY 1981	
Simulator for B-52 bomber	$116	Navigation systems for nuclear-capable aircraft	$99
Trident missile	$47	F-111	$33
Pershing missile	$1	Mark 113 fire control system	$4
		Mark 117 fire control system	$2
Other current contracts		Other current contracts	
SRAM missile		Attack submarine simulators	
B-1B bomber		F-16 simulator	
		Vertical launch system	

Nuclear Weapons-Related Programs

In FY 1981, Singer received prime contracts for primary nuclear weapons-related systems worth $165 million. Singer's contracts for secondary systems totaled at least $139 million.

Primary systems:

Simulators for the B-1 bomber, B-52 bomber and Trident submarine--The largest simulation contract ever awarded--$98 million-- went to Link Flight Division for the B-52 simulator in 1980. Link Flight has received more than $300 million on this program to date, and its total awards by 1984 could reach $350 million. Awards in FY 1981 were at least $116 million. This simulator, like many other flight simulators for military aircraft, will duplicate the entire mission profile for the plane, including the launch of Short Range Attack Missiles and Air-Launched Cruise Missiles. Without these simulators, the kind of training B-52 pilots could receive, especially in firing missiles, would be drastically reduced because of the expense and risk involved.

Singer's 1978 annual report highlighted the command and control system trainer for the Trident submarine as a major Link project that provides the Navy "with training in tactics and countermeasures, torpedo setting, firing, and post-launch control, and missile launch."

IRRC could not identify the amount of FY 1981 awards for the Trident submarine simulation contract, and for competitive reasons Singer would not provide the amount of its contract.

The company was to build a simulator for the original B-1 plane and plans to bid on the simulator contract for the B-1B.

B-1B bomber--Even without the simulator contract, the company states it has "a substantial participation in the B-1 program." The Kearfott division is developing a high accuracy inertial navigation system (Hains) for the plane. Awards are $20 million to date and could reach as much as $100 million, depending on how many planes are finally built. The division also is developing the digital multiplex units that make it possible for the B-1's avionics units to communicate with each other.

Trident missile, Pershing missile--Kearfott produces guidance system components for the Trident II and the Pershing missile.

For the Trident missile, Singer is developing an advanced inertial guidance system that can use the stars to make any necessary adjustments in the missile's course. In FY 1981, Singer received at least $47 million for Trident missile components. In FY 1983, the company received at least an additional four contracts worth a total of $20 million.

Singer's awards for the Pershing guidance system in FY 1981 totaled at least $1 million.

Other--Singer has produced guidance systems for the Short-range attack missile (SRAM) and the Subroc antisubmarine rocket.

Secondary systems:

F-111--Navigational weapons control equipment applicable to F-111D/F and FB-111A aircraft are produced by a Singer facility in San Marcos, Calif. Awards in FY 1981 were at least $33 million for this project.

The company also produces simulators for the F-111, including the FB-111 strategic nuclear bomber. Its F-111 simulator contracts were at least $2 million in FY 1981.

Navigation systems for nuclear-capable aircraft--The Kearfott Division received at least $99 million in assorted FY 1981 prime contract awards for navigational and other communications equipment for a variety of nuclear-capable aircraft, including the F-4, F-15, F-16, A-4, A-7 and P-3C. At least $45 million of this amount was for work on the General Dynamics F-16 plane. In 1982, The Wall Street Journal reported $18 million in contract awards to Singer for additional work on the F-16's navigation system.[1]

Simulators for attack submarines--Singer delivered its first submarine combat systems trainer to the Navy in 1978. According to the company's 1978 annual report, this simulator allows the Navy to train crews for the 637, 640, 686, and the nuclear-capable 688 class of submarines "in defensive tactics, including firing of torpedoes, evasive tactics, and the use of sensor equipment."

F-16 simulator--Singer first won the contract to build the F-16 flight simulator in 1977. Since that time, the company has produced 18 of these systems. The F-16 simulator, like the B-52 simulator, trains pilots in all aspects of the plane's maneuvers from take-off to landing.

In 1982, Singer received contracts worth $35 million to build an additional five simulators.

Fire control systems--The Librascope Division produces two fire control systems--the Mark 117 and Mark 113--that are the standard fire control systems for U.S. nuclear attack submarines. The Mark 113 and its successor, the Mark 117, help coordinate the launch of Subroc nuclear-armed antisubmarine rockets and conventional torpedoes.[2]

Contract awards to Singer for the Mark 117 were at least $2 million in FY 1981, and awards for the Mark 113 were at least $4 million. In May 1983, Singer received an additional contract worth $6.8 million for the Mark 113.

Singer also produces two other fire control systems--the Mark 114 and Mark 116--that play a part in the launch of Asroc weapons from surface ships.

Finally, Singer is involved in the development of a vertical launch system that will enable surface ships and submarines to fire cruise missiles, both conventional and nuclear. In 1982, Singer received contract awards worth at least $15.5 million for this system.

Singer-Government Relationship

Singer maintains a Washington office with 25 employees, all but two of them involved in marketing for one of Singer's aerospace and marine divisions. No registered lobbyists were employed as of November 1982, but a position of Director of Legislative Affairs had just been created and filled. One of the company's Washington representatives says the purpose of the office is "marketing, with legislative interface as a small part of that."

Singer has no PAC.

Singer hired 33 mid- to high-level DoD employees between 1977 and 1981, 27 of whom were former military officers. Five Singer employees transferred to mid- to high-level positions in the DoD during the same period.

In 1982, Lt. Gen. Kelly H. Burke, USAF (Ret.), joined Singer's board of directors. Gen. Burke had been the Air Force deputy chief of staff for research, development and acquisition until 1981. He now works as a consultant for various groups, including the Defense Science Board and the Air Force Scientific Advisory Board.

Contingency Planning and Prospects

Singer has not been affected adversely by defense contract cancellations in the past because as a high technology components producer, the company has not had large sums invested in any one project. When the original B-1 plane was canceled in 1977, a company spokesman said, the company was disappointed but "the impact on Singer was negligible." Singer was to have built the on-board central computer systems for the B-1, which would have brought at least $50 million to Singer over a 10-year period.[3]

A spokesman said Singer attempts to place workers in other parts of the company if their skills are compatible, and he said the company abides by any union contracts.

Diversification effort: Singer had made military products in World War II but switched back to sewing machines after the war. In the late 1950s, when many contractors were trying to become less dependent on military work, Singer moved back into defense work. Management wanted to acquire advanced technology defense research units that could spin off innovations for Singer's sewing machine business as well as bring in revenues. In 1958, Singer acquired the research firm of Haller, Raymond, T. Brown (now HRB-Singer) to meet these goals. It was grouped with Singer's Bridgeport Industrial sewing machine plant and another military technology acquisition to form the Singer Military Products Division. These three units were never able to work together, and the division was abolished quietly in 1960. In 1963, Singer tried again with another cluster of advanced technology companies that was called the Metrics Division. This group helped to increase Singer's defense business, but it failed to develop nondefense technology. In 1968, the company merged with General Precision Equipment Corp., a company that already had successfully combined commercial business (controls for washing machines) with military business (computers, inertial guidance systems, and flight simulators). But the kind of interaction between military and commercial technology once envisioned still did not materialize.

The acquisition of these advanced technology defense research units was part of a larger expansion and diversification campaign also begun in 1958, which, along with the drop in sewing machine sales, caused

Singer major financial problems. In 1975, the company wrote off its business machine and other non-sewing, non-defense operations, resulting in a $452 million loss.

Prospects: The cancellation of any single nuclear weapons system would not affect the company any more than the B-1 cancellation did in 1977. If a nuclear freeze were implemented, says a spokesman, "the negative impact would be minimal. We shouldn't be impacted like some others would be." And, indeed, the company points out that its "emphasis on training and navigation systems (as opposed to actual weapons) insulates it to some degree...from congressional and Pentagon turnabouts on weapon choices and defense contracts." Still, the company's work on the B-1, the Trident missile, and the Pershing missile would be affected by a freeze, and at least 9 percent of the company's total defense prime contracts could be lost, judging from FY 1981 awards.

An all-around decrease in defense spending might make the company more nervous. Singer is pinning its hopes to a large degree on its high technology aerospace divisions to play a major role in the company's recovery.

Singer Footnotes

1. The Wall Street Journal, Sept. 8, 23 and 28, 1982.
2. Ronald D. Pretty, ed., Jane's Weapons Systems 1982-83, Jane's Publishing Co. Ltd., London, 1982, p. 314.
3. The Wall Street Journal, July 1, 1977.

TRW

TRW is a high technology company with a foot in several markets--electronics and space, car and truck, and industrial and energy. Of these, the electronics and space segment--which produces TRW's computers and satellites--is the largest, a position it has gained over the last five years.

How TRW's Mix Has Shifted

	Sales (in billions)		Operating Profits (in millions)	
	1978	1982	1978	1982
Car and truck	$1.5	$1.5	$206	$129
Electronics and space systems	1.2	2.2	84	170
Industrial and energy	1.1	1.4	102	127
Total	$3.8	$5.1	$392	$426

Source: Business Week, Nov. 15, 1982

TRW is based in Cleveland. It ranks 103rd on the Forbes list of the nation's top companies. Net sales were $5.13 billion in 1982, a 3 percent decrease from 1981. Earnings went down 14 percent, from $229 million to $196 million. The electronics and space systems segment increased its sales and earnings, but drops in car and truck and especially industrial and energy sales caused the overall decline in the company's performance.

Government and Defense Business

Defense dependence: The U.S. government is TRW's most important customer. In both 1981 and 1982, sales to government agencies accounted for close to one-third of the company's sales. TRW's next three largest customers--General Motors Corp., Ford Motor Co. and United Technologies Corp.--are on a different tier. They accounted for approximately 4 percent, 4 percent and 2 percent, respectively, of TRW's 1982 sales.

Data on TRW
(dollar figures in millions)

	1978	1979	1980	1981	1982
Net sales	$3,787	$4,560	$4,984	$5,285	$5,132
Net earnings	$174	$189	$204	$229	$196
Sales to U.S. government	NA	NA	$1,190	$1,404	$1,651
Sales to U.S. government by electronics & space segment	$598	$698	$954	$1,153	$1,366
Sales to Defense Department as a percentage of total sales	11%	10%	12%	12%	15%
Sales to other government agencies as a percentage of total sales	NA	NA	NA	15%	17%
Department of Defense contract awards*	$325	$437	$508	$517	$869
Ratio of DoD contract awards to total sales+	.09	.10	.10	.10	.17
Government backlog	NA	NA	NA	$1,300	$2,400
Total TRW employees	93,353	97,935	94,051	91,941	85,099

* U.S. fiscal year, ending Sept. 30.
\+ U.S. fiscal year awards compared with calendar year sales.

TRW's largest government customer is the Department of Defense. Over the last six years, TRW's defense sales have averaged about 12 percent of its total business. In 1982, they accounted for 15 percent, about half of TRW's government sales. The other half went to a number of agencies, primarily NASA.

TRW's backlog and research and development costs also reflect the company's emphasis on government business. In 1982, government orders made up 80 percent of TRW's backlog. According to The Christian Science Monitor, 80 percent of the company's $1 billion in 1981 research and development costs were met by the government.[1]

The relationship between TRW and the government is not one-sided; both the DoD and NASA depend on TRW as one of their major contractors. In FY 1982, the company was the 21st largest defense contractor, with prime contract awards of $869 million, and the 18th largest NASA contractor, with prime contract awards of $44 million.

All three of TRW's business segments contract with the government, but the electronics and space systems segment performs most of the company's government work. It accounted for 83 percent of TRW's revenues from the government in 1982. The Industrial and Energy business segment accounted for 17 percent, and the car and truck segment accounted for less than 1 percent.

Spacecraft and space systems have played a significant role in the company's government business for many years. TRW has designed and built more than 175 unmanned spacecraft, including Pioneer I, the first satellite built by a private company, and Explorer VI, the satellite that transmitted in 1959 the first television picture from space.

Apart from spacecraft, the products and services that TRW sells to the government are similar to those it sells to commercial buyers. TRW's electronics components, systems and services form part of military communications, reconnaissance, and guidance and navigation systems as well as commercial telecommunications, computers and home entertainment products. The company links its computer-based and analytical services to the data-processing needs of retail stores, financial institutions and the DoD.

Defense employees and facilities: TRW says it cannot estimate the number of its employees engaged in defense work because its defense and nondefense projects overlap. If employment is roughly proportional to sales, about 13,000 of TRW's 85,099 employees worked on defense projects in 1982.

TRW's electronics and space segment's headquarters and many of its divisions are in southern California. In September 1982, a laser cut the ribbon in the opening ceremony for a new TRW facility in Cummings Research Park, Ala., across the street from the Army Ballistic Missile Defense Organization. TRW expects to employ 200 people at Cummings by the end of 1983. The facility will write advanced computer programs for Army missile agencies.[2]

None of TRW's 300-some facilities (spread over 15 countries) is owned by the U.S. government.

Nuclear Weapons-Related Programs

Thompson Products Inc., an auto valve producer that was TRW's predecessor, supplied aircraft valves to the Defense Department during World War I. The company was not involved in nuclear weapons-related systems, however, until it merged with Ramo-Wooldridge, an electronics firm, in 1958. Before the merger Ramo-Wooldridge had served as the systems engineer and technical director for the nation's first intercontinental ballistic missile program. In that role, Ramo-Wooldridge coordinated the efforts of the thousands of contractors and subcontractors on matters ranging from propulsion, guidance and reentry to data processing and site construction, a job characterized as more complex than the Manhattan Project. After the merger, systems engineering for ballistic missiles and other military projects remained part of the combined Thompson-Ramo-Wooldridge (TRW) military business.

TRW's Nuclear Weapons-Related Contracts
(in millions of dollars)

Primary Systems		Secondary Systems	
FY 1981		FY1981	
MX missile	$78	Command and Control Technical Center	$27
Minuteman missile	$33	VHSIC program	$4.6
ABRES program	$16	Defense Satellite Communications System	$3.7
Defense nuclear agency	$2	GEODSS space tracking system	$2.3
		AN/ALQ-131 ECM system	$2.3
		E-3A Awacs plane	$1.1

Other current contracts (primary):
Advanced strategic missiles program
Ballistic missiles
LoAD
B-1B fuel pumps
Laser isotope separation
Defense support satellites
Alpha program
Lode program

Other current contracts (secondary):
FLTSATCOM satellite system
Consolidated Space Operations Center
Titan III rocket
Laser research
Space Defense Operations Center
Manned space station
Milstar satellite system
Aircraft components for nuclear-capable aircraft

In FY 1981, TRW received prime contract awards for primary nuclear weapons systems worth at least $130 million. The company received an additional $41 million for secondary systems.

Primary systems:

MX ICBM--TRW's participation in the MX program, like that of many other MX contractors, spans the early development of post-Minuteman ballistic missile technology to the present.[3]

TRW has two major contracts in the current stage (the full scale engineering and development stage) of the MX program. Under the larger contract, the company is responsible for overall systems engineering and technical support. The smaller contract involves research and development on MX targeting.

In FY 1981, TRW received $78 million for these two MX contracts. TRW said that in 1982 its MX revenues accounted for approximately 2 percent of its total revenues, which equal about $103 million. In FY 1983 (through May), TRW has received contract awards worth $118 million for MX work. TRW's MX contracts are renewed on an annual basis, although renewal is not guaranteed.

TRW counsel Ted Schaffner told IRRC that about 650 TRW technical and professional employees work on the MX. Most of these are white collar workers, including many engineers who are moved to different TRW programs, both civilian and military, as the need arises. TRW's MX contracts are carried out at the company's facilities in Redondo Beach and San Bernardino, Calif.

Minuteman ICBM--Many major MX contractors also participated in the Minuteman program. TRW is no exception; it has provided systems engineering and targeting analysis for both ICBMs. In addition, TRW assisted with the Minuteman vulnerability and hardness program and command data buffer. In FY 1981, TRW received prime contracts worth at least $33 million for the Minuteman program.

Advanced Ballistic Reentry System (ABRES)--TRW received prime contract awards worth at least $16 million in FY 1981 and $23 million in FY 1982 for ABRES research and development. The ABRES program conducts research and development of reentry technology for existing or future ballistic missiles.

Advanced Strategic Missiles Program--TRW is involved in the Advanced Strategic Missiles Program, which also researches and develops reentry vehicles and ballistic missile technology for existing or future ICBMs and SLBMs. DoD spent $100 million for this program in FY 1982, which was split among approximately 40 contractors and government agencies. TRW received about $10 million, about 10 percent of the total. In FY 1983 (through May), TRW received at least $13 million.

Ballistic missiles--In FY 1983, TRW received at least $5.6 million for general material data and computer services for Air Force ballistic missile systems.

Defense Nuclear Agency--In FY 1981, TRW received $2 million for work at the Defense Nuclear Agency. This agency's programs relate exclusively to nuclear weapons systems.

Ballistic missile defense--TRW says it is involved in the low altitude defense system (LoAD) program, a small, simple ballistic missile defense system that could be deployed rapidly to defend U.S. ICBMs.

In addition, TRW is working on forward acquisition sensor (FAS) technology that would perform the warning and attack assessment functions of a more complicated ballistic missile defense concept, the layered defense system. The layered defense system would consist of two levels; the first would include FAS sensors, and the second would be a LoAD system. When launched to high altitude, the FAS would use infrared sensors to pick out incoming Soviet missiles.

B-1B combat aircraft--TRW's Industry and Energy segment, which makes aircraft engine parts for many commercial and military aircraft, will supply the fuel pumps for the B-1B bomber to the plane's prime contractor, Rockwell International.[4]

Laser isotope separation--TRW, along with Lawrence Livermore National Laboratory and Los Alamos National Laboratory, is conducting research on a process that uses laser technology to transform low-grade plutonium into weapons-grade plutonium. This process, called laser isotope separation or special isotope separation (SIS), could enrich plutonium more rapidly and less inexpensively than current methods, but it poses problems for controlling the proliferation of weapons grade plutonium.

Ballistic missile defense lasers--TRW participates in several high energy laser programs, some of which have BMD applications. In 1981, TRW participated in the Alpha laser device development program, one of the three main DoD laser research programs. The Alpha program's goal is to establish the feasibility of a laser device suitable for space operations, primarily for ballistic missile defense. In July 1982, TRW was selected to supply the hydrogen fluoride laser for the high energy laser large optics demonstration experiment (Lode), another of the three main DoD laser programs. The Lode project is working to develop the mirror and beam control optics necessary for the effective use of lasers in space.[5]

Defense Support Program satellites--TRW is upgrading four Defense Support Program satellites. These satellites use infrared sensors to detect ballistic missile launches.

Secondary systems:

TRW's involvement in secondary nuclear warfare-related programs falls into three categories: space systems, electronics, and aircraft engine components.

Space systems: Of the hundreds of space systems that TRW has built over the last 20 years, many have been part of U.S. strategic communications systems--the satellites and their supporting ground stations that give the military omnipresent eyes and ears across the globe. These strategic systems include:

Defense Satellite Communication System (DSCS)--In 1968, the United States launched its first military communications satellites (DSCS I), produced by Ford Aerospace and Communications Corp. Not long afterward, TRW won the contract for this system's second generation satellites, DSCS II, which went into orbit in 1971. They still operate the Pentagon's principal military strategic communications channels.

The DSCS II system consists of four operating satellites and two backups. It links 27 military command centers and carries voice, teletype, images and computerized data. The Air Force says DSCS "provides for voice and high data communication between virtually anywhere on earth through satellite relay" and "supports vital national security requirements for world-wide command and control, crises management, intelligence data relay, diplomatic traffic and early warning detection and reporting."[6]

The impact of satellite systems like DSCS on the military is immense. They allow political and military leaders to monitor every move in a conflict situation from the other side of the globe. For example, in 1975 President Ford used DSCS to communicate minute by minute with the Marines sent to rescue the crew of the merchant ship Mayaguez, seized by Cambodian forces in the Gulf of Siam.

In FY 1981, TRW received at least $3.7 million for the DSCS program. In FY 1983 (through May), it received at least $5.2 million. TRW's involvement in this program will end soon, however, because GE has been selected to produce the third generation DSCS satellites.

Fleet Satellite Communications System--FLTSATCOM is a global system for high priority Navy and Air Force communications. The Navy uses it to connect its land, air and sea forces. The Air Force uses it to carry its Afsatcom (Air Force Satellite Communications System) transponders (devices that receive and transmit radio signals) that command and control nuclear-capable forces.

TRW has manufactured four FLTSATCOM satellites, which the Air Force launched between 1978 and 1980. In 1982, Congress approved funding for three more FLTSATCOM satellites, which, among other uses, will serve strategic users until Milstar, a new satellite communications network, is completed in the late 1980s.

TRW received $199 million in FY 1983 prime contract awards to procure parts and materials and to produce the sixth, seventh and eighth FLTSATCOM satellites.

Ground-based Electro-Optical Deep Space Surveillance--TRW is designing and building this ground-based surveillance system, which will use powerful telescopes to relay images directly from space to the North American Air Defense Command's (Norad) master computers.

TRW describes GEODSS's capabilities:

> With computer analysis and identification of the images, the (GEODSS) systems can monitor objects in deep space with greater speed and sensitivity than was possible before. For example, the system can see objects 10,000 times dimmer than the human eye can see--even the light reflected off an object as small as that [of a] misplaced astronaut's glove.
>
> Each GEODSS unit consists of three large, powerful astronomical telescopes that relay what they see through the camera system to computers, driven by TRW software. The data is then processed and displayed for operators. Each GEODSS unit can sight about 1,000 objects in space during a single night.

TRW began work on its $62 million GEODSS contract in 1978 at its Defense Systems Group facility in California. In FY 1981, TRW received a contract worth $2.3 million for GEODSS research. In FY 1982, it received a contract worth $7.9 million for maintenance and support of the system. In FY 1983, TRW received additional GEODSS contracts worth at least $21 million. When completed, GEODSS will consist of five facilities. The first three have been built at the White Sands missile range in New Mexico, in Taegu, South Korea, and in Maui, Hawaii. The other two will be constructed at sites in the Indian Ocean and Atlantic regions.

Consolidated Space Operations Center--In June 1982, TRW's Defense Systems Group received a five-year, $70 million contract to perform systems engineering and integration work for this center. Under construction near Peterson AFB, Colo., CSOC will fulfill several roles. It will combine the military space shuttle and satellite operations into one facility, enabling DoD to coordinate more complex military missions. It will work to make military space systems less vulnerable to attack, especially nuclear attack. Finally, it will serve as the third ground communications station in the United States able to receive messages from early-warning satellites. It will be the first such station built partially underground, one of the measures intended to make the facility itself less vulnerable to attack.[8]

In August 1982, TRW received an additional $3.4 million contract for technical services for the center.

Titan III rocket--In FY 1982, TRW received $17.4 million for engineering and technical services on the Titan III, a rocket that launches satellites, including the Defense Satellite Communications System.

Lasers--In 1981, the Navy and TRW demonstrated a mid-infrared advanced chemical laser (MIRACL). In that test, the 2.2 megawatt laser achieved "the highest power levels yet demonstrated in the U.S.

laser technology program," according to Aviation Week and Space Technology.[9] It will be one of the lasers used for study at the national high-energy laser systems test facility, which will be completed soon at the White Sands Missile Range, N.M. In September 1982, TRW, along with Rockwell International and Bell Aerospace, won a DoD contract to develop a supersonic oxygen iodine chemical laser. This laser will have a shorter wave length than chemical lasers already in development, one important factor in minimizing laser power requirements while maximizing brightness. In November 1982, TRW completed an initial study of laser countermeasures devices and techniques that could be used to protect U.S. satellites.

In FY 1981, TRW received at least $19 million in DoD prime contract awards for laser programs. In FY 1982, it received at least $9 million, and in FY 1983 (through May), at least $14 million.

Space Defense Operations Center--TRW says it is one of Ford Aerospace's main subcontractors for the Space Defense Operations Center, which is part of the North American Aerospace Defense Command (Norad) at the Air Force's Cheyenne Mountain complex.

Manned Space Station--DoD has provided funds to TRW and seven other companies--Boeing, Martin Marietta, General Dynamics, Lockheed, Rockwell International, Grumman and McDonnell Douglas--to examine the possibilities for a manned space station. Each company received study contracts worth $800,000 and is to deliver a report in April 1984.

Military Strategic Tactical and Relay Satellite (Milstar)--TRW was involved in the early development of this new military communications system, but it lost the full-scale development contract to Lockheed in February 1983.

Electronic and communications systems: TRW's electronic and communications work is applied to many types of nuclear weapons-related systems from planes to computers.

Very High Speed Integrated Circuit program--TRW is developing the electronic warfare signal processor for the Very High Speed Integrated Circuit (VHSIC) program. The company says it received a contract worth $34 million for this program in 1981. In FY 1983, a contract modification brought TRW an additional $6 million.

Antisubmarine warfare--TRW says it has participated in Navy antisubmarine warfare and undersea surveillance programs for 15 years. Recently, the company received a contract to upgrade the Ocean Surveillance Information System (OSIS). An ad that TRW placed in Aviation Week and Space Technology in May 1983 said that OSIS "makes sense of the sensors to track air, sea and submarine traffic the world over."

Electronic warfare--In FY 1981, $2.3 million of TRW's prime contract awards were for work on the AN/ALQ-131 jamming pod for the nuclear-capable F-15 Eagle.

E-3A Awacs--TRW received $1.1 million in FY 1981 for management services and training studies for the E-3A Awacs plane.

Cruise missiles--TRW's Defense Systems Group has received prime contracts for work on the sea- and ground-launched cruise missiles.

Command and Control Technical Center--In FY 1981, TRW received $27 million for research and development at the Command and Control Technical Center. This center provides engineering and technical support to several command and control systems including the World-wide Military Command and Control System, an advanced communications network that ties together computers at the military command center in the Pentagon, the Strategic Air Command at Omaha, and many others.

Classified electronics: In FY 1982, TRW received at least $45 million in classified electronics prime contract awards.

Aircraft engines: TRW makes components (compressors, bearings, turbine airfoils, fuel boosters, turbine wheels, nozzle diaphragms and compressor assemblies) used on many commercial and military aircraft, including the nuclear-capable McDonnell Douglas F-15 fighter plane.

TRW-Government Relationship

Political action committee: TRW's PAC contributions to members of defense-related committees increased more than fivefold between 1979-80 and 1981-82. In 1979-80, TRW gave $9,900 (23 percent of its total contributions) to 33 candidates; in 1981-82, it gave $47,052 (35 percent of its total) to 56 candidates.

Two of TRW's largest contributions in 1981-82 went to congressional defense committee members. Sen. Harrison Schmitt (R-N.M.), then chairman of the space subcommittee and member of the defense appropriations subcommittee, received $4,500. Rep. William Chappell Jr. (D-Fla.), second-ranking member of defense appropriations subcommittee, received $1,500. Other large contributions went to Rep. James Jones (D-Okla., $3,000), chairman of the House Budget Committee, Sen. Pete Wilson (R-Calif., $5,600), Sen. Lloyd Bentsen (D-Tex., $3,000) and Rep. Richard Lugar (R-Ind., $3,100).

Washington office: TRW maintains an office in Arlington, Va., a suburb of Washington, D.C. Six lobbyists registered on behalf of TRW in 1981-82. One was the Washington Industrial Team. Two of that firm's principals, Richard Ichord and Robert Wilson, are former Representatives who until 1981 served on defense committees. Only the Washington Industrial Team listed "defense issues" as its primary legislative interest. Two others listed "aerospace and electronics," and one listed "legislation relating to contribution and indemnification for government contractors" as their primary legislative interest. The Washington Industrial Team also represents many of the other companies in this study.

Personnel interchange: From 1977-81, TRW hired 291 mid- to high-level DoD personnel, and 12 TRW employees left the company for mid- to high-level jobs at the Pentagon.

Harold Brown, Secretary of Defense in the Carter administration, works as a consultant to TRW. To avoid the appearance of conflict of interest in this role, Brown resigned from the President's Commission on Strategic Forces, a bipartisan group charged with reviewing and evaluating the nation's strategic modernization program and the MX basing mode. However, Brown did serve as a consultant to the commission and apparently played an important role in its deliberations.

Richard DeLauer, Under Secretary of Defense for Research and Engineering, is a former TRW vice president.

Contingency Planning and Prospects

Contingency planning: In 1981 and 1982, a group of TRW shareholders sponsored a resolution asking the company to appoint a committee to establish contingency plans for its MX missile contract. In response, TRW said that such plans were "unnecessary and inappropriate" because the company's diversification limited "the adverse impact of reductions in or discontinuance of a particular business or program, whether governmental or commercial." In addition, the company said that it "seeks, on an ongoing basis, to identify new products to replace contracts which are completed or discontinued." TRW Secretary Martin Coyle told IRRC that if the company's large MX contract were canceled, placing workers elsewhere in the company probably would not be a problem, especially since "we cannot hire enough engineers to do what we need to do."

Many of the companies included in this report have made similar arguments against the necessity of contingency planning, but TRW's points seem more persuasive than most. Although TRW derived about 15 percent of its sales from the DoD in 1982, its contracts were spread over a large number of different programs, which minimizes the company's vulnerability to any one contract cancellation. In addition, not only are the products and services that TRW sells to the government--such as systems engineering, satellites and computers --similar to what it sells to commercial customers, but the company itself says that its defense and nondefense projects (and employees) overlap. Thus, in TRW's case, the channels for movement between defense and commercial work in the event of a contract cancellation seem relatively well developed.

Prospects: In the short term, only TRW's MX contract appears vulnerable to budget cuts or a freeze. If the MX were canceled immediately and completely, about 2 percent of TRW's sales and about 650 technical and professional employees would be affected, judging from 1982 levels. However, the negative effects of an MX cancellation could be mitigated if TRW were able to gain systems engineering contracts for other programs and MX employees were placed elsewhere in the firm.

Budget cuts or a nuclear weapons freeze are not likely to affect directly most of TRW's space systems, many of which are part of command, control, communications and intelligence (C^3I) programs that rank high on Pentagon and congressional priority lists. Defense Under Secretary De Lauer has called C^3I the first priority among all new U.S. strategic programs. However, a freeze or a ban on space weapons could hurt TRW's future earnings potential because under such arms control restrictions, many of the advanced technologies that TRW is developing would never be produced. In addition, even research and development contracts could be curtailed. Lasers, ballistic missile defense systems, advanced ballistic reentry vehicles and other space systems would fit into this category.

TRW Footnotes

1. In the News, Nov. 30, 1982, p. 12. (Issued by TRW Staff Public Relations, reprinted from The Christian Science Monitor, Nov. 4, 1982.)
2. In the News, Nov. 30, 1982, p. 35. (Issued by TRW Staff Public Relations, reprinted from Alabama Development News, September 1982.)
3. David Gold, et al., MisGuided EXpenditure, Council on Economic Priorities, New York, 1981, p. 176.
4. Council on Economic Priorities Newsletter, "The B-1: Bomber for All Seasons," February 1982, p. 6.
5. Aviation Week and Space Technology, July 19, 1982, p. 153.
6. Air Force Systems Command, Office of Public Affairs Fact Sheet, "Our Role in Space," p. 7.
7. Aviation Week and Space Technology, March 14, 1983, p. 97.
8. Business Week, "Keeping the lines open during a nuclear war," Feb. 7, 1983, p. 116.
9. Aviation Week and Space Technology, "Laser Weaponry Technology Advances," May 25, 1981, p. 69.

Tenneco
(Newport News Shipbuilding)

Tenneco Inc., based in Houston, is a diversified conglomerate whose main lines of business are production of oil and gas, manufacture of natural gas pipelines, construction and farm equipment, automotive components, packaging, chemicals, shipbuilding, and agriculture and land management. Newport News Shipbuilding and Dry Dock Co., a subsidiary in Newport News, Va., serves primarily as a contractor to the U.S. Navy designing, building, repairing and refueling nuclear-powered aircraft carriers, cruisers and attack submarines.

Tenneco performed well during the 1981-3 recession, with revenues of $15.40 billion and net income of $819 million in 1982, compared with revenues of $15.38 billion and net income of $813 million in 1981. The company stands at number 22 on the Forbes 500 top sales list.

Tenneco classifies as its manufacturing sector Newport News and two other subsidiaries, J.I. Case, makers of construction and farm equipment, and Tenneco Automotive, makers of auto parts. Manufacturing accounted for approximately 30 percent of Tenneco's net sales and 10 percent of its pretax income in both 1981 and 1982.

Standing alone, Newport News reported $1.32 billion in 1982 revenues. This represented 32 percent of manufacturing net sales in 1982, and 9 percent of Tenneco's revenues. But Newport News's $111 million in pretax income represented 57 percent of all pretax income earned by the manufacturing sector.

The stature of Newport News as a producer of revenues and profits for Tenneco is a very recent development. Its pretax income was as low as $14 million in 1978--just 1 percent of the company's total--and its return on equity jumped six-fold during the 1978-80 period.

Government and Defense Business

The U.S. Navy is largely responsible for Newport News's record profitability. The Navy relies on Newport News as a prime shipbuilder and as the only non-government shipyard for overhauling and refueling nuclear submarines. Tenneco won $1.15 billion in fiscal 1981 defense contract awards (including $1.13 billion in awards to Newport News), placing it 15th on the DoD's prime contractor list. In fiscal 1982, the company won $845 million in awards from the Pentagon (including $803 million for Newport News), making it the 22nd largest defense contractor. The company should appear near the top of the 1983 list because of huge multiyear awards won for Nimitz aircraft carriers.

Data on Tenneco
(dollar figures in millions)

	1978	1979	1980	1981	1982
Revenues*	$8,610	$10,976	$13,102	$15,383	$15,397
Net income	$452	$571	$726	$813	$819
Shipbuilding net sales	$733**	$730	$891	$1,096	$1,324
Revenues from Navy work as a percentage of total shipbuilding revenues	67%	74%	76%	77%	90%
Revenues from Navy work as a percentage of total Tenneo revenues+	6%	5%	5%	5%	8%
Shipbuilding pretax income	$14	$33	$55	$82	$111
Shipbuilding pretax income as a percentage of total pretax income	1%	2%	3%	4%	6%
DoD prime contract awards++	$407	$1,093	$1,524	$1,151	$845
Ratio of DoD prime contract awards to total revenues^	.05	.10	.12	.07	.05
Newport News backlog	$2,046	$1,648	$3,164	$3,835	$8,520
Newport News employees	22,602	23,014	24,750	25,000	26,800
Total Tenneco employees	104,000	107,000	106,000	103,200	96,000

* Restated figures reflecting current accounting practices.
** Shipbuilding "revenues" used for 1977 and 1978.
+ IRRC estimate.
++ U.S. fiscal year, ending Sept. 30.
^ U.S. fiscal year awards compared with calendar year revenues.

Newport News builds three types of Navy vessels. It is the sole source for Nimitz class nuclear-powered aircraft carriers and for Virginia class nuclear-powered guided-missile cruisers. It and the Electric Boat subsidiary of General Dynamics share responsibility for the SSN 688 attack submarine program. The cruiser program ended with the delivery of the Arkansas in September 1980, but both the attack submarine and aircraft carrier projects are steaming along. At the end of 1982 Newport News was at work on the fourth of the Nimitz class carriers and on nine attack subs. It also counted contracts for two additional Nimitz class carriers and contracts for overhauling and refueling six nuclear-powered ballistic missile submarines (SSBNs) in its $8.5 billion backlog.

Only 5 percent of Newport News's 1982 revenues came from non-government customers. The yard is capable of building new commercial ships but has not landed any such contracts since 1974. Newport News lost more than $200 million on commercial work in the mid-1970s, dampening management's enthusiasm for the merchant end of the business. The yard's current commercial work is limited to ship overhauls. A subsidiary, Newport News Industrial Corp., which grew out of the shipyard's knowledge of naval nuclear shipbuilding, helps the commercial nuclear power industry build and repair reactors. It also accounted for 5 percent of 1982 revenues. The Navy accounted for the rest: 90 percent of Newport News's 1982 revenues, an increase from 77 percent in 1981.

Defense employees: At a time when many shipyards are trimming their work forces, Newport News has been expanding its number of employees gradually from 23,000 in 1979 to approximately 25,000 late in 1982. About 70 percent of the employees are blue-collar workers.[1] The company also invests about $70 million a year in capital improvements at its 475-acre facility on the banks of the James River. Among the capital projects are investments in robotics and computer-aided manufacturing. Such capital-intensive expenditures are a prime reason why Newport News expects not to increase its work force substantially beyond 25,000 despite the prospect of two more aircraft carrier contracts, each of which requires about 5,000 workers.[2] Management did expect to hire 1,000 more workers in 1983 and up to 2,000 in the following year.[3] At the same time, Newport News's president recently pledged that the shipyard, Virginia's largest private employer, would have no layoffs through 1984.[4]

As the shipyard's defense work has increased to more than three-quarters of its revenues, it can be presumed that at least that percentage of its employees is engaged in defense-related work. Overall, Tenneco employed 103,200 workers at the end of 1981, so defense workers comprised about one-fifth of the total.

In the 1970s, Newport News engaged in a long and ultimately unsuccessful effort to prevent the United Steelworkers from organizing the shipyard, one of the biggest plants in the South. In 1978, 16,500 production and maintenance workers voted to affiliate with the Steelworkers, and in 1979 they held a 12-week strike when the company continued to avoid negotiating with the union. A U.S. circuit court in October 1979 affirmed a National Labor Relations Board order recognizing the Steelworkers as the workers' representative. The announcement in March 1980 of a 43-month contract containing important wage and benefit increases for the 16,500 Steelworkers was widely regarded as the company's final acknowledgement of the union's importance.[5] Recently, the contract was renewed with the current 18,200 Steelworkers without a strike.

Nuclear Weapons-Related Programs

Newport News's work on strategic missile submarines dates to 1958, when the yard began work on one of the first U.S. SSBNs, a Polaris missile submarine. Since then, Newport News has built 13 more SSBNs, along with more than 20 nuclear-powered attack submarines (SSNs).

Tenneco's Nuclear Weapons-Related Contracts
(in millions of dollars)

Primary Systems		Secondary Systems	
FY 1981		FY 1981	
SSBN overhaul, repair	$160	SSN 688 attack submarines	$737
		Nimitz class aircraft carrier	$132
		Miscellaneous attack submarine work	$61
		Guided missile cruiser	$3

The yard's prime contract awards on primary nuclear warfare systems--all for work on SSBNs--totaled $160 million in FY 1981, equal to slightly more than 1 percent of Tenneco's 1981 sales. Awards on secondary and nuclear-related systems totaled $933 million. The ratio of combined primary and secondary awards to total revenues was about .07 in 1981.

Primary systems:

A growing percentage of Newport News's submarine work is devoted to repairing and refueling nuclear-powered submarines. The yard opened a new drydock in 1980 at a cost of $15 million, roughly doubling its capacity for this kind of work. Four overhaul/refueling jobs were performed in 1980 on nuclear ballistic submarines; the number jumped to seven in 1981, and contracts for six more were in hand at year-end. FY 1981 contracts for overhaul, alteration and repair of submarines that originally carried Polaris submarine-launched ballistic missiles (SLBMs) totaled $160 million. In November 1981, another $94 million award to overhaul an SSBN was announced. Further awards of $13 million and $103 million for this work were announced in 1982. The $103 million award was for modernization of the George Washington Carver SSBN to carry Trident I (C-4) SLBMs.[6]

By the end of FY 1983, the Navy was to have converted 12 submarines that originally were armed with Polaris SLBMs to carry Trident I missiles. Of these, four originally were built by Newport News. Nineteen other Polaris SSBNs, including six built by Newport News, now carry Poseidon (C-3) SLBMs. Of 544 SLBMs currently deployed by the United States, 160 are carried by submarines built by Newport News.[7]

Secondary systems:

SSN 688 submarines--In the early 1970s the Navy began procurement of the SSN 688 Los Angeles class attack submarine, a fast attack vessel armed with Subroc nuclear antisubmarine warfare depth bombs and conventional MK-48 torpedoes, designed to sink both surface ships and submarines. The Navy plans to add a new strategic capability to the SSN 688 beginning in 1984, when these submarines will carry nuclear-armed Tomahawk land attack cruise missiles. Initially, the Navy will deploy up to eight cruise missiles per submarine. Later, a new vertical launch system will be installed on SSN 688s. This system will carry 12 Tomahawks, both conventional and nuclear, without requiring removal of current weapons. The nuclear Tomahawks will give the attack submarines a strategic role.[8]

Since the program began, Newport News has won contracts on 15 of the boats, and Electric Boat has secured 20. The competition between the two yards has ebbed and flowed; Newport News built five of the first eight SSN 688s, then did not win another contract between 1978 and 1981. But in March 1981, the Navy awarded three SSN 688 contracts to Newport News without seeking a bid from Electric Boat, noting that the average cost of Newport News's first five SSN 688s had been 50 percent less than that of the first five produced by Electric.[9] The unilateral $1.5 billion award was widely perceived as part of the Navy's then-raging dispute with Electric Boat about cost overruns.[10] After it settled with the Navy in October 1981, Electric Boat received another attack submarine contract.

Newport News received between $737 million and $798 million in SSN 688 awards in 1981, $675 million of which was contained in the first installment on the $1.5 billion three-sub prize. In October 1982, the yard received an additional award of $90 million for SSN 688 work. Newport News is likely to receive a steady flow of SSN 688 business in the near-term; Congress fully supported the Pentagon's plans to order five of the submarines in fiscal years 1983 and 1984, at a cost of nearly $3 billion.

Nimitz class aircraft carriers—Newport News is the sole supplier of Nimitz class nuclear-propelled aircraft carriers. Each carrier is more than 1,000 feet long, carries 90 aircraft, and requires about five years to construct. Not surprisingly, they are the world's most expensive ships. Among aircraft deployed on Nimitz class carriers are the A-6, A-7, S-3 and SH-3, which carry tactical nuclear bombs and a nuclear antisubmarine depth bomb. Newport News delivered the third of the carriers, the Carl Vinson, in early 1982. The yard has received contracts for work on three more carriers and is well on the way with the construction of number four, the Theodore Roosevelt. The two most recent carriers were authorized by Congress in 1982 (at $3.4 billion apiece), and the Navy gave Newport News a $3.1 billion award--the largest in history--in December 1982 for initial work and purchase of long lead time materials for construction of the two carriers. The Navy hopes to win approval for a total carrier fleet of 15 over the next five years.

Newport News has been less fortunate in receiving contracts to overhaul existing carriers than it has been in getting awards to build new ones, losing a $500 million job to the Philadelphia Navy Yard in 1979.[11]

Other work--Newport News was the only contractor for the Navy's nuclear-propelled guided missile cruisers. Four of the Virginia class boats, armed with Asroc nuclear ASW rocket, were built by the yard; the final one, the Arkansas, was delivered in 1980. The Navy did make one additional contract award worth $3.2 million for cruiser work in 1981.

The shipyard built nine of 37 SSN 637 class attack submarines. These submarines, built between 1965 and 1975, carry Subroc nuclear-tipped missiles. Like the SSN 688s, some SSN 637s will be equipped with nuclear-armed Tomahawk cruise missiles.

Tenneco-Government Relationship

Political action committee: Tenneco has been aggressive politically in support of Newport News's military and merchant business. In 1977, the Shipbuilders Council of America conducted a $1 million campaign--$400,000 of which was contributed by Newport News--that unsuccessfully attempted to persuade Congress to require that a share of oil imports be carried on American-built ships. In response to criticism, Tenneco stated emphatically that it considered such lobbying proper and "intends to do so in the future."

Tenneco also was criticized for making questionable payments both at home and abroad in the years before 1976. Among the payments acknowledged by Tenneco was a $10,000 fund solicited from Newport News employees and disbursed to area political campaigns in 1968. The questionable payments scandal triggered investigations by the Securities and Exchange Commission, the Internal Revenue Service, several grand juries and the company itself, as well as a host of shareholder suits and a shareholder resolution. As a corrective measure Tenneco explicitly forbade the use of company assets to make illegal political contributions.

Since then, however, the company's PAC has been very active in making legal political contributions. The PAC gave $203,850 in 1979-80 and $454,150 in 1981-82 to congressional candidates. The major portion of these contributions has gone to conservative candidates, and 88 percent supported Republicans.

In keeping with its relatively strong ideological bent and with the multifaceted nature of the company, the Tenneco PAC has not given a large portion of its contributions to members of the congressional leadership, or to members of defense committees. Some $22,150 in 1979-80 (11 percent of the total) and $70,350 in 1981-82 (15 percent) went to sitting members of defense committees. Substantial contributions have gone to nonincumbents. Of $134,200 given to Senate candidates in 1979 through September 1982, $95,700 (71 percent) went to Republican nonincumbents, most of whom were running against incumbents. (Some of these contributions were made after the candidates won their elections.) Recipients of $5,000 or more included Republican Sens. James Abdnor (S.D.), Slade Gorton (Wash.), Charles Grassley (Iowa), Frank Murkowski (Ark.), Dan Quayle (Ind.), Steve Symms (Idaho), Paul Trible (R-Va.) and Pete Wilson (Calif.).

A member of the House until this year, Sen. Trible is known to be an aggressive advocate of Newport News's interests, and in his 1982 Senate campaign, Trible told voters that he was a "principal architect" of the Reagan shipbuilding program. Trible said in a campaign speech that he was "responsible" for the increase in shipbuilding, "and thousands of Virginians are at work because of it."[12] Campaign rhetoric aside, news accounts do credit Trible with being an important "booster" of the shipyard. Tenneco has rewarded Trible with the maximum $10,000 in campaign contributions in 1981-2. Other Virginia congressmen, particularly those on defense committees, have also received substantial contributions.

Washington office: Newport News employs the law firm of Sullivan and Beauregard to lobby for it in Washington. Two of the firm's three principals have Navy backgrounds: Henry G. Beauregard is a former assistant general counsel of the Navy for procurement, and Robert Moss also worked in the Office of the General Counsel of the Navy. Among Sullivan and Beauregard's other clients is the Shipbuilders Council of America, a trade association whose current chairman is Edward J. Campbell, president of Newport News.

Personnel interchange: Between 1977 and 1981, 97 mid- to upper-level defense officials left the government to join Newport News Shipbuilding, while two company officials moved in the reverse direction.

Contracting difficulties: While Newport News has worked to cultivate the government, its relationship with the Navy has not been entirely amicable. Between 1973 and 1976 it submitted $884 million in cost overrun claims resulting from the construction of seven attack submarines, two carriers and five cruisers. In 1977, the company received $44 million to settle two of the claims. The following year, the bulk of the claims were settled. Newport News was paid approximately $190 million by the Navy to resolve the disputes over 12 of the ships. The financial consequence of the agreement was an $18 million reduction in the company's 1978 pre-tax income, $9 million after tax, because of lower-than-expected profits on the construction. In 1979, the Navy settled the final claim by awarding Newport News $182.3 million for the Arkansas, originally expected to cost $171 million. The ship, on which Newport News earned a scant $100,000 profit, was delivered the following year, two years late.

Even though it had settled with the company, the Navy, at the insistence of Adm. Hyman Rickover, asked the Justice Department to investigate possible fraud in the size of the claims. A grand jury was empaneled in Richmond to evaluate the evidence, but in January 1982 Rickover reported there were no indictments and little possibility of any resulting from the investigation.[13]

Contingency Planning and Prospects

Like its competitor, Electric Boat, Newport News has experienced the boom/bust nature of naval construction. After several very bad years during the Carter administration, it has become healthy again as Congress has approved the Reagan administration's substantial increases in submarine and ship procurement. Both the SSN 688 submarine and Nimitz class aircraft carrier programs will bring Newport News steady work over the next few years. The long-term picture is less certain, however. Reagan's much-publicized plan to build a 600-ship Navy, requiring the construction of 133 new ships this decade, is coming under increasing attack as a result of budget pressures. The magnitude of the appropriations required in the mid-1980s has led many observers to doubt it ever will be approved.

A nuclear freeze could affect Newport News's work on modernization of older SSBNs to carry Trident I missiles, and could affect future submarine work--including submarine overhaul associated with deployment of cruise missiles on attack submarines--that the yard might bid for. However, this work is a minor proportion of the yard's activities, and the Trident conversion work is nearing completion. Likely outcomes from the Strategic Arms Reduction Talks should not have much effect on Newport News, except perhaps by affecting future contract possibilities in unforeseeable ways.

As Naval contracts have crept past 75 percent of Newport News's gross revenues, and as commercial shipbuilding's slump has become seemingly permanent, the yard has taken the logical step of redirecting its facilities to Navy use. A brand-new but vacant commercial drydock, for example, is now the construction site for the carrier Theodore Roosevelt. Newport News, however, is not likely to become as totally dependent on Navy shipbuilding as Electric Boat. It has invested substantial capital in expanding its capacity for overhauling and refueling nuclear submarines, a program less susceptible to political whims than shipbuilding. Moreover, Newport News has modern commercial shipbuilding facilities and recent experience in the commercial field--both of which Electric Boat lacks--that leave it well-positioned in the unlikely event that the commercial shipbuilding market revives.

Tenneco Footnotes

1. The Washington Post, Sept. 7, 1982.
2. The New York Times, June 1, 1982.
3. The Washington Post, Oct. 25, 1982.
4. Industry Week, Oct. 19, 1981, p. 87.
5. The Wall Street Journal, March 31, 1980.
6. The Wall Street Journal, Nov. 9, 1981, and Defense Department News Releases.
7. Norman Polmar, The Ships and Aircraft of the U.S. Fleet, Naval Institute Press, Annapolis, Md., 1981.
8. Joint Chiefs of Staff, United States Military Posture for FY 1983, p. 73.
9. The Wall Street Journal, March 18, 1981.
10. Ibid.
11. The New York Times, April 30, 1979.
12. The Washington Post, Oct. 25, 1982.
13. Statement of Adm. H.G. Rickover, Joint Economic Committee Hearings, Jan. 28, 1982, Part I, p. 10.

United Technologies

United Technologies is the quintessential conglomerate, a company whose lines of business have expanded from its traditional defense strength into a host of commercial areas. The company is best known for Pratt & Whitney engines and Sikorsky helicopters. Besides these two defense industry staples, United Technologies produces electronic and other aerospace products for the military.

Since 1973, United Technologies has aggressively pursued a policy of diversification through acquisitions, a strategy that has dramatically reduced its dependence on defense contracts. It acquired Essex Group in 1974, Otis Elevator in 1975, Amboc Industries in 1978, Carrier in 1979, Mostek in 1979 and Elektro-Finanz AG in 1982. Instead of presenting itself primarily as a defense contractor, the company now proclaims, "High technology is the common denominator of all we do." United Technologies' government sales fell from 51 percent of total sales in 1973, to a low of 22 percent in 1980. Since then, sales to the government have risen again to comprise 33 percent of total revenues.

Many of United Technologies' new acquisitions are broadly categorized as "Building Systems" or "Industrial Products." Two other industry segments contain the defense-related businesses; "Power" is dominated by Pratt and Whitney, and "Flight Systems" includes Sikorsky Aircraft and two electronics subsidiaries, Hamilton Standard and Norden Systems.

United Technologies reported sales of $13.58 billion in 1982, virtually unchanged from 1981. Earnings rose from $458 million to $534 million. In 1982, United Technologies was the 27th largest company on the Forbes 500 top sales list. It has its headquarters in Hartford, Conn.

Government and Defense Business

Defense dependence: United Technologies was the second largest Defense Department contractor in both FY 1981 and 1982, with awards of $3.78 billion and $4.21 billion, respectively. Sales to the government totaled $4.5 billion in 1982.

Almost all of what United Technologies calls its Power segment consists of Pratt & Whitney Aircraft Group, the country's leading engine manufacturer. The Power segment sold $2.58 billion in jet engines and parts to the U.S. government in 1982, compared with $1.69 billion in commercial sales. More than 20,800 Pratt & Whitney jet engines are part of military arsenals the world over. Government sales were almost

Data on United Technologies

(dollar figures in millions)

	1978	1979	1980	1981	1982
Sales	$6,265	$9,053	$12,324	$13,670	$13,577
Net income	$234	$326	$393	$458	$427
Sales to the U.S. government	$1,692	$2,082	$2,711	$3,827	$4,480
Government sales as a percentage of total sales	27%	23%	22%	28%	33%
DoD prime contract awards*	$2,400	$2,554	$3,109	$3,776	$4,208
Ratio of DoD prime awards to total sales+	.38	.28	.25	.28	.31
Total United Technologies employees	152,200	197,700	200,200	189,700	183,900

* U.S. fiscal year, ending Sept. 30.
\+ U.S. fiscal year awards compared with calendar year sales.

double the 1979 level of $1.3 billion. Operating profits in the Power segment were $420 million on total revenues of $5.27 billion in 1982.

The company's principal military engines in production are the F100, installed on the Air Force's F-15 and F-16, the TF30, used on the Navy F-14, the TF33, carried on the Air Force E-3A (Awacs), and the J52, which powers the Navy A-4, A-6E and EA-68. United Technologies is the country's leading supplier of military engines.

Sikorsky is the country's foremost manufacturer of medium and heavy military helicopters, currently producing the Army's UH-60A Black Hawk helicopter and the airframe for the Navy's CH-53E and SH-60B helicopters. The company also produced and continues to work on the Navy's SH-3. Current commercial helicopter production is centered on the S-76, used to transport executives and oil-rig personnel.

Hamilton Standard and Norden Systems, together with Sikorsky, comprise United Technologies' Flight Systems segment. Hamilton Standard makes engine and flight controls and various engine parts, and Norden produces radar, display and other aircraft equipment, along with missile propulsion systems.

Revenues of the three companies making up Flight Systems were $2 billion in 1982. Operating profit totaled $169 million.

Defense employees: United Technologies employs approximately 184,000 people worldwide. Of its 125,000 U.S. workers in 1981, at least 35,000 were employed by Pratt & Whitney, primarily in East Hartford, Conn., but also in West Palm Beach, Fla., and elsewhere. Pratt & Whitney has in the past employed close to 40,000 people, but has laid off workers as demand for its commercial engines lagged.

Sikorsky Helicopter, based in Stratford, Conn., is also one of that state's major private employers. Norden Systems is based in Norwalk, Conn. Unlike Pratt & Whitney, which does not expect immediate employment growth despite increased defense funding, Norden's high-technology systems are much in demand, prompting the hiring of 600 workers in 1982 in addition to its 1981 complement of 1,900.

United Technologies declined to provide IRRC with an estimate of the number of its workers employed on defense projects.

Nuclear Weapons-Related Programs

United Technologies is included in these company profiles primarily because of contracts for secondary nuclear-related systems. IRRC could identify no definite prime contract awards in fiscal 1981 for primary systems. Largely through its manufacture of engines for nuclear-capable aircraft, however, United Technologies is a major producer of equipment for secondary systems. Contract awards for secondary work totaled $1.41 billion in fiscal 1981.

Primary systems:

Although United Technologies did not receive identifiable prime contracts for primary nuclear weapons systems in 1981, the company does work on such systems.

Strategic bombers and support aircraft--The nation's entire current fleet of strategic bombers carries Pratt & Whitney engines. The B-52 fleet is equipped with the company's J57 and TF33 engines, while FB-111s are equipped with the TF-30 engine. The KC-135 tankers also have been powered by J57 engines, although they are being replaced by new GE engines.

Defense Department contract listings do not permit analysis of the breakdown among systems, but Pratt & Whitney has a substantial business in supplying spare parts for these and other engines. (United Technologies is the Pentagon's largest supplier of spare parts, and has been one of a number of companies recently accused of overcharging for some parts.)

The company's Norden subsidiary produces the AN/ASQ-176 offensive avionics system for the B-52 bomber. The Pentagon announced contract awards for this system of $45 million during FY 1983.

Strategic missiles--United Technologies works on the MX and Minuteman missiles and may do maintenance work on Titan II missiles.

United Technologies' Nuclear Weapons-Related Contracts
(in millions of dollars)

Primary Systems	Secondary Systems	
FY 1981	FY1981	
None	F100 engine for F-15s and F-16s	$1,310
	Titan rocket boosters	$31
	SH-3 ASW helicopter	$29
	J52 engine for A-4s, A-6s, other aircraft	$15
	M-109 howitzer	$11
	F-111 fighter	$3
Other current contracts	Other current contracts	
Minuteman missile	E-3A Awacs aircraft	
MX missile		
B-52 bomber		
FB-111 bomber		
KC-135 aerial tanker		

The Norden subsidiary has a subcontract to develop a computerized command and control system for the MX. In 1983, United Technologies' Chemical Systems Division in Sunnyvale, Calif., won a $59 million contract to remanufacture Minuteman III and Stage III motor cases with new propellants and to replace old ordnance.

The Sunnyvale facility also provides substantial support for the Titan launch booster program (discussed below under secondary systems); it is impossible to tell from DoD listings whether any of the technical services or components provided also support the remaining Titan missiles.

United Technologies' Hamilton Standard subsidiary has a major subcontract for compressors on the air-launched cruise missile program.

Secondary systems:

Fighter aircraft--The work-horse of Pratt & Whitney's engines is the F100, which drives both the F-15 and F-16. This fighter engine alone accounts for nearly a fifth of United Technologies' revenues. Both the F-15 and the F-16 are equipped to carry nuclear as well as conventional ground attack missiles. The F-15 Eagle, built by

McDonnell Douglas, carries two engines, and General Dynamics' F-16 Falcon carries one. Both planes (and hence their engines) are in current production. F100-related contracts awarded in fiscal 1981, not including foreign military sales, amounted to $1.31 billion or 92 percent of the United Technologies FY 1981 contract awards identified by IRRC as nuclear-related.

Continued contract awards are assured, as Congress authorized $1.24 billion to procure 39 F-15s and $1.71 billion for 120 F-16s in FY 1983. The government has continued to rely on the F100 despite serious problems its fighters have experienced with the engine. During the late 1970s, pilots discovered that the engine had a tendency to stall at high speeds and precipitate crashes. By 1982, United Technologies had received $500 million to fix the F100. The Air Force has also taken the precautionary step of authorizing General Electric to develop the F101 DFE as an alternative engine. Although the GE engine is not yet in production, both companies are well aware that the Air Force's continuing need for an F100-type engine may eventually result in head-to-head competition. By the time the F101 DFE is ready for production, about 2,000 of the 4,158 F100 engines the Air Force plans to buy--at a cost of $2.7 million each--will remain to be procured, a market in excess of $4 billion. United Technologies has countered the General Electric bid to break its fighter engine monopoly by obtaining $25 million in development funding over the last two years to build two improved versions of the F100. The PW1120 is being developed for foreign and export fighter aircraft; the PW1130, a more powerful variant, is designed for the next generation of fighter aircraft.

United Technologies also produced the TF30 engines that power nuclear-capable F-111 fighters. Fiscal 1983 prime awards for the TF30s used on F-111s totaled at least $7.9 million. The TF30 engine also is used on the F-14, which is in current production, and is not nuclear-capable, so positive identification of further F-111 awards is difficult.

In addition to the engines, Norden produces display and other equipment used on F-111s.

Attack aircraft--Another Pratt & Whitney engine, the J52, is used in two attack aircraft, the A-4 and the A-6E, and in an electronic countermeasures aircraft, the EA-6B. The A-6E and the EA-6B are currently in production by Grumman. The A-4 and the A-6E are nuclear-capable.

Contract awards on the J52 engine in FY 1981 totaled at least $15 million. The Pentagon announced in fiscal 1983 that it would award Pratt & Whitney $145 million for J52 work. (Because IRRC has not included the EA-6B in its secondary classification, these contracts have been excluded from the figures on total secondary contracts.)

Norden produces radar equipment used on the A-6. The subsidiary received fiscal 1981 contract awards of $3.2 million for such work.

Awacs--Although the Air Force E-3A Advance Warning and Control System (Awacs) does not deliver nuclear weapons, it does direct them, and it is considered by the Pentagon to be both a tactical and a strategic system. The Awacs aircraft is a flying command, control and communications center, made up of electronic and radar devices installed on a modified Boeing 707. As the supplier to Boeing of $681 million in commercial engines in 1981, many of which are installed on 707s, Pratt & Whitney quite logically is also the contractor for the four TF33 engines that each E-3A carries. In FY 1983, as in the two previous years, Congress approved funds for two more Awacs planes. In addition, the United States is committed to funding part of the acquisition of 18 E-3A's by NATO.

Space systems--Pratt & Whitney also has a presence in the space program through its work on Titan rocket boosters and on the Boeing-produced Inertial Upper Stage. Norden works on both programs, which are used to boost military and other satellites into space. Titan awards in FY 1981 totaled $31 million.

Helicopters--Sikorsky produced the nuclear-capable SH-3 Sea King helicopters, which are now being phased out in favor of the new SH-60 Seahawk. Until now the Sea King has served as the Navy's principal ship-based antisubmarine warfare (ASW) helicopter; a number had been modified to test and carry weapons that will be standard equipment on the SH-60B. Sikorsky garnered $29 million in 1981 prime contracts to maintain and modify the Sea Kings. SH-3s carry B57 nuclear depth charges.

The frame, but not the engine, for the Navy's new SH-60B Seahawk helicopter is built by UT's Sikorsky branch. It is not clear whether the Seahawk, another ASW aircraft, will carry nuclear depth charges. Sikorsky received $60 million in SH-60 awards in fiscal 1981. (These are not included in IRRC's aggregate figures, since the nuclear status of the SH-60 is unclear.)

Howitzer--Norden Systems received $11 million in 1981 contract awards for manufacture of the M109 howitzer gun, which can use both conventional and nuclear shells.

United Technologies-Government Relationship

Political action committee: United Technologies, like most other major defense contractors, maintains a political action committee. Like its counterparts, the company favors with its contributions members of Armed Services, Defense Appropriations, and Science and Technology committees and subcommittees. It also gives proportionately larger sums to members in the Connecticut and California districts where it operates large plants. Unlike the PACs of some other dominant defense firms, however, United Technologies' PAC is considered quite partisan:

In 1981-82 it gave $137,225 to 139 Republican candidates and only $67,050 to 78 Democrats.

Overall, the PAC gave $140,400 in 1979-80 and $204,000 in 1981-82 to congressional candidates. In the latter period, 38 percent of the total, or $78,400, was given to voting members of defense committees.

Washington office: United Technologies' Washington office is widely considered to be one of the most sophisticated and effective of its kind. It is headed by Clark MacGregor, a former Republican Representative from Minnesota and Nixon's 1972 reelection campaign chairman, described as "the prototypical Washington insider" by The Wall Street Journal. MacGregor directs the company's PAC and is the principal adviser for the U.S. Chamber of Commerce's PAC as well. Another UTC lobbyist and MacGregor's top assistant is Hugh Witt, who spent 18 years in procurement and the Defense Department before founding the Office of Federal Procurement Policy at the Office of Management and Budget. In addition to MacGregor, Witt and two other senior lobbyists, the company maintains a staff of 37 professionals in Washington who attend to the individual needs of UTC's many divisions.

The company also employs three outside lobbying firms to assist in its Washington efforts, including two run by former members of Congress who were among UTC's favorite recipients of PAC money: Cederberg and Associates, run by Elford Cederberg, former ranking Republican on the House Appropriations Committee, and the Washington Industrial Team, two of whose principals, Richard Ichord and Robert Wilson, were senior members of the House Armed Services Committee until 1981.

United Technologies has used these considerable lobbying resources to win several significant victories in recent Congresses. The Connecticut delegation is given credit for helping to steer both the Army and Navy heavy-lift helicopter programs in Sikorsky's direction,[1] and MacGregor was reported to be an important factor in persuading wavering Republicans to approve the 1981 sale of Awacs to Saudi Arabia.[2]

Personnel interchange: United Technologies' management includes perhaps the leading example of the revolving door between the government and the defense industry--Alexander Haig. Haig became president and chief executive officer of United Technologies in 1980, after serving stints as Deputy Assistant to President Nixon for National Security Affairs, White House Chief of Staff, and Supreme Allied Commander in Europe. In 1981, Haig left UTC to become Secretary of State; after his exit from the government in 1982 he became a consultant to United Technologies on domestic and foreign business policies.

United Technologies' roster of former military officials also includes vice president William J. Evans, formerly Commander-in-Chief of the

U.S. Air Force in Europe, and Eugene V. McAuliffe, previously an Assistant Secretary of Defense and now president of United Technologies-Europe.

Between 1977 and 1981, 68 mid- to high-level Defense Department employees transferred to United Technologies. Three UTC employees became mid- to high-level DoD officials.

Contingency Planning and Prospects

United Technologies declined to provide IRRC with information about possible contingency planning in the case of military contract cancellations, so it is not clear how employees might be provided for.

The company has protected itself by diversifying aggressively into commercial areas over the last decade. Rather unusually, this expansion has not been planned to take advantage of the company's aerospace expertise. As a result, United Technologies is a company with two distinct faces--an aerospace contractor taking bigger slices out of the growing defense pie, and a far-flung commercial industrial conglomerate.

The two personalities are not unrelated, nonetheless. Even though the company has cut nearly in half the percentage of its revenues that used to come from defense contracting, the combined commercial recession and defense boom almost guarantee that, in future years, as in 1981-2, defense contracting will be the company's major profit center. Moreover, not all of United Technologies' commercial and military operations diverge. Pratt & Whitney controls 70 percent of the commercial jet engine market in addition to its dominant defense posture. Sikorsky builds commercial helicopters using the same technology and facilities that serve the military. Both subsidiaries therefore retain flexibility to adapt their production mix to the vagaries of their two markets.

UTC has relatively little to fear from even a strong nuclear arms control proposal along the lines advocated by freeze proponents. It would lose some missile contracts, like the MX and air-launched cruise missile, but these are small relative to the company's other business. Norden would be most affected, but even that subsidiary would continue to have plenty of work on unaffected defense programs.

United Technologies Footnotes

1. The New York Times, March 26, 1978.
2. The Wall Street Journal, April 1, 1982.

Westinghouse Electric

Westinghouse Electric is a highly diversified industrial company that was incorporated in 1872. Initially Westinghouse was engaged primarily in the sale of equipment used to generate, transmit, distribute and control electrical energy. The company since has expanded its business base, and now engages in a broad range of activities, from the management of a broadcasting and cable communications network, to the bottling and distribution of beverages, to the production of weapons systems. Westinghouse also is the nation's leading manufacturer of nuclear power equipment.

Westinghouse divides its business into four major operating segments: Industry Products; Power Systems; Public Systems; and Broadcasting and Cable. Westinghouse employed 142,250 persons worldwide in 1982. The company has its headquarters in Pittsburgh.

Westinghouse had sales of $9.75 billion in 1982, up 4 percent from 1981, making it the 44th largest corporation on the Forbes 500 top sales list. The company's increased sales during a recession year were based in part on what Westinghouse called a "banner year" for defense. Defense sales were $1.5 billion, up from $1.3 billion in 1981.

The company's net income was $449 million in 1982, a 3 percent increase over 1981.

Government and Defense Business

Some 82 percent of Westinghouse's government sales are made through its Public Systems Co.; those sales account for about half of Public Systems' total sales. Total Public Systems sales were $2.66 billion in 1982, and operating profit totaled $245 million, up substantially from $180 million in 1981. Public Systems accounted for about 35 percent of Westinghouse's operating profit before general corporate expenses in 1982.

Public Systems' main business is the design, production and maintenance of electronic systems, which Westinghouse points out is "the fastest-growing part of the defense market." Public Systems is a leading contributor of radar, electronic countermeasure, and fire control systems for such programs as Awacs, the F-16 fighter, the B-1 bomber and a variety of ships. Public Systems also develops launching systems for such missiles as the MX and Trident and the Tomahawk cruise missiles.

Data on Westinghouse Electric
(dollar figures in millions)

	1978	1979	1980	1981	1982
Sales and operating revenues	$6,780	$7,443	$8,514	$9,367	$9,745
Net income	$311	$331	$403	$438	$449
Sales to the U.S. government	$750	900	1,300	1,400	1,850
Government sales as a percentage of total sales	11%	12%	13%	15%	19%
DoD prime contract awards*	$539	$659	$932	$1,125	$1,492
Ratio of DoD prime awards to total sales+	.08	.09	.11	.12	.15
DoE defense program prime contract awards*	NA	NA	NA	$145	$167
Ratio of combined DoD, DoE defense prime awards to total sales+	NA	NA	NA	.14	.17
Total Westinghouse employees	142,000	145,000	146,000	148,000	145,000

* Contract awards for U.S. fiscal year, ending Sept. 30.
+ Ratio of awards during fiscal year to calendar year sales.

Power Systems accounted for 12 percent of Westinghouse's government sales in 1981. The main business of Power Systems is the design, development, manufacture and distribution of nuclear energy systems and associated fuel and services; power generating apparatus and service; and transmission and distribution equipment for the electric utility industry, industrial companies and the construction market. Under contracts with the Energy Department, Power Systems manages the Bettis Atomic Power Laboratory and the Waste Isolation Pilot Plant (WIPP). Bettis, along with General Electric's Knolls Atomic Power Laboratory, is responsible for research and development of naval nuclear propulsion plants, which power submarines and some surface ships. The Bettis Laboratory does some work directly for the Defense Department, in addition to its DoE responsibilities. WIPP is a pilot program for the disposal of radioactive waste generated by the nation's defense programs.

In October 1983, Westinghouse won the contract to manage the uranium reprocessing facility at the Idaho National Engineering Laboratory. The facility reprocesses spent fuel from naval and research nuclear reactors.

Westinghouse received Defense Department contract awards of $1.12 billion in fiscal 1981 and $1.49 billion in fiscal 1982, making the company the 13th largest DoD contractor in 1982. Energy Department defense program awards totaled $145 million in fiscal 1981 and $167 million in fiscal 1982. Thus, total defense contract awards were $1.27 billion in fiscal 1981 and $1.66 billion in fiscal 1982. The ratio of defense awards to sales was .136 in 1981 and .170 in 1982.

Westinghouse did not provide IRRC with an estimate of the number of its employees that were involved in defense production.

Nuclear Weapons-Related Programs

Westinghouse is a major contributor to the MX, Trident and cruise missile programs, and to the Trident submarine and B-1 bomber programs. The company also is involved in a number of nuclear-related and dual-capable systems, notably Awacs, the F-16 fighter and attack submarines. IRRC identified FY 1981 contract awards of $135 million on primary nuclear systems and $702 million on secondary systems. The latter category includes DoE awards for the Bettis laboratory and the WIPP project.

Primary systems:

Trident submarine--While the Energy Department says that GE's Knolls Laboratory has primary responsibility for development of the Trident nuclear propulsion plant, the Westinghouse-managed Bettis Laboratory also is making a major contribution to the program. The Bettis Laboratory actually includes facilities in two locations, at the Bettis site in West Mifflin, Pa. (near Pittsburgh), and at the Naval Reactors Facility at the Idaho National Engineering Laboratory. Bettis employed 3,570 workers in FY 1982, according to DoE. The DoE-sponsored operating budget in fiscal 1982 was $197 million. DoE contract awards to Bettis totaled $135 million in FY 1981 and $155 million in FY 1982. The laboratory receives additional support from the Defense Department. Westinghouse's current contract to manage Bettis runs to September 1988.

Defense Department contract awards to Westinghouse for development work on the Trident propulsion system totaled $67 million in FY 1981. The amount increased to $73 million in FY 1982 and $94 million in FY 1983. (DoE awards to Bettis are all under one contract. Because much or most of Bettis's work is on non-Trident systems, including propulsion systems for nuclear-capable attack submarines and surface ships, and on general research, IRRC included these awards under the "secondary" category.)

Trident missile--Westinghouse manufactures the launch tubes that house the Trident submarine's sea-launched ballistic missiles. DoD awarded at least $40 million in prime contract awards during FY 1981 to the company for work on Trident SLBM launch tubes. DoD announced FY 1983 awards totaling $28 million for work on launch tubes for the new Trident II (D-5) missile, and another $9 million for work on Trident I launch tubes in Poseidon submarines. The Trident missile work takes place in Sunnyvale, Calif.

Westinghouse Electric's Nuclear Weapons-Related Contracts
(in millions of dollars)

Primary Systems

FY 1981	
Trident submarine (DoD awards)	$67
Trident missile	$40
B-52 bomber components	$26
Ballistic Missile Early Warning System	$2

Other current contracts
- MX missile
- B-1B bomber components

Secondary Systems

FY1981	
F-16 fighter components	$207
SSN-688 attack submarine (DoD)	$149
Bettis Laboratory (management)	$135
AN/ALQ-131 ECM system	$108
F-4 fighter components	$41
AN/ALQ-119 ECM system	$29
E-3A Awacs aircraft radar	$10
Waste Isolation Pilot Plant (management)	$10
Defense Meteorological Satellite Program	$5
Tomahawk missile launch system	$5

Other current contracts
- Nimitz-class aircraft carrier equipment
- Very High Speed Integrated Circuit program

MX missile--Westinghouse is developing the launch canister for the MX missile. The MX is to be enclosed in the canister, which allows for easy transport and is considered part of the missile's launch system. DoD contracting information shows no prime contracts awarded to Westinghouse during FY 1981 for MX-related work. In FY 1982, however, the department announced an $80 million award to Westinghouse's Sunnyvale, Calif., plant for MX canister development. Since then, DoD has announced further awards totaling $59 million.

Strategic bombers--Westinghouse is active in both the B-52 and B-1B bomber programs. The Air Force is upgrading B-52s with the addition of tail warning sets (designated AN/ALQ-153). These sets are radar systems installed in the tail section of the bombers to detect and warn of approaching missiles and aircraft. The system automatically ejects flares and chaff designed to confuse electronic systems of hostile missiles and aircraft, luring them away from the B-52. The Pentagon chose Westinghouse's system over those of competitors late in 1977, and the company delivered the first sets in 1980. DoD plans to procure 321 ALQ-153 systems. DoD awarded at least $26 million in B-52 contract awards to Westinghouse in FY 1981.

Westinghouse also is developing tail warning sets for the B-1B and FB-111 bombers.

Rockwell International awarded Westinghouse a subcontract for production of a B-1B bomber radar system in 1981. The B-1B terrain following and navigation radar being developed by Westinghouse is a modified version of a small modular system used on F-16s and F-4s. Westinghouse also is providing electrical generating systems for the B-1B bombers.

Oak Ridge complex--Westinghouse is one of three finalists in the running to replace Union Carbide as manager of the Energy Department's Oak Ridge nuclear power and weapons complex.

Other--DoD presented Westinghouse with a $1.6 million contract in FY 1981 for research and development on a ballistic missile early warning system (BMEWS).

Secondary systems:

Idaho National Engineering Laboratory--Westinghouse Electric won a contract in October 1983 to replace Exxon at the Idaho National Engineering Laboratory. Under terms of the contract, Westinghouse will operate the reprocessing plant and certain other facilities at INEL. The plant reprocesses spent fuel from the Navy's nuclear propulsion program and from government research reactors producing highly enriched uranium. In that process, the plant also handles nuclear waste from the naval program.

Westinghouse will take over full management on April 1, 1984. The budget for the plant is $100 million a year, and the contract runs for five and a half years. EG&G, which has operated other portions of INEL, will continue its role.

The Energy Department says that the highly enriched uranium produced at the plant (planned at a total of 1,650 kilograms in fiscal year 1984) is shipped to the Oak Ridge Y-12 plant. At Oak Ridge, most of the uranium (1,500 kilograms in fiscal year 1984) is "converted to metal form for reuse as fuels in the Savannah River production reactors and for use in the weapons program." A minor portion may end up in uranium parts used in nuclear weapons, but most apparently goes to Savannah River to fuel the reactors there that produce plutonium and tritium for nuclear weapons, according to the Energy Department. An INEL spokesman told IRRC that the plant has produced more than 18 tons of enriched uranium 235 since 1952. (Exxon has told IRRC that much of the reprocessed fuel is used again in naval and research reactors.)

Tomahawk sea-launched cruise missile--Westinghouse's experience with missile launch systems is being applied to the Navy's Tomahawk sea-launched cruise missile program. In 1981, DoD announced that the company would develop a vertical launch system for use in conjunction with Tomahawk cruise missiles based on submarines. DoD awarded Westinghouse an initial Tomahawk contract of $5 million in FY 1981; since then, the department has awarded the company at least $43 million for Tomahawk launcher work.

F-16 fighter--Westinghouse is a major contractor on General Dynamics' F-16 fighter program. The F-16 is a dual-capable tactical aircraft. The company's Electronic Warfare Division in Baltimore, Md., is the lead contractor for the AN/ALQ-131 and AN/ALQ-119 electronic countermeasures (ECM) pods. (These ECM systems, which are used to confuse enemy radar and other electronic systems, are also provided to other aircraft, and are discussed under separate headings below.)

The Pentagon awarded a production contract in 1981 for the country's next generation ECM system, the AN/ALQ-165 airborne self-protection jamming system. This system, developed jointly by Westinghouse and ITT, will enter the production phase in 1984 and will be installed on nuclear-capable aircraft like the F-16, the McDonnell Douglas F/A-18 and AV-8B, and the Grumman A-6 and F-14. Westinghouse expects sales of airborne self-protection jamming systems to generate more than $1 billion of new business for the company in the years to come.

In 1975, General Dynamics selected Westinghouse as the supplier of the F-16 fire control system, the AN/APG-66. This modular radar is similar to those developed for B-1B bombers and F-4 fighters. Westinghouse began full-scale production of the APG-66 system in 1977; the company delivered its 1,000th radar set to the Air Force in January 1982. Existing and anticipated orders will continue production into the 1990s.

In addition to the above, Westinghouse has developed a reliable solid-state electrical generating system for the F-16.

The Pentagon listed $207 million in FY 1981 contract awards for the F-16. (Some work on F-16 systems may have been included under the ALQ 131 and ALQ 119 headings.) DoD announced F-16 prime contract awards of $260 million in FY 1983.

F-4 fighter--Westinghouse has been manufacturing aircraft fire control systems for use on the Air Force's F-4 since 1959. In recent years, the company has provided upgraded ECM and fire control radar systems to enable the nuclear-capable F-4 to function into the 1990s.

Among Westinghouse systems installed on the F-4 are the ALQ-131, the ALQ-119 and the AN/APQ-120 fire control system. The APQ-120, the company's newest F-4-related weapons control system, provides improved targeting capability. Westinghouse now is modifying the APQ-120 system with a new digital computer.

Some $41 million in contract awards were listed by the Pentagon for the F-4 in FY 1981. The Defense Department announced awards to Westinghouse of $15 million in FY 1983.

AN/ALQ-131 ECM system--The AN/ALQ-131 ECM pod is used on several nuclear-capable aircraft, including the McDonnell Douglas F-4 and F-15, the General Dynamics F-16 and F-111 and the LTV A-7. A team of electronic companies led by Westinghouse manufacture the ALQ-131, which is designed to jam the radar and guidance systems of various anti-aircraft defense systems. The Air Force expects to order more than 1,000 ALQ-131 systems by 1986. In FY 1981, the Pentagon listed $108 million in prime contract awards under the ALQ-131 category. The Pentagon announced $133 million in ALQ-131 contract awards to Westinghouse in FY 1983.

AN/ALQ-119 ECM system--One of Westinghouse's early ECM systems is the AN/ALQ-119. The company has manufactured more than 1,600 ALQ-119 systems since 1970. The ALQ-119, which first saw action over the skies of Vietnam in 1972, is used widely on the McDonnell Douglas F-4, and can be installed on the General Dynamics F-111 and F-16. Westinghouse has continuously modified and upgraded existing ALQ-119 systems, and DoD awarded at least $29 million to the company for modifications during FY 1981.

Attack submarines--Westinghouse has been a major contributor to the SSN 688 and other attack submarine programs through the production of nuclear-powered propulsion systems. SSN 688s will soon be carrying both conventional and nuclear cruise missiles. The company's Plant Apparatus Division near Pittsburgh manufactures the nuclear power plants under DoD contracts. Research and development work is done at GE's Knolls and Westinghouse's Bettis laboratories.

In FY 1981, DoD awarded prime contracts totaling at least $149 million for SSN reactor work by Westinghouse. The Pentagon announced awards of $244 million to the company for this work in FY 1983.

Aircraft carriers--The Westinghouse Plant Apparatus Division also produces nuclear reactors for propulsion of aircraft carriers. While no prime awards to Westinghouse were recorded in FY 1981, the Pentagon announced $290 million for work on nuclear propulsion systems for Nimitz-class aircraft carriers in FY 1983. The Nimitz carriers themselves are being built at Tenneco's Newport News shipyard.

Westinghouse also manufactures radar for aircraft carriers.

E-3A Awacs aircraft--Westinghouse is the supplier of the primary radar system used in the E-3A Sentry Awacs aircraft. The surveillance radar system cost $7 million per unit in 1977. The company now is modifying the system to enable it to track ships at sea. DoD presented Westinghouse with at least $10 million in prime contracts during FY 1981 for Awacs radar work; awards in FY 1983 totaled at least $43 million.

Defense Meteorological Satellite Program--The principal sensor system used on the Defense Meteorological Satellite Program is made by Westinghouse. Contract awards for this work totaled at least $5 million in FY 1981 and $6 million in FY 1983.

Very High Speed Integrated Circuit program--Westinghouse is the head of a team of companies developing a new generation of computer micro-chips in the Pentagon's Very High Speed Integrated Circuits program, one of the military's most significant technology development efforts. VHSIC will have 100 times the capability of today's chips, according to Westinghouse. The Pentagon hopes to begin incorporating VHSIC into military electronic systems in 1984.

Waste Isolation Pilot Plant--The Waste Isolation Pilot Plant is a project to store and dispose of radioactive waste from defense programs. WIPP, which is located in southeastern New Mexico, will result in the storage of waste for the indefinite future in bedded salt, 2,150 feet underground. Westinghouse received awards of $10 million in fiscal 1981 and $12 million in fiscal 1982 to manage the project.

Westinghouse-Government Relationship

Political action committee: The Westinghouse Employees Political Participation Program gave $136,000 to congressional candidates in 1981-82. Some $42,250, or 31 percent of the total, was given to members of defense committees. Contributions were split fairly evenly between Democrats and Republicans; the overwhelming majority went to incumbents.

Major recipients of Westinghouse PAC support in the 1981-82 period included defeated Sen. Howard Cannon (D-Nev.), then a high-ranking member of the Armed Services Committee ($6,000); Sen. John Heinz (R-Pa.), who represents Westinghouse's home state ($5,500); and Sen. James Sasser (D-Tenn.), a member of the Armed Services Committee ($5,500).

Washington office: Westinghouse supports a large Washington office. A listing of Washington representatives by Columbia Books names eight members of the company's Washington office and 20 firms hired as Washington counsels or consultants. Westinghouse's concerns with the federal government are varied, and include other priorities besides defense--most notably nuclear power regulatory policy.

Among firms representing Westinghouse are the Keefe Co. and the law firm of Patton, Boggs & Blow, two of Washington's more influential lobbying groups. The Washington Industrial Team, which represents many large defense contractors, lobbies for Westinghouse on defense issues. The Washington Industrial Team includes former U.S. Reps. Richard Ichord and Robert Wilson, who served on the House Armed Services Committee until 1981.

At times, Westinghouse appears willing to make substantial efforts to influence defense programs in which it has an interest. In response to a shareholder resolution, Westinghouse said that it hired a public relations firm at a cost of $75,000 "to conduct public opinion research and to consult on media matters" in "an effort to further the sale by Westinghouse of its Awacs radar equipment for incorporation into aircraft to be sold by the United States government to the government of Saudi Arabia."

Personnel interchange: From 1977-81, Westinghouse hired 83 mid- to high-level Defense Department employees, and six Westinghouse employees left the company for mid- to high-level jobs at the Pentagon.

Contingency Planning and Prospects

Contingency planning: In a 1970 letter to a Senate subcommittee, then-Westinghouse Vice President Charles H. Weaver noted that "Westinghouse has had a number of spin-offs" from its defense production, notably the application of technology from the naval reactor program to civilian electrical needs. Nevertheless, Weaver expressed the view that:

> A significant problem in conversion of some defense and space technology is that it doesn't convert directly--it requires additional development to adapt it for use in the civil area. Defense and space systems generally are overdesigned for civil use and consequently are usually too costly for direct use. Further development for conversion can also be very costly.[1]

Weaver wrote that finding markets is a major obstacle for conversion planning. He added that a guaranteed market "could be helpful" in conversion, especially in "very large, high risk programs."

Since 1970, much of Westinghouse's work has been in highly sophisticated and expensive electronic systems. The technology used for these military systems could be difficult to use cheaply for commercial applications, as the Council on Economic Priorities' Robert DeGrasse and others have observed.[2] The company's work on missile launching systems also would be difficult to tie to commercial uses.

Westinghouse declined to provide IRRC with further information on its contingency planning or methods for assisting workers affected by military cutbacks.

Prospects: Westinghouse is sufficiently diversified within the defense market that the company should be fairly well insulated against cancellations of specific programs, even as the defense share of Westinghouse sales climbs above 20 percent. Unless there is a general reversal of the arms buildup, Westinghouse's defense business should continue to improve in the next few years. Westinghouse is a major contributor of military electronic systems--the fastest-growing segment of the defense market--and the company is one of the most important contractors on such naval programs as the Trident, SSN 688 and Nimitz-class aircraft carriers. Demand for naval nuclear reactors should be strong in the next several years.

A nuclear freeze would substantially reduce Westinghouse's Sunnyvale, Calif., work by ending the MX, Trident II and cruise missile programs. The Trident submarine program would be at least indirectly affected by a freeze, although freeze proponents do not consider the submarine to be a part of their proposal. The SSN 688 submarines might lose their cruise missile role, either through a freeze or through the Start process if an agreement along the lines proposed by the USSR were approved. Such a role redefinition would not stop the SSN 688 program, however.

Westinghouse Footnotes

1. National Economic Conversion Commission, "Responses to Subcommittee Questionnaire," Senate Subcommittee on Executive Reorganization and Government Research, Government Printing Office, Washington, September 1970, p. 133-4.
2. Robert DeGrasse, Military Expansion, Economic Decline, Council on Economic Priorities, New York, 1983, p. 106-118.

Department of Energy Contractors

Allied

After a much-publicized four-way merger battle, Allied Corp. acquired Bendix Corp. early in 1983. The controversial acquisition gave Allied a major role in the nuclear weapons industry through its inheritance of Bendix's Kansas City Plant, a nuclear warhead components facility that Bendix has managed for the government since 1949.

Allied, formerly Allied Chemical, has been one of the most aggressive corporate conglomerates in recent years, especially since former United Technologies President Edward Hennessy became chairman of Allied in 1979. Since his arrival at Allied, Hennessy has pushed the company into high technology and defense areas; his actions culminated in the purchase of Bendix, the 32nd largest defense contractor in fiscal 1982. Allied's aggressive moves into the defense field led an E.F. Hutton analyst to remark that "Hennessy is trying to turn Allied into a small United Technologies."[1]

The merger battle that resulted in the Bendix acquisition began in April 1982 when Bendix started buying up stock in Martin Marietta. In August 1982, Bendix announced its intention to acquire Marietta. Bendix's advances were not well-received by Marietta, which retaliated by announcing its intention to acquire Bendix. Before the battle was over, United Technologies and finally Allied had entered the fray.

Allied's ultimate victory swelled the size of the consolidated company by two-thirds. The combined company would have ranked about 40th on the Forbes list of 1982 sales leaders. Bendix brings to Allied businesses in aerospace, electronics, automotive products and industrial products. The enlarged Allied has divided its business into five segments: chemical, oil and gas, automotive, aerospace and industrial and technology. Aerospace, including the Kansas City Plant, accounts for about one-fifth of company billings.

Allied's net sales in 1982 (not including Bendix) were $6.17 billion, and net income was $272 million. Bendix's net sales in the company's 1982 fiscal year, ending Sept. 30, were $4.11 billion, down from $4.42 billion in fiscal 1981. Net income dropped substantially at Bendix in its last independent year, from $453 million in 1981 to $138 million in 1982. Bendix attributed the decline to substantially lower sales of its industrial products and modestly decreased automotive sales, offset in part by "slightly" increased profits in the aerospace-electronics businesses.

Data on Allied

(dollar figures in millions)

	1978	1979	1980	1981	1982
Allied sales*	$3,016	$4,332	$5,519	$6,407	$6,167
Bendix sales+	$3,223	$3,413	$3,864	$4,425	$4,113
Kansas City Plant prime contract awards+	NA	NA	NA	$376	$429
DoD prime contract awards to Bendix	$220	$297	$322	$458	$592
Total combined DoD, DoE defense awards to Allied and Bendix	NA	NA	NA	$873	$1,064
Ratio of DoD, DoE defense awards to combined Allied and Bendix sales^	NA	NA	NA	.078	.099
Bendix sales to the U.S. government	NA	$618	$750	$866	$919
Employees at the Kansas City Plant	5,900	NA	6,300	6,815	7,116
Total Bendix and Allied employees (except those at Kansas City)	108,000	123,000	125,000	128,000	106,000

* All figures for Allied exclude Bendix. Allied's fiscal year ends Dec. 31.
\+ Bendix (before the merger) and U.S. fiscal years end Sept. 30.
^ Includes Kansas City Plant contract awards in total sales figures.

Bendix's aerospace sales tripled in the decade before the Allied purchase, and Bendix said in 1981 that it expected increased defense orders resulting from the current military buildup to begin to have a major impact on sales and profits in fiscal 1983.

Aerospace sales currently total about $2 billion, including the Kansas City Plant, compared with total corporate sales of something over $10 billion. The Kansas City Plant accounts for about 20 percent of aerospace sales.

Government and Defense Business

Most military sales by the new Allied Corp. are made by Bendix, which was the 32nd largest Defense Department contractor in fiscal 1982, with prime awards totaling $592 million. Another $44 million was awarded to Allied, mostly to Allied's Bunker Ramo-Eltra subsidiary. Bunker Ramo, acquired by Allied in 1981, and Eltra, acquired in 1979, make electrical and electronic products, including acoustic analysis equipment for submarine warfare and electronic warfare components.

In addition to the DoD contracts, Bendix received contract awards of $429 million in FY 1982 from the Energy Department for management of the Kansas City Plant. All military awards to Allied and Bendix, including the Energy Department awards, totaled $1.06 billion in fiscal 1982. The ratio of military awards to total corporate sales for the combined companies was .099.

Most of Bendix's defense production is by the company's aerospace-electronics group, which oversees the Kansas City Plant. The primary operations of the aerospace-electronics group are the manufacture of components and systems for commercial, military and general aviation and for defense and space programs. Bendix's name became famous in the aviation field through its sponsorship of the Bendix Transcontinental Air Races in the 1930s.

The current product line is highly diversified, ranging from aircraft wheels and landing gear to missile subsystems and devices that monitor atmospheric pollution. Activities related to defense and space programs include systems for guidance and control of missiles and space vehicles; fuel controls and electric-generating and navigation equipment for military ground vehicles.; acoustic submarine detection equipment; test and checkout equipment; and field engineering, management and support services.

Nuclear Weapons-Related Programs

Allied works on primary nuclear warfare systems through its management of the Kansas City Plant for the Department of Energy and through certain Defense Department contracts. Awards for the Kansas City Plant totaled $376 million in FY 1981 and $429 million in FY 1982. IRRC identified DoD prime contract awards to Allied and Bendix for primary nuclear weapons systems totaling $12 million in fiscal 1981. The ratio of primary awards to combined Allied/Bendix sales was .035 in 1981. Awards for secondary and nuclear-related work totaled at least $131 million in fiscal 1981.

Primary systems:

Kansas City Plant--Allied's most important involvement in nuclear weapons production is through its operation of the Kansas City Plant, part of the Energy Department's nuclear weapons production complex. Non-nuclear components for nuclear warheads and bombs are manufactured at the plant.

The Energy Department describes the plant as follows:

> The plant is a highly diversified, technically oriented operation embracing the full spectrum of work on non-nuclear products—from research on new materials to the production of complex and reliable weapons components. Production activities are directed toward three basic areas: electrical

> and electronics work, mechanical products and plastic products. To support its primary production mission, the plant develops processes and materials. It also engages indirectly in energy research and development by providing developmental hardware for research programs conducted at the Department of Energy laboratories.[2]

A Bendix brochure on the facility states that its activities "are typified by relatively small quantities of highly complex and highly reliable parts which are fabricated to meet the exacting standards characteristic of components and assemblies for nuclear weapons." Weapons components produced at the plant include radars, timers and high energy pulse devices. In addition to such production hardware, the plant supplies small numbers of development items for the Sandia and Lawrence Livermore nuclear weapons laboratories.

The Energy Department says that the full-time equivalent staff at the facility was 7,116 in FY 1982. Bendix reports the current staff level at 7,334 workers.

In 1981, the staff included 936 scientists and engineers, 1,019 other professionals and 687 technicians. Production workers at the plant are organized by the Machinists Union. Some 3,150 Bendix production and maintenance workers are covered under the Machinists contract, according to the Corporate Data Exchange. Bendix says the plant is among the five largest employers in the greater Kansas City area.

Bendix has operated the plant since it was established in 1949. The current contract was renewed in 1981 and expires in December 1986. Allied would not comment to IRRC on whether it expects to renew the contract. DoE says the plant's total operating costs were $322 million in fiscal 1982. The plant's total operating budget for FY 1983 is $497 million, in addition to $59 million for construction and capital costs. In fiscal 1980, the company's net fees for operation of the plant were approximately $3.3 million, and a Bendix official estimated recently that Bendix's actual earnings from the plant after taxes and corporate deductions are "in the neighborhood of $300,000."

The Kansas City Plant is 12 miles south of downtown Kansas City. It occupies more than 2 million square feet of floor space. Bendix says that the government's total investment in the plant is approximately $150 million.

Missiles and strategic bombers--The Bendix aerospace-electronics group's production for the Defense Department includes wheel and brake systems and other work for the B-52 and B-1 strategic bombers and work on the Minuteman ballistic missile. DoD reports prime contract awards of $16 million on the Minuteman and $14 million on the B-52 to Bendix in FY 1982. Most of the Minuteman work takes place in Baltimore; the B-52 awards are spread among several locations.

Bendix produces power generators, control assemblies and instruments, and engine starters for the B-1 under subcontract to Sperry and Rockwell International. Most work under these subcontracts takes place at the company's Teterboro and Eatontown, N.J., facilities.

Bendix is a major subcontractor on the Pershing II missile. Bendix produces motor generators, repair parts, guidance computers and other equipment for the Pershing. Work is performed at the New Jersey facilities.

Bendix also provides components for versions of the F-111, including the strategic bomber variant of the plant (FB-111). In addition, the company provides research services on ballistic missile defense systems.

Secondary systems:

Allied's work on secondary systems includes provision of sonar equipment for the SH-3 Sea King helicopter, which has an antisubmarine warfare role and is equipped to carry B57 nuclear depth charges. Bendix received at least $32 million in SH-3 contracts in fiscal 1981.

Bendix received contract awards totaling at least $41 million in FY 1981 for work, including maintenance and repair tasks, on radar equipment for the nuclear-capable F-15 fighter aircraft. The company also received awards of at least $13 million for provision of components for F-15 and F-16 (also nuclear capable) engine components. In addition, Bendix produces fuel system components for the F-111, mentioned above, and for the P-3 ASW and E-2C electronic aircraft.

Finally, Bendix provides components for a number of radar systems. For example, Bendix was the prime contractor for the AN/FPS-85 long range radar. This very large radar, first put into operation in 1969 (and subsequently enhanced), is located in Florida. It monitors space objects over the Gulf of Mexico, Central America, the northern portion of South America and portions of the Pacific Ocean. The FPS-85 is one of the main elements of the U.S. ICBM early warning system, and it also serves as a crucial component of the SLBM detection system. In addition, the radar is one of two main sensors of the Spacetrack system, which detects, tracks and identifies all objects in space for the U.S. Air Force.

Much of Bendix's radar and other electronic work is classified, so contract awards on current systems are difficult to determine. However, the company received at least $43 million in classified electronic awards in FY 1981, including $19 million for communications security equipment, according to DoD records. Bendix also received awards totaling at least $8 million for operation and maintenance services at three naval research laboratory satellite tracking stations.

Contingency Planning and Prospects

Contingency planning: In response to shareholder resolutions and IRRC inquiries, Bendix and Allied have indicated a willingness to make some efforts to assist workers in the event of layoffs at the Kansas City Plant, but Allied says that "since the Kansas City Plant and all the equipment in it are owned by the government, the corporation would have no control over the future use of the plant."

Thus, Bendix and Allied have opposed shareholder resolutions, sponsored by church groups, calling for consideration of conversion planning for the Kansas City Plant. The most recent such resolution was considered at Allied's 1983 annual meeting. The resolution called for the Allied board of directors to hold a special meeting to consider Allied's involvement in nuclear weapons production. At the meeting, Allied was to "give special consideration to an exploration of alternative employment opportunities for those persons presently employed there." Allied did not respond to this request for consideration of conversion planning, except (as noted above) to say that the government has responsibility for the physical facility. The resolution received support from 2.9 percent of the shares voted.

Christine Pagano, a spokesman for Allied, told IRRC that in cases requiring reductions in the work force, the company "traditionally has made every effort" to place people within the company or elsewhere and to provide other assistance. The same policy would apply in the event of reduction in work at the Kansas City Plant, Pagano said.

The plant itself has diversified over the years into energy research, but it remains primarily dependent on nuclear weapons work.

Prospects: Allied's work for the DoD is quite diversified, and the company as a whole seems well protected against cuts in any given defense program. DoD nuclear weapons-related contracts are not large in relation to the company overall. It is possible that the company might encounter some difficulties in the face of large cutbacks in overall Pentagon spending, particularly if aircraft such as the F-15 were eliminated, but such cuts seem unlikely.

Allied's work for the Energy Department at the Kansas City Plant could be reduced substantially by a sweeping nuclear weapons freeze. Apparently neither the company nor DoE has planned for the possibility of a sharp reduction in defense work for the plant, so it seems likely that a reduction also would result in layoffs, rather than renewed emphasis on alternative energy projects.

Allied Footnotes

1. Fortune, March 7, 1983, p. 7.
2. DoE, "Capsule Review of the DoE Research and Development and Field Facilities" (Washington, 1980), p. 31.

American Telephone & Telegraph

AT&T's Western Electric subsidiary manages the Sandia National Laboratories for the Department of Energy. Sandia is the largest of the nation's nuclear weapons research and development facilities and is based in Albuquerque, N.M.

AT&T is the parent company of the Bell System, an association of companies, each separately managed, that provide service to about 80 percent of the nation's telephones. All of the system's 21 principal telephone companies are wholly owned by AT&T, as is Western Electric Co., which has as its principal business the manufacturing of telecommunications equipment. Bell Laboratories, jointly owned by AT&T and Western Electric, provides research and development services.

In January 1982, AT&T and the Department of Justice signed a consent decree that calls for a restructuring of the Bell System. As a result of the agreement, AT&T is divesting its interest in the local service operations of Bell companies, and the government has agreed to drop an antitrust suit that had been pending against AT&T since 1974. The divestiture is scheduled to be completed in January 1984.

AT&T's net income was $7.28 billion in 1982, up 6.7 percent from $6.82 billion in 1981. AT&T's rate of return on average total capital was 10.0 percent in 1982. The corporation's operating revenues were $65.76 billion in 1982, up from $59.08 billion in 1981. AT&T's earnings per share decreased 0.8 percent from $8.47 in 1981 to $8.40 in 1982.

Government and Defense Business

AT&T was the 25th largest Defense Department contractor in fiscal 1982, with prime contracts of $753 million--a figure that does not include nuclear weapons work for the Energy Department, such as that done at Sandia. Including the defense portion of Sandia contract awards (assumed to be about 75 percent of the total based on the breakdown of Sandia operating costs), total defense awards were about $1.4 billion in fiscal 1982. The ratio of defense awards to AT&T's total revenues was about .02.

The Defense Department contracts were principally for communications equipment and services, and included $252 million that was awarded to Western Electric. At least $100 million of this was for work on undersea acoustic detection systems, which provide continuing monitoring and surveillance of hostile and potentially hostile submarines.

Data on American Telegraph & Telephone
(dollar figures in millions)

	1978	1979	1980	1981	1982
Operating revenues	$60,700	$60,405	$59,361	$61,647	$65,093
Net income	$5,273	$5,674	$6,080	$6,823	$7,279
DoE prime contract awards*	NA	NA	NA	$682	$795
DoD prime contract awards*	$457	$570	$597	$695	$753
Ratio of combined DoD and DoE defense prime contract awards to operating revenues+	NA	NA	NA	.022	.024
Total DoE outlay for Sandia	NA	NA	NA	$480	$526
DoE outlay for defense programs at Sandia	NA	NA	NA	$350	$420
Employees at Sandia	7,478	7,618	7,847	8,018	7,950
Total AT&T employees	961,000	1,030,000	1,044,000	1,042,100	1,015,900

* U.S. fiscal year, ending Sept. 30.
+ U.S. fiscal year awards compared with calendar year revenues.

Other important Western Electric defense production includes work on the Nike Hercules air defense missile, which has both nuclear and conventional versions; and on ballistic missile submarine sonar and radar systems. A major contract won in 1982 is for full-scale engineering development of an advanced signal processor for ships and submarines.

At the Sandia Laboratories approximately 20 percent of work performed is for agencies other than the Department of Energy. Some 90 percent of that effort is for the Department of Defense and the Nuclear Regulatory Commission. Sandia expects to do more work for DoD in the near future. DoD programs performed at Sandia include development of detection and security systems for the Defense Nuclear Agency, the Tactical Air Command and the Navy's nuclear storage sites. The lab also researches warhead reentry vehicles for the Air Force as well as particle beam technologies that may be used for disarming enemy missiles in flight.[1]

Sandia's work for the Defense Department totaled about $131 million in fiscal 1982, and is expected to grow to $160 million in FY 1984. Defense contracts accounted for 2 to 3 percent of Western Electric's sales in 1982, and 1 to 2 percent of the division's net income, according to an AT&T spokesman. (Western Electric's total net income in 1982 was $337 million.) Total Western Electric sales to the U.S. government were $374 million in 1982. Approximately 3.6 percent of the division's research and development expenses were dedicated to the defense business in 1982, the spokesman said.

The Defense Department had urged the Justice Department to drop the antitrust suit that resulted in the current divestiture, contending that good military communications depend on the existence of a single U.S. phone company, with manufacturing and advanced research laboratories and phone operations combined. In 1981, Secretary of Defense Weinberger strongly opposed a proposed agreement that would have required AT&T to divest much of Western Electric.[2]

Spokesmen for DoD also expressed concern over the fate of Bell Laboratories, which is supported by AT&T operating companies. Bell Labs is considered one of the best research facilities in the world. In 1971, more than 30 percent of the laboratory's revenues came from defense work. That percentage steadily decreased to a low of 2 percent in 1976. The DoD still considers state-of-the-art research done at Bell Labs to be important to national security.[3]

The Defense Department's concerns were lessened by the terms of the consent decree, which provided for continued AT&T ownership of the Long Lines Department, Western Electric and Bell Laboratories. Bell Labs will endure a loss of 4,000 employees and a budget reduction of 25 percent, or $1.5 million.[4]

Bell Labs, seeking to reestablish its revenue base, intends to expand its defense work quickly from the current level of about 4.5 percent of revenues to about 10 percent. The laboratories will now have more to offer AT&T from additional defense work than in previous years. Under a 1956 consent decree, Bell Labs was obliged to provide all interested companies with licenses to its patents at reasonable fees. Under the new deregulation decision, Bell Labs will not have to provide licenses to all those companies while Western Electric will be free to market any proprietary products that come from the Labs.[5]

Nuclear Weapons-Related Programs

Sandia National Laboratories: Sandia National Laboratories operates three main facilities: its headquarters and laboratory in Albuquerque, N.M.; a smaller laboratory in Livermore, Calif.; and a test range near Tonopah, Nev. The Sandia Corp., which operates Sandia National Laboratories, is a wholly owned subsidiary of Western Electric Co. Operation of the laboratories is governed by a three-party contract, first signed in 1949, between Western Electric, Sandia and the Department of Energy (earlier the Atomic Energy Commission). The contract has been renewed at five-year intervals. The current contract expires in September 1988. The Bell System operates Sandia on a no-fee, no-profit basis.

Established in 1945 to assist the Manhattan Project, Sandia Laboratories was originally part of the Los Alamos Scientific Laboratory, operated by the University of California. In 1949, at its request, the university was relieved of the operation of Sandia, and the Atomic Energy Commission asked the Bell System to take over. President Truman wrote to the president of AT&T that operation of Sandia by the Bell System would "render an exceptional service in the national interest."

A 1980 AT&T report on Sandia says that Sandia's national security responsibility "involves the conception, design, development and testing of nuclear weapons systems. Sandia is not responsible, however, for design and development of the nuclear explosive parts of the weapons. This is the responsibility of laboratories operated by the University of California at Los Alamos, N.M., and at Livermore, Calif. Sandia performs no manufacture or assembly of atomic weapons. Sandia, however, is responsible for assuring that the weapons systems are manufactured according to specification and for their reliability and safe handling and storage."[6] In the words of its director, Sandia does "those things which make a nuclear explosive into a weapon."[7]

In a brochure explaining its purpose, Sandia states that its national security concerns are:

> developing and maintaining the scientific and engineering expertise that will assure viability of the nation's nuclear ordnance; conducting research that will generate new nuclear weapon concepts; designing and developing nuclear ordnance in conjunction with other national laboratories; verifying that the weapon stockpile remains a credible deterrent through continual assessment of safety and reliability; modifying weapons as necessary to meet new requirements; and developing and applying advanced technologies to protect nuclear materials from theft.[8]

Sandia's nuclear ordnance work principally is on safeguarding, arming, fuzing and firing systems, as well as improving aerodynamics and structures. While Sandia does not assemble or manufacture any weapons, it is responsible for assuring that each item is produced according to specifications. The laboratories also train military personnel in the use and maintenance of the weapons. Sandia says that it is "involved with a nuclear weapon from its inception until its retirement from the stockpile."

Sandia currently is working on a number of nuclear weapon deployment strategies. Among these are methods that enhance the potential for using nuclear weapons for tactical, or battlefield, purposes. One of the projects involves delivery systems that send bombs deep into the earth before detonating. An information booklet put out by Sandia says: "Such weapons could be used to create barriers and craters to impede troop advances, or to destroy targets below ground; at the same time, they would reduce the spread of radioactive materials. These systems utilize extensive terradynamics research and development pioneered at the (Sandia) Labs."

Sandia has made major contributions to the development of smaller, lighter missile warheads with miniaturized components. The Navy's Poseidon and Trident missiles, as well as other missiles, rely heavily on this technology. Sandia also is extensively involved in space and laser warfare research. The laboratories are developing powerful laser and particle beams for controlled thermonuclear fusion research.

In addition, Sandia is pioneering programs to safeguard nuclear weapons. One safeguarding concept resulted in technology that permits destruction or disabling of a weapon when tampering is detected. Another involves the use of security locks, known as Permissive Action Links (PAL), which contain microelectronic logic systems that are small enough to be embedded in critical weapon components.

The testing of nuclear weapons and their effects on related defense systems is part of Sandia's research work. Extensive study has been done to solve the problems of electromagnetic pulse (EMP), a major problem confronting U.S. strategic forces. While there is some debate about the effects of EMP, some experts believe that a single nuclear explosion in the atmosphere is capable of disrupting all domestic electronics and communications systems, both military and civilian.[9] Sandia Labs uses both underground nuclear explosions and special laboratories simulation facilities for such testing. Sandia is also the only testing facility for missiles that employ parachute-assisted reentry systems. Spokesmen for the labs expect that their testing activities will increase.

George C. Dacey, president of Sandia Labs, testified to Congress that "we have made substantial progress in a number of areas, and I think none of that could have been made had we not been able to test." He strongly urged Congress not to push for a comprehensive test ban treaty with the Soviet Union. The Reagan administration recently announced that it had decided not to enter into such a treaty largely because of the support within the defense and scientific community for continued testing.[10]

Sandia's operating budget was $680 million in fiscal 1982 and is expected to grow to $867 million in 1984 and $927 million in 1988. Total Energy Department outlays at Sandia were $526 million in 1982; $420 million of that went for defense programs. The defense portion of Sandia's budget increased 20 percent between 1981 and 1982, while other programs were funded at roughly constant levels. Energy Department contract awards to Sandia in fiscal 1982 totaled $795 million.

More than half the nondefense portion of the Energy Department expenditure on Sandia supported conservation and renewable energy programs. A spokesman for AT&T stressed that much research has both energy and defense uses, and so the line between the two functions is blurred. Major energy programs include fossil, solar, inertial fusion and fission energy, the company says. In addition, Sandia conducts major projects in advanced nuclear fission energy research and nuclear fuel cycle safety. On a lesser scale, Sandia is also pursuing work in geothermal and magnetic fusion energy, energy environmental studies, energy conservation and basic energy sciences.

Literature distributed by Sandia explains that, "Because our Laboratories' mission is engineering-oriented, efforts to achieve practical application of our work are an integral part of most of our projects. We have always worked closely with industry, with the result that technology transfer often occurs as a by-product of carrying out a project." Sandia has responded to efforts by Congress to increase the private sector use of technologies developed at government facilities. The laboratory sponsors meetings and enters into joint efforts with industry to test new concepts. The company reports that employees have been known to transfer between the lab and industry.

Sandia employs about 8,000 workers, including about 6,860 at the Albuquerque facility and 1,100 at Livermore. About 25 employees are on loan from Western Electric and Bell Laboratories. Sandia's 1981 expenditures included $187 million for the Albuquerque payroll and another $30 million for the Livermore payroll.

At the end of fiscal 1981, Sandia's payroll included 2,544 technical staff members, most with backgrounds in electrical and mechanical engineering, physics, and computing. The work force also included 2,098 "technical staff aides" and 825 non-technical staff members. The lab expects to increase its staff 5 percent by FY 1985 to correspond with increased funding for weapons activities.

Purchases by Sandia in New Mexico totaled $103 million in fiscal year 1981, of which more than 97 percent went to local Albuquerque firms. Sandia is the largest private employer in the Albuquerque area.

All assets of Sandia are owned by DoE. Acquisition costs of Sandia assets as of October 1982 totaled $592 million.

Defense Department nuclear weapons work: Under contracts with the Defense Department, Western Electric works on several nuclear weapons-related systems. One such product is the AN/BQR-15 sonar, which is used on ballistic missile submarines. DoD awarded Western Electric at least $27 million for work on this sonar in fiscal 1981.

Western Electric also works on an underwater surveillance system called Sosus. The system consists of networks of passive detectors in the Atlantic and Pacific oceans. Fiscal 1981 contract awards to AT&T for Sosus totaled at least $47 million.

AT&T also is a major contractor on the Nike Hercules dual-capable missile. Awards for U.S.-owned Nike Hercules totaled $1.4 million in fiscal 1981.

American Telegraph & Telephone Footnotes

1. Much of the information on the Sandia Laboratories used in this report is from the Sandia National Laboratories Institutional Plan FY 1983-1988, April 1983.
2. The Wall Street Journal, Jan. 11, 1982.
3. Business Week, July 5, 1982.
4. Fortune, June 27, 1983.
5. Business Week, op. cit.
6. Background on Sandia National Laboratories, a report prepared by AT&T in response to a shareholder proxy resolution, April 1980, revised March 1982.
7. House of Representatives, Hearings before the Committee on Armed Services on the Department of Energy National Security and Military Applications of Nuclear Energy Authorization Act of 1984, HR 2496, p. 105.
8. Sandia National Laboratories, a report on the laboratories distributed by AT&T and the U.S. Government Printing Office.
9. Business Week, op. cit.
10. House Armed Services Committee hearings, op. cit.

E.I. du Pont de Nemours

E.I. du Pont de Nemours and Co., manager of the Savannah River Laboratory and nuclear materials production plant, is a large, diversified producer of chemical and petroleum products. Du Pont is now the ninth largest company in the United States, according to Forbes, as a result of its 1981 acquisition of Conoco Inc., a petroleum company, for $7.2 billion, in the largest merger in U.S. history. Du Pont is based in Wilmington, Del.

In 1982, its first full year of combined operations, Du Pont recorded total sales of $33.33 billion, 46 percent more than its 1981 sales (not including Conoco) of $22.81 billion. Net earnings, however, declined 17 percent from $1.08 billion in 1981 to $890 million in 1982. The company attributed the decline to the costs of financing the merger and "depressed markets" in the chemicals industry.

Government and Defense Business

Du Pont without Conoco was the 94th largest Defense Department contractor in FY 1981; the new combined company became the 50th largest contractor in FY 1982, with contract awards of $326 million. Most of the increase stems from the acquisition of Conoco, which won DoD contract awards for petroleum products totaling more than $106 million in 1982. In addition, Du Pont's Remington Arms Division nearly doubled its contract for managing the Army's Lake City Ammunition Plant in Independence, Mo.

Despite these substantial DoD contracts, most of Du Pont's defense work is managing the Savannah River Plant and Laboratory for the Department of Energy.

Nuclear Weapons-Related Programs

The Savannah River Plant and Laboratory in Aiken, S.C., which is owned by the federal government, is the nation's only source of tritium and is the primary source of weapons-grade plutonium, materials required for nuclear warheads and bombs. Research performed at the facility concentrates on improving the production of radioisotopes and the safety of nuclear operations.

Du Pont's involvement with the Savannah River Plant began in 1950 when the Atomic Energy Commission requested the company to design,

Data on Du Pont
(dollar figures in millions)

	1978	1979	1980	1981	1982
Total sales	$10,646	$12,650	$13,744	$22,810	$33,331
Net income	$797	$965	$744	$1,081	$894
DoE defense program prime contract awards*	NA	NA	NA	$483**	$673
DoD prime contract awards*	$89	$102	NA	$133	$327
Ratio of DoE defense program and DoD prime contract awards to total sales+	NA	NA	NA	.02	.02
Gross operating costs at Savannah River	$250	$285	$320	$390	$460
Employees at Savannah River	5,850	5,770	6,100	6,600	6,675
Total Du Pont employees++	133,400	137,000	136,000	117,000	165,000

* U.S. fiscal year, ending Sept. 30.
** For purposes of comparison with other companies, IRRC estimates that $374 million out of FY 1981 DoE prime contract awards was used for "primary" nuclear systems.
+ U.S. fiscal year awards compared with calendar year sales.
++ Excludes employees at Savannah River and other government-owned plants.

construct and operate the present facility in order to expand the nation's capacity to produce the material for nuclear weapons. At that time, only one plant, the Hanford plant in Richland, Wash., produced nuclear weapons materials. The urgency of the request was underscored by the start of the Korean war and the desire to develop the first thermonuclear weapon, the hydrogen bomb, before the Soviet Union. The government believed Du Pont would be the most capable of developing the Savannah plant quickly.

The company stated in a 1979 report on Savannah River that Du Pont was "an almost unique choice for the project both because of its experience in designing, constructing and operating the original nuclear production site at Hanford and because it possessed the integrated research, design, construction and operating force capable of undertaking a project of this magnitude under the auspices of a single company." Production began in 1953, and the first plutonium shipment left the plant a year later.

The plant site occupies 200,000 acres in the sparsely populated Aiken, Allendale and Barnwell counties in South Carolina near the Georgia border. The plant's present facilities include:

-- five nuclear reactors moderated and cooled by heavy water, three of which are active;

-- a heavy water production plant, not currently active, that recovers heavy water from raw water at the rate of one ounce per 52 gallons;

-- two processing plants, the only operating ones in the country, which extract plutonium and reusable uranium from used nuclear fuel from the defense program;

-- the Savannah River Laboratory.

The plant's primary function is the production of plutonium and tritium, which are then shipped to various government-owned weapons production facilities. Production requirements at the plant are determined by the U.S. government through the Department of Energy. Radioactive materials such as tritium must be replaced periodically because of radioactive decay, while changes in military, energy and civilian demand determine the need for plutonium.

The Savannah River Laboratory provides developmental and technical assistance primarily to the plant's production operations and assists the Energy Department's nuclear weapons program in all areas of the nuclear fuel cycle--including fuel fabrication, isotope production, reactor physics and engineering, fuel reprocessing, waste management, environmental monitoring and heavy water production.

In response to the Reagan administration's plans to enlarge the nuclear stockpile, one of the two dormant reactors at the Savannah plant, called the "L" reactor, is being recommissioned. The reactivated L reactor will meet part of the need for additional weapons-grade plutonium. Renovation of the reactor, the company reports, is 95 percent complete, but the government's attempt to restart the reactor without a full environmental impact statement has caused considerable controversy and delay. (See below.) The other working reactors are being upgraded on a continuing basis without extended shutdowns.

Fifteen percent of work at Savannah River centers around civilian, usually biomedical and industrial, products. Isotopes produced at the facility are used for cancer therapy, smoke detectors, oil well logging and a variety of other purposes.

Du Pont manages all operations at the plant for DoE on a nonprofit, cost-reimbursement basis. Operating costs at the Savannah facility for FY 1982 were $460 million, 85 percent of which were for defense-related activities. Capital expenditures in FY 1982 were $75 million. Operating costs for FY 1983 were expected to be $524 million and capital expenditures $310 million. DoE contract awards to Savannah River totaled $483 million in FY 1981 and $673 million in FY 1982.

Company officials say that Du Pont commercial businesses receive no direct benefit in technology transfer based on work performed at Savannah River, and that the company maintains an "arm's-length relationship" between Savannah River and Du Pont's other operations.

The Savannah River complex, the largest single payroll in South Carolina, employs 6,800 workers, including 1,400 scientists and engineers. According to Sen. Ernest Hollings (D-S.C.), the Energy Department has played on the need for Savannah River jobs in pushing for restarting the L reactor there, over some local opposition. Hollings said that DoE officials "threatened to block new jobs-producing facilities" at the plant if the L reactor were delayed.[1]

The government is considering construction of a new production reactor to assure adequate supplies of tritium in the 1990s and beyond. The cost is estimated at $4 to $16 billion.[2] The Secretary of Energy has expressed interest in beginning the preliminary environmental impact study process for such a reactor at Savannah River, at Hanford, and at the Idaho National Engineering Laboratory. Many members of Congress, including the majority of the House Armed Services Committee, are skeptical about the need for such a facility.

Savannah River also has been considered a potential site for a possible special isotope separation (sometimes called laser isotope separation) facility. The SIS process, now under research and development at Lawrence Livermore and Los Alamos, offers a potentially inexpensive alternative for purifying and enriching plutonium using laser technology. Most work on SIS has been conducted at the Lawrence Livermore and Los Alamos laboratories, but Du Pont has conducted a small research and development effort in this area.

Based in part on the support of Du Pont engineers at Savannah River and Rockwell engineers at Hanford for pursuing SIS technology, the House Armed Services Committee demanded a quick DoE commitment to building a demonstration facility, and in mid-1983, the Energy Department chose Hanford as the site. Savannah River remains a likely candidate for an eventual full-scale SIS plant, which may be built late in the decade.

L reactor--The plan to reactivate the L reactor has been surrounded by controversy over the environmental impact of the operation. The Energy Department has resisted the idea of preparing an environmental impact statement (EIS) on the reactor start-up, claiming that there would be "no significant impact." Even Savannah River officials have testified, though, that the reactors there have caused environmental damage, especially from the discharge of hot water.[3] In 1982, the Natural Resources Defense Council and the state of South Carolina filed suit to block start-up of the L reactor until EIS requirements were met.

In 1983, Environmental Protection Agency officials said they agreed with the DoE finding of no significant impact, even though EPA scientists warned that the reactor could contaminate drinking water wells in nearby communities with radioactive cesium and other chemicals. An EPA radiation expert reported that scalding water discharged from the plant would carry radioactive wastes and destroy 1,000 acres of wetlands. The EPA scientists recommended in memos that the plant not be reopened unless the government conducted a major environmental impact study.[4]

In June, Congress passed legislation requiring that an expedited but full EIS on the L reactor be prepared. The final EIS is due in December 1983. If plans go forward, the reactor will operate in 1984.

Security problems--Press reports have called attention to possible security problems at the Savannah plant. In September 1982, The Washington Post reported that a "threat assessment team" hired by DoE had discovered a number of weaknesses in the plant's security system. The team found similar weaknesses at other vital defense plants. As a result, DoE has enhanced security procedures at all such plants, including Savannah River.

Du Pont Footnotes

1. The Congressional Record 1983, p. S8186.
2. House of Representatives "Report on DoE National Security and Military Application of Nuclear Energy Authorization Act of 1984," (Report 98-124, Part 1), May 13, 1983, p. 19.
3. Testimony of Dr. Charles Gilbert before the House Armed Services Committee, "Hearings on HR 2496 Department of Energy National Security and Military Applications of Nuclear Energy Authorization Act of 1984," March 2, 1983, p. 174.
4. The Washington Post, March 16, 1983 and The Congressional Record 1983, p. S8186.

EG&G

EG&G, a fast-growing and diversified company, provides a variety of technical and scientific products and services to commercial, industrial and governmental customers. The company designs and produces sophisticated mechanical, electro-mechanical and electro-optic products and components; conducts environmental investigations and surveys; and is involved in biomedical studies.

Many of EG&G's sales are to the Department of Defense. The company performs extensive services for the Department of Energy's Nevada Test Site (NTS), a nuclear weapons testing area northwest of Las Vegas. The firm also is operating manager of the Idaho National Engineering Laboratory (INEL) for DoE. Most INEL activities are related to the nuclear energy industry, but the company also supports the defense nuclear materials program at INEL through work on processing nuclear waste. (Other, more substantial defense-related activities at INEL are performed by Exxon, and beginning in the spring of 1984 will be performed by Westinghouse Electric.)

EG&G's total sales for 1982 were $801 million, an 11 percent rise from $719 million in 1981. Net income increased 16 percent from $34.6 million to $40.2 million in the same period. Fortune ranked the company seventh in total return to investors during 1982 and 10th in total return to investors in the 1972-82 period. The firm is based in Wellesley, Mass., and conducts operations across the country and overseas.

Government and Defense Business

EG&G reports that during 1982, government contract sources accounted for $23.5 million, or approximately 40 percent of EG&G's income from operations, up from $18.9 million, or 33 percent, in 1981. Net sales and contract revenues from the government rose 25 percent from $342.2 million in 1981 to $428.6 million in 1982.

Department of Energy activities: EG&G has three contracts with DoE for the management of the NTS and INEL. Under all three contracts, EG&G is reimbursed for its allowable costs and receives its fee in two parts--an agreed-upon base fee and an award fee unilaterally determined by DoE based upon DoE's evaluation of EG&G's performance. EG&G is moving toward fees based entirely on performance. The combined management fees to EG&G for INEL and NTS were $9.3 million in 1982. All these contracts have five-year renewable terms.

Data on EG&G
(dollar figures in millions)

	1978	1979	1980	1981	1982
Total sales	$449	$534	$626	$719	$801
Net income	$17	$22	$27	$35	$40
DoE defense program prime contract awards*	NA	NA	NA	$613	$611
DoD prime contract awards*	NA	NA	NA	$38	$93
Net sales and contract revenues from government contracts	$214	$245	$284	$342	$429
Income from government contracts	$11	$13	$16	$19	$23
Ratio of income from government contracts to EG&G's total income	NA	NA	NA	.33	.40
Number of EG&G employees at NTS	3,803	3,871	4,498	5,513	5,821
Number of EG&G employees at INEL	3,893	3,978	3,982	3,682	3,505
Total EG&G employees	14,732	15,277	16,811	18,062	18,312

* U.S. fiscal year, ending Sept. 30.

Department of Defense activities: EG&G's many subsidiaries produce a variety of products and provide numerous services for DoD. Some divisions such as EG&G Ortec in Oak Ridge, Tenn., produce radiation detection and monitoring systems for industrial consumers as well as DoD. EG&G's Special Projects subsidiary holds a three-year contract for electronic warfare testing and training support at the U.S. Naval Weapons Center at China Lake, Calif. Another division, EG&G Washington Analytical Services Center, provides planning, engineering and management support to DoD and foreign government defense agencies. The center provides hardware and software engineering, quality assurance, configuration management, documentation and training for the Polaris, Poseidon and Trident nuclear submarines. The company also is active in developing antisubmarine warfare and mine countermeasure systems. Total DoD prime contracts to EG&G in FY 1982 were $93 million, a substantial rise from $38 million in FY 1981.

NASA programs: EG&G also does an extensive amount of work for NASA. The company provides institutional and technical support services at the Kennedy Space Center including management of technical operations, administrative services, data processing and data management, utilities, facilities, and health and safety services relating to manned and unmanned space launch activities. Under a multi-million-dollar subcontract with Martin Marietta, EG&G Services Co. participated in the engineering designs related to ground facilities for the Air Force Space Shuttle launch program at Vandenberg Air Force Base in California. In late 1982, EG&G Florida was selected by NASA to provide base operations at the Kennedy Space Center under a cost-plus-incentive/award fee contract that should total more than $80 million in 1983.

Nuclear Weapons-Related Programs

IRRC estimates that DoE and DoD contract awards to EG&G for primary nuclear systems totaled $399 million in fiscal 1981. Awards for secondary systems are more difficult to estimate because most came through EG&G's work at INEL on the processing of nuclear waste, mostly from the naval reactors program, but the total is less than $30 million.

Nevada Test Site: At the 800,000-acre Nevada Test Site, two of EG&G's subsidiaries have independent contracts with DoE. EG&G says funding for NTS has increased substantially over the last four years. The EG&G Energy Measurement Group, with headquarters in Las Vegas, is the sole prime contractor for management of the facility. EG&G's Reynolds Electrical and Engineering Co. provides construction, mining, drilling and maintenance functions in support of DoE's nuclear weapons testing program at NTS. EG&G reports that its increased work in this area stems from a decision to renew its emphasis on national defense and nuclear weapons work.

Nuclear tests at NTS began in 1948. Since then the government has conducted nuclear weapons tests in the Pacific, the Colorado Rockies, the Aleutian Islands and Mississippi, as well as in Nevada. In the 1950s, above-ground nuclear explosion experiments were performed at the site.

In 1958, the United States, the USSR and Great Britain placed moratoriums on nuclear weapons testing. Testing resumed, however, in 1961 after the Soviet Union unilaterally ended its moratorium. The exact number of tests performed at NTS is classified, but the government has acknowledged 610.[1] The Stockholm Peace Research Institute says there were 17 nuclear explosions in Nevada in 1982.[2]

As a result of the partial test ban treaty negotiated with the Soviet Union in 1963, all nuclear weapons tests are performed underground. Such testing will continue in the light of a 1983 decision by the Reagan administration not to enter into a comprehensive test ban treaty.

EG&G's Energy Measurements Group performs most of the technical instrumentation services involved with the actual testing of the weapons including the timing and firing of underground explosions; diagnostic and other measurements of underground nuclear detonations; design, development, production and operation of instruments and systems used in connection with weapons testing; and data processing and analysis.

The Energy Measurements Group is also a member of the Nuclear Emergency Search Team (NEST), which is responsible for locating lost or stolen nuclear materials and handling technical problems associated with extortion threats involving radiation dispersal or improvised nuclear devices. The other primary members of NEST are the DoE

Nevada Operations Office, Lawrence Livermore National Laboratory and Sandia National Laboratories.

Payments to the Energy Measurements Group for work performed at NTS totaled $112 million in FY 1982, up from $86.5 million in FY 1981. Its current five-year contract runs through December 1987.

Reynolds Electrical and Engineering provides support and maintenance services to the underground nuclear weapons test program, to DoE's weapons design laboratories and to certain other DoD activities at NTS. These services include deep-hole drilling, tunneling and mining; evaluation of radioactive waste disposal techniques; special facilities construction; feeding, housing and transporting personnel and providing them with medical services, safety services, personnel radiation monitoring, training, communications and utilities.

Reynolds Electrical prime contracts for work performed at NTS totaled $306 million in FY 1981 and $260 million in FY 1982. The current contract runs through 1988.

Idaho National Engineering Laboratory: DoE says that EG&G performs research and development at INEL in the areas of reactor physics; reactor safety technology; materials and heat transfer; magnetic fusion; energy conservation and nuclear waste management.[3] EG&G provides support services to all contractors at INEL, including Exxon Nuclear. About $25 million of EG&G's INEL outlays in fiscal 1982 were identifiable as being for DoE's defense program, mostly for waste management support services. Total DoE contract awards to EG&G for work at INEL were $221 million in FY 1981 and $239 million in FY 1982. DoE expects EG&G's INEL operations to shrink about 25 percent in the next three years. The EG&G budget outlay projection for FY 1985 is $185 million.

Under the Defense Waste Management program, EG&G provides storage for low-level radioactive wastes at INEL produced in the testing of government nuclear power reactors and in the naval nuclear propulsion reactors program. Solid waste is stored in shallow land burial sites. The company also is actively removing stored waste from above the Snake River Plain aquifer in order to comply with environmental standards. EG&G maintains a national data base for all DoE solid radioactive waste under the same program.

Also at INEL, EG&G is developing production technologies using domestic resources, substitute materials and engineering and conservation practices to meet DoE's concern that certain essential defense-related materials are produced in adequate quantity only in nonaligned countries. Factors contributing to this situation, DoE says, include a lack of abundant resources, refining and production capability in the United States, and an inability to compete with foreign producers.

DoE is considering building a new production reactor at INEL to produce nuclear weapons materials and generate electricity for civilian consumption. It says a new reactor is necessary to replace and/or supplement the aging weapons material reactors at the Savannah River Plant in South Carolina and the "N" Reactor at the Hanford facility in Washington, and also to increase electric power by the year 2000. Total budget outlays for the construction and operation of the plant in FY 1982-8 are projected at $1.37 billion.

EG&G had 3,850 employees at INEL in FY 1982. The number is expected to decrease to 2,147 by FY 1985 and 1,840 by FY 1988.

DoD nuclear weapons activities: EG&G's work for the Defense Department includes provision of sonar systems for the surface fleet and for the ballistic missile submarine program. IRRC estimates that in FY 1981 DoD prime contract awards to EG&G for primary nuclear weapons systems were $6.4 million, and prime awards for secondary systems were at least $3.1 million.

Impact of a nuclear moratorium: While 40 percent of EG&G's government income (and 16 percent of total income) is attributable to its DoE contracts for managing the Nevada Test Site and the Idaho National Engineering Laboratory, the company believes that a significant weapons reduction agreement or test ban treaty would not threaten its financial health. EG&G's 1982 10-K form says that the company's "income would be materially reduced," but that "such a ban or a moratorium would not have a material adverse effect upon the company's business or income as a whole. The company's experience indicates that a significant amount of work in support of other programs and stand-by facilities would continue under EG&G's existing contracts."

EG&G Footnotes

1. Department of Energy, DoE's Nevada Operations Office: What It Does and Why.
2. Stockholm International Peace Research Institute, World Armaments and Disarmament: SIPRI Yearbook 1983, Taylor and Francis, New York, 1983, p. 98
3. Department of Energy, Idaho National Engineering Laboratory, Institutional Plan, FY 1983-FY 1988.

Monsanto

Monsanto is the fourth largest chemical company in the United States. Its 147 manufacturing plants, laboratories and technical centers produce chemicals, agricultural products, man-made fibers, electronics materials, industrial process controls and other capital equipment. Monsanto's products include herbicides, fibers for carpets, upholstery and clothing, silicon for semiconductors, analgesics, detergents, oil and gas. Monsanto Research Corp., a subsidiary of Monsanto, operates a Department of Energy facility that produces nuclear weapons components.

Monsanto's net sales fell 9 percent from $6.9 billion in 1981 to $6.3 billion in 1982. Net income fell from $445 million to $352 million. The company attributed these drops to "recessionary trends" but emphasized that Monsanto performed better than the industry average. The company ranks 74th on the Forbes top sales list. It is based in St. Louis, Mo.

Government and Defense Business

Monsanto's government business primarily consists of one contract with the Department of Energy. Under this contract, Monsanto manages the DoE's Mound Facility in Miamisburg, Ohio, which conducts DoE weapons and energy programs. Monsanto says that about three-quarters of the Mound Facility's programs are defense programs related to the production of nuclear weapons. The rest are a variety of civilian programs that involve fossil and fusion energy, the development of instruments and controls designed to prevent theft of nuclear materials, the marketing of non-radioactive isotopes to the scientific community and the assembly of isotopic heat sources that power NASA space vehicles.

The DoE reimburses Monsanto for the facility's operating costs and pays the company a management fee. In 1982, Mound's operating costs totaled $118 million and the management fee was $4.7 million. Net income after taxes for the operation of Mound amounted to $2.5 million, or about 1 percent of the company's total net income. For 1983, DoE has awarded Monsanto $135 million in prime contract awards, which represent an estimate of operating costs and fees through the end of the year.

Monsanto also receives small contracts from the Department of Defense under which the company provides chemical products, fuels and

Data on Monsanto
(dollar figures in millions)

	1978	1979	1980	1981	1982
Total sales	$5,019	$6,193	$6,574	$6,948	$6,325
Net income	$303	$331	$149	$445	$352
DoE defense program prime contract awards*	NA	NA	NA	$106.9	$134.5
DoD prime contract awards*	NA	NA	NA	$2.3	$2.5
Ratio of DoE defense program and DoD prime contract awards to total sales+	NA	NA	NA	.16	.22
Gross operating costs at Mound	NA	NA	$75.7	$92.8	$118.2
Defense activities at Mound	NA	NA	$54.3	$69.5	$92.6
Non-defense activities at Mound	NA	NA	$21.4	$23.3	$25.6
Employees at Mound	NA	NA	NA	1,952	2,060
Total Monsanto employees	62,851	63,926	61,926	57,391	52,199

* U.S. fiscal year, ending Sept. 30.
+ U.S. fiscal year awards compared with calendar year sales.

lubricants to the military. These contracts totaled $2.3 million in FY 1981 and $2.5 million in FY 1982.

Nuclear Weapons-Related Programs

Monsanto began its involvement in nuclear weapons production in 1943. At that time, it managed three projects in the Dayton, Ohio, area that performed initial work on the Manhattan Project. At one of the sites, Monsanto scientists purified polonium, which served as a source of neutrons that would ensure initiation of the chain reaction necessary to a nuclear weapon.

In 1947, the first permanent government atomic energy facility was built in Miamisburg, Ohio, and Monsanto became its first manager. It was named the Mound facility for the large Indian Mound adjacent to the site. It now stands as one of 11 facilities that make up the nation's nuclear weapons complex. Its work has expanded from the study of radioisotopes such as plutonium to the modernization and safeguarding of nuclear weapons components.

Today, Mound's main activity is the development, production engineering, manufacture, surveillance and evaluation--in other words, the full production and maintenance--of non-nuclear components for U.S. nuclear weapons. The new components that Monsanto manufactures--detonators, timers, firing sets and test equipment--are sent to other plants in the DoE complex where they will become part of nuclear warheads. Mound also tests components that have been stockpiled for a number of years to make sure they are still in good condition.

In addition to this main weapons program, the Mound:

-- manufactures a small amount of nuclear components for weapons;

-- assembles the small isotopic heat sources that provide power in a weapon;

-- recovers and purifies tritium, a radioactive isotope of hydrogen, from nuclear waste, some of which is shipped to DoE's Savannah River plant where it is used in hydrogen bombs;

-- produces devices, called safing devices, designed to safeguard the nation's nuclear weapons from illicit use, tampering or accidental detonation.

Howard Charbeneau, Monsanto's public relations manager at the Mound Facility, told IRRC that Mound's workload is "way up, especially in the weapons component area." Charbeneau said this growth has to do with the modernization of the U.S. nuclear deterrent and includes the production of new advanced safing devices as well as weapons components. He said the growth results from decisions made six or seven years ago during the Ford and Carter administrations, and not directly from the Reagan administration's policies. He said he could not provide more detail because of security regulations.

Monsanto's 1981 report on the Mound Facility said that "several events" had broadened Mound's role in the DoE weapons complex that year. It was assigned to develop 11 new products for the "advanced artillery projectile and the air launched cruise missile programs," to produce a newly developed safing device, and "for the first time" to host "a final design review for a major weapon system."

DoE last renewed Monsanto's Mound contract in 1978 for the five years ending Sept. 30, 1983. Charbeneau told IRRC that a new contract would be signed soon, probably for another five-year period. "The new contract won't differ much from the old one," he said. The Monsanto Research Corp., a wholly owned subsidiary, is in charge of this contract.

Defense Employees

Monsanto employed 2,060 people at the Mound facility in FY 1982. Of these, 24 percent were scientists and engineers, 16 percent were other professionals, 24 percent were technicians and 36 percent were lower-level workers.

UNC Resources

UNC Resources, a diversified resource and manufacturing company, manages the steam and plutonium producing "N" Reactor for the Department of Energy at the Hanford Production Operations in Richland, Wash. The company also produces nuclear fuel and related components for use by Navy nuclear-powered warships.

Formerly known as United Nuclear Corp., the company was the nation's largest independent producer of uranium until 1978. Since that time, the company has responded to a drop of more than 40 percent in the price of uranium by suspending its mining operations and by acquiring a number of small manufacturing companies. Whereas the company's uranium business once accounted for almost two-thirds of its total revenues, uranium sales represented only 25 percent of total revenues in 1982. The company's nuclear manufacturing work, which included some products for the commercial nuclear industry before 1983, has grown steadily in the last several years to almost $134 million in 1982. UNC is based in Falls Church, Va.

Recent UNC acquisitions include machine tool companies and companies that serve the petroleum industry. Swift Group Inc., or "Swiftships," the largest of UNC's recent acquisitions, manufactures marine vessels used in support of the offshore oil and gas industry and in military and specialty applications. In addition, UNC has increased its gold and silver mining operations in Alaska, and the company recently purchased a gold and silver mine in Oregon. The company reports disappointing short-term returns from its acquisitions, but expects a more profitable future with the recovery of the oil and gas exploration industry.

UNC's total sales were $354 million in 1982, up 27 percent from $277 million in 1981. The company lost $14 million in 1982 after taking a $6.9 million profit the year before. The company says the 1982 loss reflects the depressed mining, oil service and machine tool markets.

Nuclear Weapons-Related Programs

UNC's nuclear weapons-related work is done under contract to the Energy Department. UNC received contract awards for work at Hanford of $84 million in FY 1981 and $133 million in FY 1982. It appears that most of these awards were for nondefense work. Only fuel-grade plutonium for use in research and breeder reactors was produced at Hanford between 1973 and 1982. In 1982, operations at the N reactor

Data on UNC Resources
(dollar figures in millions)

	1978*	1979*	1980*	1981	1982
Sales	$247	$292	$274	$277	$354
Net earnings (loss)	$32	$40	$2	$7	($14)
DoE prime contract awards to UNC for Hanford+	NA	NA	NA	$84	$133
Total UNC employees	5,560	5,140	3,700	4,470	4,380

* UNC's fiscal years ended March 31 of the following year up to and including fiscal 1980. Figures report for 1981 and 1982 are for the full calendar years.
+ U.S. fiscal year, ending Sept. 30.

were modified for production of weapons-grade plutonium because of the anticipated increase in numbers of nuclear weapons. The Energy Department defense activities budget for fiscal 1984 includes $226 million for UNC's operation of the N reactor.

In the secondary systems category, UNC reports that its revenues for nuclear manufacturing work totaled $117 million in calendar 1981, and that almost all of this was for nuclear fuel and related components for the Navy's nuclear-powered fleet. A small amount, though, was for systems and components for commercial nuclear plants.

The Hanford 'N' reactor: The company's UNC Nuclear Industries subsidiary has operated the N reactor since 1973. A 50 percent-owned UNC subsidiary operated the facility between 1965 and 1973. At the N reactor, UNC manufactures fuel cells of slightly enriched uranium from which it produces plutonium for use in the U.S. nuclear weapons stockpile and in research and breeder reactors.

The heat generated by the plutonium reactor is used to make steam for the neighboring Washington Public Power Supply Systems electrical generating plant. A UNC spokesman wrote to IRRC that the "N reactor has produced more than 56 billion kilowatt hours of electricity, which we believe places it about fourth among world reactors in electricity generation."

Congress first allocated funds for the N Reactor in 1958. Plutonium production began in 1963 and steam generation began in 1966. Between 1973 and 1982, the N reactor produced only fuel grade plutonium for use in research and breeder reactors. When UNC modified the reactor in 1982 to produce weapons-grade material again, it won the praise of the Energy Department for completion a year ahead of schedule.

In addition to operating the N reactor, UNC personnel provide engineering and development services at Hanford.

The Department of Energy expects to renew its contract with UNC in December 1983. UNC and DoE have agreed to an incentive fee basis for the fuel fabrication portion of the Hanford contract. UNC receives an annual fee of slightly more than $2 million for its services at Hanford. The company employed 1,750 at Hanford as of Sept. 30, 1983, up from about 1,300 one year earlier. A UNC spokeman told IRRC that "expansion is essentially complete."

Naval products division: Under contract to DoE, UNC's Naval Products Division in Montville, Conn., produces nuclear fuel and related components for nuclear-propelled surface ships and submarines. DoE supplies UNC with enriched uranium from which the company manufactures nuclear fuel elements. The elements are assembled with other components to make a reactor core. The manufacture of the cores is conducted primarily under fixed price incentive fee contracts that contain escalation provisions.

UNC's nuclear manufacturing revenues were $134 million in 1982, up 15 percent from $117 million in 1981. As noted above, a small portion of this is for commercial nuclear components and systems. Employment in the Naval Products division is about 1,200.

UNC says it "has applied the technology developed at UNC Naval Products to obtain several significant aerospace contracts from other government agencies as well as from commercial customers."

Aircraft engines: The company's Technical Products Division, located in Uncasville, Conn., produces components for the General Electric F101 engine, used on the B-1B bomber.

Union Carbide

Until April 1984, Union Carbide will be a major factor in the nuclear weapons industry by virtue of the company's management of the Energy Department's huge Oak Ridge (Tenn.) complex. A large part of Oak Ridge's work is performed at the Y-12 nuclear weapons components plant. Union Carbide announced in 1982 that it planned to withdraw as Oak Ridge contractor as part of a long-term effort to pare down operations to the company's core businesses. A successor to Union Carbide was to be chosen in December 1983 from among three candidates: Martin Marietta, Rockwell International and Westinghouse Electric.

Union Carbide, the 47th largest U.S. company on the Forbes list of sales leaders in 1982, produces chemicals, plastics, industrial gases, metals, carbons and consumer products. Its 1982 sales of $9.06 billion represented an 11 percent decline from 1981 sales. Net income was down 52 percent in 1982, to $310 million.

Nuclear Weapons-Related Programs

Union Carbide's nuclear division, under a single contract with the Department of Energy, operates four government-owned facilities in Oak Ridge, Tenn., and Paducah, Ky., which together employ some 18,000 people. The total annual budget for the complex is about $2 billion. Operating costs at the Y-12 plant were $334 million in 1982 and were budgeted by the Reagan administration to rise to $562 million in 1984.[1]

Until recently, the company's annual fee for managing the Oak Ridge complex was $8 million. A company official estimated in 1982 that after provision for nonreimbursable expenses and income tax, the company earned a $1 million profit on the operations in 1981. Currently, Union Carbide earns an annual fee of $12 million.

Union Carbide has been contractor at Oak Ridge since 1943, when the government first asked the company to operate a gaseous diffusion plant there. The company undertook management of the Y-12 plant in 1947.

The Oak Ridge complex includes two gaseous diffusion plants that produce enriched uranium, and the Oak Ridge National Laboratory. These three facilities are devoted primarily to civilian purposes.

Data on Union Carbide
(dollar figures in millions)

	1978	1979	1980	1981	1982
Sales	$7,870	$9,177	$9,994	$10,168	$9,061
Net income	$394	$556	$890	$649	$310
DoD prime contract awards*	NA	NA	NA	$33	$35
Ratio of Y-12 plant operating costs and DoD prime contract awards to total sales+	NA	NA	NA	.03	.04
Gross operating costs at Oak Ridge Y-12 plant	$159	$181	$223	$275	$334
Employees at Oak Ridge Y-12 plant	4,625	4,900	5,069	5,171	6,097
Total Union Carbide employees	103,229	110,255	116,105	117,031	113,371

* U.S. fiscal year, ending Sept. 30.
+ In calculating total FY 1981 defense contract awards for comparison with calendar year corporate sales and with contract awards to other companies, IRRC substituted Y-12 plant operating costs because the contract under which Oak Ridge is managed includes other nondefense components of the Oak Ridge operations. Total awards under the contract that funds Oak Ridge were $994 million in FY 1981 and $1.09 billion in FY 1982.

The fourth facility--the Y-12 plant--is devoted primarily to nuclear weapons work. The Y-12 plant is a highly sophisticated development, engineering and manufacturing facility, and, according to the Energy Department, its basic mission is support of the nuclear weapons program through fabrication and certification of components for nuclear bombs and warheads, development and fabrication of test hardware for the three weapons design laboratories and conduct of related process development activities. Y-12 supplies most of the uranium and lithium parts used in nuclear weapons. The parts produced at the plant are shipped elsewhere for assembly.[2]

Because of the plant's experience in precision design and production, it has also manufactured such products as highly reflective mirrors for the controlled fusion energy program, wind tunnel components for the U.S. Air Force, and several items used by the astronauts in lunar exploration. The Y-12 plant also has developed biological disposal techniques for waste products such as nitrates, and oil and machine coolant wastes. Union Carbide employs 6,097 workers at Y-12.

In addition to the Y-12 program, the Oak Ridge gaseous diffusion plant in Paducah (one of two such plants within the Oak Ridge complex managed by Union Carbide) provides enriched uranium to the nuclear weapons program. The FY 1984 budget for this purpose is $71 million.

Finally, the Oak Ridge National Laboratory, which is primarily dedicated to civilian energy research, is slated to receive $35 million in the administration's defense activities budget for fiscal 1984.[3]

Union Carbide does little work outside the Oak Ridge complex directly for the U.S. military. Defense Department prime contract awards to the company in fiscal 1982 totaled $35 million, up from $33 million in fiscal 1981. The largest portion of those awards went to buy chemical bases for liquid propellants. Carbide does continue to operate a large uranium mining and milling business.

Union Carbide's management of the Oak Ridge facility: In announcing Union Carbide's decision to cease management of the Oak Ridge complex, DoE praised the company's performance as an "exceptionally effective contractor for almost 40 years." Recently, however, the press has called attention to a variety of problems at Oak Ridge.

While the DoE consistently has given the facility very high marks for safety and waste management, a radiation leak in May 1981 caused the evacuation of 125 workers. Plant officials called the evacuation an isolated incident.[4]

Tennessee state environmental officials, however, have discovered streams and ponds with dangerously high concentrations of heavy metals, chemical solvents and radioactive debris. The officials were concerned that the toxins had been accumulating over many years and were now leaching into underground aquifers. A recent state investigation revealed that 2.4 million pounds of mercury was lost into the surrounding earth, air and water over the course of 13 years from the Y-12 plant.[5]

The situation at Oak Ridge appears to reflect a much broader problem concerning waste management by the federal government, which produces more toxic wastes than the three top chemical producers combined but faces far less stringent disposal regulations than private industry. Corporate contractors that manage DoE sites which are considered vital to national security are exempt from federal regulations governing waste disposal. Inspection and evaluation of such sites are performed by DoE itself rather than an outside agency.

A Union Carbide official, The Washington Post reported, conceded that the DoE report giving the Y-12 plant a clean bill of health was "defective." He insisted, however, that the disposal procedures at Oak Ridge do not pose a threat to Union Carbide employees or surrounding communities. He expects the problem to be alleviated when Congress allocates the remaining $1.4 million of the $7.8 million needed to construct a new waste treatment facility.

Decision to discontinue management of Oak Ridge: In response to a 1983 shareholder resolution, Union Carbide explained its reasons for not renewing the contract:

> The decision not to renew the contract was solely a business decision, based on a previously announced intention to concentrate the corporation's resources and management attention on commercial businesses in which it has achieved a leadership position. Special religious or ethical arguments were not a factor in the decision to withdraw.

Some observers have speculated that the relatively low management fee was a factor in the company's decision, but Carbide spokesman Harvey Cobert told IRRC that the fee "wasn't really a consideration."

Union Carbide executive vice president Robert Kennedy told The Wall Street Journal that the Oak Ridge operations took more in management attention "than the return to the shareholders would justify." Company officials also expressed some frustration that Oak Ridge's identity had become more closely tied to the government than to Union Carbide. Cobert said that early on in the company's management of the facilities, the government needed industry to provide management skills. "Over time," he said, "the government has provided more and more direction and management. The corporation felt [its] role was not as necessary any longer."[7]

The Department of Energy was pleased to receive numerous inquiries and six final bids by major corporations for management of the Oak Ridge facility. DoE recently announced that Rockwell, Martin Marietta and Westinghouse were the finalists for the $10 billion, five-year contract and that it would announce its decision by Dec. 9.

Some industry analysts believe that the companies are seeking heightened prestige through association with the Oak Ridge Laboratory. In addition, under a revised contracting procedure, the companies may receive a higher fee than has Union Carbide. According to Nucleonics Week, the new contractor could earn between $14 and $28 million a year, depending on whether it chooses to put its compensation "at risk" by being judged on performance.[8]

Union Carbide Footnotes

1. House of Representatives Committee on Armed Services, "Hearings on HR 2496: Department of Energy National Security and Military Applications of Nuclear Energy Authorization Act of 1984," March 1 and 2, 1983, p. 261.
2. American Friends Service Com., "Makers of the Nuclear Holocaust" (1981), p. 13.
3. House of Representatives, "Hearings on HR 2496" op. cit., p. 261.
4. The New York Times, May 28, 1981.
5. The Washington Post, Aug. 17, 1983.
6. Ibid.
7. Nucleonics Week, May 6, 1982, p. 3.
8. Nucleonics Week, Aug. 11, 1983, p. 1-2.

Appendix A
Guide to Nuclear Weapons – Related Systems

This appendix is a guide to the nuclear weapons delivery and related systems that IRRC identified in the course of preparing this report.

As discussed in Chapter I, IRRC has developed two categories for classifying nuclear-related systems: primary systems and secondary systems. With this two-tiered system, IRRC could include both a broad and a relatively narrow definition in its analysis. "Primary" systems include strategic nuclear weapons and support systems (satellites, aerial tankers and other equipment primarily designed to support strategic nuclear systems) and tactical nuclear weapons. The "secondary" category includes dual-capable systems and certain "defense wide" support systems that affect both nuclear and conventional systems. Each entry includes a description of the system, IRRC's classification and a list of current contractors (and subsidiaries in parentheses). The current contractors section includes companies receiving major contracts since 1980.

Sources used to prepare this appendix included: Fiscal Year 1984 Arms Control Impact Statements, Arms Control and Disarmament Agency; Jane's Weapons Systems 1982-83, Jane's Publishing Co. Ltd., London, 1982; Military Posture for FY 1983, the organization of the Joint Chiefs of Staff; Report of the Secretary of Defense Caspar W. Weinberger to the Congress, Feb. 8, 1982, and Feb. 1, 1983; The Ships and Aircraft of the U.S. Fleet by Norman Polmar, Naval Institute Press, Annapolis, 1981; the Defense Department's Directorate for Information, Operations and Reports (DIOR); and the Natural Resources Defense Council.

A-4 Attack Aircraft

The A-4 "Skyhawk," a dual-capable aircraft, was developed in the 1950s principally as a nuclear strike aircraft to be deployed from aircraft carriers. Some 3,000 of the lightweight aircraft were delivered to the Navy and the Marines between 1956 and 1979. The Navy now uses the A-4 for utility and training roles, and the Marine Corps uses it as an attack plane. The A-4 is equipped to carry the B28, B43 and B61 nuclear gravity bombs and the B57 nuclear depth bomb.

IRRC classification: Secondary.

Current contractors: IBM, McDonnell Douglas, Signal (Garrett), United Technologies (Pratt & Whitney).

A-6 Attack Aircraft

The A-6 "Intruder" is a dual-capable attack aircraft based on aircraft carriers. The A-6 can carry B28, B43 and B61 nuclear gravity bombs and the B61 nuclear depth bomb.

IRRC classification: Secondary.

Current contractors: Conrac, Grumman, Hughes Aircraft, IBM, Litton, Signal (Garrett), United Technologies (Norden and Pratt & Whitney).

A-7 Attack Aircraft

The carrier-based A-7 originally was developed to replace the A-4. It also is nuclear-capable; it can carry the B28, B43 and B61 nuclear gravity bombs and the B57 nuclear depth bomb. It is slated to be replaced by the F/A-18 Hornet.

IRRC classification: Secondary.

Current contractors: General Motors (Allison), IBM, Litton (Itek), Loral, LTV (Vought), Rolls Royce, Texas Instruments.

AN/ALQ-119 Electronic Countermeasures System

Used on nuclear-capable aircraft including the F-4 and the A-10, F-16 and F-111.

IRRC classification: Secondary.

Current contractors: Litton, Raytheon, Westinghouse.

AN/ALQ-131 Electronic Countermeasures System

Used on a number of nuclear-capable aircraft including the F-4, F-15, F-111 and A-7. Production started in 1976. By 1986, the Air Force will have ordered more than 1,000 of the systems.

IRRC classification: Secondary.

Current contractors: Litton, General Electric, TRW, Westinghouse.

AN/ALQ-153 Tail Warning Set

Under production for B-52, FB-111 and other nuclear-capable aircraft, this radar detects missiles and aircraft that are approaching from behind, and then automatically ejects flares and chaff to confuse and divert the electronic systems of the approaching craft.

The first two systems have been installed in B-52 aircraft. More than 300 systems are scheduled to be produced by 1985.

IRRC classification: Secondary.

Current contractor: Westinghouse.

AN/ALQ-155 Countermeasures Set

The ALQ-155 is part of a program to improve the avionics of the B-52 bomber fleet. The first sets were delivered in January 1979.

IRRC classification: Secondary.

Current contractor: Northrop.

AN/ALQ-161 Electronic Countermeasures Subsystem

Part of the B-1B's defensive avionics system.

IRRC's classification: Primary.

Current contractors: Eaton (AIL), Litton Industries, Northrop, Sedco Systems.

AN/ALQ-165 Airborne Self-Protection Jammer

A part of a new generation of electronic countermeasures systems designed for the F-16, F-18, A-6, and AV-8B dual-capable aircraft, among others.

IRRC classification: Secondary.

Current contractors: ITT, Westinghouse.

AN/APG-66 Fire Control System

The AN/APG-66 is the fire control system for the F-16 dual-capable aircraft.

IRRC classification: Secondary.

Current contractor: Westinghouse.

AN/APQ-120 Fire Control System

Used on the F-4 Phantom.

IRRC classification: Secondary.

Current contractor: Westinghouse.

AN/APQ-161 Radar

Radar for the F-111F dual-capable bomber.

IRRC classification: Secondary.

Current contractor: General Electric.

AN/ASQ-176 Avionics System
An offensive avionics system used on the B-52 bomber.

IRRC classification: Primary.

Current contractor: United Technologies (Norden).

AN/BQQ-5 Sonar
The primary sensor system for the SSN 688 Los Angeles class of nuclear attack submarines.

IRRC classification: Secondary.

Current contractors: General Electric, Gould, Hewlett-Packard, IBM, Raytheon, United Technologies (Norden).

AN/BQR-19 Sonar
A sonar system used in Trident ballistic missile submarines.

IRRC classification: Primary.

Current contractor: Raytheon.

AN/BQR-21 Sonar
Sonar used on ballistic missile submarines and selected attack submarines to detect and track other submarines.

IRRC classification: Secondary.

Current contractor: Honeywell.

AN/FPS-50 Radar
One radar in the Ballistic Missile Early Warning System (Bmews). (See Ballistic Missile Early Warning System.)

AN/FPS-85 Long-Range Radar
The FPS-85 is one of the main elements of the U.S. ICBM early warning system, and it also serves as a crucial component of the submarine-launched ballistic missile detection system. In addition, it is one of the two main sensors of the Spacetrack system. The FPS-85 began operating in 1969 and is located in Florida.

IRRC classification: Secondary.

Current contractors: Allied (Bendix), IBM.

AN/FPS-115 Radar (See Pave Paws Radars.)

AN/SLQ-32 Electronic Countermeasures System

Used on more than 240 Navy surface ships, including destroyers and guided missile cruisers, to protect them from missile attacks.

IRRC classification: Secondary.

Current contractor: Raytheon.

AN/SPS-49 Long-Range Surveillance Radar

The primary detection radar aboard many surface ships, including guided missile cruisers.

IRRC classification: Secondary.

Current contractor: Raytheon.

AN/WLR-8 Electronic Warfare Receiver

A tactical electronic warfare and surveillance receiver designed for surface ships and submarines. It is believed that five of the 13 WRL-8 systems ordered in 1977 were installed on Trident ballistic missile submarines.

IRRC classification: Secondary.

Current contractor: GTE.

AN/WLR-9 Sonar Detection Equipment

A sonar used in ballistic missile and attack submarines.

IRRC classification: Secondary.

Current contractor: United Technologies (Norden).

AV-8B Harrier Attack Aircraft

The AV-8B is a dual-capable aircraft that can take off vertically and land on short aircraft carrier runways. Scheduled to replace the A-4, it is designed to provide air support for the Marine Corps in amphibious operations. The AV-8B can carry the B57 and B61 nuclear weapons.

IRRC classification: Secondary.

Current contractors: British Aerospace, McDonnell Douglas, Rolls Royce.

Advanced Ballistic Re-Entry Systems (Abres)

The Air Force's advanced ballistic re-entry systems program develops reentry technology for existing or future missile systems. The Abres program is funding the development of an advanced maneuvering reentry vehicle (AMARV) for the Air Force similar to the Mark 500 under development for the Navy. A maneuvering reentry vehicle could be capable of eluding ballistic missile defense systems by performing evasive maneuvers during its reentry into the earth's atmosphere.

IRRC classification: Primary.

Current contractors: Honeywell, McDonnell Douglas, TRW.

Advanced Cruise Missile (ACM) (See also Cruise Missile.)

The ACM will use radar-evading "Stealth" features along with greater speed and accuracy to make it a more formidable weapon than its predecessor, the air-launched cruise missile. Because of these improvements in speed and accuracy, the ACM will be a potential first strike weapon. Its range might enable the military to launch it from within the continental United States to targets within the Soviet Union.

In 1983, the Reagan administration decided to end the production of ALCMs at an early date and develop the ACM instead. Although the Air Force has kept figures on the program classified, some analysts estimate that 1,500 to 3,000 missiles will be built.

IRRC classification: Primary.

Current contractor: General Dynamics.

Advanced Strategic Missile Systems (ASMS)

An Air Force research and development program that pursues ballistic missile and reentry vehicle technology for future use on existing or future ICBMs, IRBMs and SLBMs.

ASMS contracts with about 40 contractors and government laboratories. In FY 1984, this program will focus on developing early penetration aids for the Minuteman III and MX missiles.

IRRC classification: Primary.

Current contractors: About 40 contractors, including TRW.

Advanced Technology Bomber (See "Stealth" Bomber.)

Aegis Class Destroyer (CG47) (See Destroyers.)

Air Force Satellite Communications System (Afsatcom)

Afsatcom is a military space-based communications system that is used to communicate with U.S. nuclear forces around the world. It consists of ground and air terminals as well as communications equipment placed on military fleet satellite communications system and defense satellite communications system satellites.

Among other uses, Afsatcom will be incorporated into Minuteman missile launch control centers to improve communications between the centers and higher command authorities.

IRRC classification: Primary.

Current contractors: General Electric, Rockwell International, Stanford Telecommunications, TRW.

Aircraft Carriers

All aircraft carriers built after 1959, including the new Nimitz class, have nuclear-capable aircraft--the A-6, A-7, S-3 and SH-3--on board.

IRRC classification: Secondary.

Current contractors: General Electric, Tenneco (Newport News), Westinghouse.

Airborne Warning and Control System (Awacs) (See E-3A Skywarrior.)

Air-Launched Cruise Missile (ALCM) (See also Cruise Missile.)

The ALCM is a small, low-flying, nuclear-armed unmanned aircraft. Launched hundreds of miles from its target, the ALCM (also designated AGM-86B) guides itself by comparing topographical features measured in flight with preprogrammed terrain information.

By the end of 1984, ALCMs will be deployed on more than 90 B-52 planes. Eventually, ALCMs will be part of the B-1 as well as the B-52 arsenal.

Boeing won the contract to produce its version of the ALCM after a 1980 "fly-off" competition with General Dynamics' air-launched version of the Tomahawk cruise missile. Boeing's victory was short-lived, however. Early in 1983, the Defense Department announced that it was cutting ALCM production from about 3,400 to about 1,750 in favor of the advanced cruise missile (ACM), to be built by General Dynamics. As of early 1983, 192 ALCMs had been deployed.

IRRC classification: Primary.

Current contractors: Boeing, McDonnell Douglas, United Technologies, Williams International.

Alpha Project (See Space Laser Triad.)

IRRC classification: Primary.

Current contractors: Rockwell, TRW.

Antisatellite Weapon (Asat)

The antisatellite weapon now under development is a miniature homing vehicle, a small device that would be launched from an F-15 fighter plane, home in on a target satellite and destroy it by colliding with it at high speed. The development of this system has important ramifications for nuclear war because it potentially could be used to destroy early-warning satellites, thus allowing a nuclear attack to be carried out undetected.

Ground-testing of the weapon began in FY 1982. It is slated to be operational by the end of the decade.

IRRC classification: Secondary.

Current contractors: Boeing (missile), McDonnell Douglas (F-15 aircraft).

Antisubmarine Rocket (Asroc)

The Asroc is the primary antisubmarine weapon for U.S. destroyers and other ships. It has a range of about six miles and can be armed with a one-kiloton nuclear depth charge or a non-nuclear torpedo.

Asroc has been deployed on all U.S. Navy cruisers, destroyers and frigates (except the Oliver Hazard Perry class) from the early 1960s. More than 20,000 Asrocs have been manufactured. The conventional version is used by many foreign countries.

IRRC classification: Secondary.

Current contractor: Honeywell.

Artillery-Fired Atomic Projectiles (Afaps)

Afaps are small tactical nuclear projectiles launched from howitzer guns. Currently, the U.S. stockpile includes 1,200 8-inch Afaps and 925 155-millimeter Afaps. Afaps under production and development include an 8-inch shell containing the W79 warhead, an enhanced radiation or "neutron" warhead. (See Howitzer.)

Atlas Booster

Developed from the Atlas ICBM, this space vehicle now is used in combination with the Centaur booster to launch military and civilian satellites and spacecraft. Some satellites propelled by the Atlas/Centaur combination, such as Navstar, FLTSATCOM and Defense Meteorological satellites, perform communication or navigation functions related to nuclear weapons. The Navy plans to order several Atlas/Centaurs during the 1980s.

IRRC classification: Secondary.

Current contractors: General Dynamics, General Electric, Rockwell International.

Attack Submarines

Five of the 10 active classes of nuclear-propelled attack submarines--the Los Angeles SSN 688 class, the Lipscomb SSN 685 class, the Narwhal SSN 671, the Sturgeon SSN 637 and the Permit SSN 594--carry the nuclear antisubmarine rocket. The Sturgeon and the Los Angeles class submarines will be equipped with nuclear-armed Tomahawk cruise missiles in the next two years or so.

The first nuclear-capable attack submarine, the Permit class, was commissioned in the early 1960s. Plans call for the production of eight more Los Angeles class submarines from FY 1982-84.

IRRC classification: Secondary.

Current contractors: General Dynamics (Electric Boat), General Electric (propulsion and electronic systems), Singer (simulators), Tenneco (Newport News--Sturgeon and Los Angeles class), Westinghouse (propulsion systems).

B-1B Bomber

More than 20 years after initial research and development, the B-1 bomber is being assembled. Planned as a follow-on to the B-52 after Rockwell International's B-70 was abandoned, the B-1 has faced substantial criticism, and in 1977, President Carter canceled the program. President Reagan revived the B-1 as part of his strategic program in 1981.

Carter canceled the B-1 because he believed that the development of cruise missiles obviated the need for a "penetrating" bomber; upgraded B-52s could continue to perform traditional bomber missions, despite their age, if they were used as "stand-off" cruise missile carriers. In addition, Carter knew that a more advanced penetrating bomber using "Stealth" radar-evading technology was in the early research stages. The Air Force, however, has always been dedicated to maintaining the role of the penetrating bomber, and in league with B-1 manufacturer Rockwell International and congressional supporters of the program, the Air Force kept up pressure to revive the B-1.

The new B-1 is designated B-1B, to distinguish it from the B-1A, which Carter canceled. The B-1B has improved range and payload characteristics, and will operate at subsonic speeds. The new version also incorporates some "Stealth" technology. The cost of the B-1 has risen from $45 million each when Carter canceled it to more than $200 million each. The first B-1B will be delivered in the mid-1980s; all 100 currently planned are to be delivered by the end of the decade. The B-1B is expected to assume a cruise missile carrier role in the 1990s as the Advanced Technology Bomber is deployed.

The B-1B is now the largest single Defense Department program. There are more than 5,000 subcontractors and suppliers for the B-1B. Many observers speculate that pressures will be strong to keep the B-1B production line open beyond 1988.

IRRC classification: Primary.

Current contractors: Allied, Avco, Boeing, Eaton, General Electric, Martin Marietta, Northrop, Raytheon, Rockwell International, Singer, Sperry, Westinghouse.

B-52 Bomber

Some 316 B-52 bombers make up the major portion of the nation's current strategic bomber fleet. Work on the earlier versions of the plane, also known as "Stratofortress," began in 1955, and 744 planes had been delivered to the Air Force by the time production ceased in 1962. The B-52 G and H versions were the last B-52s built. Earlier versions have been retired or shifted to reserve forces.

The government has spent considerable resources upgrading the B-52 fleet. The B-52G and B-52H versions are being equipped with modern digital avionics systems, along with state-of-the-art sensors and subsystems, hardening against electromagnetic pulse (EMP) and upgraded electronic countermeasures equipment. Meanwhile, the Air Force has equipped two squadrons of B-52Gs to carry air launched cruise missiles (ALCMs) on external wing pylons--a job that will be completed by the end of 1984--and in 1985, the Air Force will begin equipping each of B-52Hs with external and internally carried ALCMs. The new avionics system will help align, target and launch the ALCMs.

For now, the B-52G will continue to carry Short-Range Attack Missiles (SRAMs) and gravity bombs as well, although Boeing expects eventually to fit the bomb bay where these weapons are carried with an internal rotary launcher that would carry an additional eight ALCMs. The Air Force spent $1.3 billion on B-52 modernization in FY 1981-83.

IRRC classification: Primary.

Current contractors: Allied, Boeing, Colt Industries, Emerson Electric, General Electric, Hewlett-Packard, Honeywell, Hughes Aircraft, IBM, ITT, Lear Siegler, Litton, Motorola, Northrop, Pneumo (Cleveland Pneumatic), Singer, Standard Manufacturing, Sundstrand, Textron, Varian Associates, United Industrial (AAI), United Technologies (Pratt & Whitney).

BQM-74C Target Aircraft

This target aircraft, along with the MQM-74C, is used to train pilots of nuclear-capable planes including the F-15, F-4 and F-16 to shoot down air-to-air cruise missiles, which the drones simulate.

IRRC classification: Secondary.

Current contractor: Northrop.

Ballistic Missile Defense Program

Although the production of a ballistic missile defense system is prohibited by the ABM treaty, both the United States and the Soviet Union continue to conduct research on ballistic missile technology.

The U.S. ballistic missile defense program has two complementary elements: the advanced technology program (ATP) and the systems technology program (STP). The ATP is working to advance all ballistic missile defense technology. The STP's purpose is to develop, design and test ballistic missile defense concepts that could be deployed rapidly if necessary, especially in defense of U.S. ICBMs. The STP uses the ATP's developments to research and test BMD components in as realistic an environment as possible. STP projects include the LoAD and layered defense systems. ATP projects include the Defense Optical Tracker. (See separate entries.)

IRRC classification: Primary.

Current contractors: Control Data, Honeywell, McDonnell Douglas (STP), Rockwell International (ATP).

Ballistic Missile Early Warning System (Bmews)

Bmews consists of three large radars located in Greenland, Alaska and England, designed to detect a ballistic missile attack on North America.

The information collected from Bmews is transferred to the North American air defense combat operations center. Bmews and other ground-based radar systems act as back-ups for space-based sensors.

IRRC classification: Primary.

Current contractors: Electronic Space Systems, Felec Services, General Electric, ITT (Federal Electric), RCA, Westinghouse.

Ballistic Missile Submarines

The Navy has built five classes of ballistic missile submarines, usually identified by the kind of missile they carry: the Polaris, the Poseidon or the Trident.

The Polaris submarines were built in the early 1960s; now all have been withdrawn from the strategic missile role. The Poseidon submarines were built in the mid- to late-1960s by General Dynamics' Electric Boat and Tenneco's Newport News shipyards. There are 31 Poseidon submarines in the current ballistic missile fleet, of which 12 have been retrofitted with the more capable Trident I missiles. Each Poseidon submarine carries either 16 Poseidon or 16 Trident missiles, each of which has several warheads.

The first two Trident submarines, also known as the Ohio class, entered service in 1982 and 1983. The Navy plans to buy at least an additional 12 Trident subs. They will be armed with the Trident I missiles until the Trident II missile is developed. Each Trident submarine will carry 24 Trident I missiles, each with up to eight warheads.

IRRC classification: Primary.

Current contractors: General Dynamics (Electric Boat), General Electric, IBM, Rockwell International, Singer, Sperry, Tenneco, Westinghouse.

Blue-Green Laser

The Navy and the Defense Advanced Research Projects Agency are sponsoring a joint effort to develop technology using blue-green lasers to communicate with submarines at operating depths. Such laser technology also could be developed for other uses, such as antisatellite weapons.

IRRC classification: Primary.

Current contractors: Avco, Rockwell International.

C-10 Tanker/Cargo Aircraft (See KC-10.)

C-135 Stratolifter (See KC-135 Aerial Tanker.)

Centaur High-Energy Upper-Stage Booster

The Centaur is used in combination with the Atlas booster to launch military and civilian satellites and spacecraft.

IRRC classification: Secondary.

Current contractor: General Dynamics.

Cobra Dane Radar

Cobra Dane is a huge radar system that monitors the initial and intermediate launch phases of Soviet ballistic missile flights to the Kamchatka peninsula and Pacific Ocean.

Cobra Dane, which is located on Shemya Island in the Alaskan Aleutian islands, started operation in 1977.

IRRC classification: Primary.

Current contractor: Raytheon.

Cobra Judy Radar

Designed to complement Cobra Dane's abilities, Cobra Judy is specially designed to monitor an attacking ballistic missile's final flight stages. Cobra Judy is the first phased array radar system to be based on a ship. It is mounted on the Observation Island, an old U.S. Navy freighter.

IRRC classification: Primary.

Current contractor: Raytheon.

U.S. Cruise Missiles Under Development

Manufacturer	Missile	Warhead	Range (nautical miles)
Boeing	ALCM (air-launched cruise missile)	Nuclear	1,500
General Dynamics	ACM (advanced cruise missile)	Nuclear	classified
General Dynamics/ McDonnell Douglas	Tomahawk cruise missiles:		
	1) GLCM (ground-launched cruise missile)	Nuclear	1,300-1,500
	2) SLCM (sea-launched cruise missile)--"land attack"	Nuclear	1,300-1,500
	3) SLCM (sea-launched cruise missile)--"land attack"	Conventional	700
	4) SLCM (sea-launched cruise missile)--"anti-ship"	Conventional	300
	5) MRASM (medium-range air-to-surface missile)	Conventional	300

Source: Richard Betts, ed., Cruise Missiles: Technology, Strategy, Politics, The Brookings Institution, 1981.

Common Strategic Rotary Launcher

This is a launcher under development for potential use with the B-52, B-1B and advanced technology bombers. Initial deliveries are planned for FY 1986.

IRRC classification: Secondary.

Current contractor: Boeing.

Cruise Missile

The cruise missile is a small, self-piloted jet airplane that will be deployed in ground-, sea- and air-launched versions. Unlike conventional ballistic missiles, it does not fly in an arc, but maintains a steady position as low as 50 to 100 feet off the ground, low enough to evade most radar systems. The cruise missile's guidance system is expected to navigate the missile to within 100 feet of its target after flights of up to 1,500 miles.

Because it is so small, the cruise missile can be produced relatively cheaply (in Pentagon terms) in large numbers. It also can be launched from almost any platform. Several versions of the missile are now under development. (See chart.)

In its 1982 Yearbook, the Stockholm International Peace Research Institute stated that "the largest increase in the number of U.S. nuclear warheads since MIRVing may result from the massive cruise missile program." And, when the sea-launched cruise missile (also known as the Tomahawk cruise missile) is deployed in numbers, SIPRI says, it "will make every major U.S. naval vessel a potential strategic nuclear factor."

IRRC classifications: Primary for air-launched and ground-launched (Tomahawk), secondary for sea-launched (Tomahawk).

Current contractors: (See individual entries for Air-launched, Ground-launched and Tomahawk cruise missiles.)

Defense Meteorological Satellite Program (DMSP)

These meteorological satellites are a group of satellites--usually two in orbit at one time--that collect weather data for military uses including the final targeting calculations for ICBMs. Some of the data collected are also made available to the public through the Commerce Department's National Oceanic and Atmospheric Administration.

IRRC classification: Secondary.

Current contractors: Barnes Engineering, General Tire & Rubber (Aerojet-General), Harris, Hughes Aircraft, RCA, Westinghouse.

Defense Satellite Communications System (DSCS)

In the 1960s, the military launched its first communications satellite system, designated the DSCS. It was followed by the DSCS II in the 1970s. In the 1980s, the DSCS will be replaced by the third generation DSCS III satellites.

The DSCS system can reach virtually anywhere on earth through satellite relay. The system supports both tactical and strategic national security requirements including world-wide command and control, crisis management, intelligence data relay, diplomatic traffic and early warning detection and reporting. It operated the Pentagon's principal strategic communications channels. Part of the DSCS III satellite is devoted to the Air Force Satellite Communications (Afsatcom) system which links together strategic forces.

IRRC classification: Secondary.

Current contractors: Aerospace Corp., General Electric, TRW.

Defense Support Program Satellites

These satellites are designed to detect ballistic missile launches by using infrared sensors to detect the heat of their rocket engines. The Titan space vehicle launched the first satellite in 1971.

IRRC classification: Primary.

Current contractors: General Tire & Rubber (Aerojet-General), TRW.

Designating Optical Tracker (DOT)

DOT would monitor, detect and track incoming ICBM reentry vehicles as part of a ballistic missile defense system. It is being developed under the systems technology program. (See Ballistic Missile Defense Program.)

IRRC classification: Primary.

Current contractor: Boeing.

Destroyers

Since the mid-1940s, the Navy has built six classes of destroyers: Gearing, Sherman, Spruance, Adams, Coontz and Kidd. All of these vessels carry the nuclear-capable antisubmarine rocket (Asroc). A new class of destroyers, the Arleigh Burke class, will be built later in this decade. It will have a vertical launch system on board that can carry 90 missiles, including the Tomahawk cruise missile, the Standard 2 missile and the Asroc, all of which can be armed with conventional or nuclear warheads. The contract for the first ship will be awarded sometime in 1985.

IRRC classification: Secondary.

Current contractor: Litton Industries (Ingalls Shipbuilding) for Kidd and Spruance classes.

Distant Early Warning (Dew) Line

The Dew line is one of the earliest parts of the nation's early warning radar systems. It consists of an array of radars that stretch across the northern border of North America.

The line is now being upgraded to improve its effectiveness; all the current 31 radar sites will be replaced with new equipment under Seek Igloo and other programs.

IRRC classification: Primary.

Current contractors: AT&T (Western Electric), Felec Services, Raytheon, Sperry.

E-3A Awacs Aircraft

Based on a commercial Boeing airliner, the E-3A is an airborne command, control and communications (C^3) and surveillance center. It carries a distinctive "radome" mounted on top that looks like a flying saucer. Its sophisticated radars allow it to provide surveillance of an immense area of air space. For example, the Awacs can detect approaching aircraft so far in advance that it can send fighter planes out to intercept them.

Awacs aircraft are used in two capacities: a tactical battlefield surveillance plane that could direct nuclear weapons in a battlefield nuclear conflict, and a supplement to North American air defense until Dew line radars are improved and the OTH-B radars are completed.

Twenty-five of the 34 E-3As ordered by the Air Force had been delivered by the end of 1981. Five Awacs aircraft have been sold to Saudi Arabia.

IRRC classification: Secondary.

Current contractors: Boeing, Felec Services, General Electric, Hazeltine, IBM, Northrop, TRW, United Technologies (Pratt & Whitney), Westinghouse Electric.

E-4 Advanced Airborne National Command Post (AABNCP)

The E-4s are modified Boeing 747s that in wartime would serve as airborne command platforms from which the president or other officials could command the country's strategic forces.

The United States has four of these planes. They are outfitted with low frequency, very low frequency and super high frequency communications equipment and are hardened against the effects of nuclear detonation, including electro-magnetic pulse (EMP).

IRRC classification: Primary.

Current contractors: Boeing, Electrospace Systems, General Electric.

EC-130Q Tacamo Radio Relay Communications Aircraft

A modified version of the C-130 transport aircraft, the EC-130Q plane is a strategic communications platform used to communicate with submerged ballistic missile submarines as part of the Navy's Take Charge and Move Out (Tacamo) program. Tacamo communications equipment transmits signals that are highly jam-resistant.

IRRC classification: Primary.

Current contractors: Lockheed, Rockwell International.

EC-135 Command Post Aircraft (See KC-135 aerial tanker.)

Extremely Low Frequency Communications Program

The ELF program now consists of a large ELF antenna buried under rock in northern Wisconsin that can send messages to SSBN and SSN submarines. The Navy wants to expand this antenna into a large grid system that would consist of 56 miles of antenna in Michigan, tied to the existing antenna and test facility in Wisconsin. This expansion is part of the Navy's effort to upgrade peacetime communications to operating submarines and to support transition to wartime operations.

IRRC classification: Primary.

Current contractor: GTE.

F-4 Fighter Aircraft

The F-4 "Phantom" once was the first line fighter aircraft for the U.S. Navy, Marine Corps and Air Force, designed for both nuclear strike and conventional roles.

Now many F-4s have been replaced by newer planes, but it still serves with all three services. The Air Force and Navy versions can carry the B28, B43, B57 and B61 nuclear weapons. The F-4 production line stopped in 1979 after manufacturing more than 5,000 planes. F-4s also are in service with many foreign countries.

IRRC classification: Secondary.

Current contractors: City Investing (Hayes International), Digital Equipment, Fairchild Industries, Flameco Engineering, Ford Motor, General Dynamics, General Electric, Goodyear Tire & Rubber, IBM, Lear Siegler, Litton (Itek and Litton Systems), Loral, McDonnell Douglas, Raytheon (Beech Aircraft), Signal (Airesearch and Garrett), Singer, Sundstrand, Texas Instruments, United Industrial (AAI), Varian Associates, Westinghouse.

F-15 Fighter Aircraft

The F-15 "Eagle" is a dual-capable aircraft that serves as tactical fighter aircraft and an air defense plane for North American air defense. It also will serve as the launch platform for the antisatellite weapon under development. (See Antisatellite weapon.)

The F-15 entered service in 1976. It can carry the Genie missile.

IRRC classification: Secondary.

Current contractors: Allied (Bendix), Colt Industries, Ex-Cell-O, General Electric, Goodyear Tire & Rubber, Hewlett Packard, Honeywell, Hughes Aircraft, Litton, Loral, Magnavox, McDonnell Douglas, Moog, Northrop, Pneumo, Signal (Garrett), Sperry, Sundstrand, United Technologies (Pratt & Whitney).

F-16 Fighter Aircraft

The F-16 "Falcon" is a new plane, designed to be the combat fighter of the 1980s. It is a lightweight, high performance tactical plane that was supposed to be lower cost than its predecessor, the F-15. However, during its development, its price tag has soared. Still, the Air Force recently increased its order to about 2,000 planes.

The F-16 is designed for conventional and ground attack missions. It can be armed with the B43 and B61 nuclear weapons. It is deployed in the Air Force, as well as in some NATO countries.

IRRC classification: Secondary.

Current contractors: Allied (Bendix), Colt Industries, Dynamics Research, Ex-Cell-O, General Dynamics, General Electric, General Motors, Goodyear Tire & Rubber, Lear Siegler, Marconi Avionics, McDonnell Douglas, Northrop, Pneumo, Sargent Fletcher, Singer, Sundstrand, Teledyne, Tracor, United Technologies (Pratt & Whitney), Westinghouse.

F-104 Fighter Aircraft

The F-104 "Starfighter" is a nuclear-capable plane that now is in service abroad. In the mid-1950s, the F-104 was chosen as NATO's common fighter plane. Although primarily an interceptor, the F-104 is capable of delivering nuclear weapons, including the B-23, B-43, B-57 and B-61 nuclear weapons are listed among the F-104's arsenal. No F-104s are retained by the Air Force.

IRRC classification: Secondary.

Current contractor: Lockheed.

F-105 Fighter Aircraft

The F-105 "Thunderchief" was designed as a long-range strategic fighter bomber. This nuclear-capable aircraft became operational in 1958 and flew missions in the Vietnam war. It now is part of the Air Force reserve forces. It can carry the B-61 nuclear weapon.

IRRC classification: Secondary.

F-106 Fighter Aircraft

The "Delta Dart" is an older nuclear-capable plane soon to be replaced by F-15s. Its production was completed in 1960. It now serves as part of the nation's strategic air defense forces. It can carry the Genie nuclear weapon.

IRRC classification: Secondary.

Current contractor: Hughes Aircraft.

F-111 Fighter Aircraft

The F-111 has three variants: the F-111 tactical fighter plane, the FB-111A medium range bomber aircraft and the EF-111A electronic warfare aircraft.

The F-111 is a dual-capable fighter plane in service with the Air Force that can carry the B-43, B-57 and B-61 nuclear weapons. Sixty FB-111As form part of the nation's strategic bomber force along with the B-52s. The FB-111As carry the B-61 nuclear gravity bomb or the W-69 short-range attack missile.

IRRC classification: Primary (FB-111A); Secondary (F-111).

Current contractors: Allied (Bendix), American Electronic Labs, Eaton, Ford Motor, General Dynamics, General Electric, Grumman, IBM, Litton, Martin Marietta (including International Laser Systems), McDonnell Douglas, Raytheon, Rockwell International, Sanders Associates, Singer, Sundstrand, Teledyne, Texas Instruments, United Technologies (Pratt & Whitney, Norden).

F/A-18 Fighter/Attack Aircraft

The F/A-18 "Hornet" is a lightweight aircraft that is designed for use on aircraft carriers. It is scheduled to replace some of the F-4, A-7, A-4 and AV-8A planes now in service. Congress approved orders for 84 F/A-18s in 1984 and another 84 in 1985.

Although it will serve primarily as a carrier-based, conventionally armed aircraft, it is one of the many nuclear-capable planes in the nation's arsenal. It can carry the B-57 and B-61 nuclear weapons.

IRRC classification: Secondary.

Current contractors: Advanced Logistics Management, Allied (Bendix), Control Data, General Electric, Harris, Hughes Aircraft, K-Systems (Kaiser Aerospace & Electronics), Litton, McDonnell Douglas, Northrop, Texas Instruments.

FB-111 (See F-111.)

Fleet Satellite Communications System (FLTSATCOM)

FLTSATCOM is a dual Air Force/Navy satellite system for high priority communications. The Navy uses it to connect its land, air and sea forces including antisubmarine warfare platforms and ballistic missile submarines. The Air Force uses it to carry its Afsatcom (Air Force Satellite Communications System) transponders--devices that receive and emit radio signals--for the command and control of nuclear-capable forces. One channel also is used by the National Command Authorities. The system consists of four orbiting satellites and one spare.

IRRC classification: Secondary.

Current contractors: Aerospace Corp., TRW.

Forward Acquisition System (FAS)

As part of the layered defense antiballistic missile system, the FAS would detect and track attacking warheads before they entered the earth's atmosphere.

IRRC classification: Primary.

Current contractors: McDonnell Douglas, TRW.

Frigates

The Navy has more than 70 frigates in active commission, with an additional 12 ships, the new Oliver Hazard Perry class, planned for FY 1982-1987. All of the active frigates carry antisubmarine rockets, except the new Oliver Hazard Perry class.

IRRC classification: Secondary.

Current contractors: Advanced Technology, Penn Central (Automation Industries), Bath Iron Works, Gibbs & Cox, Sperry, Todd Shipyards.

Genie Missile

Developed in the 1950s, the Genie is an unguided missile armed with a 1 to 5 kiloton nuclear warhead. It is now used with various air- craft, including the F-106 fighter. Production ended in 1962.

IRRC classification: Primary.

Ground-Based Electro-Optical Deep Space Surveillance (GEODSS) System

A ground-based surveillance system, under development, which will use powerful telescopes to relay images directly from space to the North American Air Defense Command's (Norad) master computers. GEODSS is designed to spot an image the size of a soccer ball at 25,000 miles in space and to track about 1,000 space objects in a single night.

IRRC classification: Secondary.

Current contractor: TRW.

Ground-Launched Cruise Missile (GLCM) (See also Cruise Missile.)

The GLCM is a variant of General Dynamics' Tomahawk cruise missile, altered so it can be launched by mobile ground platforms. Like all cruise missiles, the GLCM flies at low altitudes and is guided by a terrain countour matching guidance system. It has a range of approximately 2,500 kilometers and will be armed with the new W84 warhead.

GLCMs were scheduled to be placed in Europe starting in December 1983. Plans called for 464 missiles to be deployed in Britain, the Federal Republic of Germany and the Netherlands. Another 96 missiles will be built for tests, training and replacements.

IRRC classification: Primary.

Current contractors: General Dynamics (Convair), GTE, McDonnell Douglas, Williams International.

Guided Missile Cruisers

Like destroyers, all the guided missile cruisers built after 1960 carry the nuclear-capable antisubmarine rocket (Asroc). The newest class of cruisers is the Ticonderoga class, now under construction at Litton's Ingalls shipyard and at Bath Iron Works in Bath, Maine. The first Ticonderoga ships will carry the Asroc, and later ships will have vertical launch systems that can launch Tomahawk cruise missiles, among other weapons. The Navy wants 24 of these 9,000 ton ships, and the first two have been completed.

Some of the Virginia class cruisers, the Ticonderoga's predecessor, will be retrofitted with vertical launch systems and Tomahawks.

IRRC classification: Secondary.

Current contractors: Bath Iron Works, Litton Industries (Ingalls Shipbuilding), RCA, Syscon.

Honest John

A dual-capable unguided missile, Honest John is a battlefield weapon that was developed in the early 1950s. It can be armed with the W31 nuclear warhead, with a 1 to 20 kiloton yield. This weapon is now deployed in Greece and Turkey.

IRRC classification: Secondary.

Howitzer

Several artillery-fired atomic projectiles (Afaps) are available for use in 8-inch and 155 millimeter howitzers (short cannons). Nuclear-capable howitzers include the M110, M110E2, M115, M109, M109A1, M114A1 and M198.

IRRC classification: Secondary.

Current contractors: Condec, FMC, Firestone Tire & Rubber, General Motors, Goodyear Tire and Rubber, Harsco (Bowen-McLaughlin-York), Standard Products, United Technologies (Norden).

Inertial Upper Stage (IUS)

The IUS is a system under development designed to transport satellites to points in space beyond the range of launch vehicles such as the Space Shuttle and Titan III rocket. The IUS has direct military applications in enhancing the nation's ability to place military satellites into orbit, especially in the high orbits where most early warning and communications satellites are placed. IUS systems performed successfully in Space Shuttle tests late in 1982.

IRRC classification: Secondary.

Current contractor: Boeing.

Integrated Operational Nuclear Detonation Detection System (Ionds)

Ionds is a set of sensors that will be placed on Navstar (radio navigation) satellites in order to determine the size and location of any nuclear detonation worldwide. In peacetime, Ionds will contribute to monitoring compliance with the partial nuclear test ban treaty and will monitor and collect intelligence information. In wartime, it would provide rapid reports on the effects of nuclear attacks, allowing weapons to be targeted appropriately. (It is also called Nuclear Detonation Detection System--Nudets.)

IRRC classification: Primary.

KC-10 Aerial Tanker

The KC-10 "Extender" is a derivative of the McDonnell Douglas DC-10 commercial aircraft. Orders for 44 KC-10s have been authorized from FY 1983 through FY 1987. The plane will be used for refueling strategic and tactical aircraft.

IRRC classification: Secondary.

Current contractors: General Electric, McDonnell Douglas.

KC-135 Aerial Tanker (and Variants)

Following its decision to purchase the B-52 bomber, the Air Force determined that it needed a new jet tanker for in-flight refueling of its intercontinental bomber force. In 1955, the Department of Defense chose a modified Boeing 707, later designated the KC-135, to serve this purpose. The KC-135s have undergone extensive modification since then. In FY 1983-89, 300 aircraft will be modernized and equipped with new engines. The investment will increase their payloads and enable the tankers to operate into the next century.

Variants of the KC-135 include the C-135 (a cargo plane), RC-135 (a reconnaissance aircraft), and the EC-135, which is equipped with electronic equipment and serves as a command post.

IRRC classification: The KC-135, RC-135 and EC-135 are all considered part of the nation's strategic forces, and therefore are primary nuclear systems. The C-135 is not considered nuclear-related, but there are few current expenditures on the cargo plane.

Current contractors: Avco, Boeing, Chromalloy American, City Investing (Hayes International), Curtiss-Wright, E-Systems, General Electric, General Motors, Pneumo (Cleveland Pneumatic).

Kidd Class Destroyers (See Destroyers.)

Lance Missile

The Lance is a dual-capable battlefield weapon that replaced the Honest John and Sergeant missiles. A new enhanced radiation warhead (neutron bomb) under production is designed for the Lance.

IRRC classification: Secondary.

Current contractor: LTV (Vought).

Large Optics Demonstration Experiment (Lode) (See Space Laser Triad.)

IRRC classification: Primary.

Current contractors: Honeywell, Lockheed, TRW.

Layered Defense System

This is a ballistic missile defense system, under development, with two tiers. The first tier would consist of long-range interceptor missiles that would target attacking missiles before they entered the earth's atmosphere. The second tier would be a backup system, similar to a LoAD system (next entry), that would attempt to destroy any warheads the first tier missed.

IRRC classification: Primary.

Current contractor: McDonnell Douglas.

Low Altitude Defense System (LoAD)

A relatively short-range antiballistic missile system, also known as Sentry, that would destroy attacking warheads inside the atmosphere. The main advantage of this system is that it is small and simple. It is a version of part of the former Safeguard antiballistic missile system.

IRRC classification: Primary.

Current contractors: Lockheed, Martin Marietta, McDonnell Douglas (prime contractor), Raytheon, TRW.

MQM-74C Target Aircraft (See BQM-74C Target Aircraft.)

MX Missile

The MX intercontinental ballistic missile, undoubtedly the most controversial U.S. weapons system in the last few years, carries three times the throwweight and has twice the accuracy of its predecessor, the Minuteman III. Each MX will be able to deliver up to 10 nuclear warheads, each with an estimated yield of 330 kilotons. The Reagan administration has named the MX the Peacekeeper.

Work on the MX began more than 10 years ago. The goals of the MX missile development have been to provide U.S. forces with a survivable ICBM with the ability to destroy hardened military targets--particularly missile silos--in the Soviet Union. The MX reentry system--the Avco-produced Mark 21--theoretically provides each warhead with a better than 90 percent chance of destroying a Soviet missile in its hardened silo.

Critics say that the missile, in combination with other systems, will give the United States a theoretical first strike capability. Current plans call for placing the first MX missiles in existing (though hardened) Minuteman III silos; meanwhile, further research will be done on alternative basing modes.

Orders for the first 21 MX missiles will be placed in FY 1984, and the first 10 missiles are supposed to be operational by FY 1986.

IRRC classification: Primary.

Current contractors: Avco, Boeing, General Electric, General Tire & Rubber (Aerojet General), GTE, Honeywell, Hercules, Martin Marietta, Morton Thiokol, Northrop, Rockwell International, TRW, United Technologies, Westinghouse Electric.

Manned Orbiting Space Station

Several companies are under contract to study the feasibility of a manned orbiting space station that could have several nuclear-warfighting applications, ranging from serving as a space dock for the repair of defense satellites to serving as a platform for space-based antisatellite or antiballistic missile weapons.

IRRC classification: Secondary.

Current contractors: McDonnell Douglas, Rockwell International, TRW.

Mark 4 Ballistic Missile Reentry Vehicle

The Mark 4 is the reentry vehicle for the Trident I (C-5) missile. It uses a W76 warhead with a 100 kiloton yield.

IRRC classification: Primary.

Current contractor: Lockheed.

Mark 11 Reentry Vehicle

The Mark 11 is a single-warhead reentry vehicle used on the Minuteman II missile. Current variants in use are the Mark 11B and 11C. (See also Minuteman II.)

IRRC classification: Primary.

Current contractor: Avco.

Mark 12 Reentry Vehicle

The Mark 12 is a multiple independently targetable reentry vehicle (MIRV) used on the Minuteman III missile. Current variants in use are the Mark 12 and the Mark 12A. The Mark 12A is an improved version that was considered as a candidate for the MX missile; it may be used on future missiles. (See also Minuteman III.)

IRRC classification: Primary.

Current contractor: General Electric.

Mark 21 Reentry Vehicle

The Mark 21 is a new multiple independently targetable reentry vehicle (MIRV) to be deployed on the MX missile. (See MX.)

IRRC classification: Primary.

Current contractors: Avco, General Electric.

Mark 113 Fire Control System

This is the baseline fire control system for all U.S. nuclear attack submarines and some strategic ballistic missile submarines. It controls the submarine rocket weapons and all conventionally armed torpedoes.

IRRC classification: Secondary.

Current contractor: Singer.

Mark 114 Asroc Fire Control System

The Mark 114 is used on destroyers, frigates and other ships to prepare antisubmarine rocket weapons for firing.

IRRC classification: Secondary.

Current contractor: Singer.

Mark 116 Fire Control System

This is used on the Virginia class of guided missile cruisers to launch antisubmarine rockets.

IRRC classification: Secondary.

Current contractor: Singer.

Mark 117 Fire Control System

This system is a successor to the Mark 113, used in some of the newer SSN 688 attack submarines.

IRRC classification: Secondary.

Current contractor: Singer.

Mark 500 Reentry Vehicle

The Mark 500 is an advanced reentry vehicle that would be capable of eluding ballistic missile defense systems by performing evasive maneuvers during its reentry into the earth's atmosphere. Although no plans exist to produce the Mark 500, a testing program has been undertaken to ensure that such a vehicle could be produced rapidly if the Soviets deployed a ballistic missile defense system that could render U.S. reentry vehicles ineffective.

IRRC classification: Primary.

Current contractors: General Electric, Litton, Lockheed, Rockwell International.

Midgetman Missile (See Small ICBM.)

Military Strategic Tactical and Relay System (Milstar)

Milstar is a communications system, under development, that will consist of eight satellites designed to serve both strategic and tactical forces with worldwide, highly jam-resistant, survivable communications. Milstar operates at extremely high frequencies (EHF), and the Defense Department considers it a pivotal program in its work to strengthen and refine space systems that can survive jamming and nuclear attack, including the effects of electromagnetic pulse (EMP).

IRRC classification: Secondary.

Current contractors: General Electric, Lockheed, Raytheon.

Minuteman II Missile

The Minuteman II (also designated LGM-30F) is a three-stage intercontinental ballistic missile carrying a single warhead with a yield of 1 to 2 megatons. The Minuteman II is the second in a series of Minutemans built by Boeing. It was first deployed in 1966.

A total of 450 Minuteman IIs are deployed in Montana and South Dakota; the Air Force has no plans to retire any of these missiles in the forseeable future. The Minuteman II is more accurate and has a longer range than its predecessor, the Minuteman I.

The Minuteman II warhead is the W56, and the reentry vehicles used on the missile are Avco's Mark 11B and Mark 11C. Boeing assembled the missiles.

IRRC classification: Primary.

Current contractors (for both Minuteman II and Minuteman III missiles): Allied (Bendix), Allis Chalmers (American Air Filter), Avco, Boeing, GTE, General Tire & Rubber (Aerojet-General), General Electric, Harris, Honeywell, Logicon, LTV, Motorola, Northrop, Rockwell International, TRW, United Technologies. (Note: Most recent expenditures have been on the Minuteman III.)

Minuteman III Missile

The mainstay of the nation's land-based strategic forces is the Minuteman III ICBM (also designated LGM-30G), which accounts for 1,650 of the 2,143 ICBM warheads in the American stockpile. There are 550 Minuteman IIIs, each of which carries three warheads. Some 250 Minuteman IIIs carry Mark 12 multiple independently targetable re-entry vehicles (MIRVs), and the other 300 carry the higher-yield and more accurate Mark 12A. The Mark 12 carries W62 warheads, each with a yield of 170 kilotons. The Mark 12A features the 335 kiloton yield W78 warhead.

The accuracy of the Minuteman III gives it considerable ability to destroy hardened military targets. The Air Force has gone to considerable lengths to improve the missiles since they were first deployed in the late 1960s. Just between FY 1981 and FY 1983, more than $336 million was spent on such improvements.

IRRC classification: Primary.

Current contractors: See Minuteman II.

Navstar Global Positioning System (Navstar)

Navstar is a space-based radio navigation network of 18 satellites. When completed, it will allow users to determine their position within tens of feet, their speed within fractions of a mile per hour and the time within a millionth of a second. Users may include civilian aircraft and conventionally armed weapons as well as land- and sea-launched ballistic missiles. The Air Force's Office of Public Affairs calls Navstar "an excellent example of the unique capability of space to enhance the conduct of traditional military missions."

Navstar also will conduct geodetic surveys to determine the earth's gravitational pull, an important variable in a ballistic missile's flight path, and will carry Iondds, a sensor system that will determine the exact number, size and location of nuclear detonations worldwide.

IRRC classification: Secondary.

Current contractors: General Dynamics, McDonnell Douglas, Rockwell International.

Nike Hercules Missile

One of the earliest nuclear-capable air defense systems, the Nike Hercules served as the primary U.S. anti-aircraft defense weapon in the late 1950s and early 1960s. It can be armed with the W31 nuclear bomb, which has a 1 to 20 kiloton yield. It soon will be replaced by Raytheon's conventionally armed Patriot.

IRRC classification: Secondary.

Current contractors: AT&T (Western Electric), General Electric, Hewlett Packard.

Nimitz Class Aircraft Carrier (See Aircraft Carriers.)

Nuclear Detection System (Nudets) (See Integrated Operational Nuclear Detonation Detection System.)

Ocean Surveillance Information System (OSIS)

OSIS interprets the sensors that track air, sea and submarine traffic all over the world.

IRRC classification: Secondary.

Current contractor: TRW.

Over The Horizon Backscatter (OTH-B) Radar

The Over the Horizon Backscatter radars will be an important addition to the North American strategic defense system, Approved for production by the Air Force in 1982, these radars are designed to provide long-range early warning of bombers approaching North America at all altitudes. In tests, OTH-B radars demonstrated the ability to detect aircraft 500 to 1,800 nautical miles away by bouncing high-frequency radar waves off the ionosphere. They operate at high frequencies.

The first OTH-B system will be built in Maine, the second in an as yet undesignated West Coast site.

IRRC classification: Primary.

Current contractor: General Electric.

P-3 'Orion' Antisubmarine Warfare Aircraft

The P-3 Orion is designed to detect, track and, in times of war, destroy enemy submarines. It is a complex system of advanced sensors, avionics and computer equipment, one of the most sophisticated antisubmarine warfare aircraft flying. It carries a mixed array of weapons including torpedoes, air-to-ground missiles, antiship missiles, mines and depth charges, including the B57 nuclear weapon.

The P-3 entered service in 1962 and now is a part of all Navy patrol squadrons and many naval reserve squadrons. It also is in service in many foreign navies. The P-3 production line is still open; the Navy requested another 23 planes be authorized in FY 1982-84.

IRRC classification: Secondary.

Current contractors: Boeing, City Investing (Hayes International), Cubic, General Dynamics, General Electric, General Motors (Allison), IBM, Lear Siegler, Litton, Lockheed, Loral, Magnavox, McDonnell Douglas, RCA, Signal, Singer, Sperry, Texas Instruments, United Industrial (AAI), United Technologies.

Pave Paws Radars

Pave Paws are huge strategic radar systems that stand ready to detect attacks from Soviet ballistic missile submarines. Like the other land-based phased array radars, Pave Paws is a backup system for space-based sensor systems. It relays information to the strategic air command, Norad and the National Command Authorities and is considered an important addition to the Worldwide Military Command and Control System (WWMCCS). Its secondary role is to support the Spacetrack program.

Pave Paws is located in Otis Air Force Base in Massachusetts and Beale Air Force Base in California and is under construction at Robins Air Force Base in Georgia.

IRRC classification: Primary.

Current contractor: Raytheon.

Payload Assist Module (Pam) Booster

The Pam booster takes satellites from their launch vehicles (Space Shuttle or others) and puts them into their designated orbit. The Pam booster will be used to place Navstar satellites into orbit. It is similar to the Inertial Upper Stage system (see entry above).

IRRC classification: Secondary.

Current contractor: McDonnell Douglas.

Pershing 1a Missile

The Pershing 1a is an intermediate-range ballistic missile deployed in West Germany. Martin Marietta began developing the original Pershing in 1958, and the Army deployed the weapon in Europe six years later. The Pershing 1a is an improved version of that original missile system. It has a maximum range of 460 miles and can deliver warheads with yields ranging from 40 to 400 kilotons. Martin Marietta has produced 575 Pershing 1as, of which 180 currently are deployed in West Germany. The Army is equipped with 108 reloadable Pershing 1a launchers, and an additional 72 are in the West German armed forces. Some U.S. Pershing 1as were slated to be withdrawn and replaced by the more advanced Pershing II starting in December 1983.

IRRC classification: Primary.

Current contractors (for both Pershing 1a and Pershing II missiles): Allied (Bendix), Goodyear Tire & Rubber, Hewlett Packard, Martin Marietta, Morton Thiokol, Rockwell International (Collins).

Pershing II Missile

The Pershing II has a range of approximately 1,000 miles, more than twice that of its predecessor, the Pershing 1a. This extended range puts Moscow and much of the western portion of the Soviet Union within six minutes' reach of European-based American missiles.

The new Pershing is the first ballistic missile that can be guided in its final flight stages, which makes it theoretically 10 times more accurate than its predecessor and a threat to hardened military targets. Thus, its warhead is relatively small--10 to 20 kilotons--in comparision with the Pershing 1a's warhead.

The 108 mobile Pershing II missiles were scheduled to be placed in West Germany by the end of 1983, barring negotiation of an arms control agreement before then.

IRRC classification: Primary.

Current contractors: See Pershing 1a.

Polaris Missile

The Polaris submarine-launched ballistic missile was the nation's first generation sea-launched ballistic missile. Lockheed manufactured three versions of the Polaris in the early 1960s; the last recently was removed from U.S. service, but the missiles continue to be deployed by Great Britain.

IRRC classification: Primary.

Current contractors: General Tire & Rubber (Aerojet-General), Lockheed.

Polaris Submarine (See Ballistic Missile Submarines.)

Poseidon Missile

The Poseidon submarine-launched ballistic missile was the first U.S. missile to have a multiple independently targeted reentry vehicle (MIRV). The most recent version of the Poseidon, the C-3, became operational in the early 1970s. The C-3 can carry up to 14 reentry vehicles, but only 8 to 10 normally are installed. The reentry vehicles carry the W68 warheads, which have a yield of 40-50 kilotons. The Poseidon's range is approximately 2,500 nautical miles.

The C-3 is now being replaced with the Trident I missile.

IRRC classification: Primary.

Current contractors: Data-Design Laboratories, Figgie International (Interstate Electronics), General Electric, Penn Central (Automation Industries).

Poseidon Submarine (See Ballistic Missile Submarines.)

Precision Location and Strike System (PLSS)

PLSS is designed to locate, identify and guide strikes against air defense systems and other radars. It can be placed on the F-4 or F-16 dual-capable aircraft.

IRRC classification: Secondary.

Current contractor: Lockheed.

Project ELF (See Extremely Low Frequency Communications Program.)

RC-135 Reconnaissance Aircraft

The RC-135 reconnaissance aircraft is the plane that received considerable publicity in the fall of 1983 in the Soviet destruction of a Korean passenger aircraft. The RC-135 crossed paths with the Korean jetliner shortly before that jetliner crossed into Soviet airspace, and the Soviets claimed confusion between the two planes. RC-135s routinely fly just outside Soviet airspace near ICBM and other sensitive strategic locations to keep tabs on Soviet developments.

IRRC classification: Primary.

Current contractors: See KC-135.

S-3 Antisubmarine Warfare Aircraft

The S-3 "Viking" antisubmarine warefare aircraft is the carrier-based counterpart to the P-3 Orion (see entry above). It carries fewer weapons than the P-3, but it can be armed with the B-57 nuclear depth bomb. It entered service in 1974.

IRRC classification: Secondary.

Current contractors: General Dynamics, General Electric, Lockheed.

SH-3 Helicopter

The SH-3 "Sea King" is the Navy's principal carrier-based antisubmarine warfare helicopter. It can carry the B-57 nuclear depth bomb as well as conventional weapons. It is now being phased out in favor of the new SH-60B Seahawk helicopter.

IRRC classification: Secondary.

Current contractors: Allied, General Electric, United Technologies (Sikorsky).

SH-60B Seahawk Helicopter
The Seahawk is a light airborne multi-purpose system (Lamps) helicopter with antisubmarine and electronic warfare capabilities. It will operate from guided missile cruisers, destroyers and frigates. It is not clear whether the Seahawk will carry nuclear depth charges. The Navy requested funding for 27 Seahawks in FY 1983 and 21 in FY 1984.

IRRC classification: Secondary.

Current contractors: General Electric, United Technologies.

SPN/GEANS Inertial Navigation System
Originally designed for the B-1 bomber, this system will give the B-52 bomber fleet the highly accurate navigational data necessary to launch air-launched cruise missiles.

IRRC classification: Primary.

Current contractor: Honeywell.

SR-71 Reconnaissance Aircraft
The SR-71 "Blackbird" is a strategic reconnaissance aircraft, capable of flying three times the speed of sound. The Blackbird was developed in the mid-1960s for many of the reconnaissance missions that had been assigned to the U-2. It serves the Strategic Air Command.

IRRC classification: Primary.

Current contractors: Lockheed, United Technologies (Pratt & Whitney).

SSN 637 Sturgeon Class Attack Submarines (See Attack Submarines.)

SSN 688 Los Angeles Class Attack Submarines (See Attack Submarines.)

Safeguard Antiballistic Missile System
The Safeguard antiballistic missile system was completed in 1974 at Grand Forks, N.D. Congress voted to shut it down in 1975, in part because of the antiballistic missile treaty.

IRRC classification: Primary.

Sea-Launched Cruise Missile (See Tomahawk Cruise Missile.)

Seek Igloo Radar Program
The Seek Igloo radars are scheduled to replace old Distant Early Warning (Dew) line radars in Alaska. Seek Igloo radars will consist of a mix of short range and long range radars along the Dew line. (See Distant Early Warning Line.)

IRRC classification: Primary.

Current contractor: General Electric.

Sentry ABM System (See Low Altitude Defense System.)

Short Range Attack Missile (SRAM)

First deployed in 1972, these nuclear missiles are carried on B-52 and FB-111 planes. With a range of 100 miles, the SRAM increased the B-52's ability to penetrate Soviet airspace. (Later, of course, cruise missiles became even more important in extending the B-52's service life). The B-52 can carry up to 20 SRAMs and the FB-111A can carry six. The SRAM nuclear warhead, the W69, is about the same size as that of the Minuteman III warhead and has a yield of 170 kilotons.

IRRC classification: Primary.

Current contractor: Boeing.

Small ICBM

President Reagan's Commission on Strategic Forces (the Scowcroft Commission) proposed this single warhead missile as a follow-on to the MX as a means of stabilizing the nuclear environment. The missile is planned for deployment beginning in 1992.

IRRC classification: Primary.

Current contractors: Boeing, General Dynamics, Martin Marietta and McDonnell Douglas are reported to be preparing bids to develop this missile.

Space Defense System Program

This is an Air Force project, in the research and development stage, which is developing an antisatellite weapon. (See Antisatellite weapon.)

Space Laser Triad Technology Demonstration Program

The space laser triad is a three-part program aimed at demonstrating key technologies necessary for a space-based laser weapons system, with ballistic missile defense in mind. Funded by the Defense Advanced Research Projects Agency, it is now in the research and development stages. The test program for this project will be conducted with use of the Space Shuttle.

The Alpha Project's goal is to establish the feasibility of a chemical laser that could operate in space, possibly for ballistic missile defense.

The Large Optics Demonstration Experiment (Lode) is charged with demonstrating an optics system that can direct and control a laser beam, using a mirror system.

Talon Gold hopes to demonstrate a system that can detect, track and aim a laser at incoming hostile ICBMs or other targets.

IRRC classification: Primary.

Current contractors: Honeywell, Lockheed, Rockwell, TRW.

Space Shuttle

The Space Shuttle is the first space launch vehicle that can be reused. It also can put heavier, larger satellites into orbit than any of the expendable Titan boosters it will replace.

The Shuttle will launch both commercial and military satellites.

IRRC classification: Secondary.

Current contractors: General Tire & Rubber (Aerojet-General), Lockheed, Martin Marietta, McDonnell Douglas, Morton Thiokol, Northrop, Rockwell International.

Spacetrack

Spacetrack is the Air Force's worldwide detection, identification, tracking and reporting system, which records data on all space objects, in part to support satellite attack warning and verification. Four GE-produced radar at two sites--Shemya Air Force Base, Alaska, and Diyarbakir, Turkey--comprise half of the Spacetrack system. The Shemya radars, however, are being replaced by the Raytheon-produced Cobra Dane radar. (See entry above.) In the future, Darpa's Maui optical site (see section on Facilities, below) and the ground-based electro-optical deep space surveillance system (see entry above) will be part of the Spacetrack system.

IRRC classification: Secondary.

Current contractor: General Electric.

Spruance Class DD-963 Destroyers (See Destroyers.)

Standard 2 Missile (SM-2)

The SM-2 is the latest version of a shipborne anti-aircraft missile that will be produced in both nuclear and conventional version. It will replace the Terrier missile (also nuclear-capable) on guided missile cruisers, aircraft carriers, frigates and other ships.

The SM-2 is designed to destroy a number of targets, most notably nuclear-armed Soviet cruise missiles. Initial deployment is planned for 1987.

IRRC classification: Secondary.

Current contractor: General Dynamics.

'Stealth' Bomber

Not much is known about this highly classified plane except that it will incorporate "Stealth" technology to reduce its cross-section on a radar screen, making it almost impossible for current Soviet air defense to detect. Stealth technology includes propulsion improvements, use of lightweight, radar-absorbing materials and improved electronics.

The Air Force plans to procure the Stealth as a successor to the B-1B in the 1990s. Despite some pressure to get some version of the Stealth in the air sooner, maybe as early as 1988, the Air Force has been reluctant to provide the funds required to speed up the program.

IRRC classification: Primary.

Current contractor: Boeing, General Electric, LTV (Vought), Northrop.

Submarine Rocket (Subroc)

Subroc is a nuclear antisubmarine weapon. It was deployed first in 1965, and it is carried on all attack submarines commissioned since 1962: the Permit, Sturgeon, Narwhal, Lipscomb and Los Angeles classes. Each submarine carries four to six subrocs, armed with W55 nuclear depth charges. The yield is 1 to 5 kilotons. The subroc has a range of 25-30 nautical miles. It will be replaced in the late 1980s by a new antisubmarine weapon.

IRRC classification: Primary.

Current contractor: Goodyear Tire & Rubber.

Take Charge and Move Out (Tacamo) Program

Tacamo consists of EC-130Q aircraft fitted with very low frequency communications equipment that can relay emergency messages from the National Command Authorities to submerged ballistic missile submarines. It is considered to be the primary means of SSBN communication during and after nuclear attack. The SSBNs received these messages by trailing a receiver just below the surface. Some EC-130Q aircraft are always airborne.

IRRC classification: Primary.

Current contractor: Lockheed, Rockwell International.

Talon Gold Project (See Space Laser Triad.)

IRRC classification: Primary.

Current contractor: Lockheed.

Teal Ruby Experiment

The Teal Ruby experiment will be carried on the Space Shuttle sometime in 1984. It will test a prototype of a sensor system that is designed to detect enemy bombers by the heat they emit into the atmosphere. The sensors would represent a major advance in space-based alarm systems.

IRRC classification: Primary.

Current contractor: Rockwell International.

Terrain Contour Matching (Tercom) Guidance System

This guidance system is what makes the Tomahawk cruise missile a highly accurate weapon. It compares the aberrations in the contour of the terrain over which the missile flies with a series of maps stored in its memory. It then makes the necessary course corrections and keeps the missile within 200 feet of its target.

IRRC classification: Secondary.

Current contractor: McDonnell Douglas.

Terrier Missile

The Terrier is a dual-capable missile that has been deployed on aircraft carriers, destroyers and cruisers. It will be replaced by the Standard 2 missile.

IRRC classification: Secondary.

Current contractor: General Dynamics.

Ticonderoga Class (CG-47) Guided Missile Cruisers (See Guided Missile Cruisers.)

Titan II Missile

The oldest and largest U.S. intercontinental ballistic missile, the Titan II (also designated LGM-25C) carries the W53 warhead, with an estimated yield of 9 megatons. Martin Marietta produced the Titan II, which was introduced in the early 1960s; General Electric produced the missile's Mark 6 reentry vehicle. There are now about 40 active Titan IIs, down from a full force of 54. Two missiles were lost in silo accidents, and five have been retired; the remaining missiles will be retired by 1987, according to current plans. Some will be used as space launch vehicles after that time.

The Titans are the only liquid-fueled ICBMs in the U.S. inventory, and they are relatively inaccurate. The Titan IIs are expensive to maintain, and their highly toxic fuel mix has caused significant problems, including two explosions which killed three soldiers and injured 41. The second explosion, in 1980, blew the warhead off the missile. There is widespread agreement that the missiles should be retired, although the Air Force is improving them in the meantime.

Each Titan weighs 330,000 pounds, four times the size of the Minuteman. Titans are deployed in Arizona, Arkansas and Kansas.

IRRC classification: Primary.

Current contractor: General Tire & Rubber (Aerojet-General), McDonnell Douglas, Martin Marietta.

Titan III Space Launch Vehicle

The Titan III space vehicle is a modified Titan II ICBM that is used to launch military satellites into orbit. Although the reusable Space Shuttle is now available, the expendable Titan III serves as an alternative.

The Titan III has launched many military satellites, most recently several of the Defense Satellite Communications system satellites and the Defense Support Program satellites.

IRRC classification: Secondary.

Current contractors: General Motors, General Tire & Rubber (Aerojet-General), Martin Marietta, United Technologies.

Tomahawk Cruise Missile (See also: Cruise Missile.)

Several versions of the Tomahawk cruise missile (also called sea-launched cruise missile) are being built, both conventional and nuclear. (See chart under Cruise Missile entry.) Plans call for the production of approximately 4,000 Tomahawks. The first nuclear Tomahawks will be deployed on attack submarines and surface ships beginning in 1984.

IRRC classification: Secondary. (Contracts for the nuclear versions are impossible to distinguish from the conventional versions, so IRRC has counted all Tomahawk contracts in the secondary category.)

Current contractors: General Dynamics, Litton Industries, Lockheed, McDonnell Douglas, Williams International.

TR-1

The TR-1, an upgraded version of the U-2 strategic reconnaissance plane, will perform both strategic and tactical surveillance and reconnaissance missions.

IRRC classification: Secondary.

Current contractors: Lockheed, United Technologies.

Trident Submarine (See Ballistic Missile Submarines.)

Trident I Missile

The Trident I submarine-launched ballistic missile is the Navy's newest ballistic missile. Delivery of the Trident I, also known as the C-4, started in 1979. By 1984, 12 Poseidon class submarines had been modified to carry the Trident I. The Navy's new nuclear powered ballistic missile submarines (SSBNs), also designated Trident, are armed with the C-4.

The C-4 is a long-range missile, with a maximum range of 4,600 miles. The Trident I allows U.S. submarines to operate further from the Soviet Union, thereby dramatically increasing the area of the ocean in which they can patrol and yet remain within striking distance of targets in the Soviet homeland. This in turn complicates the Soviet Union's antisubmarine warfare efforts and provides the sea-based leg of the U.S. triad with an additional measure of security.

Each Trident I can deliver eight 100 kiloton warheads, roughly double the aggregate explosive power of the Poseidon C-3. An improved guidance system makes the Trident much more accurate than the Poseidon. At the end of FY 1981, the Navy had procured 450 Trident I missiles.

IRRC classification: Primary.

Current contractors: Data-Design Laboratories, Draper Laboratories, Dynamics Research, FMC, General Electric, Hercules, Honeywell, Hughes Aircraft, Figgie International (Interstate Electronics), Lockheed, Morton Thiokol, Raytheon, Singer, Westinghouse Electric.

Trident II Missile

The Trident II, or D-5, will have a range of about 6,000 miles, will carry up to 14 warheads, and will deliver even more explosive power than the D-5. The most significant improvement, however, is the D-5's guidance system. Coupled with the new Navstar global positioning system, the Trident II supposedly will have the accuracy to destroy hardened military targets for the first time, and thus will be a counterforce weapon.

Deployment of the D-5 aboard Trident SSBNs is expected by the late 1980s. Eventually, all Trident submarines will be fitted with the Trident II.

IRRC classification: Primary.

Current contractors: General Electric, Lockheed, Westinghouse Electric.

U-2 Strategic Reconnaissance Aircraft

The U-2 is the famous strategic reconnaissance aircraft that CIA pilot Francis Gary Powers was flying when he was shot down over the Soviet Union in 1960.

IRRC classification: Primary.

Current contractor: Lockheed.

Vertical Launch Systems

Vertical launch systems installed on surface ships and submarines will allow those vessels to increase the number and kind of missiles they can carry at sea, including Tomahawk cruise missiles. The first vertical launch systems will be placed on the new SSN 688 attack submarines and the first five Ticonderoga (CG-47) cruisers in the next two years or so. They also will be retrofitted on the DD-963 Spruance class destoyers.

IRRC classification: Secondary.

Current contractors: Litton, Martin Marietta, Singer, Westinghouse.

Very High Speed Integrated Circuit (VHSIC) Program

Very High Speed Integrated Circuits will form the base of the next generation of military electronics, improving the capability of weapons systems while lowering their costs. VHSICs will have applications for all kinds of military systems, especially electronic warfare, communications and radar.

IRRC classification: Secondary.

Current contractors: Honeywell, TRW, Westinghouse.

Worldwide Military Command and Control System (WWMCCS)

WWMCCS is an advanced communications network of 35 computers at dozens of sites around the world. They tie together computers at the military command center in the Pentagon, the Strategic Air Command at Omaha, the National Command Authorities and many others.

IRRC classification: Secondary.

Current contractors: Honeywell, IBM.

FACILITIES

Command and Control Technical Center

This center provides engineering and technical support to several command and control systems including the World-Wide Military Command and Control System (WWMCCS). (See separate entry, above.)

Consolidated Space Operations Center (CSOC)

The Consolidated Space Operations Center, under development near Colorado Springs, Colo., will fulfill several roles. It will combine military space shuttle and satellite operations into one facility, enabling the DoD to coordinate more complex military missions. It will work to make military space systems less vulnerable to attack, especially nuclear attack. Finally, it will serve as the third ground communications station in the United States that is able to receive messages from early-warning satellites. It will be the first such station built partially underground, one of the measures intended to make the facility itself less vulnerable to attack. Navstar and Milstar master control stations will be located at the site.

Defense Nuclear Agency

This agency is charged with investigating the effects of nuclear weapons. The purpose of its research is to determine how military systems would survive after a nuclear attack, to predict how best to destroy enemy targets, and to develop means to enhance the survivability of U.S. forces. Current research includes the effect of nuclear dust on cruise missile and aircraft engines and how to superharden missile silos and vehicles.

Kwajalein Test Site

This is a facility that provides support for strategic offensive and defensive missile and related development test programs, including ballistic missile defense.

Darpa Maui Space Tracking and Identification Station

The purpose of this station is to identify and correlate space objects. It soon will become part of the Spacetrack system.

Space Defense Operations Center (Spadoc)

The Space Defense Operations Center was established in 1980 at the North American Aerospace Defense command at the Cheyenne Mountain complex to manage space defense operations. It tracks, identifies and catalogs all space objects and coordinates all space-associated commands and agencies.

PRIMARY SYSTEMS

AN/ALQ-161 electronic countermeasures subsystem
AN/ASQ-176 avionics system
AN/BQR-19 sonar
AN/FPS-50 radar
AN/FPS-115 radar
Advanced ballistic reentry systems program
Advanced cruise missile
Advanced strategic missile systems program
Advanced technology bomber (Stealth)
Air Force Satellite Communications system (Afsatcom)
Air-launched cruise missile (ALCM)
Alpha project (Part of the space laser triad demonstration program)
B-1B bomber
B-52 bomber
Ballistic missile defense program
Ballistic missile early warning system (Bmews)
Ballistic missile submarines
Blue-green laser
Cobra Dane radar
Cobra Judy radar
Defense Support Program satellites
Designating Optical Tracker (Dot)
Distant Early Warning System (Dew line)
E-4 Advanced Airborne National Command Post
EC-130Q Tacamo aircraft
EC-135 Command Post aircraft
Extremely low frequency (ELF) communications program
FB-111 fighter/bomber
Forward Acquisition System (FAS)
Genie missile
Ground-launched cruise missile (GLCM)
Integrated Operational Nuclear Detonation Detection System (Ionds)
KC-135 aerial tanker aircraft
Large Optics Demonstration Experiment (Lode) (Part of the space laser triad demonstration project)
Layered defense system
Low altitude defense system (LoAD) (Sentry ABM system)
MX missile
Mark 4 reentry vehicle
Mark 11 reentry vehicle
Mark 12 reentry vehicle
Mark 21 reentry vehicle
Mark 500 reentry vehicle
Midgetman missile
Minuteman II missile
Minuteman III missile
MX missile
Over the Horizon Backscatter (OTH-B) radar
Pave Paws radars
Pershing Ia missile
Pershing II missile
Polaris missile
Polaris ballistic missile submarine
Poseidon missile
Poseidon ballistic missile submarine
Project ELF
RC-135 Reconnaissance Aircraft
SPN/GEANS inertial navigation system
SR-71 reconnaissance aircraft
Seek Igloo radar program
Short Range Attack Missile (SRAM)
Small ICBM
Stealth bomber
Submarine rocket (Subroc)
Take Charge and Move Out (Tacamo) program
Talon Gold project
Teal Ruby experiment (Part of space laser triad demonstration program)
Titan II missile
Trident I missile
Trident II missile
Trident ballistic missile submarine
U-2 strategic reconnaissance aircraft

SECONDARY SYSTEMS

A-4 attack aircraft
A-6 attack aircraft
A-7 attack aircraft
AN/ALQ-119 electronic countermeasures system
AN/ALQ-131 electronic countermeasures system
AN/ALQ-153 tail warning set
AN/ALQ-155 countermeasures set
AN/ALQ-165 jammer
AN/APG-66 fire control system
AN/APQ-120 fire control system
AN/APQ-161 radar
AN/BQQ-5 sonar
AN/BQR-21 sonar
AN/FPS-85 long range radar
AN/SLQ-32 electronic countermeasures system
AN/SPS-49 radar
AN/WRL-8 electronic warfare receiver
AN/WRL-9 sonar
AV-8B attack aircraft
Aircraft carriers (selected)
Airborne Warning and Control System (Awacs)
Antisatellite weapon (Asat) (Also called Space Defense System program.)
Antisubmarine rocket (Asroc)
Artillery-fired atomic projectiles
Atlas booster
Attack submarines (selected)
BQM-74C target aircraft
Centaur high-energy upper stage booster
Common Strategic Rotary Launcher
Defense Meteorological Satellite Program
Defense Satellite Communications System (DSCS)
Destroyers (selected)
E-3A Awacs aircraft
F-4 fighter aircraft
F-15 fighter aircraft
F-16 fighter aircraft
F-104 fighter aircraft
F-105 fighter aircraft
F-106 fighter aircraft
F-111 fighter aircraft
F/A-18 fighter aircraft
Fleet Satellite Communications System (FLTSATCOM)
Frigates (selected)
Ground-based Electro-optical Deep Space Surveillance (GEODSS) system
Guided missile cruisers (selected)
Honest John missile
Howitzers (selected)
Inertial Upper Stage
KC-10 aerial tanker aircraft
Lance missile
MQM-74C target aircraft
Manned Orbiting Space Station
Mark 113 fire control system
Mark 114 Asroc fire control system
Mark 116 fire control system
Mark 117 fire control system
Military Strategic Tactical and Relay System (Milstar)
Navstar Global Positioning System
Nike Hercules missile
Ocean Surveillance Information System (OSIS)
P-3 antisubmarine warfare aircraft
Payload Assist Module (Pam) Booster
Precision Location and Strike System (PLSS)
S-3 antisubmarine warfare aircraft
SH-3 helicopter
SH-60B helicopter
Sea-launched cruise missiles
Space Defense System Program
Space Shuttle
Spacetrack
Standard 2 missile
Terrain Counter Matching (Tercom) Guidance System
Terrier missile
Titan III space launch vehicle
Tomahawk cruise missiles
TR-1 reconnaissance aircraft
Vertical launch systems
Very High Speed Integrated Circuit (VHSIC) program
Worldwide Military Command and Control System (WWMCCS)

Appendix B
Glossary

ALCM
Air-launched cruise missile. (See Appendix A.)

ASW
Antisubmarine warfare.

ATB
Advanced technology bomber (also known as the "Stealth" bomber). (See Appendix A.)

Arming device
A device that prepares a warhead, bomb, or other explosive to detonate when triggered.

Asat
Antisatellite weapon. (See Appendix A.)

Avionics
Electronics applied to aviation and astronautics.

Awacs
Airborne warning and control system. (See Appendix A.)

Backlog
The dollar value of orders officially accepted, but not yet filled.

Ballistic missile
A missile that follows a bullet-like trajectory.

Basing mode
The manner in which weapons systems are deployed and ready for use.

Booster
The part of the missile or space vehicle that contains the rocket engine and fuel.

Carrier-based aircraft
An aircraft that is deployed on an aircraft carrier.

Command, control and communications (C^3)
A system of procedures and equipment used by a commander in planning, directing and controlling military forces.

Composite materials
A family of strong plastics that can be used to build lighter airplanes and missiles, thus increasing their range and durability and decreasing their cross-section on a radar screen.

Conventional weapon
A weapon that is not nuclear or biological and in most cases that is not chemical.

Conversion
A blueprint for the orderly transfer of capital, labor and other resources from one kind of production to another. (See Chapter VI.)

Counterforce
The ability to destroy military targets, especially ICBM silos.

DARPA
Defense Advanced Research Projects Agency.

Deploy
To place in a desired area.

Depth charges
Explosives designed to activate under water at a specified depth.

Diversification
A firm's expansion into new businesses through merger, acquisition or internal development, usually in order to spread financial risk among many ventures.

DoD
Department of Defense

DoE
Department of Energy

Dual-capable
Capable of firing either nuclear or conventional munitions.

Electro-magnetic pulse (EMP)
A burst of electromagnetic energy created by a nuclear explosion that can disrupt and even destroy electronic components.

Electronic countermeasures (ECM)
Measures used to negate the effectiveness of enemy radars, missiles or aircraft. One branch of electronic warfare.

Electronic warfare (EW)
Military use of electronics in a warfighting context.

Enrichment
The process of increasing the concentration of one isotope of a given element so that it is better able to sustain a chain reaction.

Extremely high frequency communications equipment (EHF)
Communications frequencies that are almost impossible to jam; used in strategic communications systems, such as the Military Strategic Tactical and Relay (Milstar) satellite system.

Extremely low frequency communications equipment (ELF)
Communications frequencies that also are almost impossible to jam; used in many strategic systems including submarines and the E-4 airborne command post.

Fire-control system
Equipment that plans, prepares and controls the firing of missiles or other weapons.

Fuselage
The central body of an airplane.

Fuzing device
A mechanism designed to start the explosion of a weapon, analogous to the match that lights the fuse.

GLCM
Ground launched cruise missile. (See Appendix A.)

Gaseous diffusion
A process for enriching uranium to weapons-grade quality.

Hardened
Constructed to withstand the blast, heat and radiation effects of nuclear explosions.

Heavy water
Water containing deuterium, which makes up part of the fuel in a nuclear fusion reaction.

Howitzer
A cannon that combines certain characteristics of guns and mortars.

Intercontinental ballistic missile (ICBM)
A land-based missile capable of delivering a warhead to intercontinental ranges, more than 3,000 nautical miles.

Intermediate Range Ballistic Missile (IRBM)
A ballistic missile with a range from about 1,500 to 3,000 nautical miles.

Inertial Guidance System
The basic guidance system for ballistic missiles. By using gyroscopes, it guides a missile or a spacecraft over a predetermined path without outside information.

Infrared sensor
Device that uses infrared wavelengths and can detect objects by identifying their temperature.

Jamming system
A system that uses electronics to impair the use of other electronics equipment. Jamming systems protect aircraft by preventing radar and other tracking systems from locating them accurately.

Kiloton
A measure of the explosive power of a nuclear weapon; equal to 1,000 tons of TNT.

Launch platform
A platform--land, plane or ship--from which missiles and other weapons can be launched.

Megaton
A measure of the explosive power of a nuclear weapon; equal to 1 million tons of TNT.

Multiple Independently targeted Reentry Vehicle (MIRV)
One of several reentry vehicles carried on a single ballistic missile which can be directed to a target that is independent of the other vehicles.

Mutually assured destruction (MAD)
The concept that stability between the superpowers will reign as long as each side has the assured capacity to "destroy" the other.

National Command Authorities
The President and the Secretary of Defense serving together as civilian commanders of all U.S. forces.

Norad
North American Air Defense.

Nuclear materials
The plutonium and other radioisotopes used in nuclear weapons and nuclear power plants.

Payload
All the devices--weapons, penetration aids, chaff, flares--that are ejected from a missile, plane or other delivery vehicle.

Penetration aids
Decoys used to divert attention from a missile, aircraft or other weapon in order to increase its chances of reaching its target.

Political Action Committee (PAC)
A committee, sponsored by a corporation, union or other group, that solicits contributions from members of the group and makes contributions to political candidates.

Prime contract
In the context of the government, any contract in which a government procuring agency is directly involved.

Propulsion
The forward push given to missiles and rockets.

Radioisotopes
Radioactive elements, either natural or man-made.

Reconnaissance aircraft
Aircraft that observe and report on enemy positions and activities in either war or peacetime.

Reentry vehicle
The part of a missile that carries the nuclear warhead and reenters the Earth's atmosphere in the final portion of the missile's trajectory.

Sea-launched ballistic missile (SLBM)
A ballistic missile launched from a submarine.

Sea-launched cruise missile (SLCM)
A cruise missile launched from a surface ship or a submarine.

SSBN
A ballistic missile submarine that is nuclear-powered.

SSN
An attack submarine that is nuclear-powered.

Signal processor
A device that interprets electronic data.

Simulator
A device that simulates the behavior of an aircraft or a submarine or other system. Used for training or research purposes.

Special isotope separation (SIS)
An experimental and potentially inexpensive process for purifying and enriching low-grade plutonium into weapons-grade material. (Sometimes called laser isotope separation.)

Stealth
New technologies that incorporate improvements in design and countermeasures to help aircraft and missiles avoid radar detection by reducing their radar cross-section. Stealth technologies include improvements in propulsion, use of composite and radar-absorbing materials and refined avionics.

Strategic
Weapons and forces are strategic when they are capable of affecting another nation's warfighting ability outside of a battlefield context.

Subcontract
In the context of the defense industry, a contract given by a prime contractor to another company for part of the work required in the prime contract.

Submarine tender
A ship that provides maintenance and support for submarines.

Tactical
Weapons and forces are tactical when they are fighting opposing forces in a battlefield context.

Throwweight
The useful weight that the main propulsion stages of a missile can set in motion toward a target.

Tritium
A radioisotope of hydrogen that is part of the fuel in a nuclear fusion reaction.

Upper stage
One of the later stages in the multi-stage rocket.

Yield
Energy released in an explosion. For nuclear weapons, this is measured in terms of the kilotons or megatons of TNT required to produce the same energy release.

Company Index

92 002